THE
Simple Living Guide

THE Simple Living Guide

A Sourcebook for Less Stressful, More Joyful Living

JANET LUHRS

Broadway Books   New York

BROADWAY

Broadway Books titles may be purchased for business or promotional use or for special sales. For information, please write to: Special Markets Department, Bantam Doubleday Dell Publishing Group, Inc., 1540 Broadway, New York, NY 10036.

BROADWAY BOOKS and its logo, a letter B bisected on the diagonal, are trademarks of Broadway Books, a division of Bantam Doubleday Dell Publishing Group, Inc.

Library of Congress Cataloging-in-Publication Data

Luhrs, Janet.
    The simple living guide: a sourcebook for less stressful, more joyful living / Janet Luhrs.
        p.   cm.
    Includes index.
    ISBN 0-553-06796-6 (hc)
    1. Simplicity.   2. Conduct of life.   I. Title.
BJ1496.L84   1997   97-13486
646.7—dc21   CIP

FIRST EDITION

Designed by Holly A. Block

Photo credits: pp. 21, 51, 52, 167, 204, 224, 238, 264, 313, 337, 380, 383, 432 © Paul Joseph Brown; p. 86 © Clyde Mueller; pp. 149, 341, 371 © Janet Luhrs; p. 297 © Daniel Sheehan; p. 391 © Ecology Action; p. 396 © Jane Freeman. Woodcut credits: pp. xii, xx, 26, 60, 90, 130, 242, 302 © Dave Albers; pp. 152, 170, 208, 268, 374, 402 © Julie Paschkis; p. 350 © Margaret Chodos-Irving.

97 98 99 00 01 10 9 8 7 6 5 4 3 2 1

You can subscribe to *The Simple Living Journal* by sending a check or money order to: Simple Living, 2319 North 45th Street, Box 149, Seattle, WA 98103. A one-year subscription in the United States is $16.00, $21.00 (U.S. funds) in Canada, and $24.00 (U.S. funds) in all other countries.

Simple Living is a quarterly publication that is filled with stories about people who have slowed down and created rich lives, and it includes tips and articles to help readers on the journey. *Simple Living* also includes a community bulletin board where readers throughout the world can connect with each other via study circle and pen pal listings.

This book is dedicated to my favorite kids in the whole world—
Jessica and Patrick—and to my family: Mom, Dad, Don, and Karen.

Contents

Thank you

Thank you very much to friends, colleagues, volunteers, and others who helped with this book.

First, thanks to my kids, who inspire me always to remember the important things in life and to my parents for teaching me the value of simplicity.

Thanks to my friends for putting up with me when I had to keep saying, "We'll get together soon, I promise!"

Thanks to the wonderful volunteers at *Simple Living* for keeping the newsletter running while I was buried in manuscripts (and even when I'm not buried in manuscripts): Patty Lowry, Nancy Reifler, Valerie Neck, and Lisa Ely, and to the paid people who also kept things running: Heidi Wolf, Teryl Heller, Wendy Cleary, and Marin Bjork. Even though Ruth Pickering isn't currently volunteering at *Simple Living*, thank you very much for all of the endless hours in the past and for continued friendship. And thanks to Magrit Baurecht for always coming up with good designs and page layouts for *Simple Living*.

Thanks to people who helped with some of the chapters.

Money—thanks to Barbara Ahern and her dad, Bob Ahern, for reading and rereading the chapter over and over and for creating all the graphs and charts. Thanks to Barbara for explaining investments and good sense to me. Thanks to Ron Bryan for helping me figure out how to calculate compound interest, and thanks to Mona Ahern for proofreading all those facts and figures. By the way, Barbara, thanks for making sure I kept exercising.

Resources—thanks to my buddy Taso Lagos for reading and annotating all of those books and for our many walks around the lake where we solve the problems of humanity and analyze the meaning of life. Sometimes we even solve our own problems.

Virtues—thanks to my inspirational mentor, Linda Kavelin Popov, for sharing the virtues with me and for encouraging me and so many others to unearth our virtues within.

Health and Exercise—thanks to Ruth Streeter for researching simple exercise and for finding that terrific quote from *Business Week* about how Americans like to drive to the store and then use treadmills at home. I couldn't have said it better.

Inner Simplicity—thanks to Rodney Smith, who inspires lots of people with his gentle teachings of insight meditation, for helping to make sure I had the inner simplicity chapter right.

Gardening—thanks to Kathryn True for her excellent research. If it weren't for Kathryn, I'd have told everyone to pave their yards over with cement and then paint it all green.

Work—thanks to my friend Larry Gaffin whose work as a career counselor has helped people pursue their dreams, and who helped me organize the chapter.

Editing—thanks to the staff at Broadway Books, especially Betsy Thorpe and Janet Goldstein. Your ideas, comments, and support helped make the Guide even better.

Best agent award goes to Theresa Park, who inspired the whole thing and introduced me to Broadway Books!

The whole book—thanks to my simplicity colleagues and mentors for helping me to see that there is another, wonderful path to take: Duane Elgin, Cecile Andrews, Vicki Robin, and the crew at New Road Map Foundation, and thanks to the memory of Joe Dominguez. I have learned so much.

THE

Simple Living Guide

Introduction: Living Deeply

*I went to the woods because I wished to live
deliberately, to front only the essential facts
of life, and see if I could not learn what it
had to teach, and not, when I came to die,
discover that I had not lived.
I wanted to live deep and suck all the
marrow of life . . .*

—HENRY DAVID THOREAU

When I first got involved with voluntary simplicity, I heard this quote from Thoreau over and over. It was supposed to symbolize the movement, somehow. I listened and thought it sounded right, but I didn't really and truly get it. First I thought it meant that anyone who wanted to honestly simplify had to go live in the woods. After all, how could anyone live simply in the midst of the hustle and bustle of a city? I was so enamored of simplicity and so excited to get right to it that I signed up for a class on how to build log houses. My little dream was that my family would go off and live in a log cabin in the woods, simply ever after. Everything would take care of itself from there on.

Six years later I'm still living in the same house in the same city. I still look pretty much the same. But inside I've changed. And lots of little details have changed. I've edited and published a journal titled *Simple Living* since 1992. I have interviewed countless people who have simplified their lives in every way imaginable. I talked to dozens and dozens more for this book. I read everything

I could get my hands on about the subject. And I spent a lot of time thinking about what it all meant. Now, finally, I really, deeply understand the quote. The key word is not *woods*, it is *deliberately*. What the heck does that really mean? This one word, in my opinion, is the hallmark of a simple life.

People and reporters often ask me what I think simple living is all about. They want to know how low an income they can live on. They want to know if they should keep their condo in the city. Does simple living mean giving up their car? Does it mean never traveling? Does it mean living in poverty? Do you have to go meditate on top of a mountain in Tibet to be *really* simple? Do you have to live in an austere house? Must you live an austere existence? Can you never go to restaurants or movies?

Simple living is about living deliberately. That's all. You *choose* your existence rather than sailing through life on automatic pilot. Your existence can be in the woods, in the city, as a carpet cleaner, a doctor, an office manager, a retired person, a single person, a parent of six, a person in his 20s, a person in her 80s. You could have any level of income, but you hang on to a good chunk of your income, whatever it is. Simple living is about having money in the bank and a zero balance on your credit card statement. If you want to travel, you are conscious enough about your choice that you are willing to give up something else. I've chosen to have kid's science projects, newspapers, and my sister's slippers cluttering the living room rather than living an austere existence. Someone else might like austerity because it brings a sense of peace and order. Either way, we've chosen these things *consciously* . . . they didn't just "happen." Simple living is about making deliberate, thoughtful choices. The difference is that you are fully aware of why you are living your particular life, and that life is one you have chosen thoughtfully.

As I got deeper into writing this book, the *deliberate* theme became so loud and clear that I even thought about changing the title from *The Simple Living Guide* to *Yes You Can!* This was because literally every single person I interviewed had consciously and with clear purpose designed their lives to coincide with their ideals. They live *deliberately*. They know full well what they want out of life, and they take creativity and determination to impressive heights in order to accomplish their dreams. Not one of them waited around for someone else to make things better, and not one of them blamed other people or other systems for keeping them from what they deemed important. Nor did any of them absentmindedly wake up one day wondering how their life came to be. They live consciously . . . deliberately . . . and thoughtfully. This is what Thoreau meant when he said "I wanted to live deep and suck out all the marrow of life . . ."

◆　　　◆　　　◆　　　◆　　　◆

Living deeply means living consciously . . . being fully present, fully aware. If you buy a big house, you are fully aware of the yin and yang trade-offs involved. (Yin and yang is a Chinese phrase that means opposites. Often this means that any choice we make has opposite effects—one positive, one negative.) The yin of a big house is that it is pleasant and comfortable, maybe even impressive. The yang is that you need to work many, many more hours at your job in order to pay for it, and that means giving up other parts of your life. When you live deliberately, you are totally aware of this balance before ever signing a paper. When you live on automatic pilot, you skim the surface of life and see only the immediate gratification of this house. Then you wonder, months or years later, why you are on the treadmill of work and spend, work and spend.

Living deeply means living intimately . . . closely tied to the people, places, and things in your life. When you simplify, you'll have space and time to know and love people in a deeper way. You'll present your authentic self to the world and will create a life that is authentic for you. You'll surround yourself with people who like and love you for who you are deep inside, rather than the professional or other kind of persona you project to the world. Simplicity and *living deeply* means shedding all of those outward layers of image and busyness that keep us from being close to ourselves and other people. It is a more authentic life. Simplicity is living from your essence . . . your core. You can discover this essence only when you slow down and begin to live deliberately, consciously. This book is about the different paths people have taken in order to slow down and live more fully. There are many of these paths.

When you live deeply, consciously, sucking the marrow out of life, you will live a full, robust, honest, and intimate life. When you skim over the surface, never stopping to really, deeply feel or think about what you are doing, or when you simply react to one event after another, you will discover, as Thoreau laments, that you have not lived. This is the essence of simplicity . . . to live with full awareness and with passion.

Simplicity is not just one thing, one path. There is not an easy recipe for simplicity. There is not a perfect way to live simply. There is not a certain amount of money that you need to live on in order to be a bona fide graduate of simplicity school. You don't flunk if you own a car; you don't earn honors if you plant a garden. Simplicity is not so much the outward trappings of your life; it is the inner you making decisions. Not the outer you, the one that says you need a certain car or certain house or certain clothes or certain job or degree in order to look good to the world. Not that one, because that is the one that lives far from your essence. That is the one so many of us in Western culture have been trained to follow. The one that gets us into debt and overcommitting our time trying to maintain that outer image. The one that keeps us up at night worrying about how we're going to continue maintaining this image that takes so much money, energy, and time. The one that overrides the quiet voice of our essence that is begging to be heard.

Simplicity is the first step we can take to quiet that loud, outer voice. We can't hear the inner pleas when we work 40 to 60 hours a week at a job we'd rather leave, when we're busy maintaining our expensive cars and houses, when we spend countless hours shopping for more outer trappings, when we zoom from one appointment and commitment to another, and when we drop, exhausted, at night in front of the TV because we have nothing left. We can't hear anything then.

Simplicity means stopping for a moment and asking what the heck we are doing with our lives. Simplicity asks whether we need to follow the status quo just because everyone else is doing it. Simplicity asks: Is it right for me? For us? If not, then simplicity gives us the inner strength we'll need to say no. Maybe you say, "I don't want that promotion I've been working toward for so long. I just thought that was the way to go: Work hard and get promoted, then you've supposedly made it." Supposedly made what? "Maybe I don't want to work the increased hours the promotion will demand. Maybe I'd really rather figure out a way to work part time so I can be with my kids more, or so I can read all those books piling up on the shelf, or so I can ski more, or see my friends more, or have time to work at the soup kitchen. Maybe I don't even like this job. But I thought I should go for it because that's what people do. Maybe I don't want to live like that anymore. Maybe I wanted this car so other people would think I've made it, but this will mean I'll have to work six more years at my job to pay for it." Simplicity asks: Is it worth it? Maybe it is. Maybe it isn't. Simplicity gives you the space and consciousness to find out. "Maybe I'm wondering why I never seem to have time for my family and friends, or for my garden, or for just pondering the meaning of life. For so long I've just accepted that lack of time is part of modern life. That's just the way it is." Simplicity says no it isn't.

Thoreau says: "We must learn to reawaken and keep ourselves awake, not by mechanical aids, but by an infinite expectation of the dawn. . . . The millions are awake enough for physical labor; but only one in a million is awake enough for effective intellectual exertion, only one in a hundred millions to a poetic or divine life. To be awake is to be alive."

When I first learned about simplicity, I didn't know what *awake* meant. Surely I was awake or I wouldn't be able to drive my car, talk on the phone, take out the garbage. Now I know that being asleep means at least two things: You can really be asleep, like at night when you are in bed. But you also can be

28 Secrets to Happiness

- ❖ Live beneath your means and within your seams.
- ❖ Return everything you borrow.
- ❖ Donate blood.
- ❖ Stop blaming other people.
- ❖ Admit it when you make a mistake.
- ❖ Give all the clothes you haven't worn in the last three years to charity.
- ❖ Every day do something nice and try not to get caught.
- ❖ Listen more; talk less.
- ❖ Every day take a 30-minute walk in your neighborhood.
- ❖ Skip two meals a week and give the money to the homeless.
- ❖ Strive for excellence, not perfection.
- ❖ Be on time.
- ❖ Don't make excuses.
- ❖ Don't argue.
- ❖ Get organized.
- ❖ Be kind to kind people.
- ❖ Be even kinder to unkind people.
- ❖ Let someone cut ahead of you in line.
- ❖ Take time to be alone.
- ❖ Reread a favorite book.
- ❖ Cultivate good manners.
- ❖ Be humble.
- ❖ Understand and accept that life isn't always fair.
- ❖ Know when to say something.
- ❖ Know when to keep your mouth shut.
- ❖ Don't criticize anyone for 24 hours.
- ❖ Learn from the past, plan for the future, and live in the present.
- ❖ Don't sweat the small stuff.

asleep during the day by not paying attention. I can drive my car but be thinking of a discussion I had yesterday with my neighbor. I will notice almost nothing on the way to the store because I am on automatic pilot and am thinking of the discussion. I miss all of life that I have just whizzed past. I don't even feel my hands on the steering wheel. I can talk on the phone while I am stirring my dinner on the stove, thinking about what to put into the pot next and only half aware of what my friend is saying. I miss the intimacy of her voice, of what she is really saying, really needing. I can stay on the surface of that relationship. I can wonder why I don't feel deeply intimate with the people around me. I can get tired of living a perfunctory life. I can take out the garbage on automatic pilot and not even be aware that I just walked out to the sidewalk holding a heavy can. I can be asleep this way.

I can never get in deep and really, truly experience each and every event in my life. I can touch the garbage can, I can touch the onion I am cutting, I can look at the person I am talking to, but I can do this without feeling much of anything, without noticing much of anything. I can accept a job and not really feel or think about what it means in the big scheme of my life. It pays the bills right now, it uses my skills, the people seem nice. The end. Or I can accept a job and know just how it fits in and just how it feels, down to my core. If I am living deliberately, I have been conscious with my money so I have some in the bank; then I can even turn down the job until a real match is made.

I can feel the smooth, round, brittle paper skin of the onion as I cut it. I can notice that my friend's eyes seem a little sad as he is talking to me. He doesn't say anything a little sad, but I can see it. Maybe I can reach out to him. Maybe then he and I won't wonder why we don't feel very fulfilled around each other anymore. This is simplicity. This is living deliberately. This is being awake. This is taking in every bit of life: the good, the happy, the dark, the sad. All of it. Sucking the marrow out of life. Not just leaving it on the banquet table for the next person to sample carefully and then put down, marching swiftly on to the next item.

We don't need to go shopping for this full life. It is right in front of us, waiting. All we need to do is notice. We're too caught up in our daily lives to find the time or space to notice. How did we get this way? When did we decide that more and bigger stuff would give us a better life? When was the last time a busy calendar gave anyone more serenity? Do we really get more joy from worrying about, rearranging, and dusting our things than we do from visiting with a friend in an intimate way? Do our soulful, intimate friends really care whether our houses are decorated in the latest style and whether we spent an extra five minutes worrying about a certain vase? Do we like ourselves more if we move up from a medium-size to a big-screen television set? Will that make zoning out every night a little more pleasant? Is zoning out what we always dreamed was the meaning of life?

When simplicity friend and colleague Joe Dominguez, author of *Your Money or Your Life*, died this year, our mutual friend Duane Elgin, author of *Voluntary Simplicity*, delivered the most profound yet simple remembrance at Joe's service. The few lines he read summed up the essence of a deliberate, intimate life: "Joe did not care if you made a bunch of money. He wanted to know if you had enough money to share your life freely with others. Joe did not care 'who you knew.' He cared if you knew yourself and if you could be true to your soul's integrity. Joe did not care how many college degrees you had. He cared whether you were willing to show up, each day, in the school of life and learn your soul's lessons. Joe did not care how old you were. He cared if you were old enough to be wise about life and to meet its challenge with humor, inventiveness, and truth. Joe did not care about your guru or astrological sign. He wanted to know if you were in touch with your soul's fire and whether you were willing to take a stand for what you love and believe."

What's happened to the rest of us? Where is our fire?

A certain level of material comfort is necessary. We all need our own nests, food, and clothing in order to survive. We need some kind of work to do, paid or unpaid. And as human beings, we need more than the bare minimum; we need a certain level of aesthetics. The trouble is, most of us don't know when to stop. We get to a certain level of comfort and then think, "This feels nice, I'd better strive for some more." The next thing we know we're buried in debt, stress, and complication. Then we've lost our fire, our passion for life.

I had a wonderful interview with a couple one time. The husband's philosophy on life was this: "The bottom line for us is, if you can become self-sufficient in the basics of life, which are shelter, nutritious food, and clothing . . . if you have these things covered, then all you have to do with the rest of your time is make yourself a peaceful person, rather than spending that same time buying things you don't need."

I had another interview with a friend who has lived in Nepal and the United States. She said: "We seem to be awfully busy here in the U.S. But at the end of our lives have we really achieved more than the simple farmer, and will we remember that we bought 12 pairs of pants instead of 2?"

Will we?

1
Time

It is not enough if you are busy. The question is, What are you busy about?

—HENRY DAVID THOREAU

I read the most heartwarming letter in the newspaper once. The letter said it all about how I feel about our big "time crunch" in modern America. It was from a 51-year-old man and was written about his mother. He wrote that after his father's death, a mentor came into his life. One of the things this mentor advised him to do was call his mother every day just to hear her voice, to let her hear his, to hear about her day, and to tell her that he loved her.

The man said that he eats one meal a week with his mom, usually dinner, sometimes lunch or breakfast. One week he didn't share a meal with her, so he went to see her during an evening before she was to leave on a trip and spent 20 minutes looking over her maps from AAA. His mom told him how relieved she was that they had looked over her route so she knew where she was going. Then he wrote about some of the things he did when he shared dinner with his mom—changed batteries in her garage door opener and cleaned her garage. He wrote: "Today I have a priceless relationship with my mom, thanks to the advice of my mentor.

I'm as attentive to her as my father would be if he were alive—I am indeed my father's son."

This letter brought tears to my eyes. Every other headline in newspapers and magazines screams about our modern day "time famine." Nobody has enough time for anything . . . everybody is running in frenzied circles from one important activity to the next. Everybody is exhausted. We use Day-Timers to make dinner dates with our best friends. Then I read this letter and wonder: What the heck is going on?

Our Intimacy Famine

Our time famine is really an intimacy famine. It is much easier to stay busy and frantic than it is to love and know ourselves and others deeply. We're busy because we want to be busy. Staying busy appears to give our lives meaning (just look at all of the things I have accomplished and all of the things I do in my life!), and staying busy is safe. We don't need to really get in and look at our lives when we're rushing from one thing to the next.

What to do? We need to look at this mythical "time famine" as an addiction and get off the drug. There is no time famine that we ourselves don't create. Time crunches are indeed addictive. Our bodies and minds get used to operating on high adrenaline every day. When we have a small hole of open time, it is very uncomfortable, similar to the discomfort an addict feels without the drug. We fill it immediately because then we can keep running at our familiar fast pace. We may complain, but it is a familiar pace nevertheless. Recall the phrase "If you want something done, ask a busy person." This is because busy people have acclimated their bodies to operating at high speed, so it is easy for them simply to stuff one more thing into an already crammed-full day. On one hand, it's terrific to be efficient. There is nothing like asking someone to do something for you, knowing that it will get done in a timely manner. There is nothing more frustrating than asking a slothlike person to do the same thing and having them give you excuse after excuse as to why it didn't get done.

All that aside, there is a middle ground. It is a new way of looking at time. It is looking within and taking responsibility for every single time crunch we are in and examining each one carefully. Why? What are we running from? Intimacy? Why? Does this quote from Austin Dobson sound familiar: "Time goes, you say, Ah no! Alas, Time stays, we go."

We want to be like the man who wrote the heartwarming letter about his mom, but we're doing something else instead. What are we doing and why?

Maybe it's our mom we want to see more, or our dads, our children, our partners, neighbors, friends, grandparents, and on and on. Maybe it's ourselves. It's easier to stay frenetic and complain about not having time for other people than it is to actually do something about it. It takes great effort to drive over to our mom's house and pore over AAA maps. It's much easier to sit on our rears and watch TV. It takes lots of empty time to play Monopoly all day with our nine-year-old kids. (Think of all the important chores and tasks I really *should* be doing!) It requires a lot of our emotional selves to have heart-to-heart talks with people rather than the usual, "How're ya doing? Great. Great. Gotta run."

It takes *time* to build friendships and relationships of any depth. With every automated teller that replaces a live one, we lose one more opportunity to interact with a real human being . . . all in the name of efficiency.

We even streamline our social gatherings. As Steffen Linder wrote in *The Harried Leisure Class*,

> People have a surprising liking for large banquets, conventions and cocktail parties. To be the only guests to dinner is normally considered less flattering than to be invited with many others. Efforts to economize one's time in this way lead in due course to one's having numerous acquaintances and no friends.

We can't take the time to be sensitive to others and truly care for them when we are in a constant hurry. Relationships take time to nurture. Let's put technology in its place—use it, but don't let it run our lives and destroy our contact with other human beings. Take the dishwasher, for example. Before dishwashers, it was customary for two people to wash dishes in the sink together. One washed and the other dried. Ever thought about the chatting and bonding that went on during these nightly episodes? Ever thought about the sensuality of rubbing dishes in a tub of warm, soapy water? Now what do we have? A lone person hurriedly cramming dishes into the dishwasher so he or she can get on to the next task quickly. The dishwasher is one modern convenience that I stopped using except after dinner parties. Turns out I *like* this meditative time to run bubbles over dishes and warm my hands. It gives me kind of a rhythmic moment to ponder the meaning of life in a way that high-tech loading cannot give.

After the dishes are crammed into their respective slots in the dishwasher, what else do a lot of us do in the evening? Sit in front of the tube, on average of four or five hours a night. No human bonding there. Remember those evenings spent taking tea and chatting together? Playing cards together? Going for walks together? (We remember them only in our imaginations because now and then we see a reenactment in a movie or somewhere.)

A speeded-up life not only robs us of time to connect with others, but it also makes us impatient and angry. We don't have time to listen to our partner's point of view. We don't have time to wait for a bank teller who is just learning. We don't have time for our children. We don't have time for ourselves. When we're overscheduled, we become selfish, because our whole day is spent trying to catch up and our night is spent trying to recuperate. We all know where a selfish life leads: to isolation and loneliness.

> *If one sets time aside for a business appointment or a social engagement, that time is accepted as inviolable. But if anyone says, "I cannot come because that is my hour to be alone," one is considered rude, egotistical, or strange. What a sad commentary on our civilization.*
>
> —ANNE MORROW LINDBERGH,
> *GIFT FROM THE SEA*

When we slow down and make space in our lives, we notice little things. We can be aware when our partner's mood has changed simply by watching his or her eyes. When we're in a hurry, or recuperating from being in a hurry, we don't have time to take note of the minute changes and fluctuations of daily life. It is awareness of these minutiae that make for a deep, meaningful life. I remember in the middle of my divorce a woman whom I knew only peripherally showed up at my door one day with a bottle of scented bath oil. She told me to take care of myself. You can't imagine how touched I was by this small act of human kindness. It was only because she had open space in her own life that she was able to be sensitive to what was going on in other people's. Later, as my life calmed down and opened up after the divorce, I was able to return a kindness to another friend who had been going through a tough time. I felt that she could use a little nurturing, so I packed a little bag with scented bath soap, scented candles, and bath salts, and told her to take care of herself.

Whenever I read about people who survived a near-death experience, most often they say that it was the little kindnesses that were most important when they looked back over their lives. It wasn't that a kid became an Eagle Scout; rather, it was the kid taking time to help an elderly woman across the street. It wasn't that a woman made it to the top of a corporation; rather it was the time she spent reading to a homeless child at a day-care center. None of these little kindnesses can happen until we open our lives.

Reclaiming Our Time

If we want to open ourselves to intimacy, then we need to change the way we look at and use our time. Take the seemingly innocuous example of reading. Eknath Easwaran, author of the book *Take Your Time*, used the following example to illustrate the old way of thinking about time versus the new way of thinking. The old way is this: When we have more and more things piling up that we feel we *must* read, we run out and sign up for a speed reading course. That way we can digest more information more efficiently. The new way is simply this: *Stop trying to read everything*.

Impossible, we say. This is the information age. I have to keep up (for my job, my school, social reasons . . . fill in the blanks). Then we turn to articles and books on working and living more efficiently. Let me run through a few examples from one "get organized" book: If you have five extra minutes that are actually unscheduled (heaven forbid), you can do the following: (1) Make an appointment; (2) Write a short note; (3) File your nails; (4) Water the plants.

If you actually have an astounding *10* minutes of free time, you can fill it up even more! Here's how, according to the book: (1) Repot a plant; (2) Hand-wash some clothes; (3) Dust the living room; (4) Straighten up your desk.

The advice goes on. *Double up on tasks*. While your clothes are drying, you can polish your silver. Make a bed while waiting for the water to boil. While waiting in your car for the kids, you can quickly clean the car, sort through the mail, and clip coupons. I'm exhausted. We're all exhausted. When do we get a break?

How do we look at time in a new way? Here are some ideas: (1) Take a close look at intimacy; (2) Adopt a new attitude; (3) Do one thing at a time; (4) Think of time as sacred; (5) Question "time-saving" gadgets; (6) Look at the big picture; (7) Leave your job at work; (8) Religious or not, rest one day a week.

Take a Close Look at Intimacy

We stay busy for a lot of reasons. One is that staying busy makes us feel important. We should rethink the paradigm that a busy person is important. Remember the Woody Allen film *Play It Again, Sam*? Woody Allen's friend called his answering service every now and then during his nonwork time in order to report his current location. Doing so made him look important.

When you think about it, looking and feeling important is really another way to keep from being intimate. If we look important, then our hidden message to the world and ourselves is that we expect people to relate to us as if we

are somebody important (better), and not as the human beings we are deep inside. That, too, is easier, but, as we all know, not at all satisfying in the long run. When we talk to someone we think is more "important" than we are, we are not communicating on a heart-to-heart, real level. All remains pleasant on the surface, and nobody has to know what's really going on inside.

The most extreme example I have ever heard about the use of importance as a way to intimidate and thus not get close was about our past president Lyndon Johnson. I took a tour of the old presidential jet he used to fly in. The tour director took us to a conference table in the middle of the plane. The table was surrounded by built-in seating on three sides. The fourth side was for Johnson's special chair. Ahem. Turns out that his chair and the table could be electronically raised and lowered. The built-in seating on the other sides was not operable. Why this design? we asked. The tour operator told us that this way, Johnson could raise both the table and his chair when he wanted to intimidate people, and he could lower it when he wanted to visit with friends. You can imagine how this worked. When his chair and table were higher, the people on the other side wound up looking like little kids peering up over the too-high dining room table.

The next time we pack our schedules in order to look important, let's stop and ask ourselves if we want to relate to people in Lyndon Johnson style or in human being style. Which is more personally, inwardly, and deeply gratifying?

When we are tired of relating to the world in this nonintimate way, we can make changes in how we fill our time. First, we need awareness. Why are we accepting one more appointment, taking on one more class, buying one more item that will cause us to work more hours to pay for it, even thinking of buying a larger house, and so on? Get to the deep motivation for each big and little item on your agenda. Run out the logic of each one to the end. If I buy this larger house, it will give me immediate gratification, no doubt. But keep going. It will up my monthly mortgage payments for the next 30 years. What will that mean? I'll have to work more. What then? I'll have less time to hang out on the front porch peeling apples with my kids or mother while we chat away in the sunshine. Or: I want to take just this one class. Yes, the immediate gratification is terrific. What next? I won't be home. Do I have a spouse or children? That's one more night I won't see them. Do I complain about not having enough time for them? Hmmm. Or: So and so has invited me to be on this committee. It meets weekly, monthly, whatever. I really need to do this for my professional (or whatever) image. Makes sense until you run the logic to the end. Is my image more important than my daily life? More important than poring over AAA maps with my elderly mother? Think hard about this stuff. Some will make logical sense, some will not.

There is another reason why we stay busy: fear. We are afraid of down time because we're afraid to discover who we are. A meditation teacher once told me that we make our lives complex so we don't have to experience what is really going on. When we live simply, we slow down and see and feel. This may be uncomfortable at times; we are quiet and mindful and see the pain, dissatisfaction, and wanting. We think we're happy because we're not paying attention. We're so used to rushing through life on automatic pilot that we don't take the time to get to know ourselves. When we rarely take the time to nurture ourselves, we can be pretty empty inside.

We're so accustomed to having to accomplish something at all times that it is scary to stop. Stephan Rechtschaffen, M.D., author of *Timeshifting: Creating More Time to Enjoy Your Life*, often asks his patients to imagine they have a free moment and are sitting on their couches, prepared to do nothing. How do they feel?

"I think about everything I should be doing and get incredibly anxious," they commonly reply.

Rechtschaffen says that when we first try to relax, we don't feel relaxed at all. Instead of joy or serenity, we feel anxiety and guilt. So we jump from the couch and get busy because we sense, consciously or not, that this vague discomfort is merely the leading edge of a wave of negative emotions that have been waiting there all along. People often tell Rechtschaffen that they get busy fast because as soon as anxiety intrudes, they fear the "slippery slope." They're afraid to allow their emotions free rein; they worry that there will be no end to them, that the floodgates will open and they'll be consumed. Rechtschaffen says:

> We're afraid of solitude because we're afraid of the feelings that will rise before we can be at ease, afraid to confront who we are when stripped of our "doing" nature. We feel a need to be surrounded by people, by activity; to entrain with another's rhythm—anything but solitude. . . .
>
> Solitude takes practice. It requires facing down loneliness and realizing that there is nothing more important you can do. Far from being an indulgence, quiet, solitary contemplation—"doing nothing"—is as restorative as any elixir.

As Eknath Easwaran says, it is this very emptiness that drives us to pack in even more, seeking desperately to fill the void in our hearts. We need to do just the opposite: Slow down and live completely in the present. We'll begin to notice colors. We'll actually *see* birds in trees. We'll really *hear* music. We'll listen deeply to people as they speak to us . . . and we'll develop compassion and sensitivity toward other people as a result. We'll feel our feelings and get to know ourselves, rather than stuff our feelings as we rush on to the next project. This is called intimacy.

Adopt a New Attitude

Remember the old *I Love Lucy* episode about the candy factory? When Lucy and Ethel got a job wrapping candy in a factory and the manager kept speeding up the conveyor belt? At first, Lucy and Ethel were able to keep up the pace, but as the belt increased in speed, they were no longer able to keep up. Soon they began stuffing candy into their hats, down their shirts, into their pockets, and in their mouths so the manager wouldn't notice that they weren't keeping up. Sounds like our modern lives, doesn't it?

Enough already. Take the reading example. How about reading fewer books and taking the time to enjoy and savor each one? What's wrong with taking a whole Saturday afternoon to laze around with feet on the couch, reading? To enable ourselves to have this open time, we need first to accept the fact that none of us can possibly read and digest everything that flies in our doors. We can't possibly. So, rather than increasing our speed even more and trying to zoom through all the material (retaining about 1/16th), we need to get selective about what we will read. Very selective. Easwaran said this in *Take Your Time*:

> Make wise choices about what you read: Read only what is worthwhile. And then take the time to read carefully. I like to read slowly with complete attention; I don't even like background music or a cup of coffee at my side. And when I reach the end of a chapter or a section, I close the book and reflect on what I have read. I would much rather read one good book with concentration and understanding than skim through a list of best-sellers which I will not remember and which will have no effect on my life or my understanding of life. One book read with concentration and reflected upon is worth a hundred books flashed through without any absorption at all.

The classic bank line vignette offers another illustration of the power of changing our attitudes. You go to the bank. You see a line. What do you do? Grumble and growl that you must wait in line? Thump your foot? Fidget? Fret over the zillion things you have to do that day? Start mentally picking apart the person in front of you as being a jerk for getting there before you? All of the above? (The reason I can throw out these examples so quickly is because I've been there, done that.)

You realize, of course, you do have another choice. Take it. We all know the line will not go one bit faster simply because we are thumping, fretting, and fidgeting. What will go faster is our pulse rate, and you know what too much of that leads to. Adopting a new attitude means that we can *enjoy this moment of rest*. Our lives have become so speeded up by technology and pressure that we rarely have time to stop. Yet our bodies and souls *require* breathing space in order to function and survive. In his book *Timelock*, Ralph Keyes says: "The cumulative effect of eliminating one opportunity after another to catch our breath is to create a breathless society."

Think about this: As we fret and stew in the bank line for 5 or 10 minutes, we complain that we have no time for meditating or "down time." Hold the phone! We can use the bank line (or red light or doctor's waiting room) time as "down time." We do not need to assume the lotus position in a quiet sanctuary in the Himalayas in order to breathe, or simply *stop*. We can use our everyday, natural pauses like bank lines instead.

We can do even more than be thankful for this unexpected moment to breathe. We can go a step further by helping the other stressed people in line. Eknath Easwaran said that one time he was in a high-stress post-office line right before Christmas. Everyone was thumping and stewing. Finally Easwaran turned to the man behind him, who was really fretting, and asked if he would like to take his place in line. The man was completely taken aback, then began to relax. He apologized for being in such a hurry. The atmosphere of the whole line changed. If we don't want to change places in line, we can at least try to be friendly as a way to build solidarity in the moment.

I had a great lesson in this one time from my friend Laura. She and I were at a gathering of friends one time and I didn't feel well. So we located one of those walk-in medical clinics. We went in, and the receptionist told us it would be a good half hour to one hour before I could be seen. My first reaction was to fret, stew, and then immediately make mental plans to run to the nearby mall and do some errands during the waiting period. Laura, on the other hand, looked forward to a whole 30 to 60 minutes to sit and breathe. She talked me into doing the same. That was a wonderful learning experience for me. I learned for the first time that I did not have to cram activity into every second. It was so delightful to sit on my rear that day that I have done it ever since, whenever one of those moments arises.

Do One Thing at a Time

Before automated everything, people had time to assimilate and digest what was going on. Now we are bombarded every minute with information from computers, faxes, beepers, and cellular phones . . . and it's always urgent. We cook our meals in microwave ovens. Why? Not so we can relax, but so we have time to accomplish even *more*. We read books like the one I mentioned on organizing so we can get ideas on all the things we can do while our meal is zapping and our car is idling.

There actually is a modern-day term for doing two or more things at once: multitasking. This way you seemingly get more accomplished but never really get engrossed in any one thing. You're not enjoying the pleasure and sensations of cooking when you're zapping food in the microwave while paying bills. You're not really paying close attention to the state of your bank account when your mind is on the dinner. You're not really giving a friend the undivided attention he or she deserves when you're doing some other chore while talking.

When we try to do two or more things at once, we do none of them well, and we don't really experience anything. We are forever distracted and not really paying attention to any one task. Then we begin to worry. While walking out the door in the morning with our minds already on the job and not on the process of walking out the door, we worry that we may have forgotten to lock the door. We worry that we forgot to turn off the oven, because our minds were elsewhere while cooking. We worry we aren't doing our best at work because we are only putting part of ourselves into our projects. One time I was at home, getting ready to go visit a friend who lived a good distance away. I was doing at least two things at once in order to get ready to go. I wasn't paying mindful attention to anything. It wasn't until I got to my friend's house that I realized I had no idea whether I unplugged the coffee machine or not. I had cause to worry, since my neighbor's house had burned down as a result of a malfunctioning coffee machine. So I had to call a friend down the street to see if she would go peek in the window to check my machine. A little awareness would have saved me a lot of worry and my friend the hassle of traipsing over to my house. Once we learn really to focus and pay attention to one job at a time, we get a terrific benefit: No more worrying because we know we have done the best we could with each task.

I'm your average type B+ or A− person, and I need to remind myself constantly to do one thing at a time. If I'm stuck in traffic, my tendency is to open a book or other reading material and try to snatch glances at the page while the car idles. If I'm on the phone, my tendency is to sweep the kitchen floor or stir a pot. Do I want someone giving me that kind of halfhearted attention while they're on the phone with me? And why am I doing this to myself? Why not relax and simply enjoy the conversation? Why not catch my breath? It always feels better when I do.

Multitasking very much impacts our level of intimacy with other people. I thought a lot about this one weekend. I had made plans to spend the afternoon with one friend. Our plans were to get together late in the afternoon on a Saturday and go somewhere about an hour away. We had an event to attend and weren't sure how long it would take.

About two hours before I was ready to leave, another friend called me and said she had an extra ticket to a dance performance that night. Would I like to go? Sure I wanted to go. A free ticket to something I'd like to see? You bet.

Before I said yes, I thought about my first friend's feelings. Even though the first friend and I only made plans for the late afternoon and not necessarily the evening, I knew how I felt when people double-booked themselves with me. It has happened to all of us, and we've probably done it to others. We'll make plans with a group of friends to go to some daylong event, like hiking on a Saturday afternoon. Some of those times one of the people will invariably double-book and make separate evening plans that necessitate the rest of us having to leave the hike earlier than we'd like, in order to make sure the double-booker gets back on time. They make these plans *after* making the original plan.

Without question, I have been guilty of this double-booking offense, and I always resent it when it happens to me. Usually the double-bookers make plans without checking with the hiking (or whatever) group first. They allow just enough time for the hike and drive without an extra minute to spare. What was originally planned as a leisurely afternoon turns into yet another tightly scheduled event.

As much as I wanted to go to the dance performance, I wound up saying no to the invitation. I said no out of respect for my first friend, and I also said no for myself. Even if the first friend could have cared less about whether we rushed back or not, I personally didn't want to rush. Enough. Enough. Enough. I wanted to savor the first event and let it roll out naturally. I figure life is fast enough and I have enough schedules to follow that I didn't need to pack more in on a Saturday afternoon.

It's not easy saying no. We're so used to thinking we should be able to taste every darned thing on the banquet table that we wind up not enjoying any of it. There are thousands of seductive activities waiting for our attendance every day. We hate to miss any of them. But simple living has taught me one thing: It is not only fine to miss a good portion of the things, it is better. Doing less allows us to enjoy each event thoroughly, and when we single-book with others, it shows them that they are important.

Think of Time as Sacred

Sacred time is our time. We own our time. Most of us don't see it that way— we give it away all over the place and then wonder where it went. In order to make your time sacred, you need to learn about setting boundaries. I became acquainted with this idea while in law school. A law school friend got a part-time job working for one of the professors. This was a fairly prestigious connection—the professors didn't ask just anyone to help them. Because of the prestige, it is very easy for students to get off-balance and take on more than they can handle. They want to please the professors at all costs. Nevertheless, this particular friend impressed me to no end when the professor asked that she do a particular project in a specific amount of time, and my friend politely said no.

Students rarely said no to professors. But my friend calmly went to the professor and said that in looking at all of the other work she needed to do within that time, she would not be able to do both. The professor not only didn't fire my friend, she went a step further and respected her for knowing her limits.

I have seen what happens when we don't set limits. I had another friend who had a job in the business world. She let insecurity rule and did not know how to say no to more work than she could reasonably take on. As a result, she was forever running overtime in a tizzy, trying to catch up, and staying exhausted. This was because she was too afraid that if she said no, it would mean that she wasn't competent and might get disrespected or fired. Au contraire. I've been on both sides of this equation. As a boss, I thoroughly respect people who work hard and efficiently and also are aware of their limits. I have had employees say no to me, and when I know they are hardworking, efficient people, I respect them. I would much, much rather they said no because then I know they know their limits and what they can handle in order to do a good job. I love knowing I can ask for a certain project to be done in a certain amount of time, and it will get done and get done well. I am not impressed by someone scrambling overtime and in a frenzy to get something done for me or anyone else. This doesn't mean you would never agree to work overtime. It does mean that if you do agree to work overtime, you know your capabilities and are fully aware that this is a special occasion and will require extra hours. With full consciousness, you are willing to go forward. This kind of awareness is vastly different from those people who operate on autopilot, always saying yes out of insecurity and always running in a tizzy to catch up.

You can say no with good conscience only if two factors are present: (1) You work mindfully when you do work (and as a result you'll work hard and efficiently), and (2) you are aware of what you are doing in your life and what is important to you. If you say your family life is important, for example, then why are you at your office every other night until 7:00 P.M. catching up on all of the work you couldn't say no to? If you say you love to work in your garden but just can't find the time, why are you signing up for another committee or class? You need to get out of reactive mode and into centered mode. Structure your time around what is important in your life.

Perhaps it would be a good idea some day, fantastic as it sounds, to muffle every telephone, quiet every motor, and stop all activity—just to give people a chance to ponder and reflect on what life is all about, why they are living, and what they really want.

—James Truslow Adams, historian

Saying no applies to both work and personal time. I am equally impressed by people who set limits on their personal time. I have a friend who, with her family, decided that every Thursday night would be family night. They all agreed that they would stay home that night. On more than one of these Thursday nights I have attempted to intrude by asking my friend to do X or Z special, enticing activity with me. She has steadfastly said no, because she respects her sacred time. I may be disappointed for the moment, but I respect her very much for setting and sticking to her boundaries.

We need to be able to discriminate between activities. In India, there is a saying: "Lack of discrimination is the greatest danger." When we lack discrimination, we do not know when to throw ourselves into something and when not to get entangled in it. We say yes to every other activity or task that comes our way because we think we need to accomplish . . . constantly. We can't keep up with what we have on our plates. Then anxiety sets in. We need to look at every new temptation very carefully and ask ourselves what it will do to our lives. If it is absolutely necessary, or if it will add to our lives in a positive, not frenetic, way, then we should say yes. Otherwise, our lives will be better off if we allow more open, free-flowing time by saying no.

A man named Duncan Caldwell once said this: "Americans have more time-saving devices and less time than any other group of people in the world."

How could this be true? After all, it *is* faster to cook dinner with a microwave than a regular oven. It *is* faster to chop with a food processor than a knife. It *is* faster to mow the lawn with a power mower than a push mower. What gives?

It is faster for a particular job to use a convenience tool, yes. But when we look at the big picture, we actually lose time. Here is why. Consider the lawn mower. Before any lawn mower was invented, people didn't even have lawns, so there was no lawn to mow. Now we all think it is our constitutional right to have a private lawn . . . and pay the price two or three times. One price is the extra work we need to do in order to earn the money to buy a lawn mower. A second is the time we spend repairing the things. A third is what we do on Sunday mornings instead of relaxing: We're out there schlepping up and down on our lawns with a mower in front of us. If we had no lawn, we would save lots of time. Go through your kitchens and add up the money you have spent on convenience gadget-o-matics. (Once again, I speak from experience.) How much do you earn at your job? How many additional hours did you spend at your job earning the money to buy all of these items? How many additional hours do you spend cleaning these items? How much larger a kitchen do you need to pay for in order to store these items? And finally, how much more do you expect yourself to do in the kitchen because you have these sophisticated machines?

The University of Michigan did a survey once and found virtually no difference in time spent on housework between those who owned many appliances and those who didn't. I know firsthand how this works. Take my automatic, $200 juicer that I *had* to buy one day. (Fresh juice would make me healthier and thus, give me a better life. It seemed logical at the time.) After whizzing up some carrot juice, do you have any idea how incredibly much more time it takes me to pull the pieces of that thing apart, clean them all, and reassemble, than it does to grab a confounded carrot out of the refrigerator and eat it raw? Come now. Am I healthier? Heck no, because I never want the hassle of using the darned thing. But maybe yes. Now I eat the original thing: carrots. Do you know it takes an entire shelf in my kitchen cabinet just to store the juicer? Then there's the laundry mystique. In our grandmother's time, doing the laundry was a big deal. Because it was such a big deal, people didn't have as many clothes and didn't wash them as often. Now that it is so easy to throw a load into the washing machine and dryer, we think nothing of changing our clothes two or more times a day. And now we *expect* that we will look spotless at all times. In that same study, the researchers found that laundry took the average mid-1960s woman one hour *more* a week than the woman in the 1920s.

So what am I saying? I'm not advocating getting rid of all appliances. I am saying think about the big picture before you purchase your next "time-saving" device. Some devices are worth it, many are not. I happen to be a person who uses my food processor regularly. The amount of use I get from it, plus the fact that it is fairly easy to clean, makes it worth it to me. For others, this is not so. Then there are the tool collections found in many basements. I have a friend whose husband went out and "had to buy" an expensive machine that would make a stairway banister. The wife waited and waited for the banister to be made, and finally hired a handyman to make it with his own tools. We all have these stories.

Big appliances like dishwashers are another time-clutter addition. If you must have a dishwasher (don't feel guilty, I have one too), buy one that is easy to maintain. The more sophisticated the machine, the more it will cost you to repair. When I needed a new one, I asked a dishwasher repairman which brand was the simplest to repair. It wasn't the one with all the latest bells and whistles. When you see a miracle chop-o-matic advertised on TV, think twice. A good-quality chef's knife will last forever, is a snap to clean, takes little room to store, and probably costs far less. Plus, that act of chopping gives you some meditative down time to focus on what you are doing. (Take your mini-stress breaks where you find them.)

Look at the Big Picture

In a classic book, titled *How to Get Control of Your Time and Your Life,* by Alan Lakein, the author asks us not to concoct a more elaborate method of using our DayTimer but to stop and look at the big picture. Consider: What do you want out of your life? What if you had six months to live? Would you spend your time as you spend it now? Don't look at how you could maximize little increments of time; look instead at your whole life. Ralph Keyes summed up Lakein's theory in his book *Timelock:*

> Only by making time to step back can we spot the clutter in our lives. In the process we may come to realize how welcome a distraction that clutter can be. And how addictive it is to be rushed and busy. Thinking about such matters doesn't just take time; it takes courage. Bigger things in life are more

Lake Timebegone

by Julie Ristau and Ellen Ryan

A farmer in Minnesota sat at the kitchen table with his daughter, now a city dweller, who had come back home to the farm, as always, during the harvest. Gazing out the window at the ripened fields, she recalled the stories she had heard about horse-drawn plows, the hand-picking of corn, and the threshing teams that went from farm to farm. She remembered back to the four-row combine her father had bought 20 years ago; and how her grandfather, sitting atop a load of corn harvested by the new wonder machine, shook his head in amazement. "I can remember when us brothers worked together and we would feel like we were really moving if we had picked three acres in a day," her grandfather said.

She now asked her father to reflect about how harvesting has changed over the years. He tipped back his mug for the last swallow of coffee and answered, "Everyone has to get it all out by the end of October now."

"Why?" she asked.

"Because they have the machinery to do it."

She remembered her dad out plowing in the cold as late as December, and how his cheeks shone ruddy red when he'd come in for supper and call it a day. Back then Thanksgiving was really a celebration of the harvest and of the fact that everyone in the community was almost done for the year.

Although her father had always farmed on a small scale, plenty of farmers had started accumulating more land in the 1960s and '70s. More acres meant larger equipment, and suddenly the narrow iron bridges on country roads were torn out to make way for wider tractors and combines. Scores of cottonwood trees along the creeks were ripped out overnight so that there would be more tillable soil and the big machinery could turn around more easily. . . .

As a 16-row combine swallowed up a cornfield across the road, she continued the conversation with her brother, who now farms the family's land. "In the past few years," he said, "if you haven't been done harvesting by Halloween, you're in trouble." The solution, it seemed, was to avoid depending on the mercy of nature by picking up the pace and working faster than the weather did. Big machinery and working around the clock made it possible.

Once farmers didn't have options like these. They simply did what they could with what they had. They could only "get it out" as fast as their family could work. More is possible now, and farmers judge themselves accordingly. With 40-row equipment, harvest may soon begin and end on a sunny morning in mid-August.

Ristau and Ryan are co-directors of the Minnesota Rural Organizing Project. 612-645-6159.

frightening to deal with than smaller things. There's more at stake; more to lose. Yet another reason to keep our calendars filled with little tasks is that it's easier to get a grip on little tasks. Busyness can keep us from having to reflect, risk intimacy, or face the void. We haven't got the time. . . . We're never forced to ask ourselves what really matters.

In his book *The 7 Habits of Highly Effective People,* author Stephen Covey asks us to imagine we are at our own funeral. What would we like people to say about us? That we were on all sorts of committees and made a small or large fortune? That we drove an exotic and important-looking car? That we lived in a sprawling house filled with totally cool things? What? That we were a devoted friend, parent, child, and partner? What exactly did we do that made us devoted? Were we kind? Were we a good listener?

He also asks readers to write their own mission statement about what is important in their lives. A mission statement usually is thought of as something a business writes in order to make better use of its time, money, and energy. Covey asks us to do the same for our lives. If we have a clue about what we want out of life, we are more likely to make our many daily decisions in alignment with a set of deeply held values. Thus, if your mission statement includes spending more time with your children or partner, you will be able to choose jobs that will allow you that time, and when you are on the job, you will be able to take on only those projects that fit in with your plan. Don't think this can't be done, because it can. I have a friend who had just graduated from engineering school and had two small children. She turned down a higher-paying, more prestigious job to go to a lower-paying firm that had a more positive work/family balance. If you have a mission statement or some clue about what you want out of life, you can bring that awareness with you when you apply for jobs. Believe me, any boss worth working for will respect you more if you know yourself and your boundaries than if you go in there willing to do any wild cartwheel just to get and keep a job. Centered bosses like centered employees. Centered people like centered friends.

Leave Your Job at Work

Like most things in life, technology has it's yin and yang (positive and negative). The positive is convenience and speed. Every now and then, convenience and speed are useful, no doubt. But the negative is that technology has enabled us to be tied to work almost constantly. We've all seen these things, and many of us have done them: talking on the cell phone while driving, while waiting in line at the post office; no joke, a friend told me she saw a man with a cell phone scrunched in his shoulder *while playing a pickup basketball game!* Beepers are on everybody's belts. You used to be able to spot the physicians among us by their telltale beeper; no more. Now everybody has an emergency about everything.

Forget about taking your phone off the hook. (Remember that?) Now our voice mail systems are ready 24 hours a day to gather messages, phone off the hook or not. And if that isn't fast enough, we can E-mail and fax each other. We *will* get through, whether someone want us to or not. And forget about relaxing on an airplane now. (Remember trashy paperbacks you'd buy at the airport bookstore?) Now we take our offices with us via laptop computers.

And natural down times are no more. Think about what happens during snow days, for example. Prior to electronic everything, we got to take the day off and lounge around all day. We couldn't get to work because the roads were closed, so nobody expected us to work. What happens now? Sorry. E-mail, beepers, faxes, computers, and who knows what else are there, ready and waiting to hook us up to our jobs. We are now expected to keep working right on through everything. Why? Because we *can*. No other reason. I read in one report that after the San Francisco earthquake in 1989, many people who were cut off from their offices wound up working from home via computers even before they had a chance to sweep up all the broken glass.

What's wrong with this picture? In the name of efficiency, we've given up control over our time . . . we've given up the security of isolated moments and have become prisoners of our movable offices.

We can set aside certain hours of the day to unhook from technology. I understand that in Japan, some offices created "no communication time" where people can't communicate with each other electronically for an hour a day. It's sort of like an abbreviated siesta. We can refuse to use a cell phone or beeper. (I still manage to get through life just fine without a beeper on my belt or cell phone in my car. Those old-fashioned telephone booths continue to stand, ready to serve, whenever the need may arise. In exchange, I have given myself the gift of quiet time in my car.) We can refuse to take work home, save for emergencies. Or we can structure our work time at home and allow ourselves 30 minutes a night, or one weekend day a month. For those of us who work in home-based businesses, we can set limits on which hours we are "at work." The statement that has always had the most impact on me is this: If we can't get our work done in 8 hours, we can't get it done in 10 or 12 either.

Remember this rule when you take your mental work home and worry and think about what you should be doing. Give yourself, say, 20 minutes to spend on worrying or thinking about your job when you get home. After the allotted time is up, push it out of your mind. But during the worry/thinking period, really get in there and worry and think like heck. Sit quietly with your worry for 20 minutes, and turn it over and over in your mind. Take a look at all sides. Then turn it off. This program works because you are giving full attention to all the worries and thoughts you may have about your job. When you are finished, you know you have worried and thought about things the best you could possibly do. It's like sprinting rather than jogging. After you sprint, you often drop in a heap, exhausted. Same thing. You get the worry out and then you can drop it until the next time. If you continue to worry or think after the allotted time, maintain your awareness and say no to yourself. Push the thoughts out of your head. Keep doing this and, eventually, practice will make perfect and you'll be able to confine your work thoughts so they do not pervade your whole life.

An American legislator sponsoring a bill that would prohibit employers from firing or even disciplining employees who refuse to work overtime asked: "Should individuals' time be ruled by the large corporations that they work for, or should people have the basic right to live their own lives, on their own time?"

Don't wait for some law to be passed until you take control of your life and time. Create your own inner law and then follow it.

Religious or Not, Rest One Day a Week

There are other ways to stop. One is to follow ancient religious customs such as observing the Sabbath. Sabbath is the seventh day of the week, Saturday, observed as the day of rest and religious observance among the Jews and in some Christian churches. Most Christians observe the first day of the week, Sunday. According to the Bible, the temporal pattern of working for six days and then resting on the seventh is a divine pattern, closely linked to the Creation of the World: "And on the seventh day God finished His work which He had made; and He rested on the seventh day from all His work which He had made."

Religious or not, it makes good sense to take off one day a week to rest. If you are religious, you can use the time for spiritual matters. If you are not religious, you need to put a big "x" through every Saturday or Sunday on your calendar (or whatever day fits for you—but keep it regular), so you can't schedule work on that day. Use it for rest and relaxation. Go have fun with your family. Goof off. Read all day. Just don't work. I got to know a religious family who observes the Sabbath so strictly that they don't even cook on Saturday. They do their cooking ahead the night before. After services, they pack up the food and take off for a family hike. In poor weather they find other restful family activities to do.

19

We all need this break. Our bodies and minds need it desperately. We simply can't keep racing 24 hours a day, 7 days a week, and expect to stay sane and healthy. In order to observe your day of rest, you need to be diligent about setting limits for yourself. There is *always* more work to be done, whether it's around the house or at the office. So give yourselves a break.

Fill Your Pot

When we don't take time for ourselves, we can't give to others. I know this isn't easy. Once my friend Renee went to the doctor complaining of exhaustion. She was (and still is) raising four children. The doctor told her to remember to take time out to care for herself. Renee slumped further into her chair and announced, "That's one more person I have to take care of!"

Sad, but true. I know the feeling well, and that's with only two kids. But I know I have more to give my children and everybody else when I take time out for myself. I know I can't keep going and going and doing and doing and expect to be a decent human being. Taking time for myself doesn't mean that I need to schedule an entire weekend off or go to Tahiti once a month. (Hmmmm, not a bad idea. . . .) It means taking the time to rejuvenate as I

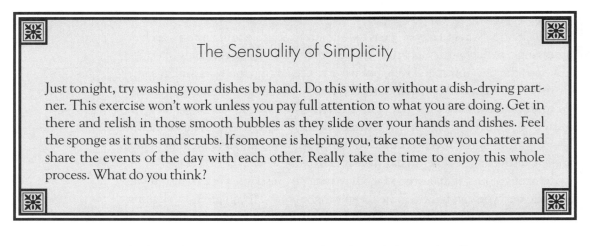

The Sensuality of Simplicity

Just tonight, try washing your dishes by hand. Do this with or without a dish-drying partner. This exercise won't work unless you pay full attention to what you are doing. Get in there and relish in those smooth bubbles as they slide over your hands and dishes. Feel the sponge as it rubs and scrubs. If someone is helping you, take note how you chatter and share the events of the day with each other. Really take the time to enjoy this whole process. What do you think?

find it. Like meditative time hand-washing dishes and really paying attention to what I'm doing. A walk outside for a half an hour with or without a friend. Twenty minutes meditating. (More on this in the chapter on inner simplicity.) I know that when I am stressed, I have little to give others. What a lousy way to live. I call rejuvenating filling up my bank account. Virginia Satir, author and psychologist, describes it as the stew pot theory: "Nothing is more wonderful on a cold day than dishing out bowls of hot stew. It's nurturing, it's love, it's friendship. But at some point, you have to stop dipping and fill up the stew pot. Nurture yourself, so you can then nurture others."

Whichever term you use, remember the principle. Take time for yourself and you will have something to give to others.

BOB AND JODY HAUG: LIVING THEIR OWN AMERICAN DREAM

Bob Haug once had it all, according to traditional American standards: big house on a lake, boats, cars, a successful business, more money than he needed. His path to this success was direct and unblinking. College, hard work, visions of the good life just ahead. Like so many others, he never thought about pursuing any other kind of life. What other kind of life was there, anyway?

Bob and Jody Haug in their kitchen.

One day, 20 years ago, Haug gave it all up and left. He now lives the antithesis of that traditional dream: very little money and a place just large enough to turn around in. No lake and an old car. But something else entered the picture that wasn't there before—contentment like he'd never felt before. Today, Bob and his wife, Jody, live an unburdened and peaceful life. They spend very little and need very little. Although they have just enough money and modest living quarters, the Haugs say life is immeasurably rich and full of meaning, and they wouldn't trade it for anything.

Bob and Jody Haug live in the small basement of their house. The main and upper floors are rented to two other families. The space for the Haugs is just big enough for their needs without an inch to spare, and that is just how they like it, because they have no need for anything more.

The living area is centered around a large wooden table that is surrounded by built-in, padded benches, all built by the Haugs. Bob says this is the center of the room because people congregate at the dining room table anyway, so why not make it comfortable and the focus of the room? There are only two other chairs in the room. Next to the table is the compact and efficient kitchen, with no walls in between. Their Norwegian-style dish drainer is built in directly above the sink, so when they wash dishes, they simply put them in the drainer to drip dry into the sink. The drainer doubles as a cabinet. There are no doors on the kitchen cabinets because the couple didn't think dishes needed to be hidden. Their stove is small because it works as well as a large one.

The Haugses' bedroom is simply a bed built into an alcove. A tiny closet separates it from the office section of the house. The closet is tiny because they don't need a lot of clothes. The bathroom is just a bit larger than the head of a boat and, indeed, even has a boat-size sink. "Why do we need a bigger one?" Bob asks. Down the hallway, the Haugs built an innovative guest room for their constant swarm of visitors (two from Norway just left and a lady from Japan was on her way). Inside are two built-in double-size sets of bunk beds, a small closet and shelf, all built by the Haugs. A movable wall separates that guest room from an adjoining one, with another built-in bunk bed. This way, the Haugs say, either one large family can use both rooms, or separate visitors desiring more privacy can partition the rooms into two. A third bedroom is for their 16-year-old son. Each bedroom is just large enough to fit a bed, closet and shelf, desk space and no more. And each room seems to do the job just fine.

The Haugs even managed to build into this space a root cellar, where they store all of Bob's fresh-picked and canned produce from the garden, and a fully equipped shop where they can do their own building and repair work. Jody has a good-size area for her knitting and sewing projects, and both share the office area, complete with a computer. They can manage in a small place only because they don't have any wasted space.

"When you're planning a house," Bob says, "start with what you actually do instead of what your preconceived ideas are, so what you build and use is really functional. I've seen people with living rooms where they covered the furniture with plastic. Well, as far as I'm concerned, they might as well cut that room off and throw it away. If you need extra space, go outside or take off for the weekend!"

Bob remembers the house he once lived in during his affluent days, which had a picture window larger than the length of his entire present house. But he has never once regretted leaving his old life. "Not one second of darkness," he says. "In fact, I look back in horror thinking about living that way again."

Bob's life used to be a paragon of the American dream. "I owned an office supply business in the Midwest," he says. "And I was making more money than I knew what to do with. I used to grab a quick lunch and sit by the river and began to ask myself why I was doing this. I had discovered that growth wasn't healthy for the little community where I lived . . . it merely resulted in increased crime, hordes of people moving in that the town couldn't accommodate, manufacturing plants springing up all over. In American vernacular, though, this was success.

"Then I wondered what I could accomplish except to make more money? But that had no value left to me anymore when there were so many other things I wanted to do, like helping people."

When his children were grown and after much soul searching, Bob left his business, cars, boats, and house to his wife, who had grown to like their standard of living and chose not to accompany him on his journey. He packed two suitcases, pocketed $100, and went to Florida because it was familiar to him. He first created a job managing a department at the University of Florida, then eventually found a job working with troubled kids. He began living simply. He learned to eat simply, forsaking all red meat and buying in bulk to save money. He bought his clothes at thrift stores and operated with only the cash he had. He learned about food packaging and how a box of cereal in the supermarket can cost more than a steak, all due to advertising and hype. "We need to stop feeding landfills with needless packaging," he says.

During his 10-year stay in Florida he saved enough money to buy himself a VW camper and left for Seattle. He has never looked back. "I've got so much more freedom now," he says. "More freedom . . . I would never trade this second part of my life because of the great freedom that I've had. I grew up with the idea that making money was the thing to do. To be economically successful was the goal, to be an upstanding member of the community . . . the pride of the people around you. I just don't feel that way anymore."

Not long after arriving in Seattle, Bob found a job and met his present wife, Jody. She had been living simply for years. The two shared a Norwegian heritage and love of the water. Later, Bob retired, and now he and Jody work occasionally, doing things they like.

"People come up to us and say 'I don't know how you folks can work only occasionally and go on all those trips to Norway,'" Bob says, "and then they go out and jump in their $15,000 car. If they had even bought a $10,000 car, that would have given them $5,000 to go to Norway!"

But the Haugs do manage frequent trips to Norway, once for nine months, and they continue their simple way of life while traveling. They camp out, stay in hostels, cook their own food, and travel lightly so they can get around on public transportation. On their nine-month trip, they found a woman who rented the basement of her farmhouse to them for $75 a month. And when they travel throughout the United States, they go in their used van, which serves as both hotel and restaurant.

"Living this way gives us freedom to do this kind of thing whenever we feel like doing it," he says. "It has given us freedom to do all kinds of things we wouldn't do otherwise."

Bob spends much of his free time growing the family food and canning it, operating a hobby business importing and distributing Norwegian folk music, and working as a volunteer for Sound Keeper for local environmental organizations.

Whenever possible, the Haugs walk. When they go grocery shopping, a mile away, they pack up a grocery bag and walk. If they need to go farther, they take the bus. The couple shares one car, but most of the time it sits in front of the house, unused. If it needs repair, both Bob and Jody know how to fix it.

For holidays and birthdays, they make gifts or exchange time or services. "Before, I used to buy all my gifts," Bob says. "Now when we make a gift for someone, we're giving something of ourselves. We have time to do that now.

"The way to live like this is to begin by kicking out all preconceived ideas of what you need. That's hard for people to do. They come into our bathroom and say 'Oh, it's too small,' but it's a matter of perspective. I say get into a boat sometime and then this doesn't seem small anymore.

"Most of us are economic slaves always looking to be entertained," Bob says. "But that's also a matter of perspective. Now I think a walk is entertainment. Not only is it free, but you actually gain health from it. I look forward to going to the grocery store because it gives me an excuse to walk. We tell people if they want to make this kind of living work, they need to separate their needs from their wants. And they need to do it with a very sharp knife."

❖ ❖ ❖ ❖ ❖ ❖ ❖ ❖ ❖ ❖ ❖ ❖ ❖

Resources

Finding Time by Paula Peisner Coxe (Naperville, IL: Sourcebook Trade, 1992)
Simple meditations for overcoming fatigue, busyness, stress, and the ticking clock—but not giving up your life to do so.

Gracious Living in a New World by Alexandra Stoddard (New York: William Morrow, 1996)
A declaration of independence for those wanting a new relationship to life. Stoddard takes life and shows it for the miracle that it is, explains why our relationship to it has been altered in our modern culture, and provides methods for finding the keys to rediscover the awe. There's a special focus on grace in our lives: getting it, earning it, relishing it.

How to Get Control of Your Time and Your Life by Alan Lakein (New York: New American Library, 1996)
Classic study on the perennial nag of balancing time and life. Helpful guide to solving some critical problems related to fatigue, stress, and willpower and opening the flowers of creativity.

Private Moments, Secret Selves by Jeffrey Kottler, Ph.D. (New York: Ballantine Books, 1990)
Solitary time need not be anxious time or time for boredom. Psychotherapist Kottler claims

that it can be the source of much creativity and inspiration as well as peace, spiritual insight, and inner enrichment.

Slowing Down in a Speeded-Up World by Adair Lara (Berkeley, CA: Conari Press, 1994)
A collection of tiny essays that bring the full impact of the insane rat race on our lives and our planet, and what to do about it. Includes many confessions of real folks about finding tranquility in a spinning treadmill we call modern life.

Take Your Time by Eknath Easwaran (Tomales, CA: Nilgiri Press, 1994)
Inspirational account of learning to slow down for the sake of sanity, self-growth, physical healing, and focusing attention. Takes a contrarian view to slowing down—it's more of an attitude than a state of being.

The Berenstain Bears and Too Much Pressure by Stan Berenstain and Jan Berenstain (New York: Random House, 1992)
What happens to the Bear family when they overcommit themselves to many time-eating activities and what they learn about slowing down.

Timelock by Ralph Keys (New York: HarperCollins, 1991)
Uncovering the brambles behind the hectic life and the remedies that are needed to remove them and clear the way for a saner, healthier, less-stressed existence.

Timeshifting by Stephan Rechtschaffen, M.D. (New York: Doubleday, 1996)
Explains how time is manufactured in the mind yet manifested in the body. Also teaches how to make wise and conscious choices about what you do and when you do it, and learning to have some say in your destiny.

2
Money

I owe, I owe, so off to work I go.

—ANONYMOUS

What does money have to do with simplifying your life? Everything. Like it or not, everything. It is the actual green bills as well as our attitudes about money that can either bury or free us.

It is easy to thumb our noses at money once we get involved with voluntary simplicity and say things like "I don't need to think about money because voluntary simplicity is about higher values." Or: "Anyone knows that money is not the source of happiness, so why spend time worrying about it?"

Voluntary simplicity is not about being broke or running away from money. It's about getting in control of your money and letting it work for you instead of against you, as it does with debt. The right attitudes and practices about money can buy you a heck of a lot of freedom.

Save That Money!

There is no secret rocket science to understanding the relationship between money and a simple life. Here is the rule: *If you don't want to work too much, don't spend the money.* Plain and simple.

Most of us remain in bondage to our jobs because we keep spending our money, which means we need to keep working in order to earn more money to spend again. Then we complain that we're stressed from working too much and tied to jobs we don't like.

When you have money saved, you have options. You can stop working for a few months to think about what you want out of life, you can work part time, or you can keep working at your job knowing that you have the option to leave. You have no choices if you have no money saved. Granted, saving money is not easy, because we live in a consumer culture that encourages us to keep spending in order to find happiness. This concept is so prevalent in our society that sure enough, of all things, in a newspaper magazine section devoted to the subject of managing your money, I ran across the following advertisement for a luxury car: "To reduce stress, you can get a cool car or a puppy. The [name of the car] is for those who refuse to drive a puppy."

Please hold the phone! What kind of hocus pocus are we gobbling up? The prescription for reducing stress is to go out and buy a car that costs more than most of us earn in two years? This is exactly how we *create* stress. We blindly accept what these ads tell us, turn on our automatic pilot button, and head for the store. On the way to the store, we turn up the volume on our rationalization button until it is the loudest voice in our heads: "This car will make me look like I've made it and for that reason it is worth going into debt. This car will make my life easier. I won't have to keep repairing my old one anymore. It is worth spending my savings. This car will impress the heck out of people who see me driving it." On and on.

If we are the average person with little or no savings and we buy this car, we have just obligated ourselves to high payments for the next three to five years or used up our savings. Either way we have just tied ourselves to our jobs for at least five more years for this "stress reducer." Add on more than five years for all of the other things we buy daily, hourly, and monthly. We then complain that we are overworked and don't like our jobs but can't quit because we have nothing to live on past our paychecks.

> *Normal is getting dressed in clothes that you buy for work, driving through traffic in a car that you are still paying for, in order to get to the job that you need so you can pay for the clothes, car, and the house that you leave empty all day in order to afford to live in it.*
>
> —ELLEN GOODMAN,
> NATIONALLY SYNDICATED COLUMNIST

Enter the simple living guide to money management. Shrieks. Moans. Groans. "I'm not going to go live in some shack and eat berries all day. No, thanks. Keep your money management plan."

Hold it! The simple living money management plan will give you back your life! There is a way to have a good life today and also save money so you can have a good life tomorrow. You can buy yourself freedom. Assuming you are employed, you can do all of this with the money you earn now.

The plan is this: Think of money as interrelated with your life—it is not some separate little entity that you sit down with once a week or month and use to, ugh, *budget*. It is part of your life. Call it the holistic approach to money, which asks you to take a look at your whole life. Are you leading the kind of life you'd always dreamed of for yourself and/or your family? Or are you running on the treadmill, spending, working, spending, and working? If you know what you want from life, you're more likely to realize that a more expensive house, car, or endless new outfits will not make your life better. You will be able to sail through stores without getting seduced by every gadget that sparkles at you. When you hang on to your money, you can start investing and earning more money. You will then have the freedom to choose the kind of life you would like rather than spending most of your waking hours working to pay off your debt or working to consume. Think of this as a financial fitness plan, similar to physical fitness. You know how much better you feel when you are physically fit?

As for your life goals, only you know what they are. Write them down. Brainstorm. What kind of life do you want? Sail the seven seas? Live in a house in the country with a dozen orphaned children? Have time to work with disabled people? Have time for your own children, parents, spouse, and friends? How much time? If you are in a profession you like, maybe you'd like to continue but donate your services instead (say legal or medical) to those in need. Maybe you'd like to work part time, or join your neighborhood playhouse and do a little acting. Often what people really want out of life are good friends, fulfilling work, family ties, and interesting experiences.

What do these things cost? Can you have them with your present lifestyle? Are you working too many hours and doing too much to be able to spend time with family and friends? Is your work fulfilling? Do you complain that you never get to take nice vacations? Meanwhile, are you making installment payments for cars, boats, and gadgets? Or spending your entire paycheck every week just making ends meet? If you say your goal is spending more time with family yet you are living in an exotic house that requires you to work like heck to make your mortgage payments, you need to rethink your priorities. It's no surprise you have nothing left over for your larger life goals. Something has to give. If you stay on your present track, you won't be able to work less and thus have more free time.

Track Your Spending

How can you achieve these goals without sacrificing today?

First, start tracking your spending. This will show you what you currently think is important. A wonderful book titled *Your Money or Your Life,* by Joe Dominguez and Vicki Robin, explains this plan in detail. Carry around a little notebook and record each and every purchase you make. If you pay $2 cash for a cappuccino, write it down. If you pay 60 cents for a pack of gum, write it down. Be sure to write clear memos in your checkbook as well. At first this will seem very tedious, but the process becomes automatic after a very short time. This procedure is the number-one way I know of to get you acquainted with your financial habits so you can begin taking control.

At the end of the month when you get your bank and credit card statements, haul out your notebook and bank records and make a spreadsheet. A spreadsheet can be as simple as a piece of paper with columns or more high tech, like a money management software program such as Quicken. Take a look at your expenses and figure out the categories where you most often spend your money. No doubt food will be one category, but don't make it quite that simple. Divide food into meals, snacks, cappuccinos, lunches out, dinners out. Bags of potato chips fall into the snack category. Go through the rest of your expenses and do your best to divide other large categories as well. Clothing is another example. If you have a job, you likely purchase clothes for work and clothes for leisure. Separate them. Add up each category. This will tell you a couple of things. One, it will show you in graphic detail where your money goes each month. No longer will you be able to complain that you don't know what happens to your paycheck. Two, it will give you an idea of your priorities. Maybe you've been taking a lot of weekend trips away and are surprised at how much money you have spent in this category over time. Perhaps you are so exhausted from work that you go out to last-minute dinners three times a week. You may be shocked when you add up this category. Maybe you spent a lot of money on tools or kitchen gadgets. These expenses tell you something about who you are.

Next, this chart will show you where you can cut back if you have nothing saved or are in debt. I once spoke to a man who was attending college. He was very disappointed when he realized he didn't have the funds to continue and would have to quit. Then he sat down and looked carefully at his expenses for the month. He was surprised to find that he could save $300 per month by cutting out miscellaneous expenses, such the latte and newspaper that he bought each morning as he commuted to school on the ferry.

On the surface, it looks as if this man needed to deny himself. After all, what is daily life if you can't indulge in a little pleasure once in a while? But he was not denying himself; he was making important choices that would lead to his larger life goal. He preferred to finish college than to drink lattes every morning. Since he didn't have the funds for both, he made a choice.

The habit of gratifying every immediate need gets many of us into financial trouble. We use the excuse, "I work hard so I deserve a reward." Take a look at the Catch 22 we have created: We work hard, so we spend money on rewards. We spend money, so we need to keep working hard.

No doubt we should reward ourselves and we should include daily pleasures in our lives, but we need to keep the rewards, pleasures, and life goals in perspective. We can do this by creating a financial plan that leads to *our life goal.* The plan should include money set aside for fun and pleasure, and it should also include money for saving and investing. While it is important to keep our life goal in focus, we also need to be mindful that goals, like life, are fluid. Yet that fluidity should not alter our saving pattern. Continue putting a given or increased amount of money aside on a regular basis no matter how often your goal may change. You'll still have a pot of money at the end for whatever your goal may be. If you do not begin saving, you will never have a pot and, thus, will have no choices.

Rethink Success

If you want to lead a truly fulfilling life, you may need to start by rethinking what constitutes success. Traditionally in our culture, success has meant driving a late-model luxury car, carrying around a gold VISA card, wearing designer watches and shoes, and living in a fancy house. No question we've all envied people who had those things, thinking their lives must somehow be better than ours. Think again. Many of the people hauling around these outward trappings of the good life are in debt up to their ears and are simply renting a lifestyle they cannot afford. Stories abound about the highly paid executives who seem to have all of the above until they lose their jobs or some calamity happens in their lives. They not only lose these material badges of prosperity, but they often lose their identities as well. When you spend the majority of your life working in order to furnish your outward appearance, you are likely spending very few hours thinking about the deeper meaning of your life and who you really are. Is success really working around the clock just to keep up this image?

Back to the balance issue. There is nothing about simple living that says you must go off and live in a shack and wear clothes that make you look as if you walked out of an old movie. Without question, many modern conveniences are wonderful. Without question, it's nice to live in comfort and have a reasonably neat, up-to-date appearance. On and on. But without question, it is not wonderful to go overboard and spend most of your time scrambling to look good to the outside world, while inside you are lying awake at night worrying about how you're going to keep it all together.

Financial success is not about being rich. It is being smart with your money and knowing when you have enough.

Create a Financial Plan

There are zillions of ways to create a financial plan. None of them will reflect reality, though, until you do the first step of charting your current expenses for at least three months. It will take that long to get a clear picture of where your money really goes. You also need to know where you can save. Maybe you've been spending more than you realized on lunches at work. One $6 lunch tab alone doesn't seem like much, but add, say, three $6 tabs a week times 52 weeks per year and you can save almost $1,000. Add up five lattes per week at $2 each and you can save over $500 a year. Only you know what you are willing to give up in exchange for a larger goal.

Next, list your fixed expenses, such as mortgage or rent, electric, water. Keep in mind that these are fixed now but can change at any time. Do you need your current house with the $1,000 or $2,000 a month mortgage? Is there a way to cut that cost? Can you move to a smaller place or rent out a room in the basement? Turn the garage into a mother-in-law apartment? What else can you do to economize but still feel comfortable? Each of us has our own level of bottom-line comfort. You have a monthly cable TV bill, but can you live without cable? How much does that cost per year? Is there something that would bring you more fulfillment over the course of time than cable TV? Would one option be, for instance, being able in a few years to quit your job or work part time? If you have little or nothing in savings and it's between cable TV and savings, think again about your goals.

Remember, you will have no choices in your life if you have nothing saved.

Get Out of Consumer Debt Fast

As quickly as possible, take the money you whittled from your expenses and get yourself out of consumer debt. Do this before starting your savings program. (This doesn't include debt for the purpose of investments such as real estate or securities, when you borrow money to make money. Borrowing money to spend money is quite a different story and is foolish.) There are three good reasons to pay off your debt first:

1. You probably are paying out a lot more in interest than you will earn by saving. Most installment or credit card interest is anywhere from 9 to 18 percent per year. That is what you are paying *out*. Most bank savings accounts pay, at most, 3 percent interest. Most Certificates of Deposits (CDs) pay about 5 percent, and the average money market fund pays, on average, 4 to 5 percent.* That is what you receive *in*. For example, if you have $500 in savings and are earning 3 percent interest in a typical passbook savings account, you will earn $15.21 in interest in the first year (compounded monthly). On the other hand, if you don't pay off your $500 credit card debt, and you pay 18 percent interest on your credit card, *you will pay the bank $97.80 in interest during that same year.* In this case, you would save $82.60 by paying off the credit card first, *before* saving any money.

2. It is difficult to sleep really well at night when you owe money. A good night's sleep is paramount to leading a simple life.

3. You are paying more than you realize by staying in debt. Add up all the interest you are paying on top of the original cost of the item you bought. If the merchant at the store had told you this was the cost of the item, would you have bought it? A good book about getting out of debt, titled *Life Without Debt*, by Bob Hammond, details these costs:

Let's say you spent $1,000 on clothing using a credit card charging 18 percent interest and made the minimum payments† to pay off the balance. It would take you almost six and one-half years to erase the debt, and your $1,000 wardrobe would actually cost you more than $1,650.

❖ ❖ ❖ ❖ ❖ ❖ ❖ ❖ ❖ ❖ ❖ ❖ ❖ ❖ ❖ ❖ ❖ ❖ ❖

*Based on the most current rates as of this printing. Check with your bank when you begin your financial program.

†Minimum payment based on $1/36$ of the outstanding balance or $20—whichever is greater.

Using a credit card charging 12 percent interest, the wardrobe would cost you $1,335—a savings of almost $300 in interest charges.

Need more furniture? If you buy $2,000 worth of furnishing with a credit card charging 18.5 percent interest and pay off the balance by making minimum payments, it will take you more than 11 years to repay the debt. By the time the loan is paid off, you will have spent an extra $1,934 in interest alone—almost the actual cost of the furniture.

Did you read this? Are a few outfits worth *six years* of your working life? Are a few pieces of new furniture worth *eleven*? Holy mackerel! Not only that, but the bank already has far more money than you do. Why are you handing over all this extra money in interest charges when you could use it a lot more than they could? Once, only once, and never again, I racked up a $6,000 credit card bill. My minimum monthly payment was $87. The bank was charging me $75.35 a month in interest alone! No wonder it takes lifetimes to pay off this kind of ridiculous debt. (Mine is paid.) Most of us don't bother to think of the real ramifications of buying on credit. We see an item we like, revert to our primal instincts of gratifying ourselves immediately, and whip out the plastic. Months or years later, we wonder why we're on a treadmill.

Take cars, as another example. Say you put $4,000 down to buy a new car worth $24,000. You finance $20,000. Say you are charged 10 percent interest for 48 months. Your monthly payments are $507.20. You have paid not $20,000, but over $24,000. Plus, you probably have zero in your bank account. So now you have a shiny new car with which to drive yourself to the job you'd like to leave but can't, because you have no money saved. Hmmm. How about if you reversed this scenario and paid $4,000 cash for a good used car, then *invested* that same $500 a month for the same 48 months at the same 10 percent interest, compounding monthly? At the end of 48 months you would have a car *plus* $29,605.92 sitting in your bank account. Hello? Is anybody listening?

To reverse your own financial picture, begin by prioritizing your debts. List them in order of those carrying the highest interest rates first. If your debts are from credit cards, shop for a card offering lower interest rates and transfer the higher rates to the lower-rate card immediately. The goal is to pay the lowest possible interest on your debt. Whichever method you use, you should pay off your loan as quickly as possible. All of the money you whittled from your expenses should go directly to this debt. Forget the minimum payment or skip a payment mumbo-jumbo that the credit card companies or banks offer you. You are still being charged interest and your debt continues to get bigger with every new interest charge. Only the bank comes out ahead with this scheme.

Pay as much money as possible on your card or loan every month. For any debt that you do not consolidate, you should figure out how much you can pay each month. Even $5 a month on these lower- or no-interest bills is better than nothing. Before enacting your plan, first contact all of these creditors and tell them what you are doing. Chances are they will be thrilled to hear that you are not running off to bankruptcy court or to Tahiti.

Another way to pay off a high-interest debt is with a home equity loan. Home equity is the credit offered to homeowners on the accumulated equity of their homes. The amount of money available for these loans is based on how much the current value of the home exceeds the current debt. Home equity loans generally carry far lower interest rates than do credit cards. Be cautious, however, before embarking on this path. Many people get their home equity loans, pay off their debts, and then turn around and start racking up new credit card debt. Now they have a new debt *plus* payments on the home equity loan! Unless you are very, very disciplined, it is better to pay your debts with other methods.

Credit Cards

The easiest way to stay out of debt is to get rid of all credit cards but one, and vow that you will buy nothing on any kind of installment plan *at least* until you have paid your debts in full. It is hoped that by that time, you will enjoy the freedom of debt-free living so much that you will not want to sign up again. It is important to have only one credit card, because the more cards you have, the more tempting it is to spend. Unless you have a business and need to keep expenses separate, why would you need more than one card other than to have a higher credit limit? Stories are endless about people accumulating more and more credit cards and racking up $20,000, $60,000, and more in debt. Then they lose their jobs. Or want to take a break. Whoops! Sorry, no can do!

After your debt is paid, your one card should be the kind with no annual fee. Why pay a bank a yearly fee for the privilege of having its card sitting in your wallet? The no-annual-fee cards sometimes carry higher interest rates, but this shouldn't matter since you will not charge anything over what you actually can pay off at the end of the month. (Remember, this card is for *after* your debts are paid. *Before* they are paid, your credit card should be one with a low interest rate. The savings from that low rate will offset any annual fee if your debts are significant. Do your math to make sure that the annual fee is offset by the lower interest rate.)

Do not use the card except for honest-to-goodness emergencies or instances where you need it, such as to rent a car. Do not use it for daily living, going out to dinner, going to the mall or hardware store. If you are undisciplined, admit it and pack your card into a zip-lock bag of water, put it in the freezer, and leave it there. By the time the ice thaws, the urge to splurge should have passed. When you get out of the habit of spending money you don't have, you can take it out of the freezer.

Note: The only people who ought to use credit cards regularly are those who are *super, and I repeat, super disciplined.* For instance, sometimes you can get free airline tickets by signing up for certain credit cards. Those cards almost always have an annual fee attached—usually $65. If you are the type of person who *always* pays your card in full each month, you could pay for everything, groceries and all, with your card. As long as you pay nothing in interest, you can get yourself airline tickets for the annual fee of $65 per year. On the other hand, if you don't pay your card in full every month, then your interest charges, plus the annual fee, would cost you as much as a ticket. Only you know how diligent you are.

Pay Yourself First

Once you are out of debt, the most important secret to attaining financial independence is this: *Pay yourself first.* Financial independence means you don't need to work for a living anymore; interest paid on money you have invested generates enough income for you to live on comfortably. There are other ways to attain financial independence, but they involve another kind of work. An example is real estate investments that require you to work as a landlord. You need to be aware of the trade-offs in any plan you choose.

No plan is worth anything unless you follow this rule. The rule is important because we are all human, and there are enticing gadgets and goodies at every turn, waiting to separate us from our money. It is absolutely the easiest thing in the world to spend money and tell ourselves that we'll save *after* we just buy this one little thing. We all know that *after* usually doesn't materialize.

The story at the end of this chapter is about two people who retired in their 30s and 40s. Both of them said that their rule had always been to pay themselves first. One of them said she began this plan in her 20s and was so religious about it that she would pay herself first even if it meant being late with a doctor's bill one month. This didn't happen often because she usually was very aware of what was coming and going, but she was human like the rest of us and goofed up once in a while. The important thing was that even her goof-ups didn't alter her pay-your-self plan. The other reason she was able to stick with the plan was because she could see its long-term reward. She had charts that showed she could invest, say, $125 a month into an account paying 7 percent interest (compounded monthly with principal and interest left intact) for 10 years, and at the end of 10 years she'd have $21,761. At the end of 20 years she'd have $65,495. She realized she could be 44 with $65,000 in the bank, or 44 with nothing. Either way, she was going to be 44 years old. This got her very excited.

How $100 Invested Monthly Will Grow at Various Annual Compound Rates of Return

YEARS	5%	7%	9%
5	$6,801	$7,159	$7,542
10	15,528	17,308	19,351
15	26,729	31,696	37,841
20	41,103	52,093	66,789
25	59,551	81,007	112,112
30	83,226	121,997	183,074
35	113,609	180,105	294,178
40	152,602	262,481	468,132

For all of you who never saw a compound interest chart, please refer to the box entitled: How $100 Invested Monthly Will Grow at Various Annual Compound Rates of Return. Make a copy and put it on your wall in a prominent place if that will help you to stick with your pay-yourself goal. Looks pretty good, doesn't it? You're in good company if you think earning money from compound interest is a smart thing. When Albert Einstein was once asked what he thought was the most powerful force on earth, he answered: "Compound interest." Benjamin Franklin described compound interest as "the stone that will turn all your lead into gold." Compound interest is no more than interest making more interest over and over again. And remember this bit of advice: Whether you invest or not, you will still be 10 years older in 10 years. Wouldn't you rather be 30, 40, 50, or 60 with an extra $10,000, $20,000, $40,000, or more in 10 years? A little discipline goes a long way.

Moans and groans. "Well, forget it. That's great for somebody in their 20s, but I'm 45 years old and have never saved five cents, so why bother now? I'll never be able to make a dent in a compound interest chart."

I repeat again: Would you rather be 55 in 10 years with $21,000 (at 7 percent interest if you put away $125 per month) or 55 in ten years with $0? What choices will you have at 55 with $0?

How much you can put away for yourself depends on your financial chart. Once you have streamlined your expenses and decided what immediate gratification you are willing to forgo in order to achieve your larger life goal, and once your debt is paid in full, earmark a given amount for paying yourself first. For those sturdy, disciplined readers among us, you can sit down each month when paying bills and write out a check to yourself along with your other bills. For the rest of the human race—probably the vast majority—set up an automatic savings plan with your bank or place of work. A bottom-line rule of thumb is that you should save at least 10 percent of your income. If not that, anything is better than nothing, so tell your employer to take out $25, $50, or what-have-you from your paycheck and put it into a savings account. That way you will never see the money and you won't miss it. You will, however, see it later after it has turned into a huge pile of money.

The moans and groans continue. "I don't have an extra $50 a month to save. Who are you kidding?" Answer: At some point in your life, you probably earned less than you do today. If not, somebody, somewhere makes $50 less than you do. How do they make ends meet? Believe me, you can find $50 to put away (after your debts are paid). At 10 percent interest (compounding monthly), in 10 years putting away $50 a month you'll have $10,327.60 in your pot. If you wait until you have more than $50 a month, you'll lose valuable savings time and probably will never get around to it. Indeed, $1 invested and reinvested in stocks since 1802 would have turned into $3 million by 1992. This is because stocks have averaged a 6.6 percent annual return since 1926. In the last five years they have averaged 15 percent annual return per year. We're talking one measly dollar here.

Here is a little rule you may be interested in: For every five years you wait to put aside retirement money, you need to double what you put away. In other words, if you need $50 a month starting at age 25 to reach your goal, you'll need $100 a month at age 30, and so on. Plus, one of the most common excuses people have who don't have any money saved is this: "Yes, yes, I will save. Just as soon as I buy X or Z, or right after I do this or that. Absolutely." As you may well know, this conversation usually goes on for years.

You'll notice I have used varying examples of rates of return for your investments. This is because every variety imaginable of return is out there waiting for you. You can earn very modest returns on a passbook savings account (3 to 5 percent) or CD (5 percent), or you can take on more risk and invest in stocks or mutual funds, which can pay you anywhere from 5 to 20 percent return.

There are two ways to save and invest your money. You can invest before or after you pay taxes. Say you are in the 28 percent tax bracket. Say you have $100 to invest. If you put your money into a retirement fund like a 401(K) (an employer-provided plan), an IRA (Individual Retirement Account), or a SEP IRA (Simplified Employee Pension Plan), you do not have to pay taxes on that $100 until you begin using the money after age 59$^{1}/_{2}$. The Internal Revenue Service is trying to reward you for saving for retirement so the government won't have to take care of you in your later years.

Save Your Raise

Here is another trick that will enable you to enlarge your savings pot. The next time you get a raise, save the whole raise with every paycheck. Think about it. If you managed to live on the previous paycheck, you can manage to live on it now. It is very, very tempting to raise your standard of living with each raise, but where will that get you? Answer: in debt or on the treadmill at a new level. We've all seen the studies where people are sure they would be happier at the next income level. The interesting thing is that this is true for *all* income levels. Those who earn $20,000 say they would be happy earning $50,000. Those earning $50,000 say they would be happy at $80,000. Those at $100,000 need $200,000. This is because they think their clothes need to be more expensive to reflect the new raise, their cars need to be more upscale, their after-work entertainment needs to be a little more elaborate, and they think they need a few more rewards at every turn. The level changes; the treadmill continues. If you are ever to have freedom in your life, do not fall into this trap. Say you receive a raise of $150 per month. If you spend the whole thing every month, at the end of 10 years, you will have a house full of clothes and gizmos, most of them long forgotten. Many of the outfits will have fallen out of style and ended up in a secondhand store. Many of the gizmos will be technically obsolete and will be in the trash heap or basement, collecting dust. All of the elaborate dinners out will be history.

On the other hand, if you save the whole $150 a month and invest it in the stock market at a 15 percent return for 10 years, you will have a pot of $41,798.59. Which would you rather have, the option to go back to school, lie in a hammock, work part time, change jobs, or volunteer, or would you rather

Is It Simple Living, or Common Sense?

by Vicki Robin

"Can't survive on $100,000 a year!"

Every year financial magazines feature "shocking" cover stories about the destitute rich who are barely squeaking by on six-figure incomes. We all know that's hogwash. But how much is too little?

A column appeared recently in a Florida newspaper about three women who worked the night shift so they could earn money for their families and care for their children while their husbands were at work. The columnist, citing various "typical" expenses, bemoaned the terrible difficulties faced by a family attempting to survive at the median-income level ($34,000 before taxes in that county). It got me thinking about some of the habits and assumptions that make the median wage in this country feel like poverty.

Lack of basic accounting skills: Our schools and parents do a poor job of teaching basic money management. People have become sloppy with their finances, especially since the advent of credit cards with astronomical limits. Personal bankruptcies have tripled in the last decade.

Job-related expenses: How much of that median income is being used to support the jobs themselves? The columnist assumed the family would need two cars for commuting. Clothing and restaurant tabs are often job-related. Some people total all of the costs of maintaining a second job and conclude it would be more economical for one parent to stay home.

Transportation: Buying and maintaining a car is a matter of intelligence and choice. An hour or two at the library reading consumer magazines will help you avoid the lemons—whether you're buying new or used. Frequent oil changes keep your engine purring. Rethinking the importance of comprehensive and collision coverage, especially on older cars, can save money. The $500 per month transportation cost assumed by the columnist could easily be halved or quartered, especially if your frugality permits you to buy your next car with cash. This allows you to bargain more effectively and to avoid paying twice—once for the car and again for the finance charge.

Health: Recently a friend needed a prescription. The first pharmacy she called charged $56 for the name brand drug and $25 for the generic. The next charged $34 and $10; the last one $26 and $7! Always comparison shop for your health-care needs, including insurance. If you opt for a high-deductible policy and self-insure for the first $500 or $1,000, you can save significant amounts of money. Under $300 a month for a family of four is reasonable. Remember, what you are buying with your policy isn't health, it's sickness insurance. A good diet, exercise, and rest as well as enthusiasm about being alive give your body health-producing messages.

Essentials: The columnist assumed family food costs of $500 per month. People who follow the program outlined in our book, *Your Money or Your Life,* easily bring their food expenses down to well below $100 per month per person. Clothes: $200 a month? When you consider the advances in textiles, many of our clothes may outlast our bodies; $75 a month is more like it. Rent: $500 a month? Yes, that is in line with the nationwide norm. Electric: $100 a month? Maybe. But is cable really one of life's necessities?

Tally my figures and you get about $18,000 a year for a family of four. Add in a generous 25 percent for incidentals and you get just under $23,000, as opposed to the columnist's $33,000. That leaves $10,000 for paying taxes, saving on education, vacations or retirement, house repairs, and so on. Living within the means of a median-income family takes setting priorities and careful accounting. It is being intelligent and responsible. It's even freeing. Instead of feeling constantly behind the eight-ball, you feel in charge. You've made a conscious decision about how to use your resources.

Vicki Robin is coauthor with Joe Dominguez of *Your Money or Your Life* (New York: Viking Penguin, 1992).

have no savings, a house full of forgotten junk, and no options? If you've been diligent about cutting your spending and you are working within a financial plan yet you still feel tight, how about agreeing with yourself to spend only say an additional $50 a month more of this raise? If you save $100 a month at 15 percent interest, you'll have $27,865.73 in 10 years. Who said simple living wasn't about living a balanced life?

Where to Save and Invest

There are two general types of investments: short term and long term. Short-term investments are those that you can dip into fairly easily, such as passbook savings accounts. These pay low interest rates. Long-term investments pay higher yields, and you need to leave them alone for long periods of time.

Before doing any serious investing, first you should put aside money for an emergency reserve account. Use your pocket change, $5 here, $10 there, and slowly build up a three- to six-month reserve of basic living expenses. This is because job searches can easily run much longer than six months. Put this money in a readily accessible (short-term) and secure account that will not charge you penalties if you withdraw early. A money market account is a good, safe place for these funds. If you want to earn higher interest and still have access to your money, you can stagger the maturity dates of your certificates of deposit (CDs). Offset the maturity dates of your CDs so one comes due every few months. If you don't need the money when it is due, roll it back in and start again.

Your long-term savings are different from your emergency fund. This should be hands-off. If it's not hands-off, your human nature will prevail, and without a doubt, you'll find all sorts of reasons why you need to spend the pot. If you make it too expensive to dip into, you'll be more likely to ignore your rationalizing voice when it starts begging you to spend the money. Luckily for you, hands-off accounts pay much higher interest rates than do short-term CDs or money market accounts.

There are many types of short- and long-term investments. The kind you choose depends on your risk tolerance level. The higher the risk, the greater return you can earn. If gambling on some high-risk stock causes you to be up at night worrying, then the benefits are lost and you are farther away from that simpler, more peaceful life that you are working toward.

The following chart explains these various levels of investments.

Safety Level	Investment	Whom to consult
Low return	Passbook savings	Bank
	Certificates of Deposit (CD)	Bank or broker
	Money market funds	Broker
	U.S. Treasury securities	Broker
	Government savings bonds	Bank or broker
Moderate Risk	High-quality bonds	Broker
Moderate Return	Blue-chip stocks or mutual funds (investing in above)	Broker
Increasing Risk	Low-quality/high-yield bonds	Broker
	Speculative stock or mutual funds (investing in above)	Broker
Highest Risk	Options Commodities	Only for the very sophisticated

One option is to diversify your investments. This way you spread the risk around. You could put a little in a higher-risk stock and a little more in a variety of secure investments. The best way to figure out what is available is by talking to people you know and trust and who have a good handle on their money. They can refer you to reputable brokers and bankers. Or you could simply start by marching in to your local bank and asking for help. Banks are always happy to take your money. But don't use your checking-around time as an excuse to put off saving money. At least open up a passbook savings or money market account at your bank while you are shopping for the best investment package. Remember, any investment is better than continually giving your money away to the tailor, the baker, and candlestick maker. Why line their pockets when you can line your own?

To get yourself fired up about how much you can earn by investing, use the Rule of 72. This tells you how long it will take for your money to double. Divide 72 by the interest rate you are getting. If you earn 8 percent, your money takes 9 years to double (8 into 72 is 9). If you invest $5,000 at 10 percent, you divide 72 by 10, which yields 7.2 years. After 7.2 years you will have $10,000.

For a good, simple primer on investments, take a look at a booklet titled *Money for Nothing, Tips for Free*, by Les Abromovitz.

Live on Less

When you start getting excited about how much money you can earn by slowing your spending and saving your money, you'll probably come up with all sorts of creative ways to continue with your present standard of living, yet do it on less. The two main rules are: Pay retail as little as possible, and plan ahead. If you wait until the last minute to buy things, you'll pay anything. If you know your washing machine is 30 years old and heading south, start looking early for good deals on a replacement machine. Don't wait until it dies and you have a load of half-washed, wet laundry staring up at you. Out of desperation you'll run out and buy the first washer you see.

Clothes are another example. Maybe you've been paying retail for your outfits and buying a lot of them. You can continue to dress nicely by putting more thought into what you are buying and by buying secondhand. Here is an example of how you can put more thought into what you are buying. I have one friend who worked in the corporate world and shopped up a storm in order to project the proper successful image. She had different-colored shoes to go with every outfit. Then she took a look at the amount of money she had donated to her feet and decided to start shopping smarter. She decided that she could continue to project a successful image by wearing only black and brown shoes. Those colors would still go with nearly all of her outfits. The money she saved on shoes went directly to her bank account. She continued to get promoted all the way to vice president wearing only black and brown shoes.

If you're not ready for out-and-out thrift stores, you can buy classy, designer fashions at secondhand designer boutiques. These places are cropping up all over and carry both men's and women's clothes. They are small, fashionable-looking stores that look like their regular-priced trendy cousins. They accept only new-looking clothes. Absolutely no one could ever tell the difference in how the clothes look. The hidden difference, of course, is that you pay half or less for the same outfit.

My friend Suzanne is a professional woman who looks absolutely elegant every single day. This is no exaggeration. Suzanne is a savvy thrift store shopper who figured out where wealthy women send their clothes when they are finished with them. She does not shop at the little designer secondhand boutiques—she shops at a regular thrift store and buys entire outfits, shoes and all, paying $10 for a skirt, $7 for a blouse. Suzanne has managed to maintain her standard of living on less. I've seen great-looking, professional men in thrift stores putting together outfits that looked like they came right out of the pages of a men's magazine. Honest! I'd never have a clue to their secret except I saw them coming out of the dressing room.

Think about your household furnishings. With a little paint and imagination, secondhand furniture can actually look more interesting and appealing than a houseful of proper designer pieces that you can't breathe around. Or mix the old with the new, and do it within a budget.

Cars offer you a terrific way to live well on less. We've all heard the statistics that new cars lose 15 to 20 percent of their value as soon as you drive them off the lot. They'll lose another 10 to 30 percent over the next two years. Why are *you* the one signing up to take this big loss?

You don't need to drop everything and take a horse to work in order to make intelligent choices about transportation. There is a wide, wide range of options between new cars and beaters. Every Sunday the classified section in the newspaper is filled to the brim with good, nice-looking, solid used cars of all types imaginable. There are, for instance, thousands of nearly new cars that, well, little old ladies drove to church on Sundays. They really are out there. These cars can be as solid mechanically as most new cars. You can buy formerly leased cars through rental agencies or go to used car dealerships that offer warranties. Once again, you can live well on less. Save your money and pay cash for a car. Worry about getting a top-of-the-line designer model when your financial goals are met. By then you may find that other things have more value to you than driving around in a $50,000 arrangement of metal.

There are endless other ways you can live well on much less. Whether you shop at retail or thrift stores, remember always to shop with a conscience. You're not saving much by being a thrift store shopper if you buy more than you need simply because you think you are getting all these great deals. The next time you are in any store and are about ready to part with your money, ask yourself what that purchase will do for your life. Really. Does the purchase have anything to do with your life goal or your values? Will it make your life any better? Could it make it worse? Are you giving up that much more freedom in order to have this thing? I use this checklist when I go shopping. Since I'm human like everyone else and succumb to consumer seduction here and there, I devised a second trick. I leave the tags and labels on for a week without touching the item. Usually after a week, my "gotta-have-it" attitude has passed and I return the thing to the store.

Pay attention to your inner voices when you shop. Mine are astounding. If it's a nifty new sweater staring at me, I can rationalize all over the place why that sweater will make my life better. I also get into the more athletic, natural-living rationalizations that seem somehow loftier than the sweater ones. I like to hike, for example, but I'm not an avid backpacker. One spring I decided I'd become an avid backpacker that summer. My local outdoor outfitter was having a sale on backpacks. I ran to the store, tried on backpacks, and walked out $200 lighter with a backpack. The thing sat unused all summer. Finally, tags still on, I returned it after realizing that the few times I backpacked, I could rent a backpack and save a bundle.

If you really are an avid backpacker and go all the time, terrific, buy a backpack. But watch your little spendthrift voice as it attempts to seduce you into buying all sorts of other gizmos and gadgets. You can save a bundle simply by paying attention.

You also can read books on saving money. Many such books tell you how to save money on everything from snacks to funerals. I list many in the reference section of this chapter. Remember, if you have a life goal (or two), then figuring out ways to live just fine on less can be a fun challenge. Even if you don't have the goal of changing the world or even your life, one immediate goal can be to see how fast you can get out of debt or see how fast you can double your money by saving and investing. If you don't have some kind of goal in mind, however, cutting costs can be no more than a dismal exercise in penny pinching.

Planning for College

There are a number of ways to plan for your child's college education. First, consider the option of having your kids pay for college, or at least a good share of it. This is possible, even today, if your kids take on full-time summer jobs, work part time during the school year, live at home or in a shared housing arrangement, and attend a local, public college. The cost of college skyrockets because parents and kids think the student should have the entire "college life" package—ritzy out-of-state college, dorm living, a car, and a myriad of other amenities that most of us managed without just fine. The option of two-year community college is a money saver as well. Tuition is much lower, and at the end of two years students with decent grades can transfer their credits to a four-year college. Ron and Mary White believed that kids should help pay for college and started all three of their children working part time at age 14. Their oldest son Sean, now 23, got his first job on weekends at a fast-food restaurant, then worked at a grocery store doing evening cleaning. Later he became a checker. Sean paid all of his tuition, living expenses, books, and supplies for a four-year public university and maintained a 3.7 grade point average. At age 15 he had saved enough money to go on a trip to Japan with an exchange student who lived there.

The Whites' second son, Colin, now 19, got his first job in a flower shop, washing windows, getting supplies, and later delivering flowers. He paid for most of his tuition and all of his supplies and books at a two-year college. He earned enough credits to transfer to a four-year public university. Their daughter BriAna, now 17, worked at age 14 as well, and pays for her own car insurance, gas, entertainment, some clothes, and a private phone line. She too will contribute to her college costs.

If you want to contribute more to your child's college tuition, consider paying off your mortgage early. You can tap into your equity when it's time to pay tuition. Home equity can provide a relatively low-cost loan, and the interest payments may be tax deductible.

Another way to pay college costs for your kids is to trade your larger family home for a smaller one. You can use the freed-up principal for tuition. If you make this move after age 55, you don't pay capital gains taxes.

You also might be surprised to find that your family can qualify for financial aid, even if you have an income of $100,000 or more. At least you should apply. Money saved in tax-deferred retirement accounts, such as 401(K) plans, usually is not taken into account when financial aid is determined. It makes sense to continue building your retirement nest even after you have children and start saving for college. Federal student loans are available to nearly everyone, at rates much lower than you'd pay on most bank loans.

One family I talked to made a plan to save enough money to put their kids through the local public college. If the kids wanted to go to a more expensive private school, the difference in the two tuition levels was theirs to pick up. Other families get their kids saving money as soon as they start working or as soon as they get an allowance. The children regularly invest a given amount of money, just like the parents do. By the time they reach college age, these kids have their own nest egg that can pay some of the costs. Teach your kids early to save money and watch their balance grow. You could also save a given amount for yourself and a given amount for your kids every month. Say you have $50 a month extra to invest. You can earmark $35 for yourself and $15 for your child. You can come up with an extra $15 by forgoing approximately seven $2 bags of potato chips a month.

Here is another way to save for college. Before you have kids, or soon thereafter, put a lump sum of money away one time, and you will have college tuition paid by the time that child is 18. Say you invest $2,000 in a mutual fund during the first year of your child's life. You invest this only once and never put in another dime. Assume a 10 percent rate of return. With compound interest, your child will have nearly $1 million when he or she turns 65. Gulp. At this rate, believe me, your child will have enough money for college. No doubt we've all blown at least $2,000 in one year. What are we doing?

I know of another family who decided to buy a rental house every time a child was born. They invested the minimum down payment, rented out the house for 18 years, and at the end of 18 years they sold the house and used the proceeds to pay for college. They had two children. If the average house costs $100,000, you need approximately $10,000 to $15,000 down payment.*

Oh? Can't come up with $5,000 or $10,000? Ready to skip this page because it only applies to wealthy people? Stay with me! You can do it!

Refer back to the first part of this chapter where you figured out how much you could whittle from your monthly expenses. Say you are the average American family earning $38,000 a year. Say you follow the minimum 10 percent savings plan. You can save $3,800 per year. That amounts to $316 per month. If you invest that $316 at 9 percent return (compound), you will have $8,500 in two years. If you keep going at the same rate, you will have $24,000

❖ ❖ ❖ ❖ ❖ ❖ ❖ ❖ ❖ ❖ ❖ ❖ ❖ ❖ ❖ ❖ ❖ ❖ ❖ ❖

*State laws vary on the amount of minimum down payments, depending on whether you will live in the home or rent it.

in five years. Voilà!—a down payment on a rental house, or a lump sum to invest in, say, the stock market, mutual fund, or what-have-you.

Cognitive Dissonance

As you begin to focus on the meaning of your life, you'll likely find that you don't need all of the things you once thought you needed in order to be happy. In fact, you'll probably find that the less you have to worry about, rearrange, dust, and insure, the more freed up you are to pursue meaningful activities. You'll start to be truly satisfied on less money. This process doesn't happen overnight, and it doesn't happen in linear fashion. You're human, so give yourself a break. You'll go through periods of spending less and enjoying the process, then you'll splurge for no good reason, then revert to saving again. This is the typical process of change.

After you ride up and down on these waves for a while, you'll enter the phase known as cognitive dissonance. This is when you do something you know you shouldn't be doing, but your human nature takes over and you do it anyway. When you reach this stage of awareness, you're well on your way to really making changes in your life.

Here is an example of cognitive dissonance. Say you suffer a heart attack. Before the heart attack, you rarely exercised and didn't think much about it. After the attack, your doctor tells you that if you don't do 30 minutes of cardiovascular work at least four times a week, you'll wind up back in the hospital. You diligently follow this plan for a month. Then you revert to your old ways and stop exercising. The difference is that cognitive dissonance has set in. Now you know you should be exercising and you feel guilty sitting on the couch. You may not move off the couch, but you feel guilty. Eventually, perhaps weeks or months later, your guilt will propel you off the couch and you will start your exercise program again. The same goes with spending less. You'll create a life financial plan and decide to save $50 a month from now on. After diligently following the plan for six months, one month you happen by a store and see just the coat you have been eyeing for a long time. It's on sale: only $100, down from $300. You don't really need the coat and didn't save for it. Your primal instincts take over and you rationalize why you must have it now, and why just this one little month and the next you won't save your $50. You buy the coat. When you get home, if you are in the cognitive dissonance stage, you'll feel guilty about your purchase. With sufficient guilt, you might return the coat and immediately march to the bank to deposit the money. Prior to cognitive dissonance, you would have shopped on automatic pilot and never given your purchase a second thought. In fact, you would have been very proud of yourself that you saved all that money by buying the coat on sale. Shortly thereafter, you also would wonder why you never seemed to make ends meet.

Financial Independence

If you stay even reasonably focused on your goals, you will, without a doubt, begin to reach an equilibrium in spending and saving. Everyone's level is different. This equilibrium occurs when you really do feel just fine living on the lowered amount of money. You no longer have to grit your teeth just to get through stores without buying every other thing that comes into view. You feel so good with this new way of living that shopping less becomes automatic. You haven't turned into a no-spending maniac or crabby miser; you simply feel good spending less. While this process has been occurring, your savings also have been growing. You are on your way to achieving financial independence.

I refer you again to the book *Your Money or Your Life,* which details the path to financial independence. In general, part of the plan is to get yourself a sheet of butcher-type paper and put it on your wall in a prominent place. (You can get the end rolls of newsprint from your local newspaper for free.) Write down the months in a year across the top of the paper. Going down the left side, write down dollar figures. These figures should start at the highest amount you have spent in a month (including all expenses, from mortgage to food) and go down to $0. Make a grid of these figures. You can create a similar grid on money management software programs. The butcher-paper grid can be the better option because it is in full view all of the time, serving as a constant reminder that you are reaching your goals. In red, put a dot on your spending for each month. If you spent $3,500 in January, put the dot on $3,500. If the interest income from your savings and investments totals $100 in January, put a blue dot on $100. Once you begin living your financial plan, your spending will go down and your savings will go up. You are financially independent when what you spend per month equals what you receive in interest from saving and investments.

There is a catch to this plan. If you begin investing via the slow and steady route and put all of your money in something totally secure, such as U.S. Treasury bills, it will take you longer to reach financial independence, because Treasury bonds pay lower returns than do higher-risk investments. You will, however, have a solid, steady result at the end that will not fluctuate. You will have a guaranteed income for life, and you'll never have to do a thing about it.

MONEY

On the other hand, if you wanted to earn higher interest so you could reach financial independence sooner, and you'd been putting your money in products such as stocks, you will have a more risky nest egg at the end because stock values go up and down regularly. If you have diversified your investments into a lot of funds, stocks, real estate, what-have you, you're fairly secure because even if one investment loses money, chances are the others will remain stable or increase. In this way, you have a better chance of counting on a given amount of investment income. If you enjoy investing and stay abreast of the market, then continue on with this method and have fun. If you don't enjoy the risk of investing, you're better off if you transfer all of your money to a stable Treasury bill. You will lose some investment income because Treasury bonds, on average, have lower returns than stocks. Simply save money for a longer period to make up the difference.

Take Time to Invest in Your Life

Remember, simple living is not about going to extremes. It is about finding balance in your life. Nowhere is this concept more important than in your dealings with money. It is vital that you develop an awareness of money and the role it plays in simplifying your life. While concentrating on saving and investing, however, don't forget another type of investment: your life.

We've all heard the Dickens tale *A Christmas Carol,* in which the miser Scrooge realizes that his obsession with building a hefty financial portfolio has cost him friends, family, and a full life. He has nothing but a pile of money until the Ghosts of Christmas visit him with a wake-up call and remind him to reach out to others.

A balanced simple life means saving and investing money *while also* investing your time in building supportive relationships with others and developing yourself as a full human being. Often we confuse a large bank balance with security. Yes, we do need a decent-size bank account for security, but we also need friends and family to be there with hugs and apple pie when the going gets rough. By spending less and getting yourself off of the work-and-spend treadmill, you can free your time and energy for this kind of "investment."

Simple living is about stuffing *some* money into bank accounts, learning to live well on less money, taking the time to build nurturing relationships, and developing yourself as the best human being you can be.

THEY PAID THEMSELVES FIRST TO RETIRE AT AGES 37 AND 44

When she was in her early 20s, Barbara Ahern's dad showed her a basic compound interest table. The table showed how a person could systematically put away a small amount of savings and yield a large amount of money at a fixed date in the future. Barbara took her dad's advice, put money aside every month, made some investments, and 23 years later, retired at age 44.

Greg Bartholomew composes his first opera.

When Greg Bartholomew was growing up, he remembers his father hated his job. He never wanted that to happen to him. Greg's plan was to work hard, save his money, and be financially independent in his 30s. This way he would never be stuck at a job he didn't like. Greg created a 10-year plan for himself and retired at age 37.

Both Barbara and Greg say that two of the most important reasons why they were able to reach their goals were the principles of *pay yourself first* and *live within your means*. Each month they put aside a fixed or additional amount of money before they spent any of it. They also kept their goal of financial indepen-

Barbara Ahern enjoys an afternoon of rollerblading.

dence in front of them at all times. This helped them get past urges to spend.

Greg's plan was to go to law school and work for 10 years. He graduated at age 25 and got a job as an entry-level lawyer earning $23,000 a year. "Compared to most people in the world, I was making good money," he says. "But compared to most lawyers, I was making very little. The most I ever earned was $60,000, but I stayed at that firm because it was more collegial than some of the other firms that pressure lawyers to make more and more money."

Still, Greg says that being a lawyer didn't offer him any meaning or substance, so he couldn't justify practicing law just to pay bills. He could justify it only if it bought him freedom in the future. He got an awakening his first month at the job. His paycheck went to purchase a car with four-year payments, a bed, and a couch. He also had $7,000 in law school loans. "When the end of the month came and I decided I hated being a lawyer and wanted to quit very badly, I realized I couldn't quit because of what I had bought. I had to keep working to pay my bills. I gave myself six months to stabilize my financial situation."

He stayed at the job and gained confidence in his abilities yet never forgot his early realization that if he continued to spend money, he would have no options and wouldn't be able to fulfill his 10-year plan. He began saving $500 a month, increasing that amount by 10 percent a year. "I stuck to it," he says, "and even put away more than that." When his company developed a 401(K) plan, he put in as much as the plan allowed and continued to save $500 to $1,000 a month. "At the four-year point," he says, "I was accumulating a lot of money."

In two years, Greg paid off his car in order to avoid heavy interest payments. "I've always been very alert to what I'm paying out in interest and what I'm receiving in interest," he says. "If the interest out is more than the interest in, I quickly change things."

When Barbara earned more, she saved more

Barbara also began saving her money. She looked at her dad's compound interest chart and saw that if she saved $125 a month, she could be a millionaire by retirement age. "That was the first trigger that I could be financially independent through systematic savings and investments," she says.

At age 25, Barbara got a job as a stockbroker and learned the mechanics of investing. She was trained to understand her clients' goals, such as college, retirement, or financial independence. "They teach you to determine what for you would be financial independence. One client might need $5 million and another $100,000. It is a very individual calculation that depends on the rate at which you consume, how many years you have left to live, plus assumptions about inflation and interest rates. In a very simplified example, if you need $1,000 a month to live, you could invest $120,000 at a 10 percent rate of return."

"I remember one incident clearly," Barbara says. "My boyfriend at the time and I were talking about a friend who had put $200,000 into a real showplace house. This was in the 1970s, when interest rates were double digit. We looked at each other and said if we put that same amount into a money market account we'd never have to work again."

Barbara began investing $50 a month from her then-salary of $600 a month. "I read somewhere about the concept of *pay yourself first*," she says, "and I practiced it. There were times when I'd even delay paying some significant doctor or electric bill just so I'd put my $50 away first. I'd wait until the next month to pay the other bill, even though I'd be charged a late fee. The late fees served as a reminder to me that I was living above my means."

Barbara's net worth at age 26 was about $2,000. She used that money as a down payment to purchase her first house.

At age 28, Barbara married Ron Bryan, a real-estate agent. Together they realized that they could be financially independent through owning and renting property. They reasoned that the typical person spends 25 percent of his gross income on housing. If they owned four typical houses outright, they would have the income of a typical person.

"Once you have that picture established in your mind, you want to move toward the goal faster because it is so compelling," Barbara says. "You find yourself doing things that enable you to reach your goals sooner. For example, we started out financing our house with a 30-year mortgage, which would have made us financially independent in our 50s. That seemed too far away, so we switched to a 15-year mortgage. On another property, we didn't switch mortgages but instead made large principal payments."

When Barbara began to earn more money, she avoided the trap of spending more money. Instead, she and her husband increased the proportion of money that went into savings. "For several years, we saved 30 percent of our income, and in the last few years, we saved more than 50 percent of our income," Barbara says. "When my company offered a 401(K) plan, I signed up for the maximum allowable. Whenever I got a bonus, we'd invest it in real estate. A lot of my coworkers would spend their bonuses on vacations, redecorating their houses, or paying off huge VISA bills. Any time the company came up with a salary deferral plan, I'd take advantage of it. The moment automatic payroll deposits were created, I used it immediately to fund retirement and savings accounts. It became easy to pay myself first because I didn't have to think about it."

Barbara remembers that saving money at that rate wasn't always easy. Other colleagues had house cleaners and yard help, and indulged in little luxuries, such as weekly massages, because the work was so stressful. Ron and Barbara gave up having a smoothly running household and decided it was worth it to accept some short-term chaos in the home in exchange for long-term financial independence.

Barbara and her husband lived on cash as much as possible. They continued to do the things they valued, such as taking vacations, but only on a cash basis. They made sure they had the money before they left. They did most of their own home repairs.

Finally, at age 44, Barbara's work was becoming less and less pleasurable, and at the same time, her investments had appreciated faster than she expected. She had reached her goal. "We didn't end up with four houses free and clear, but we did end up with a combination of rental property and other investments that yield enough to guarantee a comfortable lifestyle."

For Greg, paying into savings was part of bill paying

Two years after he began working, Greg bought his first house, lived in it, and rented out the spare bedroom. He continued with his law job, even finding a certain pleasure in it. "It wasn't the kind of pleasure you get from doing something you really like," he remembers, "but it was comfortable enough and was allowing me to reach my financial goals. I also liked the people very much."

Over the next couple of years he bought a rental condominium and he and his sister bought another rental house. He used money from refinancing his original house to purchase the additional homes. He continues to rent out his spare bedroom.

After he had worked for seven or eight years, Greg realized he needed to begin preparing himself for the day he would leave his job. He wondered how he would spend his time, how he would take care of health insurance. He knew he liked music. He worried about sitting home alone. He wanted regular activities with other people. He joined two choirs while still working. "It was really exhilarating and confirmed in my mind that I really wanted to do something with music when I quit."

Finally, in the spring of 1992, Greg gave notice at his job. He worked for the next two years part time, beginning at half time, then quarter time. "That was really good psychologically because I wasn't abruptly left at home with nothing to do," he says. "That transition period also allowed me to adjust my spending even more." Greg also began writing book reviews, short fiction articles, and working on call as an arbitrator. He says he will earn less than $3,000 this year from those endeavors.

One way Greg has been able to save money is by keeping his savings separate. His checking account is for spending money and his savings go into a money market account. "My savings were part of my bill paying," he says. "I had the deposit slips for my money market account right along with my bills."

Greg says he does not charge anything that he cannot pay off that month. His early car purchase and real estate investments are the only exceptions. "I didn't want to get locked into a routine of having to pay $50 a month for this and $30 a month for that," he says. "If I want a TV for $500, for example, I save up until I can pay cash. I don't pay $40 a month for years. When I was working, I'd plan ahead for big items and target them for my birthday or Christmas. I made choices. I didn't buy everything I wanted."

Saving money has always been fairly easy for Greg, since he equates money with his time. "There are a lot of $5 an hour jobs out there," he says. "If someone is going to blow $15 on three drinks, I think about how they're going to blow three hours of their life."

Since quitting his full-time work, Greg continues to sing with a choir and has gotten halfway through his dream of writing an opera. He constantly questions how he wants to spend his time. "When I step back, I realize I'm really lucky, because most people don't have the time to figure out how they want to spend their days. Most people don't think they have a choice, but they don't realize that they have gotten themselves into the situation. They buy bigger and bigger houses. Even now it can be hard to talk to people about my life because my problems are not as immediate as theirs.

"For the first time in my life I know that if I send my résumé out, I can be honest about who I am and I only want something I feel good about. I don't have to *pretend* to feel good about a job now. I have the luxury of saying no."

Greg's plan is to sell all the property except his original house, and live on the proceeds for a number of years. During that time he says he hopes that doing what he cares about will generate income. By then, he will own his original house free and clear.

When Barbara gets up in the morning these days, she notices a big difference. "All of my motivation for whatever I do is internal now. Before I quit, I was always responding to a current external drive of what I was going to do when, like get to the office at 8, go to a meeting at 10, pick up dinner on the way home.

"Now I get up in the morning and think about what I feel like doing that day. It's not that I have nothing I want to accomplish, but I set the time and place for what I do when. I don't have long-term goals at the moment," she says. "I just want to be healthy and fit, and send our son off into the world as prepared as he can be."

When people express envy at Barbara's situation, she reminds herself that they made choices, just as she did. When one colleague complained that she wanted to quit her job too, she made a list of the things she would have to give up if she retired. Included on that list were indulgences like expensive jewelry, mail-order steak, and a gigantic gift-giving budget. "This friend concluded that she didn't want to do without these things," Barbara says. "They apparently bring her more pleasure than retirement."

"For me, it's nice to be in a position that even if you love your job, if it goes sour or you have a bad day, you know you don't have to stay. This particular friend can't say that because she has chosen her job as means to wear nice jewelry, buy steaks, and give generous gifts. As long as you have your eyes open, great! If you say I love wearing diamonds, having a housekeeper, and a manicured lawn and love it so much it's worth working an extra 30 years, then terrific! I respect that. For me, the goal of independence was so compelling that I was willing to put up with the noise. People should never say they can't retire at age 35, 45 or 50 . . . they should realize they've *chosen* not to."

❖ ❖ ❖ ❖ ❖ ❖ ❖ ❖ ❖ ❖ ❖ ❖ ❖

Resources

Living on Less

Cheap Tricks by Andy Dappen (Brier, WA: Brier Books, 1992)
The author calls himself a "third-generation penny-pincher" who has managed to live on a "pauper's income" and support a family. He's done it with his "Eleven Food Commandments" and tricks like learning how to use your credit card to borrow money free of charge for 50 days. His tricks cover the gamut, from appliances to water.

How to Live Green, Cheap & Happy by Randi Hacker (Mechanicsburg, PA: Stackpole Books, 1994)
A wide-ranging discussion on the "eco-chic" fashion, from using the "earth gym" to the benefits of the barter system. It takes the best of the 20th century and blends it with such age-old customs as growing your own food and hiring kids to do work around the house. It also makes a case for the social benefits of recycling.

Living Cheaply with Style by Ernest Callanbach (Berkeley, CA: Ronin Publishing, 1993)
An informational resource on how to stretch money and find great bargains. The books lists popular ideas on living cheaply but with flair. Some range from the simple (avoid eating out too often, start the day with a good breakfast so you won't be so hungry so often) to the complex (the benefits of having your own solarium). Hundreds of items are listed for easy reference.

Living More with Less by Doris Janzen Longacre (Scottsdale, PA: Herald Press, 1980)
An international look at extending the value of money. It encourages a look at other cultures, particularly those in lesser-developed countries, to see how others are doing more on a fraction of what we earn in the West. We can use this knowledge to promote more "connection" in the world. An attendant study guide by Delores Histand Friesen shows practical ways to do this.

The Best of Living Cheap News by Larry Roth (Chicago: Contemporary Books, 1996)
Roth has devoted years to finding simple, practical ways to enjoying a comfortable life without paying through the nose for it, which he first shared in his magazine, "Living Cheap News." Now he's assembled the best from his publication into a book that shows how to cut costs in everyday things—from buying a house to finding a good but cheap restaurant.

The Tightwad Gazettes, Vols. I, II & III by Amy Dacyczyn (New York: Villard Books, 1996)
A gathering of practical tips from the magazine of the same name. The volumes contain hundreds of suggestions on how to do more with less, ranging from baking a great muffin to recycling old jeans into handbags. Graphs, drawings, and charts are used to make the methods shown more comprehensible and easy to follow. Some chapters also include a resource list for further information.

The Philosophy of Money

The Costs of Living by Barry Schwartz (New York: Norton, 1994)
The author gives a scholarly look at how the economy has taken a toll in our personal lives. The book covers how money can affect marriage as well as divorce, what we have gained and lost in the rise of our commercial economy, and what must be done to return the values of love and spirituality back to human society.

The Holy Use of Money by John C. Haughey (New York: Crossroad, 1992)
The book presents an argument for integrating money into one's spiritual existence. It deals with issues such as reconciling the two spheres of material and religious, how valid and appropriate tithing can be, and who should participate in the national economy.

How Much Is Enough by Alan Durning (New York: Norton, 1992)
The subtitle, "The Consumer Society and the Future of the Earth," is a more appropriate title for a book dealing with the effects of our Age of Affluence. It discusses the impact of material industrialism on the finite earth as well as on the human spirit. If we are to see a healthy earth again, we must understand our relationship to the environmental and material worlds.

Money and the Meaning of Life by Jacob Needleman (New York: Doubleday Currency, 1991)
As the title suggests, Needleman's book digs deep into our social preoccupation with money and how our attitudes have changed over the years. In his eyes, we don't understand the true value of money, therefore we don't take it seriously enough, much to our growing peril. We must foster a new attitude that regards money for what it is (information and a tool) and what it is not (the end-all of all life).

The Poverty of Affluence by Paul Wachtel (Philadelphia: New Society Publishing, 1989)
Wachtel observes how material gain is not often a component of human happiness. He

examines our society's seemingly insatiable desire for economic prosperity and growth and wonders if this has not led to a shattering of our communal and psychological lives. He asks if there is not a better way to live our lives.

Simple Living Investments by Michael Phillips and Catherine Campbell (San Francisco: Clear Glass Publishing, 1984)
Old age goes through a metamorphosis in this book about "investment" strategies that deal more with social values than number-crunching analysis. It posits that being honest about our monetary views while encouraging soulful values in our daily lives as the lynchpin to true financial success.

Whole Life Economics by Barbara Brandt (Philadelphia: New Society, 1995)
Women have long been excluded or "devalued" from the measurable economic world, according to the book. The author uses historical data and research to show how unequal pay between men and women sustains an "unfair" economy and why that must change. She also discusses how some activities (such as caring for children and helping friends) cannot be measured in money but still have a great deal of impact on our society.

Your Money or Your Life by Joe Dominguez and Vicki Robin (New York: Viking Penguin, 1993)
This book is considered the bible of determining where your money goes as opposed to where you want it to go and of showing how we are encouraged to consume.

Money and Investment Basics

First Book on Investing by Samuel Case (Rocklin, CA: Prima, 1995)
The book explains the inner workings of basic investment strategies such as mutual funds, IRAs, compound interest, taxes, and "dollar-cost average" to those who may have never heard of the terms.

How to Get What You Want in Life with the Money You Already Have by Carol Keefe (Boston: Little, Brown, 1995)
Creative money expert Keefe has written a book based on her own experiences of getting out of debt and trying to raise a family on a teacher's income. Chapters include topics on how to pay yourself first and why paying the minimum on installment bills makes the most sense.

Learn to Earn by Peter Lynch (New York: Fireside, 1996)
Investment guru Lynch teaches you how to read a stock table and a corporation's annual report. He also explains how to analyze a company like a professional investor.

Life Without Debt by Bob Hammond (Franklin Lakes, NJ: Career Press, 1995)
Debt is a national as well as a personal issue. Hammond writes about the key steps necessary to both getting out of debt and then staying out of it permanently. It explains personal bankruptcy, the perils of credit card debt, and the psychology behind debtors. There is also discussion on making wise use of investments.

Money for Nothing, Tips for Free by Les Abromovitz (Glendale Heights, IL: Great Quotations, Inc., 1995)
The book offers tips for the novice in the areas of personal finance, financial planning, investments, real estate, and insurance. Some of his tips include how installing a security system or smoke alarm in your house reduces insurance premiums, and why purchasing raw land is one of the riskiest investments anyone can make.

The Frugal Investor by Scott Spiering (New York: Amacom, 1995)
Successful strategies for a low-risk, high-return portfolio. Also, discussion on how to properly manage your investments.

Straight Talk on Money by Ken and Daria Dolan (New York: Simon & Schuster, 1995)
"Down-to-earth" investment advice for families dealing with mortgages, college tuition, insurance, and tax-free investments such as 401(K) plans.

Your Children's College Bill: How to Figure It . . . How to Pay for It
Brochure created by the Institute for Certified Financial Planners in Denver. Covers ways to

pay for college, including borrowing, financial aid, saving, and investing, plus worksheet. Call 1-800-282-7526.

Internet/On-Line Resources

Fidelity Investments Information Center
Study mutual funds, download prospectus, or for a fee, retrieve quotes.
http://www.fid-inv.com/index.html

Kiplinger's Personal Finance Magazine
Subscribe for on-line access to the newsletter.
http://www.kiplinger.com

Money Investing Update
Daily news from the *Wall Street Journal*.
http:/update.wsj.com

National Institute for Consumer Education
Consumer-oriented advice and resource lists from Eastern Michigan University.
http:/www.emich.edu/public/coe/nice/pfinance.html

Financial Software

Managing Your Money. MECA Software. Tracks budget and investments and analyzes financial decisions.

Microsoft Money. Microsoft (Windows 3.1 and Windows 95). Software to organize your budget. Also offers an option to link with Reuters News Service's Money Network Software.

Quicken. Intuit. One of the most popular software tools to balance your budget and forecast your financial future. Quicken Deluxe offers more features to calculate your money goals. Quicken Financial Planner lets you plan ahead with retirement in mind.

3

Inner Simplicity

*What lies behind us and what lies before us are
tiny matters compared to what lies within us.*

—OLIVER WENDELL HOLMES

The number-one reason why most people even think about simplifying their lives is to attain some level of inner peace and contentment. They have tried all of the outward trappings—new houses, cars, wardrobes, relationships, careers—and found that while those things bring some joy and satisfaction, the positive feelings are fleeting, and they also can bring added stress and chaos. Indeed, always looking outside of ourselves for happiness gets exhausting. The search is endless. How much richer to feel joy and contentment inside of ourselves first, before seeking pleasure outside. Then we can be more selective about choosing our outside pleasures, and those choices will come from a place of inner strength, not as a temporary "fill-up" for emptiness. When we spend all or most of our time seeking outside pleasures and neglecting our inner selves, we are left wanting more. We don't know what the "more" is, but we're vaguely aware that something is missing.

Voluntary Simplicity Is a Ticket, Not a Destination

Often when people hear about voluntary simplicity, they think a simple life *in itself* is the answer. They think that if they clear their clutter and save money, *then* they'll be more peaceful. That's partly true.

Clearing clutter and learning to live with less are merely *tickets* to your destination. They simply allow you the time and space to open yourself to the possibility of finding peace. It is difficult to find time for your inner life if you are busy running from one activity to the next, working overtime to pay off debt, or forever rearranging, dusting, and fooling with your clutter. When you remove some of those obstacles, you can begin to still yourself from the inside. You can get to know your deeper self, or your soul—that part of us that is very often sadly neglected. Think about how much time you spend looking after the needs of your mind and body. Very few of us spend more than a fleeting second here and there nurturing our souls.

Modern medicine finally has accepted the fact that the mind and body are connected and that we need to maintain both to obtain optimum physical fitness. Yet one other aspect remains: the soul. We can't see it, but we know it is there. It is our life force. When we neglect our life force, we neglect our entire foundation.

The First Step

People often ask what the first step is to simplifying their lives. The answer depends on their personal style. For example, if you are more outer directed, it's probably easier to start by clearing out the clutter from your house one drawer at a time. Or say no to half of your social commitments. Pick any chapter from this book and set to work simplifying the outer areas of your life. Once you have less to worry about in your outer life, you'll have more space for your inner life.

The other way to begin is by starting with your inner life. Take time each day for meditation. This practice slows your mind. Once you slow the inner chaos and clutter, your outer life naturally will follow suit. This route is difficult if your outer life is packed full and if you are used to finding fulfillment on the outside.

When I began my simplification journey, I thought my only route to simple nirvana was to follow Thoreau and move to a log cabin in the woods and grow my own vegetables. As I began studying and thinking about simplicity, however, I realized where I lived and what I did were not necessarily the answer. They may aid the process, but they are not the final destination. The real answer was whether I was at peace inside or not. If you're peaceful inside, you can live anywhere. If you're in turmoil on the inside, or if you are used to giving in to one desire after another, no log cabin, monastery, or clutter-free house will still your restless waters.

This point became clear to me one time when I interviewed a woman who lives alone on the top of a mountain. Her job is to check weather. When she's not checking weather, she spends time writing a book and reading. This woman couldn't be more removed from the distractions of our hectic world. She showed me pictures of her house—a peaceful, bucolic little place with gorgeous views that go on forever. But my first question to her was "With all that stillness, what about your inner demons?" She knew exactly what I was talking about. The more still your outer environment becomes, the more aware you are of what's going on inside. No more staying busy and running away from yourself. There you are.

This woman had dealt with at least a good portion of her demons by stilling her mind, but she said it was very obvious when friends came to visit who had not dealt with theirs. To them, the stillness would become suffocating, and they would want to leave earlier than planned. You can imagine living as she does with no outside distractions. You'd find out very soon who you are in there. On the other hand, living like a lot of us do, in the midst of every distraction imaginable, keeps us from ever knowing our deeper selves. Luckily, we don't need to move to a mountaintop to get to know who's in there.

Awareness

We can get to know ourselves through meditation. Most of us know by now that we don't need to sit on top of a mountain in Tibet to meditate. We can do it right in our own houses and apartments. We can meditate if we have families, and we can meditate if we have jobs. When we meditate regularly, we can become more aware of what we are doing, moment by moment. This awareness will do more than anything else to keep us off the treadmill. Without inner awareness, most of us skip and slide through life with hardly a clue about why we make certain choices. We operate mostly on automatic pilot. If you doubt this, try a little test. Take out a paper and pencil and draw a picture of your telephone, without looking at the phone first. Draw from memory. Yes!

Gotcha! Why do I know you couldn't draw your phone? Because nobody can, including me. We use these things how many times a day but have no idea what they really look like, where the numbers are placed, how the keys are shaped, on and on. The reason why we haven't a clue is because we are not fully present each moment. Usually we're doing one thing while thinking of many other things. This unawareness gets us into all sorts of trouble in our lives. We sail through a store and see a nice gizmo sitting on the shelf. Without thinking further than immediate gratification, we haul out $50 or $100 and buy the darned thing. We do the same with all variations and sizes of objects, from chocolate chip cookies to $50,000 cars.

We make social engagements on automatic and job choices on automatic. Slowly we become aware of the fleeting nature of "success" or accomplishment. The patina lasts for a very short time, and we're vaguely aware of an emptiness inside. We rush out and try to fill it with something else. All the while we're almost totally unaware of our deep motivations. Later we wonder why we're on the treadmill.

Choose Your Style

There are two general forms of meditation. In one, you focus your mind on one point. You can do this through visualization or employing a mantra. The emphasis is on focusing and relocating the mind again and again on one point. The other form of meditation is called awareness, or insight meditation. You not only focus your mind but you notice what is happening at that point of focus.

Whichever style you choose, remember to stick with it. It is as easy to search constantly for better and better meditation or spiritual styles as it is to search for better and better possessions.

Focus Meditation

There are many forms of visualization. You can sit and concentrate on your "spiritual eye," which is situated in the middle of your forehead. People who use this method think of this area of the brain as the area of consciousness. It is thought to be the doorway to our spiritual center. To meditate this way, concentrate on that point between your eyebrows while you are sitting. Imagine gazing into your spiritual center, and imagine it is surrounded by white light. Listen to the sounds inside you. Much has been written about these "spiritual sounds"; the ancient Greeks referred to them as "music of the spheres." Sit quietly, focusing on your spiritual eye and on the spiritual sounds. It is thought that these sounds are best heard through the right ear. You can visualize any number of things. Your heart can be a flower slowly opening up, or you can imagine you are at a favorite peaceful destination, such as a beach or mountain cabin.

You also can use a mantra as a way to provide focus. A mantra is a word or phrase that you repeat over and over in your mind. You can make up your own or have one given to you by a meditation teacher. Some feel that a mantra is a very special and spiritual word that should only be given by a spiritual teacher; others feel that any melodic word, phrase, or sound that has meaning for you will work to focus your concentration. A mantra you choose for yourself could be anything you think is important, such as "love" or "peace," or even a universal sound such as "aum." If you repeat the same word or phrase over and over in your mind, you have something to focus your awareness on, rather than letting random thoughts clutter your mind. If your mantra is a uniquely spiritual one given to you by a teacher, focusing on it will not only help you to slow your mind but also help you attain higher levels of spiritual consciousness.

> *Stop and listen to the heart, the wind outside, to one another, to the changing patterns of this mysterious life. It comes moment after moment, out of nothing, and disappears into nothing. Live with less grasping and more appreciation and caring.*
>
> —JACK KORNFIELD

Insight Meditation

I personally like insight meditation and find it most useful for simplifying my life. While all forms of meditation can help you feel more peaceful inside, I like the insight method because it helps me not only to focus my attention but to be aware of the here and now. A wonderful book title sums up the theory. It is called *Wherever You Go, There You Are*, by Jon Kabat-Zinn. The phrase "wherever you go, there you are" means being fully aware of, or mindful of, what you are doing moment by moment. The way to cultivate this mindfulness is through meditation, and we can meditate and be aware wherever we go and wherever we are. "Wherever you go, there you are" also means that once you learn to find fulfillment on the inside, you will not have to look outside. You always have "you" with you, and you always can be "at home" right inside yourself, no matter where you are. This doesn't mean you shun the world. It simply means that you build a strong foundation within yourself first; then the pleasures of the world are simply adornments, not sustenance. It also means that you live with more intimacy in the world. You are fully present and intimate with the things and people around you, rather than passing them by on your way to somewhere else.

The beauty of insight meditation is that you can practice it all throughout the day, while doing dishes, driving, arguing with your spouse, reading to your children, going for a walk, and standing in a bank line. Like anything, it takes practice. The practice part is taking a few minutes each day to do sitting meditation.

How to Practice Insight Meditation

Find a comfortable place in your house where you can sit undisturbed for at least 10 minutes. Before you complain that you don't have 10 or more minutes, think about how much time you spend watching TV or yakking on the phone, to name two. It is best to carve out a niche for yourself, a place that you can retreat to each day, a place that beckons you to be still. You don't need a whole room; a serene corner will do. Either prop some pillows on the floor or use a straight-back chair. You want to meditate while sitting, not lying down, because the goal is not to get so relaxed you fall asleep. You want to be fully awake yet calm. (If you have trouble falling asleep, you can use this practice while lying down at night, but that is not the point of this chapter. See "Dealing with Insomnia" in this chapter.)

We're used to seeing pictures of yogis in India sitting cross-legged on the floor meditating, but most Westerners have so much trouble adjusting their bodies to that position that the discomfort becomes distracting. Sit in a comfortable position, with your spine straight. You want to stay awake with your energy flowing in a clear pathway. You can place your arms on your lap in any style that is comfortable. Many experienced meditators like to lay their hands on their laps with palms up. This position is thought to allow more acceptance and energy to flow into you. Before ignoring this concept, think about the importance of hand positions in our daily lives. Clenched fists mean we're ready for fighting or we're feeling very angry. Greeting someone with open arms means we're accepting and open to this person. In any case, try different hand positions until you find one that feels comfortable. Do try the open palm position a few times before giving it up.

Once you are sitting comfortably, do a few deep relaxation exercises to calm yourself. There are many options. One is deep breathing. Breathe in through your nose as slowly as possible and as deeply as possible. Hold your breath for a few seconds, deeply, then slowly exhale through your mouth. Repeat three times. Another is called square breathing. Imagine a square. With your eyes closed, take in a deep breath and imagine that it is traveling up one side of the square. Count slowly to five. When you reach five, imagine your breath is at the top of the square. Don't let your breath out. Now hold your breath for another five count as it travels across the top of the square. When you reach five and the end of the top of the square, begin breathing out and imagine your breath is traveling down the other side of the square. Slowly count to five again. Now hold your breath out for another five count as it travels across the bottom of the square. It should be out completely. Repeat the square three times.

You also can do head, neck, and shoulder rolls to relax, and you can chant a particular phrase over and over to calm yourself. (Chanting simply means that you repeat a phrase or group of phrases over and over for a specified period of time.) If you follow a certain religion or spiritual belief, you can chant a meaningful phrase or prayer over and over for five minutes or so. If you are not religious or spiritual, repeat a favorite poem or other phrase. This repetition of words helps relax you and calm your busy mind.

Once you are relaxed, you can begin meditating. If you've never meditated before, try sitting for just 10 minutes after you have calmed yourself. Set a timer if you like. Ten minutes of stillness, doing seemingly "nothing," will feel like an eternity at first because we're so programmed in our culture to be "productive" every minute. Gradually build your meditation time to a goal of 45 minutes a day; twice a day is even better. For now, however, simply set aside 10 minutes once a day. It is best to set aside the same time every day to meditate so you form a habit. One option is to set your alarm in the morning 10 minutes early. Or take 10 minutes during your lunch hour at work, if you can find a quiet space. Meditate before going to bed at night, but don't do it in bed. If you have small children, take your 10 minutes when they take naps or right after they go to bed at night, before you start on the dishes or bill paying. Some parents even have trained their children to sit quietly for a family "quiet time." Personally I never was able to manage this feat with my children, but I think that was largely because I was not dedicated enough to meditation at that point to push it. Children usually know when something is really important and when it is negotiable. Whatever the case, be flexible. You are looking for only 10 minutes a day. And remember, if you never get past 10 minutes, be happy. That is 10 minutes more of quiet time that you wouldn't have otherwise; don't stress yourself over what you don't have.

Insight meditation is very straightforward because you simply sit and follow the natural rhythm of your breathing. You can focus either on the breath as it en-

Dealing with Insomnia

by Kriyananda (J. Donald Walters), Ananda Community

Insomnia is one of the miseries of the modern age. This might, indeed, be called the Age of Anxiety. People who fail to get the rest they need at night often resort to heavy doses of coffee and other stimulants to remain awake during the day. They sleep badly the following night as a result of these stimulants, and so by degrees enter a life-cycle that leaves them chronically out of tune with life (or energy)—like an eight-cylinder motor functioning on only one cylinder.

If you are troubled with insomnia, try doing a few yoga postures before going to bed. Get the energy in your body flowing smoothly, instead of leaving it gathered and blocked in local knots of tension. (Physical tension activates areas of the brain, making sleep difficult.)

Then lie in bed flat on your back. Inhale deeply; tense the whole body, equalizing the flow of energy throughout the body; throw the breath out and relax. Repeat this alternate tension and relaxation two or three times.

Then watch the breath mentally for a while, allowing its steady rhythm to soothe you, like the waves of an ocean stroking the shore on a calm day.

After some time, inhale deeply; then exhale slowly and completely and feel that you are surrendering yourself to an infinity of peace. Hold the breath out as long as you can comfortably, and repeat mentally, "*Aum,* peace, peace, amen," or, "*Aum, shanti, shanti, shanti.*" (*Shanti* is the Sanskrit word for "peace.") Visualize an ocean of peace spreading out in all directions around you—or think of peace as gathering protectively around you in great, soft clouds. Repeat this breathing process 6 to 12 times.

If after that you are still awake, continue watching the breath, calmly, passively.

Yogis say that one's bed should be arranged so that its head is not pointed toward the west. A westward position is said to induce fitful sleep and restless dreams; eastward, to aid the development of wisdom; and southward, to promote longevity.

Before sleep, and also before meditation, it is better not to eat anything. Especially to be avoided are starchy or other high-carbon foods. The heart and lungs clear the body of waste products, expelling them in the form of carbon dioxide. Starches and sugars give the heart more carbon to pump out of the body. A hard-working heart, with resultant heavy breathing, makes perfect rest impossible. If you must eat anything before going to sleep, try taking your food warm and if possible in liquid form—for example, warm milk. (Try this sleep-inducing beverage before bed: Boil a little chopped garlic in milk, then simmer it for 10 minutes.)

ters your nostrils or feel it in your abdomen. If you choose the nostril method, sit, with eyes closed, and focus all of your attention on the breath as it filters through your nose. Feel it tickle the little hairs. Feel it move upward through the nose and into the sinus area. Feel or imagine it as it enters your forehead area and flows throughout your whole head. Then feel it leaving your body the same way. If you choose the abdomen method, feel the breath as it comes into your body, and then feel your chest and abdomen expand and fill with air and then release.

Calming the Water

Soon you'll find that although this process is straightforward, maintaining focus on the breath is very, very difficult to do. Your mind will wander all over the place and most of the time, you'll totally lose awareness of your breathing. You'll be thinking about going to the bank before it closes, about the discussion you had with your boss yesterday, about what to wear to the party tonight, what color to paint your bathroom, on and on, ad infinitum.

The beauty of insight meditation starts with these random thoughts. For the first time ever, you will have a clue about the workings of your mind. Before this moment of awareness, most of us have no idea about the incredibly vast number of scattered thoughts that surge through our brains every second. Indeed, it is these thoughts that make our lives complex.

Here is why. The mind is driven by the senses, which are connected to the outer world. It is the job of our senses to put us in literal touch with our surroundings, through sight, sound, smell, and touch. When we come into contact with a stimulus, it is immediately transferred to our brains, where thoughts begin. Suddenly we become attached to the object of our senses. Everyone becomes attached to different things because of old memories and sensations. Suddenly we want the object of our desires. We must have it. And now we're hooked. We spend energy and/or money trying to attain the thing. Multiply this scenario by the hundreds, one piled on top of another. No wonder our lives are so chaotic. Stop and think about your own life. Think back on all of the actions you took just in the last 24 hours or last week, either thinking about or striving to attain desires. Those desires could be material or emotional. It doesn't matter. As Pandit Rajmani Tigunait writes in *Inner Quest:* "As long as you do not know how to withdraw the senses from the external world, you have almost no choice but to let your mind remain a victim of sensory pleasure."

We all know how transitory sensual pleasure is. We barely gratify one desire and another waits right behind, like jets lining up on a busy runway. We are constantly dissatisfied because desire never leaves us alone. To obtain any level of inner peace, we need to slow the onslaught. This doesn't mean we should withdraw from the world and enjoy no sensory pleasures. Half this book is devoted to enjoying the sensations that are right in front of us. The key is to be at peace within yourself first and to be aware of your motivations and actions rather than operating on automatic pilot.

When you begin with a foundation of inner strength and serenity, you then can choose wisely the sensual pleasures you will allow yourself to follow. Your awareness also will allow you to enjoy the simple pleasures that are waiting for you every moment. Meditating itself is a sensual pleasure. In fact, there is an old Indian saying, "Bhoga is yoga," which, roughly translated, means "delight is religion."

You'll find that with more awareness, you'll truly enjoy simpler pleasures because you will be able really to focus on them. The old adage "Stop and smell the roses" is totally appropriate in this context. When we rush through life on automatic, we don't take the time to even notice a beautiful rose. Then we go out and spend time and money paying for our entertainment. When we become more aware of the moments throughout our day, we also become aware of our surroundings, like the beautiful rose. We can take in all of its sensory beauty—the shape and softness of the petals, the intricate coloration, the heavenly smell. We really and truly *notice* this rose, maybe even for the first time. You'll find that when you begin to soak in these natural pleasures deeply, you'll have less need to chase after as many material desires as you did before.

Return to the breathing whenever your awareness returns. Accept the fact that in the beginning, your mind will wander off your breath more than it stays on it. This is part of the process. In fact, your mind will never be totally still. Another aspect of insight meditation (and, I'm sure, most other forms of meditation) is that it is about accepting yourself. If your mind wanders, simply take note of where it wandered and gently bring it back to your breath. This is the time to leave behind the achievement-oriented mind-set we've all been raised with—the one that says if you're not doing it right, you need to try harder and harder. Soon we're frustrated and feel as if we've failed.

Be gentle with yourself. Unlike so many other things in Western culture, there is no "goal" in meditation. Simply be aware of who you are as you go through the day. Not to change who you are, not to "snap out of it" or judge your mood, but simply to be aware of yourself as a whole human being.

While meditating, your mind may wander on its own or as a result of a noise or distraction. Say you're following your breath and a bus goes rumbling by, taking you from your reverie. Instead of getting angry at the bus for disrupting you, simply note to yourself "noise" or "bus," and return to your breath.

When your mind wanders on its own, you really can get to know yourself by labeling your thoughts. For instance, when I'm following my breath and I start thinking about a new house or new coat, I label it "wanting." If I rehash an argument, I may label my thoughts "anger." When I recall a pleasant moment, I label it "nice memory." Then if the memory persists to the point of my wanting to have it in my life again, I may again label my thoughts "wanting." I may feel anxious about an upcoming event. I'll label it "worrying." Sometimes I spend 99 percent of my time labeling thoughts. That's just fine, because by labeling my thoughts, I start to know what's going on inside me. I don't try to change the thoughts or get even more frustrated with myself that I'm feeling angry, worried, or desirous of something. Instead, I simply take gentle note of the thought and then, just as gently, return to my breath. Insight meditation is not about trying to change yourself, and you are not a failure if you don't feel peaceful all of the time once you've started meditating.

Jack Kornfield writes: "To be at peace requires us to be intimate with our sorrows, anger, loss, struggle, desires, pleasure, joys, and happiness."

Daily Mindfulness

You will find that after practicing insight meditation for a while, you begin taking your awareness with you throughout the day. Just as when you are "sitting" (as meditating is often called), you will find that most of the time during the day you will operate on automatic pilot and will have no consciousness of what you are thinking moment by moment. Now and then you will get a brief moment of awareness. This awareness is what can change your life. For one thing, you can hang on to a lot of your money when you are aware. When you walk through a store and see something you want to buy, but don't really need, simply label it "wanting" and move on. Perhaps you take on too many social engagements and find yourself flitting from one activity to the next to the point where you are exhausted and your schedule is packed full.

With awareness, you can label your motivation for taking on yet another engagement. Maybe you have some old feeling of being left out, and that old feeling returns whenever you are faced with deciding whether to accept another social opportunity. You could label it "fear" or "feeling left out" or whatever is appropriate. You also can take note of your pleasurable thoughts in order to become more aware of what feels right in your life. Maybe you're relaxing with a

Simplicity Is in Your Heart

by Janet Luhrs

Rodney Smith decided to learn insight meditation as a way to move into a richer part of his life. He was disturbed by how complex his thoughts were. When he looked at nature, he noticed that everything in nature is simple. "I wondered how I, as a part of nature, could be feeling such complexity internally when nature was manifesting simplicity," he said. "I wanted to find the same simplicity in me that I saw in nature."

Rodney spent three years at the Insight Meditation Society in Massachusetts. Then he spent four years in Thailand, where he was ordained a monk. He learned inner simplicity firsthand. "As a monk, you are given one little bowl, and you go out to the neighborhood to ask for food. You eat whatever they eat. If they eat vegetables, you eat vegetables. If they eat meat, you eat meat.

"You are also given one robe, and you have few possessions. One of my possessions in particular taught me a lesson in attachment to material things. I had a small Buddha carved out of bone that I really loved. I also had a good friend who I owed a lot to because he had helped me psychologically. As a gift of gratitude, I decided to give him the statue, but I couldn't do it. I loved it too much. Finally I was able to give it to him, and I found that I never missed it. There was enormous joy in giving. That joy is simplicity. When you let go of something you feel joy, because possessions tend to possess us. This was an important time in my life that allowed me to see the value of possessions. It didn't make any difference whether I had the Buddha or not. What had troubled me before was the *thought* that I couldn't give it away."

Rodney also learned that simplicity and love are the same themes. "What keeps us from connecting intimately with one another are all of our projections," he says. "If I put a lot of projections on you as to what I want, then our relationship is complicated and not from the heart. Suppose you came to me because you wanted me to be your meditation teacher. I would project that you would expect me to be wise. If I sit back and maintain an image of wise person, then I can't connect with you as a human being because I have to be a wise human. People want to connect with each other but don't because of the complexities of the mind."

We can learn from the simplicity of nature that things are just as they are. Those lessons can apply to us as human beings if we realize that thoughts are just thoughts and emotions are just emotions. We can project to the world the simplicity of who we are rather than the complexity of who people tell us we should be.

"It's not as if we have to do something to ourselves to be simple. We just have to see the limits of where complexity will take us," Rodney says. "If I sit back and act wise, for example, there is a part of me that doesn't get nourished . . . it keeps me from my heart. Once I see the limits of that, I won't do it anymore."

Rodney says that as long as we allow ourselves to be carried away in our desires, possessions, and accumulating, we'll never get to that inner core of ourselves, our hearts. That is what provides us a sense of fulfillment, caring, and concern. This can apply to material and personal accumulation. Often people feel they need more knowledge or more sophistication so they can project a smarter or more sophisticated image to the world. But every step they take in that direction takes them farther from their heart.

"It's not what you amass, it's your relationship to what you acquire that makes the difference," Rodney says. "For instance, you need to have a job, you need education in order to get the job, but you don't have to make that education or job title a rigid statement of who you are. Your naturalness can still come through even with all of that knowledge.

"Simplicity is where your heart is."

People also can play a role by adopting voluntary simplicity as their persona. Simplicity can be a cause, and you can create a division between you and everyone who isn't living like you. That creates isolation. "Simplicity of the heart doesn't lead to divisiveness," Rodney says. "When you understand that simplicity lies in the heart, you have compassion for other people's complexities. That complexity is their pain. I don't need to feel distant from them. Simplicity is tolerance . . . allowing other people to be who they are."

A simple heart is not only tolerant but is one that wants to serve as well. This is because a simple heart isn't so self-absorbed. "If I'm totally absorbed with my own needs and problems, I have no room for anyone else and I can't reach out," Rodney says.

When the mind is simplified, it is able to see things as they are, as in nature. Disappointments don't become tragedies. An example is a person who is fired from a job. If the person is someone who lives in simplicity, he or she feels the grief of losing the job and feels the fear of not knowing what to do, but he or she doesn't allow that fear to roll into complexity. Examples of that complexity would be expanding the fear to thoughts such as "How will I live like this?" or "This is the only job I'll ever have" or "I'll never find another job."

When a person lives in simplicity, his or her internal world is very sane because it doesn't generate self-induced problems.

"When you live in a world of form, you live in a world of accumulation," Rodney says. "If, on the other hand, you get involved in simplicity in a wholehearted way, it takes you to the spiritual because it takes you to your heart."

For information on insight meditation, contact: Insight Meditation Society, Pleasant Street, Barre, MA 01005, 1-508-355-4646.

good friend over a cup of tea and a brief moment of awareness enters your consciousness. You'll be aware that this is a very pleasurable sensation. Perhaps you're hiking in the woods and for a fleeting moment you realize how content you are. Maybe you are alone some evening reading a book and you realize how peaceful you feel. Think about why. Perhaps you need to free up your overcommitted schedule to find more time for these kinds of moments.

On the other hand, if you are feeling restless, stop and think about why. The usual way we deal with restlessness is to run out and get busy doing something. Stop and look at that restlessness. Meditate on it. What's the underlying feeling? You'll not only get to know yourself, but you'll simplify your life as well, because you won't be using activity as a "filler."

When you label your thoughts, you'll also discover how fleeting they are. Usually when you meditate and label your thought, it will dissipate quickly, to be replaced instantly by another one. Once a meditation teacher asked a group of us about our thoughts. She asked where we thought they came from. Of course, no one knew. They simply sailed into our conscious mind. And where did they go? No one knew. They evaporated into the air. Could we touch them? No. Did they have any form or substance? No. If we dissected ourselves, would we find these thoughts anywhere in the body? Would we see them? No. Did they rule our lives? Yes. Once we realize how truly empty these thoughts are, it becomes just a bit easier to put them in perspective.

Meditation Is Not Always Easy

Regular meditation practice is not easy. Our voice of instant gratification will nearly always find something else for us to do besides meditating. This has been my problem. When I meditate regularly, even for 15 minutes a day, I feel a sense of inner peace that pervades whatever is going on in my outside world. It gives me a serene sense of grounding. Yet, as with exercise, it's hard to keep up because I allow myself to get distracted by everything else, even though I know the results of exercise and meditating are so very worthwhile.

It also can be difficult to practice meditating regularly because of fear. Finally coming face to face with ourselves can be painful. We are not perfectly happy and content beings all of the time. We all have fears, insecurities, and dark sides right along with our positive aspects. Often it is easier to stay busy and involved in outside activities so we don't have to look at these more negative parts of ourselves. Yet all too often we know that when we ignore our difficult feelings, they will crop up somewhere else in our lives. It's kind of like plugging one geyser in a backyard and then looking up and finding 20 more springs popping up in other areas.

I find that when I have sadness in my life, for example, my first tendency is to rush around and stay busy. When I don't take the time to sit with my feelings, especially the negative ones, they lie at the pit of my stomach, and I carry a sense of unease with me. When I have that sense of unease, I become very unconscious of it after a while, but it is there because my life feels more tense. I may have a shorter fuse. I have less compassion for others. I don't concentrate as well. And my life becomes more complex in the process. Then, as the days go by, I wonder why I'm feeling blocked up and tense.

When I sit with my sadness and let it be, I still feel sad, but I also feel very calm. I may cry. Eventually I can look at the feeling and turn it over and ultimately heal. I do all of this without judging. It is perfectly normal and healthy to feel sadness at different points of our lives. Remember, living with awareness means not judging whatever feelings you have. It is simply being aware of them. Nothing more.

By stifling the feeling through busyness or some other tactic, we are, in essence, judging those feelings. We're saying that those feelings have no merit and are no good; therefore, we will do our best to get rid of them. We wonder why we live on automatic pilot treadmills and why stress and chaotic lives are a national malady.

> *Those who enter the gates of heaven are not beings who have no passions or who have curbed the passions, but those who have cultivated an understanding of them.*
>
> —William Blake

There is another component to letting ourselves experience pain of one sort or another. Matthew Fox, who writes extensively on the subjects of spirituality and human growth, once wrote that pain is the most legitimate school for compassion. So true. If we judge our own feelings of pain by ignoring them, we will not experience them in a direct way. If we haven't experienced pain, it is more difficult to have compassion for others. It is also easier to judge their pain and ignore it as well. Then we wonder why our relationships with others are superficial—why we always feel the need to put on a happy face no matter what and expect others to do the same. No one on earth is happy all of the time; in fact, it is the myriad of emotions that human beings experience that makes our lives rich.

A simple life is an authentic life. Living authentically doesn't mean we need to mope through life focusing constantly on our own problems. It simply means that when we have pain in our lives, we take a look at it, grieve, and let go. We become stronger, deeper, more authentic people in the process.

The Discipline of Meditation

If we want to reap the benefits of meditation, we need to put in a little effort. That effort comes in the form of discipline. I understood how discipline operates when a meditation teacher once told me about his stay at a monastery. The monks got up every day at something like 4:00 A.M. to meditate. They repeated the process at other set times during the day. I had been having a heck of a time fitting meditation into my "busy" day. Half the time I just couldn't seem to find any time, even for 10 minutes. By the time evening rolled in, I would realize I hadn't meditated all day, and then I was too tired. So the next day would start all over again. Only when nothing else was going on would I manage to fit in my 10 or 20 minutes. This wasn't working for me.

As soon as I heard about the monks, I instantly realized that what I lacked was discipline. It took tremendous discipline to get up at 4:00 A.M. to meditate. In return, the monks were feeding their souls. I was leaving mine empty.

Discipline is probably the most difficult aspect of your meditation practice. But remember, it is a part of your practice. You can't separate the two. Meditating once in a while when the mood strikes will not result in much benefit for you. Who wants to get up even 10 minutes early in the morning? Who wants to give up any part of a lunch hour? Who wants to take the time from a busy schedule to do "nothing"? Yet after even a week or two of regular practice, you will feel results.

Pandit Rajmani Tigunait writes in *Inner Quest:* "Don't get lost in an endless round of worldly duties and obligations. No matter how skillful you are, or how selflessly you carry out your duties, there will still be an endless number of things left undone at the end of your life. If you don't learn how to balance duties and your personal spiritual practice, you will be lost."

Pandit Tigunait suggests that regulating your life is very important, because it is difficult if not impossible to create regular, calm time for meditating when your life is chaotic and disorganized. This means going to bed at a regular hour, getting up at a regular hour, and saying no to activities that would interfere with your schedule. Say you've set the hour of 8:00 P.M. to meditate each day. Say a friend calls you at 8:00 P.M. Do you talk? Nope. You tell the friend you'll call back in 20 minutes, or however long you have set aside for your practice. So that you aren't regularly confronted with enticing interruptions, pick a time that is generally a quiet one for you. Doing so will make your life much

The Five Most Common Hindrances to Awareness and Clarity

Grasping and Wanting

There are many forms of desire. Some are beneficial, like the desire to help others or the desire to make the world a more beautiful place. Some are harmful, like the desires of addiction, greed, blind ambition, or restlessness. With awareness you can sort out your own desires and name them.

Anger

Anger is unpleasant but a part of life. We can be mildly or intensely angry at someone or even a group of people. Anger pervades our lives and affects how we treat others. We can hardly be loving and compassionate when we feel angry. Name your anger and take note of how it feels in your body. Pay attention to it. What exactly are you angry about? While meditating, sit back like an observer and simply notice.

Fear

We're afraid of many things. We're afraid to go to our boss for a raise. We're afraid to talk to someone about a problem. We're afraid someone will steal our car or break into our house. We're afraid for our children. On and on. Jack Kornfield writes in *A Path with Heart*, the way to calm fear is to name it and talk to it. He advises experiencing its energy as it moves through us, naming it, and then saying: "Oh, fear, here you are again. How interesting."

Boredom

Most of us in modern society know all about conquering boredom the busy way: call a friend, make an appointment, turn on the TV, bury ourselves in work, weed the yard, and on and on. With awareness, we don't need to let boredom run our lives. Take a look at boredom the next time you're meditating. Name it, feel it, be with it.

Judgment

We judge ourselves and others constantly. Try a little awareness the next time you enter a room. "He looks grumpy. She looks pathetic in those stretch pants. I wish I had it all together like she does. They look interesting. . . ." When you do this while meditating, either sitting or going through life, simply name it: judging.

easier. Then make your outer life schedule work around your inner life schedule, rather than the usual vice versa. No one said this was easy, but it will be much easier if your outer life is more simple and organized, and if you make the decision that inner contentment is a goal.

Attachment

When you become aware of your thoughts, you will discover that one of the most common is the thought of desire, or "wanting." We want every other thing we see. Constantly. Without consciousness, we blindly follow the thought and act on it. We don't need to. A Carmelite priest, Father Colin Stone, said: "We're a little bit like a washing machine on the spin cycle, so thrown to the edges by all our activity that we've lost touch with our center. . . . To avoid our own woundedness, we will try to fill our emptiness with materialism, activity, or addictive behaviors so we don't have to face ourselves."

There is a word for our constant desire for gratification. It is called attachment. We want beautiful things, attractive people, good food, pleasant odors, and so forth. To attain these things, we spend a lot of our energy focusing on them, dwelling on them, and going to great strides to attain them. We become "attached." In our striving, we often act selfishly or negatively. Part of our attachment is to making ourselves feel good. Sometimes we put others down in order to feel better. Sometimes we ignore those close to us in order to earn more and more money to acquire more and more power, status, or things. If we become attached to a person, we feel we want to possess or control that person in some way. When we cannot attain the goal of our attachment, we get angry or frustrated. These kinds of emotions do nothing but complicate our lives.

The problem does not lie in these objects we are attached to but in our attitudes about them. We can love people without becoming attached to them in this way. In fact, real love is not about being attached; it is about honoring and respecting the other person to be who he or she is and not trying to possess the person. The same applies to our children. When we are attached in this way to our children, we expect them to behave exactly as we think they ought to behave. We leave them no room to be unique human beings on their own. This doesn't mean we let them get into unsafe situations or do as they please; rather, it is about viewing them as separate beings with their own interests, talents, and capabilities. We can enjoy beautiful objects without obsessing about how to get them for ourselves. We can take pride in our own possessions without hanging our life on them if they are lost, stolen, or destroyed.

One way to work with attachment is to name it when you become aware that you are getting attached, and then think about the undesirable aspects of the object. If it is something you want to buy, realize that you will have less money for your own freedom if you buy the thing. You will need to take care of it, dust it, insure it, find a place for it, worry about it getting stolen. If it is a person, say your child, think about the frustration you will have if your child doesn't follow in your footsteps. If you have been successful in the business world and your child wants to be a musician, you will frustrate everyone by having the attitude that the child needs to follow your ideas of "success." When we age, we become attached to youth. It's one thing to stay healthy and in good shape; it's another to become obsessed with looking 29 or 39 forever.

You also can realize that attachment is borne out of fear. We fear if we don't cling tightly to a person, we will lose him or her. If we don't drive a certain car, we won't look successful. If we don't get the new house, we will be unhappy. Stop and look at the fear. Turn it over and over and look at it from a distance. Will you allow your fear to put you in debt to buy an item you can't afford or to cling so tightly to a person that he or she will indeed go away? Awareness will help you to name and look realistically at your fear and attachment. Without awareness, you'll probably go off and operate on automatic pilot just as before.

We find that when we are attached to anything, we become unhappy. This is because attachment is an attitude that overestimates the qualities of an object or person and then clings to it. Attempting to seek happiness through possession or attachment never ends. We always want more and better, and we're always discontented.

On the other side, being aware of attachment doesn't mean that we have no relationships or possessions. We're human beings and we need love and intimacy. We need a certain amount of possessions. The difference is our *attitude* about those people and possessions, and the amount of possessions we think we need in order to be satisfied.

Create a Vision

One way you can incorporate a meditation discipline into your life is to create a vision for yourself. Get a clear picture of exactly why you want to meditate regularly. This vision is like a mission statement that businesses write. What are your values? How will meditating help you to realize those values? As Jon Kabat-Zinn says in his book *Wherever You Go, There You Are*, this vision needs to be far more individualized than the simple thought that meditation is good for you or that meditating is a lofty thing. Kabat-Zinn writes: "Rather, it is bearing in mind what is most important to you so that it is not lost or betrayed in the heat and reactivity of a particular moment. If mindfulness is deeply important to you, then every opportunity is an opportunity to practice."

Meditate While You Work

Once you have disciplined yourself to do sitting meditation regularly, you will, I am sure, notice that you have more frequent moments of awareness throughout the day. You also can deliberately meditate as you go about your daily life. There are thousands and thousands of opportunities for awareness every second of every day. That is what the book *Chop Wood, Carry Water* is about. There is not one activity, including mundane chores such as chopping wood and carrying water, that you cannot do mindfully. When you go to the bank, you can be fully present and converse with the teller as if he or she is really there. When you do the wash, you can be mindful as you place the garments into the bin. You can stop to think about who wears these clothes. When you cook a meal, you can fully engage yourself and feel and smell each item as you cut or prepare it. If you and your spouse have a disagreement, you can be mindful about what you say rather than flying off on an automatic pilot reaction. Or if you do fly off (we're not perfect, so let's not sweat it), you can be mindful and apologize. You can do the same with your children, boss, or coworkers.

There is a way to practice daily mindfulness. It is called walking meditation. The next time you go for a walk, pay attention to each step. Try this at home before venturing outside. Walk slowly, one foot in front of the other. As you place your heel on the floor, *feel* the heel on the floor, then feel the ball of your foot touch down, and the toes. Then feel every muscle in your leg and thigh as you lift your leg to take another step. Feel the muscles putting that foot down on the ground in front of the other foot. Repeat this. Walk for 10 minutes around your house paying attention to every movement your body makes in order to walk. If you are barefoot, feel the soft rug or cold wood. When you do this a few times, you'll be ready to walk outside at a little faster pace. If you walk at a more normal pace, people won't wonder what the heck you're doing. In my opinion, simplicity has nothing to do with calling attention to yourself. No one else will have a clue about what you're doing, but inside you'll know that you are feeling every step and movement and you are practicing mindfulness.

Walking meditation is simply one more way to put you in touch with yourself and the world around you. When you are mindful, you are aware of your feelings and the environment at that moment. As a result, your mind slows and calms. Think about it. If you are focusing on every step and every sensation, your mind can't be off obsessing about some desire or other, or a worry you may have, and so on. You'll be focusing on the moment at hand. As the Buddhists say, you'll be *awake*. Believe me, when your mind is focusing on the present moment, it is naturally much more calm and centered than if it is off on the usual hundreds of tangents going in every imaginable direction.

Loving Kindness Meditation

Once you have disciplined yourself to make meditation a part of your life, you can meditate with a purpose. One in particular is called loving kindness meditation. You meditate on thoughts of love and acceptance for yourself first, and once you have filled your cup, you meditate on loving thoughts for other people. Here is how.

Take your usual meditation posture and begin centering yourself with your breathing. Then imagine that love, acceptance, or kindness begins to surround you and fill every pore. You feel the warmth of this love, as if being embraced. Breathe in this feeling and warmth, and let it radiate all throughout your body until you feel warm and accepted all over. You can stay with these feelings for as long as you like. Keep taking in deep breaths, and with every breath breathe more love and acceptance into your soul. When you are finished, you will feel more calm, peaceful, and loving.

Next you can practice the same meditation focusing on other people. Start with your family or those who are around you the most. Focus on each person and imagine swathing him or her in the same loving warmth. Doing so is easy when you are imagining someone you love and with whom you have a positive relationship. You'll need all of your compassion when you focus on someone with whom you have problems. Nevertheless, these are the relationships that need healing the most. Although difficult, continue imagining this person bathed in feelings of love and compassion. If you keep at it long enough, eventually you will make a few inroads to seeing the problem on a new level. You may even be able to see that person's side of the issue; if his or her personality simply grates on you, you may be able to see that person with compassion for the first time. Perhaps this person has wronged you. You have every right to be angry. Loving kindness meditation can help you to let go of a little of the anger and, in so doing, free up your energy to love yourself again. In any case, this meditation can change your own outlook and attitude, which will result in more calm, accepting, compassionate relationships with others. Believe me, with less personal conflict, your life will be simpler by miles.

Loving Kindness and Children

One of the best things you can do for your children is to practice loving kindness meditation regularly. If you take the time to fill your own heart and soul through this meditation, you will have more patience, love, and kindness to give to your children. Once you fill your own heart, you can focus your energies on your children while meditating. Visualize them bathed in loving feelings.

We've heard the stories about great athletes who visualize a perfect game before the actual match. Tennis players see a smooth, strong backhand over and over, or a knockout serve and so on. They visualize each detail of the game and see themselves as playing at absolutely top form. You can do the same for your children. Take the time to visualize them as little beings deserving of abundant love, compassion, and kindness. If you are having a particular problem with a child, do as the athletes do and visualize the perfect way to handle it.

The right visualization may not come for a while. No problem. Keep practicing loving kindness meditation and believe me, the right attitude will come. Often the right answer is changing our own attitude. How does that old saying go? You can do a lot more with a spoonful of honey than vinegar? Loving kindness meditation is one way to remember to focus on the honey. By doing so, you will reap the rewards of a better relationship with your children. After all, how do you like to be treated?

Recently I cut out a short article and taped it to my wall at home. I leave it there to remind me to have compassion for my children. It is written by a grown man who wrote a tribute to his father. In the tribute he salutes his father for his compassion. He retells the story of one prom night when he took his father's special car out of the garage to impress his date. He did not ask for permission. In his haste to drive away undetected, he forgot to close the driver's door. As he backed out of the garage, checking for clearance, he sprung the door from its hinges. He managed to force it closed. When he returned at 3:00 A.M. from the prom, he lay awake for hours trying to figure out how to tell his father what happened. When he came downstairs, his father was sitting in the kitchen, drinking a cup of coffee. "I took the Chevy to the body shop," his father said. "They'll have it fixed tomorrow. We can decide who'll pay for it then." His father paused. "Did you have a good time at the prom?"

What a story of compassion in action. It is so easy to lash out quickly at our children, often because we, the parents, are so stressed from our own lives that we have little patience left over for anyone else. If a few moments of loving kindness meditation can help us to be just a little more patient, a little more compassionate, and a lot more loving, we will reap rewards a thousandfold.

Develop a Habit of Being Quiet

You can also calm yourself by simply being quiet. Being quiet can be difficult in our stimulation-filled world. Think of all the noise that surrounds many of us every moment. We wake up to the noise of an alarm clock. Often we leave our radios on for the music or news. Some people turn on the TV in the morning as they prepare for work. If we even take the time to eat, we have no idea what our food tastes like because we are busy listening to or thinking about other things while we eat. We get in our cars and start up the motors. We turn on the radio. If we ride the bus, we are surrounded by people talking. Most of us work with the noise of machines (telephones, computers, copy machines, and on and on) and people. We return home the same way. Instead of being relieved for a little quiet, we can't stand it and turn on the TV for company and noise again. If we live with other people, we talk to them. Our household machines are noisy—the dishwasher, vacuum, washing machine, power tools. This goes on seven days a week! No wonder why we're exhausted, and no wonder why we have no idea what's going on inside of ourselves.

Noise has been linked to high blood pressure, heart disease, mental health problems, learning disorders, and stress. "When our days are full of TV, radio, and other chatter, noise squeezes out the silence in which to think, reflect, and find meaning in who we are and what we do," says Bruce David, Ph.D., psychologist and author of *Monastery Without Walls: Daily Life in the Silence.* "When there's no pause in the input, our heads get filled with the voices and opinions of others—be it parents, friends, or Peter Jennings. In silence, we have the chance to listen for our own voices. We make choices based on what we really want and not on what others expect.*

Plain old silence is a wonderful thing. You can connect with yourself, and

❖ ❖ ❖ ❖ ❖ ❖ ❖ ❖ ❖ ❖ ❖ ❖ ❖ ❖ ❖ ❖ ❖ ❖

*From *Prevention Magazine*, October 1996.

with the world around you, in a way you cannot do when you are constantly stimulated. Try it next time you have a choice. When driving, try driving in silence. Instead of automatically reaching for the radio dial, try instead to focus on the experience of driving. Feel your hands on the hard, smooth steering wheel, feel the seat underneath your thighs, the pedal under the ball of your foot. Really look at what you see in front of you. We think we're looking, but instead we're gazing mindlessly while thinking about heading to the grocery store to get tonight's dinner.

When you get home at night, leave the TV off. If you live alone, this may be frightening because you won't have "company." If you can get past the withdrawal stage, you will have a chance to really be with yourself. Listen to nature outside. Keep the TV off in the morning too. Enjoy the peace and quiet. Listen to your thoughts and feelings.

You also can create your own retreat right at home. Set aside an evening just for yourself where you can stay home in silence; then go a step further and set aside a whole weekend for silence. Granted, this is much easier if you live alone, but you can accomplish it if you have a cooperative family. You could have silent family retreats right at home. No need to check into an expensive retreat house. If you decide to try this, be sure to turn the ringer off the phone. If your children are too small, perhaps you and your partner could spell one another for a silent day. One parent could take the kids out for a few hours while the other stays home to bask in silence, and then switch the following weekend or month. Silence is very rejuvenating.

You'll find that when you quiet the din around you on a daily basis, you'll enjoy quality sounds much more. For instance, you can play beautiful music some evening and really enjoy it. It won't be lost in the cacophony. If you live with other people, you can take the time to enjoy the sounds of people you love rather than some mindless chattering on the TV. If you have children, listen to their banter and games. If you have a conversation with someone, you can pay quality attention to that person without the distraction of modern noise-makers like TV and machines. What a gift to someone to know that you are giving them your full attention!

As with all areas of simplifying, please don't go overboard. It's just fine to have noise in your car sometimes. It's just fine to have the TV on sometimes. With awareness, however, you'll learn to balance noise with peace and quiet.

Daniel Gottlieb, Ph.D., psychologist and author of *Voices in the Family*, says: "The goal is to learn to listen to your own inner voice and not just respond to someone else's ideas. The perfect time to be silent is when *you* decide you need it."

Being Mindful

Michael Freeman spent the first part of his life sailing through on automatic. It took a number of major life upheavals and years of soul searching for him to discover that being happy and simplifying his life were not a matter of "doing" but were a way of "being." "A simple way of life may be different for each person," he said. "You can have a house and a job or not, there is no one description of how a simple life will be. You could find a monk or a nun living in a monastery whose minds could be as busy as anyone's."

Michael tried on many of the outward costumes of life in his search for contentment. At first, he identified himself with his position and money. He devoted most of his time to achieving on the job and making money as a policeman. Although he was filled with anxiety and remorse about not spending more time with his family, he never questioned his unconscious drive to

---

The Sensuality of Simplicity

Take a shower or bath and *feel* every drop of water as it flows around your body. Relish in this experience. It may be the first time you actually have been fully present in the shower. Whenever your mind drifts off and you think about the bank, your children, your next appointment, gently bring it back to the water trickling and spraying over your body.

---

achieve more and more. "It was simply what I did," he said. "I thought I had what life offered: a sunken living room, a nice car. So I didn't give much thought to whether I was happy or not."

Then Michael's wife left him. Then he left his job. Later he was confronted with a moral dilemma at a new job. People were writing personal checks from grant money that was supposed to be used for a helping program. "For the first time I began to notice there were people starving in the world and these people at my job were concerned with their egos," he said.

So he decided to move to the woods. Then he would be happy. He moved, worked as a carpenter, and married a second time. But still, Michael Freeman was not fulfilled. He found that even people living in the woods thought that a new TV or four-wheel-drive vehicle would make them happy. He decided he needed to push himself further away from the mainstream in his search for happiness. He became self-sufficient and grew his own food, canned it for the winter, put in his own water system, used a windmill for power, and opened an organic restaurant. He couldn't have driven himself much farther from the sunken living room life.

Michael Freeman pauses for reflection.

"Now I was a slave to this new business," he said. "The restaurant was getting out of control. Like perpetual motion, it was running us."

Michael left that restaurant to partners and moved again. Still searching. He had tried the traditional outward cloaks of happiness and, still, contentment eluded him. He decided it was time to look inside. Who was Michael Freeman? Cop? Dad? Husband? Restaurant owner? Self-sufficient man of the woods? Who? He began to unload his possessions in an effort to uncover the real Michael Freeman. He moved to a cabin. He wouldn't, however, unload his carpentry tools, which amounted to a complete woodworking shop. "This was security," he said. "But also a millstone."

A fire taught him his next lesson about who he was and what he needed. One night a blaze erupted at the neighbor's place not far away. He made a conscious, awake decision that night that he would rather go and try to save the neighbor's place than worry about his beloved tools. Given the nature of the fire, he knew that if he left in time to save the neighbor's place, he would lose his tools and other belongings. "There would be no way to save my things unless I moved them first," he remembers, "but I knew I didn't have time to do that if I was going to help my neighbor."

Michael helped to save the neighbor's place. He also learned that he could live fine without the security of his tools. Miraculously, he says, the fire did not destroy his tools. But he got rid of them anyway. He moved again. Still searching. Still unloading one outer life ring after another. Who was Michael? Still looking. A friend suggested he go to a community where Ram Dass wrote the book *Be Here Now*. He stayed two years and learned about a thing called spirituality. He learned how to meditate, to be aware of thoughts, feelings, and sensations. He was finding Michael Freeman. He was experiencing his inside self. He went on a three-month retreat at a meditation center and joined the staff, where he stayed for four years. He experienced living in a monastery. And then he decided it was time to merge his inner and outer lives. It was one thing to live simply in a monastery or retreat center, it was another to live that way in the city. How could he do that?

"I am looking for a middle way now," he says. "Monasteries are one way, but householders can live simple lives too, even though it is not easy. As soon as I moved to the city, I saw how easily I could slip into the constant desires of mainstream society. We want more money, more insurance . . . constant pressures to fit into patterns. In the city, I get up and immediately think about what I have to do. I need to be aware.

"Now I begin each day by noting the day. I note that a new day is beginning. I try to stay mindful throughout the day, and at the end of the day I ask myself if I was mindful. Being mindful while eating—thinking about what I am eating and experiencing that sensation. Being mindful while walking—feeling the pressure of the pavement on my feet. Looking at my surroundings and really seeing them. Hearing the sounds. Smelling the smells. Being mindful while I am driving. The feel of the steering wheel against my palms. Or if I am hurrying, I try to be aware that I am hurrying. I try not to judge myself and say 'Oh, I shouldn't be in a hurry'; I am just aware that my heart is beating faster or my neck is tense. I try not to change it, just note the feelings."

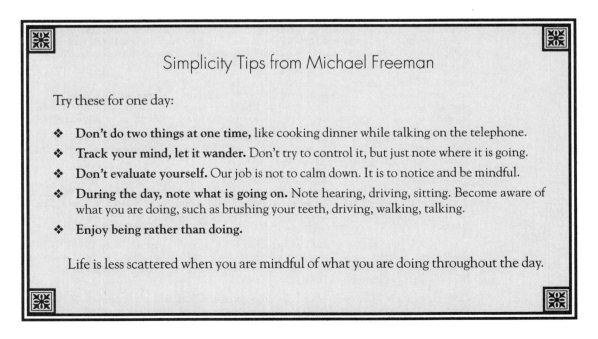

Simplicity Tips from Michael Freeman

Try these for one day:

- ❖ **Don't do two things at one time,** like cooking dinner while talking on the telephone.
- ❖ **Track your mind, let it wander.** Don't try to control it, but just note where it is going.
- ❖ **Don't evaluate yourself.** Our job is not to calm down. It is to notice and be mindful.
- ❖ **During the day, note what is going on.** Note hearing, driving, sitting. Become aware of what you are doing, such as brushing your teeth, driving, walking, talking.
- ❖ **Enjoy being rather than doing.**

Life is less scattered when you are mindful of what you are doing throughout the day.

❖ ❖ ❖ ❖ ❖ ❖ ❖ ❖ ❖ ❖ ❖ ❖ ❖ ❖

Resources

Beginning to Pray by Anthony Bloom (New York: Paulist Press, 1993)
Written by an Orthodox archbishop, the book teaches the realities and fundamentals of prayer. Nonsectarian or denominational, it offers practical viewpoints on gaining access to and assistance from God.

Buddha's Little Instruction Book by Jack Kornfield (New York: Bantam, 1994)
Inspirational teachings of Buddha as told by a Buddhist teacher and psychologist. Uses Buddha's own words to help guide the mind, body, and soul toward peace and enlightenment, as well as the six meditations.

Care of the Soul by Thomas Moore (New York: Harper Perennial, 1994)
Penned by an ex-monk, this book looks at events and how they affect the soul. It posits that much of our daily work can become more "soulful" if we learn to appreciate the needs and pleasures of inner satisfaction that do not directly deal with immediate physical and material wants. Our culture has given up its emphasis on soul for the sake of financial comfort, but in doing so has left us all feeling lonely and dry.

Chop Wood, Carry Water, by Rick Fields, (Los Angeles: Jeremy P. Tarcher, 1985)
A classic book on mindfulness in everyday life. We can bring spirituality and mindfulness to everything we do, including chopping wood and carrying water. Book discusses how to be mindful at work; in intimate relationships; with money, play, the earth, and more.

The Importance of Living by Lin Yutang (New York: William Morrow, 1937, 1996)
Introduction and explanation of Eastern philosophy of living, particularly the slower, more serene lifestyle of Chinese culture. Discerns a basic difference between Eastern and Western ideals; the West relies on rapid means to achieving a certain end, while Eastern ideology focuses on less rushed movements, the unfolding of events naturally, and the appreciation of singular moments that have nothing to do with anything but themselves.

Inner Quest by Pandit Rajmani Tigunait (Honesdale, PA: Yoga International Books, 1995)
A question-and-answer book that covers a wide range of topics, from explanations of karma, how to meditate, reincarnation, chakras, to finding higher consciousness. Based on a compilation of articles found in *Yoga International* magazine as well as the author's own life history as a yoga master.

Inner Simplicity by Elaine St. James (New York: Hyperion, 1995)
One hundred practical suggestions to unclutter the cluttered life, but find the core of something more meaningful while doing it. The topics range from learning to enjoy silence, to releasing your attachment to possessions, to learning to see problems in your life as gifts.

The Little Zen Companion by David Schiller (New York: Workman Publishing, 1994)
A compendium of anecdotes, quotes, and practical advice on following and assimilating the Zen lifestyle, whose purpose is "to perfect character."

Man's Search for Meaning by Viktor E. Frankl (New York: Simon & Schuster, 1959, 1984)
A classic written by a survivor of Nazi concentration camps. Both a testament to man's ability to overcome horrific tragedies as well as a primer for the search for personal fulfillment. The acceptance of life as loss and pain is only half of the equation; the other is what Frankl calls "tragic optimism," or the willingness to look to the future with an austere sense of hope.

Meditation for Starters by J. Donald Walters (Nevada City, CA: Crystal Clarity, 1996)
Book plus accompanying CD highlights the purpose of meditation and its benefits. Offers ways to meditate, including how to prepare for calming and relaxing the body and what happens after meditation.

Open Heart, Clear Mind by Thubten Chodron (Ithaca, NY: Snow Lion Publications, 1990)
A practical guide to Buddhism that touches on its very core: namely, the four noble truths,

the eightfold path, and the three principal realizations. Also looks at topics that affect our daily life, including love, anger, and jealousy.

A Path with Heart by Jack Kornfield (New York: Bantam, 1993)
Combines a personal journey with a look at how meditation directly relates to our biggest problems and concerns ("Meditation on Making the Demons Part of the Path," "Who Am I?" etc.). Ends with a focus on how to live a "conscious" life, including the five precepts that form the basis of a harmonized social existence.

There Is a Season by Joan Chittister (Maryknoll, NY: Orbis Books, 1995)
Uses the well-known biblical verse (Ecclesiastes 3:1, 3:13) as a meditation on our lives and how to change the outside by starting on the inside. By peering into those forces that prevent us from achieving peace and tranquility (i.e., bad habits, our own fears and apprehensions), Chittister offers us a spiritual way to living life richly and well.

To Have or to Be by Erich Fromm (New York: Continuum, 1996)
Considered an important book on personal psychology, this posthumously published book offers us a report on the battle going on between the material world (power, aggression, greed, technology, wealth) and the inner world (with its emphasis on love, human relationships, creativity, and sanctity of life). How each of us reacts to this supreme war tells a lot about our relationship to the world and to ourselves.

Voluntary Simplicity by Duane Elgin (New York: William Morrow, 1993)
What is the good life and how can it be achieved, so that we feel inwardly wealthy yet outwardly secure? Elgin invites the reader to understand the links among personal consumption, spending habits, and material motivations with our own inner needs. Enrichment is found in a life lived closer to the ground, without too many unnecessary accoutrements and with a sense of wonder and mystery about the life that surrounds us.

Wherever You Go, There You Are by Jon Kabat-Zinn (New York: Hyperion, 1994)
Founder of a stress reduction clinic, Kabat-Zinn introduces a variety of meditative practices, including the sitting, mountain, lake, and walking meditations. Practical and intended for the novice. Also offers explanations on the causes of stress and what we can do to reduce them.

4
Work

What is at the center of your life?
Carefully examine where you spend
your attention, your time. Look at
your appointment book, your daily
schedule. . . . This is what receives
your care and attention—and by
definition, your love.

—WAYNE MULLER, "HOW SHALL WE LOVE"

A single moment in the early 1970s changed forever the way Ted Butchart looked at life and work. He remembers sitting on a barricade one night at Portland State University during the Vietnam War protests. It was midnight and he sat alone, trying to sort through his feelings about the war and about the demonstrations. A man in his late 70s came and sat with Ted. "He proceeded to tell me how afraid he was to see the revolution and the students marching," Ted says. "I understood how scared he was because he thought that this could have been the beginning of an overthrow. He didn't know." It turned out that this man's most overwhelming concern was whether he would be able to continue to collect his retirement and pension checks. That was all this man had to live on.

"It gave me a lot of compassion," Ted remembers, "but that night I swore I would never allow myself to be in that vulnerable a position. I knew I never wanted to compromise my moral or ethical positions simply because of an effect they may have on my personal income. I needed to create a life that was buffered from economic ebb and flow: an apple tree and cider press rather than a pension check."

The Simple Living Theory of Work

The simple living theory about work for me is owed in large part to my dad. He taught me two of the most important rules:

1. Find something you love to do and get paid for it.
2. Live under your means. (Living under your means is when you spend less than you take home and sock away the rest.)

This, indeed, is what Ted experienced while sitting on the barricade. You need to practice both steps in order to make the simple living work theory a success. Think about it. If you don't live under your means, you have nothing saved. Then you have few choices about how to spend your time and what to do for a living. You need to keep on working whether you want to be at the job or not. You can't quit and take your time to find something meaningful because you need the income to feed and house yourself. If you not only have nothing saved but are in debt too, you really need to keep working or you'll be harassed to death by collection agencies. (Personally, I would rather die of natural causes, thank you.)

Stay with me. If you have been living *under* your means, you have been saving money. Now you have the luxury of taking time off to think about the kind of job you'd really like, or returning to school to learn a wonderful new skill, or working part time. If you've saved a bundle of money (check Chapter 2 to understand that you don't need to be born to wealthy parents to do this), you may even be able to retire early and then do *exactly* as you like. You could work just for the fun of it. Imagine that.

There is another option. Learn to live on very little and then you have the choice to work part time, on a contract or a temporary basis, or in a field that doesn't pay much but that you love. You may not be able to save much, but you'll be living the kind of life you want. You could simply work enough to finance a passion. This idea was well stated in an ad for a ski resort. It showed a picture of a person skiing down a hill. The caption read: "College degree. Good job. Big house. We all make mistakes." I must admit, this is advertising copy writing at its finest, and this is living intentionally at its best. So many of us simply go with the approved flow—college, good job, mortgage, two new cars, suburbs, and so on. We never stop for a moment to think about whether this is what we really want. Don't get me wrong; I'm hardly advocating wandering aimlessly through life with no focus. Education and good jobs can be wonderful additions to anybody's life. Education in particular is excellent insurance—you have a lot more choices when you have education, and education can open many doors that you never knew existed. Likewise, good jobs can provide much satisfaction. And indeed, a life of nothing but goofing off, whether skiing, fishing, or wandering, would probably get old after a while. Simple living is, once again, about finding balance. Can you create a life that includes lots of what you love, such as skiing, and also have something to fall back on? Can you have a job or career that allows you this kind of life? Do you need a big house and big mortgage? Not necessarily. How many people have you talked to who remember their old college days as happy ones, where they used orange crates for furniture, they could fit everything they owned in the back of a Volkswagen bug, and they enjoyed lots of freedom and a balanced life? Is there something in the middle now? I personally wouldn't want to live on orange crates, and I like having a "nest," but do we need a huge sprawling nest that costs us our lives?

Joe Puryear graduated from college and decided what he really loves to do is climb mountains. He works in an outdoor equipment store that encourages him to take time off to pursue his passion. But he plans more than that. He hopes to develop his climbing skills so sponsors will pay him to climb. And he's also taken the time to develop a personal life with his partner, Valerie. Joe has reduced his material needs in order to save money for his expeditions. His job pays very little, but it's enough to support his deliberately chosen lifestyle.

Here is how the simple living theory worked in my life. My first career out of college was as a journalist, earning very little money. Then I quit to become a freelance writer, earning even less money. I loved (and still do) writing with a passion. No kidding, I get a real thrill out of sitting up till all hours writing stories. But I knew I couldn't continue as a freelancer if I spent much money, so I lived on less. Very simple equation. I lived well (for my standards), even taking frequent vacations to places like Hawaii and Mexico, but I had zero debt, a subminimal wardrobe, and a $500 car. I never even applied for a credit card. I wanted to continue enjoying the freedom of freelancing so much that I was very happy making the trade-off of owning fewer gizmos and gadgets. The thought of getting a full-time job sent shivers up my spine, and I knew a job would have been my only option if I increased my spending. There was no way on earth I was willing to make that trade-off.

The same rule applies to everybody, no matter what they are doing. Doesn't matter what kind of reasonably paid job you have. In fact, a book ti-

> *Thomas Aquinas said, "There can be no joy of life without joy of work." Our joy of work and life can flourish when we move from an intention of "making a killing" for ourselves to that of "earning a living" in a way that contributes to the well-being of all.*
>
> —DUANE ELGIN, AUTHOR OF *VOLUNTARY SIMPLICITY*

tled *Millionaire Next Door,* by Thomas Stanley, gives some surprising facts and figures: Did you know that most people who are millionaires have very ordinary jobs, such as managing a trailer park or running a welding shop? And the second most important fact in the book is this: Far more people who are *not* millionaires drive new cars than do those who *are* millionaires. Does this give you an idea? People who managed to squirrel away huge sums of money did not do so by spending all of it. These people figured out one theory: Live on less and sock away the rest. For all of those who complain that you need to be a highly paid professional in order to have any choices in life, please refer to the *Millionaire* book. You don't need to be a millionaire to live a fulfilled, balanced life. But you do need to adopt these same principles.

Once you understand the two most important simple living theories about work, there are many nuances and fine points. For instance, you need to be willing to work hard and efficiently when you do work, you need to be open to all sorts of possibilities, you need a lot of determination, and above all, you need lots of ingenuity.

Work Is Important

Without question, work is a major part of our lives. Wilhelm Reich, the Austrian psychoanalyst and colleague of Freud's, once wrote that "Love, work, and knowledge are the well-springs of our life. They should also govern it." And Freud himself was once asked what he thought a normal person should be able to do. His answer was *"Lieben und arbeiten,"* which means "Love and work."

In the book *Chop Wood, Carry Water,* by Rick Fields, Peggy Taylor, Rex Weyler, and Rick Ingrasci, the authors quote from a Tibetan Buddhist teacher, Tarthang Tulku, who said: "Caring about our work, liking it, even loving it, seems strange when we see work only as a way to make a living. But when we see work as the way to deepen and enrich all of our experience, each one of us can find this caring within our hearts, and awaken it in those around us, using every aspect of work to learn and grow."

Much of this theory has to do with changing how we look at work. We can bring to whatever work we do a sense of passion, purpose, and awareness. Rather than tuning out during our work day and operating on automatic pilot, we can instead be fully mindful and present with each task we do. Think about this: Most people spend up to 70 or more percent of their day at their jobs. How sad to be tuned out to and, worse, dislike, that much of your life!

In *Creative Work—Karma Yoga: A Western Interpretation*, the philosopher Edmund Bordeaux Szekely describes this change of attitude:

> In the highest sense, work is meant to be the servant of man, not the master. It is not so important what shape or form our work may take; what is vitally important is our attitude toward that work. With love and enthusiasm directed toward our work, what was once a chore and hardship now becomes a magical tool to develop, enrich and nourish our lives. "Work makes the man" is an old proverb with much more truth in it than appears on the surface. Work can indeed make the man, if the man will use his God-given powers of reason to transform work into the sacred partnership with the Creator it was originally meant to be.

This attitude can breathe new life into a current job that we thought was mundane and boring. Here is how. Zen monks are trained to do manual labor, such as sweeping, cleaning toilets, and pulling weeds. This is to show that spirituality is not just something we strive to acquire by hanging out in a church or sitting for meditation. Spirituality is also about bringing mindfulness to everyday activities. Once the monks understand this, no labor, no matter how menial, is beneath their dignity. "In fact," says Roshi Philip Kapleau in *The Three Pillars of Zen*, "this work is enlightening because enlightenment in Zen is never for oneself alone but for the sake of all."

Surely we've all experienced both sides of this equation in our jobs and in our daily lives. We've had bosses who think that just because they are the boss means they no longer have to serve anybody. What a delight to find a busy boss who takes time out to serve coffee to the office staff, or help them find something, or offers to do an errand for them during lunch hour. Some people we work with joyfully take on each task as it comes, while others groan and grumble continually. (Balance, balance . . . remember, we're all human, and this means that even a normally joyful person gets crabby sometimes.)

A change of attitude can improve the entire climate in your office, and it also can make your life much richer in the process. When work is done mind-fully, any task can be another opportunity to deepen your spirituality. A new attitude can even make what you thought was a job you had to leave into a very pleasant place to work. Whether you're the boss or the employee, try this change of attitude before bailing out.

Mindful Work

We also need to be mindful and authentic if we want to change our work. If we don't take the time to be aware of how we are feeling throughout the day, we will have a difficult time finding meaningful work. Part of this mindfulness is peeling off layer after layer of our onion skin to discover who is really in there. Most of us simply go with the flow of what is expected throughout our lives. We grow up thinking it is right to get our validation from the outside. We think we should go after the highest-paying job we can possibly get in our field, so we do. Once we work in our fields as computer programmers, doctors, machinists, bricklayers, office managers, or insurance executives, we start to think of these titles as our identities. The more money we earn from these jobs, the more we identify with them as who we are. Indeed, many of us acquire our "power" from the job. We become "powerful" attorneys, or business owners, or CEOs, or managers. What happens when we lose the job? Out goes the power.

Simple living is about recognizing that degrees are degrees, jobs are jobs, and the paycheck is money. None of these things is who we are, deep inside. They are all a part of us, but they are not our total identity. When we live au-thentic lives, we find our power and identity within ourselves. Anything we add on as a result of a job is simply what it is: a job, or power related to the job, or money from the job.

Dean Ornish, author of *Dr. Dean Ornish's Program for Reducing Heart Disease*, says this change of attitude can affect our health and well-being:

> Hard work itself can be good for you. . . . But sometimes people think, "If only I can make a certain amount of money," or "If only I can get this promo-tion," or "If only I can get this acknowledgment, or this award"—whatever it happens to be—"then I'll be okay, then I'll feel good about myself, then peo-ple will love and respect me, then I won't feel so isolated." . . . It's not really what we do that leads to chronic stress and to illnesses like heart disease, it's what motivates what we do—the misbelief that somehow, something exter-nal to us is going to bring us health, and peace, and intimacy, and love.

When we spend most of our lives projecting a job-related image to the world, and when we finally take the time to notice how we are feeling inside, often we find that there is a deep, quiet emptiness that something is not right.

Simple living is very much about being authentic, and this point is crucial if we want to have a satisfying work life. Being authentic is not the image we like to project to the world but who we are deep inside. To find out who you are inside, refer to Chapter 3. Susan Wittig Albert, author of *Work of Her Own*, has an additional suggestion: Every night for several days or weeks, before you go to bed, ask yourself what you really want to do with your life. What is your purpose? You can keep a journal and write about the accomplishments you want to leave behind. And remember, your answers will change and evolve as you grow. Albert says that as long as we stay hooked on external recognition, we remain hooked on adapting to whatever is expected of us. When we do that, we do not live from our hearts and souls.

I know about this issue firsthand. After I had been a journalist and freelance writer for a few years, insecurity began to set in. I absolutely loved the balance of my life, yet I would look wistfully at those people downtown with the suits, fancy watches, and briefcases. They all looked like they were going somewhere, and I thought I was missing out. Then my best friend Laura decided to go to law school. I thought that was the end of our friendship because now she would start hanging around "more important" people.

With no awareness, I allowed this insecurity to cover more and more of me until one day, I woke up and thought, "Why shouldn't I go to law school?" I thought then I could enjoy the same status, and the world would somehow think I was important too. So I went to law school. For a while, I attempted to act like a lawyer. I bought a suit and started using a bigger vocabulary. I liked some parts of law, but there was no real fit inside where it mattered. My soul was forgotten. Then I had children and decided to stay home with them. My ego really went out the door. When I met new people, all I could admit to was being a mother and changing diapers. How interesting was that?

Inside I was happy being with the kids, yet I continued to struggle with my outside persona. Very gradually, the inner and outer personas began to merge again, integrating just as they had before law school. I started to feel just fine. Then I returned to writing at home. Finally I could admit to the world who I really was again. It felt like coming home or being ten years old again. I could quit throwing around my big-word vocabulary and began to talk like myself, saying *gosh*, *gee*, and *heck*. I am a mom and a writer and I like it just fine, thank you. I drive an old car and so what, thank you. (I haven't lost one friend because I drive an old car, by the way.) I'm back to wearing jeans and sweatshirts, and I'm very comfortable, thank you. I'm me and it feels just fine. If I ever returned to law or anything else, it would be the result of an inner-directed motivation rather than an outer-directed one.

New Definition of Success

Once you become more authentic and are less dependent on outside validation, you will begin to redefine success for yourself and the world. In the past, success was more clearly hinged on how much money a person made or how high he or she climbed on the corporate ladder. (Usually these went hand in hand.) I thought a lot about the success issue after talking with Betty Friedan at a conference. You remember Betty, author of *The Feminine Mystique*, which started the entire women's movement in the United States. Betty asked me if simplicity was a women's or a men's issue. I told her I thought it was a *human* issue.

"I wonder about that," said Betty. "I need to learn more about this, because my fear is that simple living is just a way to rationalize sending women back home again."

I consider myself to be reasonably modern. I believe in egalitarian relationships of all kinds. But I opted to go back home and be there for my children after they were born.

But Betty worried that going home meant women going back to being quiet and subservient. I told her I didn't want to come anywhere close to promoting a movement that even hinted at women returning to subservience. On the other hand, I told Betty I didn't want to promote the idea of kids being in day care 10 hours a day.

Betty's response was what opened me to an expanded view of success. She wondered why it had to be either/or: Either the women go home or the kids go to day care all day. She said we needed a new way of viewing the world.

Betty says it's time for both women and men to work together to restructure family and work. We can do this through four new paradigms: (1) a shorter work week; (2) flexible job schedules; (3) no polarization (women vs. men, blacks vs. whites, gay vs. straight, young vs. old . . .); (4) a new vision of personal success and the corporate bottom line.

If we move away from the notion of "getting ahead" in a career as a measure of the success of a human being and move toward cooperation, we can begin to reframe real "family values." At the corporate level, we can push for flex time or a shorter work week. Businesses could employ more people for the same amount of work by shortening the work week for individual workers. In exchange, workers might have to accept a lighter benefit package. (Everyone needs to shift if we're talking about societal changes.)

At the personal level, think of how we have traditionally raised men, for example. The average male of my generation was raised to believe his number-one role in life was to earn the most money possible. The amount of money in his bank account, the status of his job, and the high style of his car, for example, were what created his identity. What happens when a man does not achieve his goal? The man feels badly about himself, as if he has failed himself and those in his family. Now women are heading down the same street. As they work more, they identify more with their jobs in the same way.

This is sad. The issue swept right into the doors of my newsletter, *Simple Living,* when I accepted my first personal ad. The man wrote to me and said he was tired of women becoming disinterested in him as soon as they figured out he did not drive a Porsche and have a "status job." He wondered if there were any women out there who were interested in a man who was developing other parts of himself as a human being.

This is where Betty's theories and simple living converge. Can we create a new society where we are valued for the kind of human beings we are rather than the size of our bank accounts? This is not to suggest we all quit our jobs and live like paupers but rather that we redefine success for everybody. Success means, for example, both women and men having time to care for one another and their families. We cannot do that when we are working 10 hours a day getting ahead.

We cannot do any of this until we redefine our identities. If our identity is tied up with the kind of car we drive for example, then we *need* to work more hours in order to pay for it. So much for family values. If our identity is tied up in the height of the rung we reach on the corporate ladder, then we *need* to work more hours in order to achieve that level. But if our identity is a *combination* of what we do for a living, *plus* what kind of friend, parent, spouse, child, or community member we are, then we will begin making changes in our own lives. We will naturally spend less and buy fewer toys, because those things are no longer so much of our identity. When we spend less, we can work less. When we work less, we can take the time to become better human beings. We can have satisfying jobs and careers, and we can earn a good wage, but not at the expense of ourselves, our loved ones, and the world.

The simple living work theory is about balance. Work is one important part of your life, but not the only part. Even if you have the best job in the world that you love very much, you need to balance it with the rest of your life. Overwork has gotten so prevalent in our society that a new phrase has evolved to describe its effects: TINS stands for Two Incomes, No Sex. Everyone is too tired from working to have anything left over for the other pleasures in life, and those double-income parents are having their children raised by day care centers. Economist Juliet Schor, who wrote the book *The Overworked American*, found that in 1990, men worked two and a half more weeks per year than they did in 1970 and women worked seven and a half more weeks. Everybody loses out.

With an awareness of balance, we can have satisfying work lives and satisfying home lives. But how?

Finding Soulful Work

The Buddhists use the term "Right Livelihood" to describe work we choose to do because we want to do it, not because it is fashionable or pays a great deal of money, or because someone else approves of it. Susan Wittig Albert says right livelihood is work that is chosen thoughtfully, mindfully, and with a full understanding of our needs.* It challenges us to grow as wholehearted people and pays enough money by reasonable standards. Susan suggests that for a few months before you make a change, you should keep a journal of observations about your current situation. In it, first describe your current work objectively. Leave your editorial comments and judgments for later. Describe the surroundings, how you arrived at the job, how long you've been there, the organization, and so on. Second, add your comments and judgments. Evaluate the good and bad aspects of your job. How do those aspects affect you? Third, ask yourself what it will take to make the negative aspects more acceptable and appealing. Can you make the changes yourself, or is there someone, such as a boss, who would be willing to make them? And also ask yourself how the good aspects of the job helped you to learn and grow.

Susan says also to write down the amount of hours you really work. Don't forget to include all the lunch hours you work overtime and those hours you put in at home worrying or fretting about your job. Next take a look at how you unwind. Are you able to sit still without feeling compelled to do something? Do you have enough free time? Ask yourself how your job provides a sense of self-definition; how would you feel if you lost your job tomorrow?

This journal will provide you with a clearer sense of what you like, what you

❖ ❖ ❖ ❖ ❖ ❖ ❖ ❖ ❖ ❖ ❖ ❖ ❖ ❖ ❖ ❖ ❖ ❖ ❖

*Order Susan's tape series, *Finding Our Right Livelihood,* from Center for Renewing Work, P.O. Drawer M, Bertram, TX 78605.

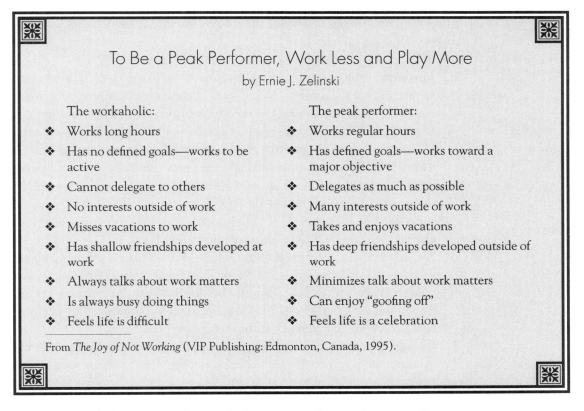

To Be a Peak Performer, Work Less and Play More
by Ernie J. Zelinski

The workaholic:	The peak performer:
❖ Works long hours	❖ Works regular hours
❖ Has no defined goals—works to be active	❖ Has defined goals—works toward a major objective
❖ Cannot delegate to others	❖ Delegates as much as possible
❖ No interests outside of work	❖ Many interests outside of work
❖ Misses vacations to work	❖ Takes and enjoys vacations
❖ Has shallow friendships developed at work	❖ Has deep friendships developed outside of work
❖ Always talks about work matters	❖ Minimizes talk about work matters
❖ Is always busy doing things	❖ Can enjoy "goofing off"
❖ Feels life is difficult	❖ Feels life is a celebration

From *The Joy of Not Working* (VIP Publishing: Edmonton, Canada, 1995).

don't like, and what you need in a job. It is a manual way of getting off automatic pilot so you can take a step back and look at your situation objectively. This is a first step to looking deeper into your heart rather than looking outside of yourself, in order to determine what is important to you.

One of the most important aspects of simplifying your life is to recognize that *you* are the one in charge. There's no sense waiting around for someone else to do it for you, or wasting a lot of energy blaming others for causing your life to be complicated. In the job arena, it is up to you to make whatever changes are necessary. If your boss or someone else in authority won't or can't make whatever changes you deem necessary to your mental, spiritual, and physical health, then you need to decide either to accept the situation or to leave the job.

Make Your Current Job Work for You

If you decide you are frustrated by aspects of your current job but are not ready to leave, do not despair. There are options available to you. For one thing, you can attempt to change the job you are in. My friend Larry Gaffin, a career counselor, offered this advice:

1. **Job portfolio change.** Stay in the job but negotiate ways with management to take on tasks and roles you find more meaningful. A woman at a major computer hardware company worked as a technical writer. She saw limits to where this job would take her professionally. She also saw a trend—that the company needed to be more customer-driven. Her manager agreed. She organized customer focus groups to make the products more user-friendly. This helped the company move ahead with its vision and her to work more directly with people, which was something she enjoyed. In redefining her job, she made herself more visible and, in doing so, avoided burnout. Her idea also became incorporated in other company divisions.

2. **Negotiate.** Areas of negotiation include shorter hours, a flex schedule, job-sharing, phased retirement, banked overtime, telecommuting. A law office manager in Los Angeles loved her job but was tired of living in L.A. She convinced her bosses to allow her to telecommute from her new home in Taos, New Mexico, with periodic trips to L.A.

3. **Change the system.** Talk to others in your company to find out if they feel as stretched as you do. If so, you can work together to present solutions to management or the company's union.

4. **Pay attention to your attitude.** Many times, what is wrong with the job is not the job or corporation but our attitude about it. Do we have realistic expectations about our job? Perhaps you can find more meaning in your job if you work to find better balance outside of work.

You also should set boundaries for yourself. If your company has an unwritten expectation that everybody works overtime, you can go to your boss in a businesslike way and state that you need to leave every day by 5:00 P.M. You may or may not prevail, but if you are in good standing at the company and you present your plan in a rational way, you at least have a chance.

Another way to improve your workplace is through companywide changes. Jim Meyerdirk was asked to execute a system called open book management (OBM) at the manufacturing company where he works. OBM is a way to get all employees involved in helping the company make money. In exchange, employees are given stock ownership and bonuses and become owners. Suddenly they have a personal stake in working more efficiently. Everybody wins. OBM started in a firm called Springfield Remanufacturing Company in Springfield, Missouri. Springfield was bankrupt when 13 employees acquired it for essentially nothing. With the use of OBM principles, Springfield was turned into a $100 million organization within 13 years.

Springfield began giving seminars about the system, and principals at the company where Jim works decided to give it a try. As production coordinator, Jim was asked to implement the program. "In order to make everybody in the company a business person, we first have to make them business literate through education," he says. "We have to train them in the fundamentals of business terminology so they can understand our financial reports. A central idea of OBM is that once people understand how the business works, they are asked to treat their individual job like a business, by predicting the financial results of their job."

If a person is a line lead, for example, he or she will be asked to predict material labor variances and control the cost of supplies. All departments have expenses they are required to control; they do so by predicting future performance.

Another aspect of OBM is game playing. A game is defined as a contest that tries to attack some area of poor performance. The employees make games out of the problem with the idea that playing games is a way to get people involved and enable them to enjoy the process. An example would be if a company was losing money due to poor inventory accuracy. It might develop a game around the idea that inventory accuracy could be improved by the people who actually have control over the inventory, usually warehouse personnel. The game's goal would be to increase inventory accuracy by, say, 10 percent.

These games offer rewards for increasing performance, rewards that go directly to the people involved in that particular department. When the goal has been realized, a new game is created for another ailing department.

"This way an employee's own performance is tied directly to the profit of the company, and the bonus system is funded by those profits," Jim explains.

With OBM, companies not only become more profitable, but morale is improved as well. Why? Because every person in the company has a say in the business. They all are empowered to make suggestions and take steps to implement their ideas. They enjoy greater job satisfaction by becoming educated and trusted with the finances of the company. All of the books, except individual salaries, are open to all. Because employees share in the increased profit, they earn more money for putting in the same number of hours.

Getting Paid

Many people confuse simple living with living in poverty. Maybe they take it a step further and think it also means not worrying about making much money on the job. Not true. Simple living is about being mindful, including being mindful about money. Being mindful means being aware of why you are working. If you are in the business of helping others, such as social work, or if you are working for a cause or organization that you believe in, money is probably not your primary motivation for working. Earn as much as is reasonable for that field, but realize that you have made a deliberate choice to work for heart over money and arrange your lifestyle accordingly.

If you are working in the business world, on the other hand, you should command the highest salary that you can get in your field. Simple living is about many things, and one of those things is being efficient. If you are going to take the time to work in business, you may as well get paid as much as is reasonable and/or possible for your efforts. My friend Jim Fulton brought this point home to me one time. When I had my freelance writing business, I had built enough experience doing a particular kind of corporate writing that I could command a very decent hourly fee. Yet I didn't have the nerve to ask for it. I called Jim for advice. "Janet," Jim yelled as only an old friend can yell at another one, "what are you thinking of? Do you realize how much other people doing the same work you are doing are making? Why are you selling yourself so short? Do I need to come over there and yell at you in person?"

That was the beginning of my change in attitude. Earning decent money does not make you less spiritual and does not mean that you can't find soulful work. Nor does it mean that you need to give up all of your values and work only for money. It simply means that if you are in the business world, you ought to work hard and efficiently so you can demand the best possible salary for that field. The only way you will be able to command a decent salary is if you build a decent reputation. You can do that by working mindfully and giving your job your full attention with a good attitude. If you are fully present at your job, you'll naturally work harder and more efficiently. It is only when we "space out" and don't stay focused on tasks at hand that we get disorganized and inefficient.

If you own or are somehow in control of a service industry, you need to be really mindful and think about the value of your service and who your customers are. For instance, I am no longer at all impressed by doctors and other professionals who have elaborate, highly decorated offices and then turn around and charge me a small fortune for my visit. Guess who is paying for the 34th-floor sweeping view and Louis XIV furnishings? Me! Sorry. I'll take my business elsewhere where I can get good, professional service with a normal office that I don't have to pay extra for.

If you are one of these professionals, you may rethink your own version of "success." If you find yourself a more moderate office and lower your overhead, you can charge your clients less. You can even set aside a certain amount for a sliding scale. You will still earn good money. The difference is that you will keep a higher percentage of the money because your overhead is lower. You'll also bring a human touch to your industry by making your services available to those with lower incomes.

Passionate Work

Cecile Andrews, author of *Circle of Simplicity, Return to the Good Life*, has thought about passion and work so much she even teaches classes titled Finding Your Passion. In fact, it was after taking one of Cecile's classes that I decided to start my *Simple Living* newsletter. I had a passion for the subject of voluntary simplicity and I had passion for writing.

Cecile believes that you naturally find passionate work when you simplify your life and open yourself and your time to noticing what you love. "When people are really devoted to a passion, they create ways to keep it alive," she says.

Cecile has been earning money from her passions since she was a high school student. She played the flute so well that she began giving lessons to younger students. She continued to earn money from flute lessons through college. Another of her passions has always been reading, so her first career was as an English teacher. She also loves to read women's mystery novels, so she gives seminars in them. "It's also important to hook your passion to something larger," Cecile says. To that end, she often uses the novels in another of her passions: women's studies. "Women who read these mysteries have images of very intelligent women using their intelligence, not physical strength, to solve problems," Cecile says. "This has been very powerful for a lot of women whose self-esteem is linked to how they feel about their intelligence."

Another way to turn your passion into a job is by volunteering first. Cecile began another career as director of Women's Studies at a community college after working first as an unpaid intern. She created the job as part of her internship.

"When you follow your passion, you don't know where it's going to lead," Cecile says. "I always tell people to do what you love to do, then figure out how to earn a living from it."

Get Paid for Your Passion

There are two ways to get paid for your passion: make it your full-time career or a part-time sideline. Beth Steinkoning loves to sail and has done two things that enable her to sail frequently. The first is that she and her four-year-old son live on a sailboat that Beth owns. If she owned a house, she couldn't afford a boat. Beth weighed her priorities and opted for the boat. Second, she earns money from three part-time jobs, rather than one nine-to-five job. One of those part-time jobs is teaching sailing on weekends. This schedule allows her more time to spend with her son and allows her to pursue her passion of sailing.

Rick Steves turned his passion into a full-time career. Rick, who has always loved to travel, created a niche for himself that allows him to travel frequently and get paid well. "You've got to travel for the love of travel and teach out of a passion of wanting others to experience and enjoy the world of travel the way you have," Rick says. He started his working life as a piano teacher. He would take summers off and travel to Europe. He did this for 10 years. In order to finance his trips, he made do with an old car and had no debt. "It was inconceivable to me to get a car that would require monthly payments," he says. "My priorities were Europe, not a new car."

But the big question for Rick was making the leap from traveling as a hobby to traveling as a job. His travel career began with his first public talk about how to travel to Europe for less. He held the class in the recital hall of his piano studio and advertised it through a local experimental college. People came. After the talk a group of students took him out for pizza and said, "Let's go to Europe as one big family." Rick's tour guide business was born. He continued to finance the travel seminars and trips with his piano business earnings. For the first tour he covered only his costs, but the experience gave him a taste for being a guide. "It clicked with me," he says. As his classes became more and popular, Rick found that he was using the recital hall more for travel lectures than piano recitals, and he finally decided to drop the piano business. He has since moved to a larger building and employs 20 people in his company, which is called Europe Through the Back Door. Every year Europe Through the Back Door organizes 80 tours. Sixty thousand people read his quarterly travel newsletter. Rick teaches people to travel to Europe "close to the ground . . . get their fingers dirty in the local culture . . . traveling in an independent, thoughtful, and efficient way."

He has published 15 books and is the biggest Eurail sales outlet in the United States, selling 7,000 train passes a year. The company has a mail-order travel accessory and book business, selling such items as money belts, phrase books, and a carry-on bag that Rick designed. "My theory is find a need and fill it," he says. Rick hosts a TV series on National Public Television titled *Travels in Europe*. His bestselling book, *Europe Through the Back Door,* sells 40,000 copies a year. And Rick continues to travel. He spends a total of three months a year in Europe, and takes his wife and two children for a month each year.

The struggle for him is finding balance. He loves his business and he loves his family. He looks at life as having four elements: family, work, personal, and social/spiritual. "You need to decide how you want to divvy up your pie," he says. "If you don't have time for all those elements, it's your own fault. I've chosen to focus only on the family and work parts and let go of the rest. You make trade-offs.

"I feel like I have a calling . . . my work translates into a lot of happy travel experiences, and I feel really good about that. I'm a workaholic and, as a result, I focus only on my family and work."

Work at Home When You Have Children

Many parents, including me, opt to create home-based businesses so they can earn money and be with their kids. You can be single or married and the same rules and job ideas still apply. In fact, 25 million Americans have joined what has been coined the Home Business Revolution. It is getting so mainstream that I no longer hide the fact that I work at home. At least half the time that I tell someone I work at home, they answer that they do too!

I personally can't think of a better way to go. When my kids are sick and home from school, no problem, they can sleep and I can work. When they go to bed at night, no problem, I can work if I need to. When they have a holiday break, I can schedule my break to coincide. I also worked part time at home when my children were preschool age. No problem, I hired a baby-sitter to entertain them while I holed up in a spare-bedroom office. I could be there when needed for a hug, and I knew how the baby-sitter interacted with my kids.

The biggest adjustment, in my opinion, is you need to let go of the super-achievement career idea of prechildren days. If you choose the option of working at home, accept the fact that you will be interrupted and won't get as much done as you would in a regular office. You may find, as I do, that there are toy trucks and leftover art projects on your desk when you go into your office to start working. You won't have the camaraderie of an office filled with adults, and you won't get a lunch break where you can wander around downtown or eat at a cute restaurant with your friends and colleagues. The reason why you won't get a lunch break is because you will learn to focus and work very fast and efficiently in the short spurts of alone time that you do have. For me, any trade-offs I have made to work at home have been well worth it.

Not getting as much done at home is so common that in the introduction to a book titled *How to Raise a Family and a Career Under One Roof,* author Lisa Roberts says: "Because this book is in itself a product of working at home while raising a young family, it is not everything I want it to be but rather everything I could give it at the time."

I know many men and women who work at home. One engineer and father of two boys set up an engineering design business in his garage. Another husband and wife operate a mail-order greeting card business from their basement. A hairdresser turned her detached garage into a very charming salon. She had built enough of a clientele in her prechildren days that she was able to pick and choose the clients she took in at home. I know a psychotherapist/mother who turned her detached garage into an office where she sees clients. A *Simple Living* subscriber wrote and told me that she and her husband built a home in the back of their airplane hangar where they operate a maintenance and small airplane rental service. She called hers a "business-based home" and was glad that her children could grow up knowing exactly what mommy and daddy do for a living. I work in a spare bedroom and use the dining room table when needed. Many people take in database or word processing jobs for all sorts of small businesses that can't afford their own regular help. You can open a day care or after-school center in your home, or be a consultant, a desktop publisher, or an Internet researcher. You can be a bookkeeper, accountant, or pet hotel. You also can work at home part time and at a job site part time. One single mom I know worked it out with her employer to be at the job site during school hours and to work at home after school. The list of things you can do at home is limited only by your imagination and ingenuity.

As Lisa Roberts says and I agree: "No benefit is greater for a parent than peace of mind. Home business offers the professional parent an opportunity to enjoy a rich family life."

Work with Heart

Michele Gran and Bud Philbrook conceived of their dream vocation on the night of their honeymoon.* They had already put money down on a honeymoon cruise when Michele decided she wanted to do something more meaningful than recline in a deck chair. "On one hand, I was pleased about that," Bud says. "On the other, I kind of liked the idea of the cruise." The

❖ ❖ ❖ ❖ ❖ ❖ ❖ ❖ ❖ ❖ ❖ ❖ ❖ ❖ ❖ ❖ ❖ ❖ ❖

*Parts of this story were taken from *Skyway News,* February 18, 1992.

meaningful honeymoon prevailed, and the couple went to a remote village in Guatemala.

Years before, Bud had worked in a village in India as part of an international delegation of professionals. He knew of a similar project in Guatemala, and after he and Michele decided that was where they'd like to go, he sent a letter asking if the couple could help out for a week.

Their first week as a married couple was spent in a hut with Michele writing a brochure explaining the community's development efforts and Bud helping the community leaders write a loan proposal to the government for a new irrigation system.

When they returned home, the *Minneapolis Star* published an article about their unconventional honeymoon. "Apparently a lot of people read that story, because they would come up to us and say 'We've always wanted to do that. How can we do it?' " Bud remembers. "We started wondering how we could bring people together with projects like this."

Bud was studying law at the time and Michele, who holds a master's degree in international communications, was working as a marketing and public relations consultant. During their spare time, they began to organize their business. In 1984 they were ready and sent their first group of Global Volunteers to Jamaica.

"It was hard to convince the first people to volunteer," Bud says. "And I can understand why. When I was giving presentations, I had to stand up there and say: 'We really don't know what we're doing, but we'd like you to do it with us.' "

Thirteen years later Global Volunteers has a worldwide staff of 25 in 13 countries and has sent more than 1,000 volunteers to places as far away as Vietnam and Tanzania and as close as Mississippi and Arkansas. Michele works full time for the organization as vice president of marketing. Bud still works as a lawyer and leads one trip each year as well as going on fact-finding missions as the organization expands to other sites.

"Most volunteers tell us 'I went to give and received more than I gave,' " Bud says. "For some volunteers, it's deeper than that. It's the recognition that there are differences in the world—languages, religions, cultures, races—but given those differences, we as global people are far more alike than we are different. . . . Once you live in a village with a group of people so foreign to you and discover that they're your friends, you can't come back home with any other conclusion. And that's powerful stuff."

Find Your Bliss at Work

Bliss is the opposite of burnout. Bliss is being in the "flow state," when you are so completely involved in what you are doing that you forget about yourself. You and it are one. When you are in this state, you tend to perform optimally. Research has shown that flow is more likely to happen at work than during leisure. There are conditions that help create this state:

A. Balance. There is a balance between your ability and the difficulty of the work. A challenge is something you can do, but it stretches you just a little. If you are a social worker, your caseload is stimulating, yet you are not overloaded. When any work is too difficult or too easy and repetitive, you are out of balance.

B. Meaningfulness. Your work is important and does not violate your values. List 20 things you love doing and analyze them. What was it about each part of the activity that you enjoyed? Find work that allows you to engage in this kind of meaningfulness. When your work is meaningful, you will enter the "success syndrome." This syndrome occurs when you, your skills, and values fit into your workplace. When you fit, other people want to help you and support your ideas. This positive atmosphere rolls you along and creates a cycle of success.

C. Purpose. Rather than thinking of your job as task-oriented, think of it as problem-

Professionals Who Switch Gears

Deborah Aaron managed to use her former career as a springboard for her new one. She had been a lawyer for many years when she knew it was time for a change. She worked for a large law firm for two years, then joined with a partner to begin their own firm. Deborah and the partner agreed they wanted balanced lives.

Seven years into the practice, however, the partner admitted he wanted to earn hundreds of thousands of dollars per year, and he didn't care how many hours and months he spent earning it. "I wanted to be a human being and not just a lawyer," Deborah says. The partnership split up, and Deborah worked on her own for a year until the day a friend told her she looked very depressed. She suggested that Deborah take a sabbatical. "I can't do that," Deborah answered. "People depend on me. I'm such a remarkable lawyer that all of my clients would be irreparably harmed if I left!"

Forty minutes later she realized she could and would take the break. She reoriented. What problem were you hired to solve? This allows you to have something to strive for and to look at the bigger picture.

D. Control. You have the ability to make an impact. If you do good work, things are better; if you do poorly, things get worse.

E. Corporate culture audit. Once you have identified your own values, assess the values of your company. This assessment requires you to listen for company buzzwords and stories. Also look at who gets ahead and why. Does this fit within your values?

F. Vision. Picture in your mind the job you would love to have in the future. If you can't get a picture in your mind, how will you get there? If it is a picture you are at all capable of doing and you believe in it, you can achieve it. Remember to base the picture on your internal, rather than external values. For instance, many people take jobs because of high pay, or because it is a prestigious place to work. What about the actual work you will do? Is it an internal fit? A good fit is like an old shoe in the back of your closet. A good fit sets you up for the success syndrome.

G. Map. Create a map to achieve your vision. Work from your destination backward. At each step, ask yourself, "Can I do this now?" If not, what do you need to do first? Keep going backward until you get to where you can do something now.

From a conversation with Dr. Beverly Potter, author of *Beating Job Burnout: How to Renew Enthusiasm for Work* (Berkeley, CA: Ronin Books, 1997).

turned to her office, looked at her cash flow, and made a list of cases she felt morally committed to completing. She accomplished her goal of closing her practice within seven months.

Deborah had the choice to take the break because she had always been a good saver. "Even in my yuppie days in the early 1980s when I was earning a good living with no spouse and no dependents, I still never spent more than I earned," she says.

Soon after quitting, Deborah fell into a black hole of depression. "I didn't know anyone else who wasn't working. I didn't know what I wanted to do. I had a vague idea I wanted to write and speak about the more human aspects of law, and I had in mind maybe I'd write a book that year."

Deborah also managed to hang on to all of her nest egg. "I didn't spend a dime," she says. "I sold the small house I'd been living in and bought a run-down larger house. I fixed it up and rented out rooms that paid for almost my whole mortgage. I was also paid on some accounts receivable that were left from my practice. Without my office overhead, I was able to pocket all of the money."

Deborah's new career started to bloom after she finally wrote her book, *Running from the Law*, three years after quitting her law practice. She began giving seminars and private consultations that helped other lawyers with their transition from law. She didn't charge for her services but did build her confidence and reputation. Her diligence and patience paid off. She now travels the country, paid by law schools and bar associations to give large seminars on the topic of alternative law careers. She also has had three books published on the subject.

"I'm much happier with the change," she says. "There is no comparison. I'm doing what I believe in—helping people to master change in a positive way, without the adversarial process. I'm dealing with positive human issues of people making choices to express who they are instead of trying to conform to other people's wishes."

Deborah's ideas of a fulfilled life have changed since she made her transition. "I had always thought that if you were doing what you love, you can't do too much of it. Now I realize that even if you love what you do, it can take over your life and whack you way out of balance.

"I noticed that when I wasn't getting paid well it was easier to control than when I started to earn good fees. Then it seemed like a shame to turn down all that money when I was enjoying what I was doing. I find it's difficult to find that balance."

For Deborah, simplicity means living a life that is as free of inner conflict as possible. "When I practiced law I had control over my time just like I do now, but I always felt a kind of gut conflict that it wasn't right for me. Now I pretty much walk around conflict-free except the problem of learning to say no to more work.

"A friend once told me years ago that her goal was inner peace. I thought that was strange and wondered how she would know if she had it. Now I understand, it's a matter of listening to your gut."

Telecommuting

Phil Campbell longed for a life in the wide open spaces of a small town but had a business to run in the city. The goodwill that he had built with his longtime employees eventually enabled him to keep his business operating in the city while he telecommuted from his little town.

Phil had owned and operated an import business for many years when he decided to buy property in rural Montana. He had gotten disillusioned with city life and, at age 53, began to look at the world with different eyes. "I noticed how complex it was to live in the city," he says. "When you're younger, you look for opportunity, action, and growth. I no longer needed that.

"I was finally able to move because I had been good to my employees all of those years," he says. "I always put them first and gave them more than I gave myself for a long time. In the end, I got what I wanted, which was the freedom to relocate, because I had valuable, trusted people working for me."

To prepare for the move, Phil devised a six-month plan. He offered the company management job to a woman who had worked with him since the beginning. He immediately gave her a raise, so she earned more than he did, and told her to run the company during the six months as if he weren't there. They traded offices, and Phil was available only for consultation and problems. At the end of the period, she was ready to take over. Phil would move to Montana and continue to do the buying and traveling, just as he always did. "I could do that from anywhere so long as I had a fax machine," he says.

One year after his move, Phil's company had the most profitable year ever. He works from an office in his house and says he gets more work done in less time because there are no distractions. But he cautions others who contemplate a similar move to spend time building trusted employees first. "You can't just hire someone off the street to run your company while you do this," he says. "It needs to be someone you trust and with whom you've built a good relationship over time. If people are serious about this, they need to start now and plan a move five years later. I had a friend who used to chide me for paying my employees so much and for being so nice to them. He also owns a business. This man can't even leave to go on vacation without having his brother take over because he doesn't trust his employees. I spent a lot of time building up a tremendous bank account of goodwill and trust. It has paid off for me because now I have my freedom."

Taking Sabbaticals

The book *Six Months Off,* by Hope Dlugozima, James Scott, and David Sharp, starts with a wonderful quote. In the 1938 movie *Holiday,* Cary Grant talks to Katherine Hepburn:

"I'm going to take a holiday for as long as I need."

"Just to play?"

"No! I want to find out why I'm working. The answer can't just be to pay bills or to pile up more money . . . I can't find out sitting behind some desk in an office. So, as soon as I get enough money together, I'm going to knock off for a while. Come back and work when I know what I'm working for. Does that make sense?"

A sabbatical can be the most sensible thing you can do if you're in a rut but can't relax enough to focus on your buried creative energy. Even if you like your job or career, sabbaticals offer a good time to catch up on hobbies, take classes you've always wanted to take, visit with friends, stare into space, or bicycle around Europe. If you have a family, you can arrange to take everyone along. Some couples spell one another—she takes a break in year one and he takes it in year two. A few employers have foresight and plan sabbaticals into the job description. While in law school, I worked at a progressive yet busy law office that had a rotating schedule so the burned-out lawyers would rejuvenate themselves regularly. If they didn't organize this system, they would suffer very high turnover of personnel. The lawyers work nine months on and take three months off every year. Like clockwork, at the end of the nine months, employees begin seriously considering quitting the job. Yet sure enough, after their three-month break, they return refreshed and ready to give their all to their new caseload. Everybody wins.

As wonderful as sabbaticals are, however, they are available only to those who follow the first rule in simple living: *Live under your means*. You can't take six or any number of months off if the VISA creditors are after you, or if the bank needs your car payments, or if the department store is calling for your Stairmaster or TV payments. You'll also have a difficult time pulling away if you have zero debt but also zero saved. What will you live on while you're pondering the meaning of life on a mountaintop in Tibet? How will you pay your rent or mortgage back home?

If you think a sabbatical is your answer, start now by paying off debt and saving your earnings. The program is explained in Chapter 2. Once you have organized your financial life, you are free to organize your sabbatical. But how?

The authors of *Six Months Off* answered the usual big questions: (1) How will you find the time? (2) How will you approach your boss? and (3) What will a sabbatical do to your career? They suggest offering to trade a raise or bonus for time off or to take an unpaid leave during a slow period. You also could offer to work overtime for a few months, or join with other employees to see if you can organize a formal sabbatical program. You don't need to be a burned-out lawyer to take a sabbatical—everyone gets burned out from working day in and day out. Any company would be better off with refreshed, vibrant employees.

If you like the sabbatical idea, you also could choose a career with built-in breaks, such as teaching, or tax preparer, or any kind of career that is structured around projects, such as carpentry, some sales positions, and consultant and freelance work.

As for your résumé, the authors of *Six Months* off say: "When first shaping your sabbatical plans, think for a second about how you'd explain it later to a future employer or your coworkers. Does it make for a good story? Or does it sound a little, well, dubious? Or—and this is even more telling—imagine yourself reading the résumé of a sabbatical taker. What would make you utter 'what a jerk' under your breath and what would leave you with admiration and low-grade envy for the person?"

Can you turn your sabbatical into a learning opportunity for your field? Can you put your skills to work in another country? That way you're continuing with your career path while also getting a break and new perspectives on life.

Ethel Whelan took a year off from her U.S. teaching job to teach school in Honduras. Her husband, Jack, was supportive but didn't want to go, so Ethel and their five-year-old son, Luke, made the move. Ethel had worked as an overseas volunteer when she was in her 20s and longed for another opportunity. Now, with a child and job, she had more logistics to contend with. "I really wanted to do this," she says, "so I decided to look at my contract. I noticed a small clause that talked about leaves. It turned out the school district even had a leave department. They were really helpful."

The contract allowed Ethel a one-year leave without pay and without penalties. She found her job through the University of Northern Iowa job fair. The fair is free and is for teachers to connect with overseas schools. Teachers need to be certified and with at least two years of experience, and the jobs are all guaranteed to be with bona fide and established international schools. The standard contract is for one to two years, with the school paying roundtrip airfare if the teacher stays the length of the contract. Teachers are also paid a small salary and are given room and board. Ethel's offer was from an English-speaking international school in Honduras. She and her son lived with a family, and Luke was able to attend the same school that employed Ethel.

Ethel says she believes there are more benefits to accepting a temporary assignment when some of the variables are unknown. "You can either take a year off and have everything perfectly lined up, or you can do the same and cover the basics like your safety and income, but leave the rest open," she says. "By leaving it open, the returns are one thousandfold because you learn more when you don't have all of the answers already given."

Ethel says her sabbatical was well worth it. The year away heightened her appreciation for what she does have in the United States and also broadened her sense of what she needs in order to be satisfied. "I discovered parts of myself that I didn't know I had, like the ability to make decisions in very uncertain conditions and the ability to adapt to situations," she says. "Oftentimes there would be no water or electricity for days at a time. I learned the beauty of reducing life to fundamentals. The people in Honduras didn't worry about why there was no water, they simply accepted it until it returned. They knew they couldn't do anything about it anyway. Their joys are very fundamental and their fears are very fundamental. If there was a monsoon, an entire village could get wiped out.

"Because of this attitude, their demands are very sane. I began to realize that it doesn't really matter why there is no water or electricity. I didn't need that information in Honduras, and I'm still walking around. I've found that the more sophisticated and urbane we are, the more we think it's important to talk about all of these details, like the city council member who didn't pay his taxes or the endless news stories about the crack in the water main. All of the attention to every little detail takes away from the rest of our lives. We get sidetracked by having to be universal busybodies.

"The first thing we see in the morning is all of this news either on television or our morning newspaper. It sets the tone of our day, even before we talk to our kids, before we meditate, before we might read a novel."

Ethel learned about paring life down to the essentials: simple fears, simple enjoyment. "At night if you want to go out, you can't choose from 45 restaurants," she says. "In Honduras, no matter how wealthy you are, there is no way you are going to have all of these choices. I've learned to accept a lot more of 'what-is' here at home."

Working Part Time and Job Sharing

Elouise Schumacher had been a full-time reporter for a major daily newspaper for many years when she realized she was getting burned out. She and two colleagues who were feeling the same way began talking about the possibility of job sharing. Everyone else in the newsroom worked full time.

"We were met with much resistance from people who didn't understand why we didn't want to work 50 to 60 hours a week," Elouise says. "You're supposed to love your job so much you're happy to do it. We wanted time to be humans and do some other things."

At the time, only one of the women had children; the other two simply wanted a more balanced life. It took almost two years for their proposal finally to be accepted, and that was only because there was a change in management. The new boss was more sympathetic to the idea. He later admitted that he too was very skeptical, but the arrangement worked better than he thought it would. He said: "I've gotten more work out of them than I did before."

Elouise agrees. "I think it's true that you work harder when you know you're going to be gone."

She says another reason why they were successful was because all three women had proven track records, and they were willing to go the extra mile to make it work. "We weren't slackers, and we were very flexible. For instance, we wouldn't just leave at five when it was our vacation time. We'd stay and finish whatever story we were working on. If needed, I came during my off time to finish up a project."

The arrangement was that two full-time jobs were shared by three people. Each reporter worked four months and took two months off. During the vacation period, they would cover each other's beats. Their health benefits continued as long as they worked one day into each month, and their vacations were paid as before.

Unfortunately, the formal job share ended when Elouise had her first child. She realized that a four-month-on, two-month-off schedule wasn't the best for raising a baby and proposed another schedule. Management did not agree and canceled the original job share. Now the other two women have an informal arrangement where they each take two months off a year, and Elouise works part time as a copy editor on the news desk. It's a shift job with regular hours, rather than project-type job that is typical of reporting, and thus is more conducive to part-time work.

"It's so much better now than if I was working full time," she says. "I can be home with my kids when they're sick, and now I really love going to work. It's a wonderful break."

Work Efficiently

Two fields that are well known for requiring long hours at the job are medicine and law. Yet not all professionals subscribe to the status quo.

My friend Laura Sealey is an attorney and the mother of three young boys. Laura supports her family of five (three boys and a stay-at-home husband) by working only 30 hours a week—four part-time days at her office and one at home. She has been able to work these hours because she is efficient. Laura is her own secretary, receptionist, file clerk, legal researcher, and lawyer. Other than her husband's help with bookkeeping, Laura has no employees. She also has a very professional yet very modest office that she shares with another attorney who also has no employees. No beautiful view, no high-rise building. Laura needs to earn far less money because she has very low overhead. Indeed, Laura has never lost a client because her office wasn't elaborate. "Just about all of the potential clients who come to see me wind up hiring me," she says.

Laura uses voice mail as her receptionist, she has organized her filing so well that she files papers as soon as they come in the door, and she types her own documents into the computer, rather than dictating to a secretary who does the typing. She accepts only those clients to whom she feels she can devote her full attention.

With rare exceptions, Laura is home every night and every weekend. "My family is my priority," she says, "so I have to work efficiently in order to be home for them."

Robert Markison is a surgeon with an at-home wife and three young children. He has turned efficiency into a high art. Markison not only owns and operates a full-time surgical practice, but he also has plenty of time for his wife and children and makes all of his own clothes, shoes, and hats as well as musical instruments. He never takes work home and rarely works more than 35 to 40 hours a week. How?

"I take the surgical worldview, which is economy of motion and efficient use of time and materials," he says. For every project, whether it is sewing himself a dress shirt or performing an operation, he visualizes the entire scheme first, from start to finish. He sees through to the end of each experience. He learned much of this from a system of self-hypnosis called autogenics. "You completely visualize an experience from the start, prefiguring the material and equipment," he says. "This way you don't have creative blocks."

Autogenics also taught him how to avoid becoming angry. "In medical school I learned how to count to 10 before getting angry. Conflict is invariably time-consuming."

Robert says efficiency also comes from working smart. One aspect of working smart is to keep paperwork to a minimum. He doesn't do business with HMOs because of the amount of paperwork they require. "I don't get into paper battles," he says. He's learned to use the computer, so he can run his office with only one employee, and he sees only those patients whom he believes sincerely want to participate in their care process and get well. He avoids caffeine because of the peaks and valleys. He says it's important to maintain a constant level of functioning, which cannot be accomplished with caffeine. He also keeps well hydrated throughout the day by drinking lots of water. This keeps the blood flowing to the brain. "A lot of people run dry during the workday," he says. "Then they get irritable."

Working smart is knowing what distractions to avoid. This includes choosing friendships with optimistic rather than pessimistic people. "Your days are very long if you're involved in a circle of doubting people either in or out of work," he says. Robert also steers clear of the Internet. "I don't engage in the Internet unless it is absolutely necessary. The same goes for all electronic appliances like cell phones. These are distractions that people get into and suddenly they can't get anything done. The Internet just adds gratuitous conflict during the day."

He's even cultivated efficient speech. He says, "Concise self-expression, whether written or spoken, is a terrific time-saver."

Robert's efficient use of time has been a bonus for patients. "Nobody waits more than five to ten minutes to see me," he says. "I don't believe it's good for anyone to wait on either side of the white coat. It's not fair. Everybody's working. Everybody's got kids to pick up or someplace to go. It's morally correct to see fewer patients and see them promptly."

Start Your Own Business

Here is the simple living theory about running your own business. Being your own boss can allow you tremendous freedom and can give you control over your life. The key, however, is that *you* need to run the business rather than allowing *it* to run you. If you are one of those business owners who devotes 16 hours a day, 7 days a week to nurturing your business, you hardly qualify for the balanced life that simple living is about. It's one thing to devote more than usual hours to get a business off the ground, or to work overtime during a particular heavy period, but often those hours continue day after day, year after year, because the business owner gets into the mind-set that no one else can run it like she or he can. This is an easy trap to fall into but it's deadly for a balanced life.

How do you run a business instead of allowing it to run you? "Set clear goals for yourself," says Jim Fulton, president of the Fulton Company, a public relations firm. Decide ahead of time what you want out of your business and your life. If your goal is to get very rich, you probably will need to work a lot of hours. But if your goal, like Jim's, is to be happy and have a balanced life, then structure your business accordingly.

"The best thing about having your own business is that you have control, and you have choices," Jim says. "You have the choice to work 16 hours a day, 7 days a week. I choose to work from nine to six Monday through Friday only. I knew when I started the business that I wanted nights and weekends for my family and friends."

In order to maintain his plan, Jim says he makes another choice every day: Rather than hanging around the water cooler or wasting time on things like office politics (who has the nicest office, who got a raise and who didn't), he works hard, smart, fast, and intelligently. And he says he consciously hired two employees who subscribe to the same philosophy. They share a very modest office so the overhead is low and no one has a more prestigious space than the other. Their goal is simply to work efficiently.

Jim advises that people can work more efficiently when they know what their personal, business, and financial goals are. He has two: First, if taking on a new client or project will mean that he will need to work evenings or weekends, he turns it down. "If someone calls me and asks if I can complete a project in two weeks, I'll say no, because I know it will mean giving up my other goal of having evenings and weekends for my family and friends," he says. Second, most of his working day should be spent either billing clients or working to bring in new clients. He judges every instance or invitation as to whether it will directly further those goals. If not, he turns it down. "Here is an example," Jim says. "I'm a public relations consultant and I belong to the Public Relations Society of America. We have a local chapter that is about 65 miles away from my office. I'd love to go to their monthly luncheons and hang out and network with other people in the field, but doing that would take six hours away from my billable time. Even though I might attract a new client here and there, I decided it wasn't worth it."

Other tips from Jim:

1. Make decisions quickly and don't look back. Whatever the decision, whether buying a new computer, getting a logo designed, or buying office stationery, make the decision quickly and then accept your decision. Jim says when he needed a new computer, he shopped for a really good one, but it isn't the best in the world. It works fine for him, and he doesn't spend any time worrying about the decision he made.
2. If you are in the service industry, work only with clients you feel good about. Stories abound about small business owners who take on clients

that ultimately waste a lot of their time and return very little. Jim recently deliberated whether to accept a particular new client. After deciding to check his hunch, he drove 170 miles round trip to meet with the man. "When I got to his place I realized I just didn't like the guy," Jim says. "He was ready to write me a check and instead, I gave him the names of six other firms. He probably thought I was crazy, but I vowed never to take on clients that I had a bad feeling about."

3. Find work that you love. "Life is a process," he says. "So you'd better enjoy what you are doing while you're in the process. Work takes up a lot of that time. I love what I do for a living."

4. Make sure something you love is something you are good at—maybe better than the average person.

5. Make sure this is something for which you can earn good money. If you are going to bother starting a business, you will need to devote a fair amount of time to it, so you ought to get paid well for your time.

Turn Your Hobby into a Business

Jim Nilsen was a commercial salmon fisherman for 20 years when he realized it was time to do something else. "My heart wasn't in it," he says. "It was time to quit." Jim had enjoyed taking photographs since he was a boy and had gotten a degree in photography during the off season. During fishing season, he shot a lot of photos on the job that were widely published in trade magazines and books. But the market was limited.

It was after a trip to Europe that Jim finally decided to quit fishing. He realized how much he enjoyed travel photography. He didn't have a market for his photos, but he knew he was through fishing. "I looked at my financial situation. I didn't have any debt, everything was paid off, I had $20,000 in the bank, and I lived in half of a duplex that I owned. My monthly expenses were fairly low. Fishing had become a habit and the money was good, but I wondered why I was going back to fishing when I didn't need to do it any longer. My guts kept telling me to go for it."

He quit and, for six months, played with the design and layout of his photos. Finally he landed on a concept of using small prints. "I was really excited," he says. "I thought I had something. I didn't know much about the market, and I had no idea how vast the arts and crafts market is. I applied to a local street fair, and that was the turning point for me. I made $3,000 in one weekend."

Jim discovered that there are thousands of arts and crafts shows around the country and thousands of people earn very good money in the arts and crafts field. He says they are dedicated, hardworking, creative professionals. Some are single, and some are couples who operate the business together, with one the creative force and the other the business person. Others are entire families who travel the country in motor homes and home school their children. The lifestyle works for Jim because his partner, Magrit, is very independent, and they have no children.

Jim did 13 shows his first year. Four years later, he averages about 20 shows a year in 10 states. He says he's making a very comfortable living that earns him at least what he earned fishing. "I have a lot more satisfaction now," he says, "and a lot more control over my time."

Each year Jim and often Magrit take a six-week photo trip to places like Greece, Guatemala, Italy, Malta, Mexico, Morocco, Spain, and Turkey. From December to February, he works at home in the studio, which is a garage detached from his house. During this season he produces photographs for the upcoming year. He works approximately five hours a day and takes lots of breaks to ski for the day or go on weeklong vacations with Magrit. He travels to the shows from March to September and again in November, camping in his van or staying in motels.

During show season, the work is hard and sometimes intense, but Jim says the positive response from customers and the freedom makes it worthwhile. "Customers really appreciate what I'm doing," he says. "It's very satisfying to have someone buy what I produce."

Temporary Work

Once you decide it is perfectly fine to project your more authentic image to the world, you will have many more career opportunities. Temporary work is one. You can make an entire career out of temporary work, or you can use it as a fill-in. Once I interviewed a woman who built a career out of temporary office work so she could take long vacations. Her first passion was travel, and temporary work was a way to finance it and be able to leave at will. She worked and traveled for 17 years, finally retiring at age 44 to travel some more.

I worked as a temporary office employee when I had my freelance writing business. It provided extra money when the writing income was slow. The vast majority of my jobs were very positive. In fact, years later, I still have friends whom I met while in my temp jobs. I also learned new skills, and temping fit with my personality—it gave me income with freedom.

Many people dismiss temping because it usually doesn't provide health benefits. So what! Provide your own. I've been buying my own high-deductible health insurance for years. If health insurance is your rationale for staying in a job you'd rather leave, or for not doing temp or contract work, please have a long talk with yourself. What kind of life is this? You spend the majority of your waking hours working for health insurance? Was this your dream as a child? When you die do you want your gravestone to read: "Here lies Jane Doe. She hated her job but worked there for years because it provided health insurance."

As for the argument that temp jobs don't allow you to move up the corporate ladder, there are two answers. One is that if you really look into your soul, you may realize that arriving at the top of a corporate ladder is not the authentic dream you have for yourself. For those who do have that dream, however, temping can indeed provide access to that ladder, because temping exposes you to a wide variety of jobs. These days, temping is no longer limited to menial labor or low-level office work. There are many high-tech and professional temp agencies. I've known a lot of computer types, for example, who do temp programming and such. I personally was offered a permanent job at more than one of the offices where I temped. It's a great way for bosses to see exactly what you are like and for you to see if the job fits you.

You can get short- or long-term temp jobs. Some are for two days, and some go on for months or more. You can find temp jobs on your own, or go through an agency. Naturally you'll be able to command more per hour if you find the job yourself because you won't have to pay an agency fee, but this means a lot more legwork. You'll need to go around to offices that could use your skills and tell them you are available. It will be the same as starting your own business. Print some business cards and résumés to leave with these people so they can call you when they have a need. Temp agencies do all of this legwork for you, at a fee. You may want to begin by visiting with a few temp agencies (look for them in the yellow pages) and work with them to come up with a list of your skills. Temps are hired to do everything from flower arranging to nuclear engineering.

Consulting

Consulting is similar to temp work in that you work when you want and where you want. The authors of the book *How to Start and Run a Successful Consulting Business*, Gregory Kishel and Patricia Kishel, describe consulting this way: "By definition, a consultant is someone who works independently, providing the specialized services and advice that organizations and individuals need to achieve their goals. The most important product any consultant has to sell is his or her ideas and information, skills, and abilities. In effect, as an independent consultant you will be paid for what you know and can do for others."

Peggy Robinson started consulting after a job search. She had 15 years experience working as an employee for conservation-oriented nonprofit agencies when she decided to move to a new city. She didn't get a full-time job offer but was offered work as a consultant at a couple of the firms she contacted. Six years later Peggy has so much consulting business she is considering hiring a full-time assistant and moving into larger working quarters. She also has created a strategy for attracting and keeping clients:

First, narrow your focus and create a specialized niche. "When I first started consulting, I realized I had a wealth of experience in how nonprofits worked. I had done everything, so I knew I could do anything," Peggy says. "But I found that people wanted consultants who could do something specific. They need a solution to a specific problem. The more clearly you can define your niche, the more likely it is you will find consulting work."

If you are an accountant, for example, you want to tell your clients that not only can you balance their books, but you also can manage their finances so they can save on taxes.

Second, no matter what your field, you need to show potential clients that you can help them financially. Let them know how your services will net them the increased income that will pay for your services; explain how your services will save them money; and show how they will earn more money by utilizing your ideas. For example, if you offer services as a financial consultant, you also should get to know bankers and lenders so you can help clients who may need to grow their business by borrowing money. Peggy works with both nonprofit agencies and foundations that offer grants to her clients.

Third, maintain visibility in your field. Peggy regularly offers training workshops at conferences. A recent client explained that she hired Peggy because she had heard her speak over a year ago. When Peggy first started her business, she regularly attended trade meetings and found that many successful consultants had more work than they could handle and were happy to refer clients to Peggy. She also maintained visibility by significantly lowering her hourly rate in the beginning to get the kind of jobs that would help to establish her as a member of the professional community.

The Sensuality of Simplicity

The next time you go to your job, spend the day doing your work mindfully. Be fully aware of what you are doing and how you are feeling throughout the day. Naturally, since we're all human, your mind will wander frequently. When you are mindful, you will have some awareness that your mind has wandered, and you can gently bring it back to the present. When you are mindful, you will do each task with full attention and to the best of your ability. Take note of your attitude while doing each task—do you feel good about it? Can it be accomplished in a different way? This will help you either to make your current job better or to get the awareness you'll need in order to make a change.

BALANCING LIFE WITH PART-TIME WORK

She was a groundbreaker...and a determined one. In 1971 Arlie Hochschild was offered a job as an assistant professor at the University of California at Berkeley. She replied that she would be delighted to accept but didn't want to work full time. She was told that the university had never hired part-time faculty before, but because they liked her qualifications, they would consider it for perhaps three to four years only, even though rules did not permit such a schedule. Arlie persisted. She enlisted the aid of the Berkeley Women's Caucus, who went to the dean and announced that if the university was going to hire women, they would have to change their rules to permit part-time work. He agreed to make an exception. But neither Arlie nor the caucus was satisfied. They did not want Arlie to be simply "an exception." They wanted the rules changed. Finally the dean agreed to offer part-time work to women. Still not enough. Men needed to be given the option as well.

"We finally made the breakthrough that men and women could work part time," Arlie says. "I wound up sharing my position with another woman. It was very successful for us, because we were refreshed and got more work done."

Arlie Hochschild in her office.

At home, Arlie and her husband shared the work and child care. While the children were small, the family lived very modestly in a one-bedroom apartment and used the dining room as a second bedroom.

Arlie says she has always been pleased with her choice, yet she acknowledges the internal struggle she has had with tempering her own desire to work more hours.

Her experience led her to write a book about the exhaustion faced by full-time workers with families. The book is titled *Second Shift: Working Parents and the Revolution at Home.* "More and more parents are coming home after the first shift (paid job) to the second shift (diapers and dinner)," Arlie says. "Family life was supposed to be a refuge from the job, not an extension of it."

Arlie says the second shift is an extension of industrial life in many ways. In the last 30 years, two trends have been present: the work day has lengthened (this includes less vacation, more overtime, more commute time), and women entered the labor force. Women take less time off after birth now and work during the summer. "Even for the hours we are at home, we're mentally still at work," Arlie says. She finds that now, when we do turn our attention to home, we do so in an industrial way, with strict schedules for kids and adults (day care, lessons, and so on). With this perspective, we created the "quality time" notion: "I'm a good parent if I devote the hour between 8 and 9 P.M. strictly to my child."

"Quality time is like work now," Arlie explains. "We treat it like another thing to do. It is delineated, bounded, and set apart from diffuse, free-flowing family time."

The longer we are at work, the more pressed we are to "work" at home, such as doing two things at once and delegating family tasks to services (cleaning, birthday party planning . . .). We also have eliminated family events, such as dinner together. "In the short run, these seem like solutions," Arlie says. "But they are the problem . . . they are what turns family life into the second shift."

She reminds us of a typical second-shift morning: The harried parent is constantly reminding the child to "get ready, quick, quick, mom has to be at work at 8:00!" Or "Hurry, hurry, you have half an hour to take your bath. Quick! Quick!" Our children react by dawdling and refusing to leave when it's time.

Often parents who work every day unwittingly create little debt collectors in their children. In exchange for not being available during the day, for example, they will promise their children a weekend at the family cabin where they can finally have unstructured time. Or they will trade time on an upcoming Saturday afternoon for lack of time now. Thus, the family copes with Monday through Friday with the promise of Saturday. The children collect not bills but love, payable at a later date. As for families with two working parents, time becomes a third partner in the marriage: You pick out two days to get home late and I'll pick out two days. . . .

The bottom-line question, Arlie says, is: Will you move into a high-powered sector that takes time away from your family or not? The issue is ambition versus a desire for nurturing and relationships. But Arlie is quick to note that these decisions are not easy. She sees the answer in work share and 35-hour work weeks.

❖ ❖ ❖ ❖ ❖ ❖ ❖ ❖ ❖ ❖ ❖ ❖ ❖ ❖

Resources

Books

American Dream, American Burnout by Gerald Loren Fishkin, Ph.D. (Long Beach, CA: Loren Publications, 1994)
Discusses the social, financial, and psychological effects of burnout and how our lives are deeply affected. Looks at our relationship to work as a significant factor in people becoming listless and exhausted and what must be done to prevent this from escalating.

Beating Job Burnout by Dr. Beverly Potter (Berkeley, CA: Ronin Publishing, 1993)
A psychological profile of burnout, its causes, and how to deal with it. Skills that help to offset exhaustion are discussed, including the role control plays in our lives, learning to pace oneself, developing social support, and finding a path with heart.

Career Crash by Barry Glassner (New York: Simon & Schuster, 1994)
The changing face of American business and how we are coping. Real-life examples of people who have been "downsized" and how some found opportunities while others became mired in crisis. Gets to the core of why this change is occurring.

Finding a Path with Heart by Dr. Beverly Potter (Berkeley, CA: Ronin Publishing, 1995)
Traversing through the myriad of obstacles on the way to finding work enjoyable and rewarding is easier than you think. This book tells how to find more pleasure in work than in leisure.

The Great Game of Business by Jack Stack and Bo Burlingham (New York: Doubleday, 1994)
Stack, CEO and president of Springfield Remanufacturing, wrote this book to explain the system of open book management. He also tells the story of how Springfield was brought back from the grave and turned into a $100 million company by using OBM techniques.

How to Be a Weekend Entrepreneur by Susan Ratliff (Phoenix: Marketing Methods, 1991)
Setting up a weekend business, such as craft booths at local fairs, and how to run and maintain it properly. Provides detailed advice on how to handle such a business and how to create growth. Includes listing of craft fairs, trade shows, and swap meets.

How to Raise a Family and a Career Under One Roof by Lisa M. Roberts (Moon Township, PA: Bookhaven Press, 1997)
The author, wife, entrepreneur, and mother of four speaks from practical experience in sharing her life story on mixing business and family. Sprinkled with checklists and suggestions on helpful tools as well as holes to avoid.

How to Start and Run a Successful Consulting Business by Gregory Kishel and Patricia Kishel (New York: John Wiley & Sons, 1996)
Details the necessary steps to take (including relevant forms, charts, contracts, and legal forms) to launch a proper consulting company, including promoting the business, record keeping and accounting, and going international.

Job Shift by William Bridges (New York: Addison-Wesley, 1994)
Shift in corporate structures and behavior has set the groundwork for the jobless future, a time when secure jobs as we know them shall have evaporated. Strategies on coping with this coming tide of economic change and how it will affect our entire lives.

The Joy of Not Working by Ernie J. Zelinski (Chicago: Login Publishers Consortium, 1995)
Self-management techniques that seek to energize life outside of work and how that can sustain a healthy life as well as promote inner creativity. Topics range the gamut—from how slavery to work can be avoided and how to have a pleasant life on only a few dollars a day.

Make Money with Your PC by Lynn Walford (Los Angeles: Aproprose, 1992)
How-to guide on starting a personal computer–related company, including what software to buy, how to comply with IRS rules, company promotion, and establishing a reputation. Also, practical tips on properly managing your new company.

100 Best Retirement Businesses by Lisa Angowski Rogak (Dover, NH: Upstart, 1994)
Realistic descriptions of 100 business possibilities, ranging from raising llamas to repairing expensive yachts. Each business suggestion includes an interview with someone who has worked in that field.

Open Book Management by John Case (New York: HarperCollins, 1996)
Case, a chief writer for *Inc.* magazine, uses lots of case stories to promote the idea of open book management. Also includes the philosophy behind the movement.

Six Months Off by Hope Dlugozima, James Scott, and David Sharp (New York: Henry Holt & Co., 1996)
How to take six months off from your job and what that can mean for your personal, financial, and business future. Takes prospective sabbatical takers on a step-by-step course on asking for time off from work, surviving on no income, and using the time to reboot your life.

Temp by Deborahann Smith (Boston: Shambhala, 1994)
Inside life of a "temp" by someone who has lived the experience. Deals with determining whether you are suited for temporary work and how to survive in the vast temp world. Other topics include how to dress properly, being fired, dealing with sexual harassment, and going permanent.

Un-Jobbing by Michael Fogler (Lexington, KY: Free Choice Press, 1997)
Questions the values that lead us to lead stressed-out lives and the difference between work and jobs. Advice on how to free yourself from the paycheck and find greater fulfillment in the money-making world. Looks at how overconsumption might be the cause of all our ills.

What Can You Do with a Law Degree? by Deborah Arron (Seattle: Niche Press, 1997)
Find more options with a lawyer's degree, whether in or out of law. The book lists several fields that can be rewarding places to put such a degree to good use and tells how to investigate those fields.

What Color Is Your Parachute? by Richard Nelson Bolles (Berkeley, CA: Ten Speed Press, 1994)
Perspectives in job hunting and choosing and changing a career, including topics such as how to find the person who has the power to hire you as well as learning to conduct a productive interview. Advice also offered on starting your own business and working out of your home.

Work of Her Own by Susan Wittig Albert, Ph.D. (New York: G. P. Putnam & Sons, 1992)
A woman's guide for career planning and business opportunities, looking at how work and career options affect today's female population. By reflecting on a woman's values, the book looks at how internal modes affect the day-to-day work existence and how to carefully choose a career path that makes the most sense.

Miscellaneous

Families and Work Institute
Offers many books on work and family, including leave issues, families in transition, dependent care issues, and family work issues. Contact: 330 Seventh Avenue, 14th floor, New York, NY 10001, 1-212-465-2044.

Family Care Resources
Offers help for parents balancing work and family. Write: P.O. Box 3707, MS 3W-JM, Seattle, WA 98124-2207.

Labor News for Working Families
Provides resources to unions to develop workplace policies for families, including child care, elder care, domestic partner benefits, family leave, flexible work schedules, and more. Write: Labor Project for Working Families, 1.1.R.-2521 Channing Way, Berkeley, CA 94720.

Shift Toward Better Families, Communities and Jobs
Newsletter about new ways to work. Contact: P.O. Box 2741, Iowa City, IA 52224.

Working Mother magazine
October 1996 is special issue on 100 Best Companies for Working Mothers.

5

Simple Pleasures and Romance

*At night I went out into the dark &
saw a glimmering star & heard a
frog & Nature seemed to say, Well
do not these suffice?*

—RALPH WALDO EMERSON

I went to a winter solstice gathering one time, and everyone sat on the floor in a circle. We were celebrating the darkness. People told their stories about what darkness meant to them. The first thought that came to my mind was about three heavenly evenings I spent in nature. One was walking along a quiet, country road at night watching fireflies darting to and fro in the bushes. The second was sitting outside on a veranda on a warm summer evening in a house that was in a junglelike area. I remembered my passions soaring just listening to the crickets, frogs, and other nocturnal creatures that rhapsodized all throughout the evening and into the dawn. I wanted and needed no other sound, no other stimulation. The third was swimming in a warm inlet of the ocean that was inhabited by fireflylike organisms called pyrodinium (Greek for "whirling fire"). They would give off a surreal greenish light in the water when disturbed, and they would look like diamonds when you thrust the water up into the air.

There are other moments in nature that I remember fondly as well. I still remember the evening I spent languishing in a natural hot spring. It was so comforting to feel the lukewarm water flow all around my body. I rubbed my torso onto a flat stone, laid my back onto the earth, and shifted the mud around with my toes. The spring was in the middle of an ancient forest, surrounded by enormous old trees, ferns, moss, plants, and rocks. You could hear nothing but the river below and the birds. The next morning as I ate breakfast outside, I watched an osprey soar by with a fish in its mouth. I thought to myself, This is living; this is the real thing.

Sometimes the real thing is also inside. I love to read beautiful children's stories to my children. Our imaginations create the look of the characters and setting together. I like hanging out playing Monopoly with Grandpa and my son, and listening and watching as Grandma teaches piano to my daughter. I like to have family dinners with my brother, sister, parents, and kids. I relish late evenings with my sister, when we talk about the meaning of life. Sometimes we share a glass of wine, sometimes we talk over candlelight. I love to hold hands with someone special at the movies. And I love being ridiculous, as when I have pun contests with my aunt and cousins. Of course, there's nothing I like better than saying I love you.

These are the simple pleasures of my life, the memories that stand out, the thoughts and actions that make my life feel very rich. These simple pleasures are a highlight of living a less complicated existence; they can be easily missed in a life that goes by at 90 miles per hour. Some are so small that they lie unnoticed right at our feet when our minds and bodies are racing. When my life gets too busy, these are the first things to go and the first things I miss. I start feeling kind of hard-edged and disconnected. Awareness helps me slow down and get back to opening my life.

I scan through my favorite memories again. I can't find any of my favorite moments where I got all dressed up and spent a fortune to be entertained, or where the action was loud and fast. Instead, I find friends gathered for dinner or a game of Pictionary. I find a springtime hike in a meadow painted with wildflowers. I find time spent with a friend who needed to talk through a problem, and I remember I'm glad I was there. I find a silly game of softball with Jim and Laura and our kids in Jim's backyard. I find lots of walks with friends where we philosophize, discuss the meaning of life, and sort out our stuff. In my memory, I keep finding these kinds of easy, simple pleasures; I still can't find the complicated, expensive ones. They are there, but they don't stand out as favorites.

Simple pleasures. Simplicity is about streamlining your life so you have time for the things that matter . . . so you no longer feel the need to be entertained constantly. There is enchantment right in front of you, waiting for you to notice. All it asks is that you slow your inner clock and question the level of stimulation you really need.

There are lots of ways to nurture simple pleasure. First, you'll need to slow your own life so you have the time and space to even think about these things. A lot of what makes life pleasurable is sharing little intimate moments with other people. Connecting with others doesn't need to be a big, involved ordeal. If it's a housemate or partner, connecting can be doing chores together. If you're a parent with little children, connecting with your partner means setting aside special time to be alone together. Nothing elaborate. I loved hearing one wife tell me that she and her husband made sure their kids were in bed every night by 8:00 P.M. because that was special grown-up time. Every night her husband would brush her long hair as she read stories to him. How much simpler and how much more pleasurable can you get?

A *Simple Living* reader wrote a story about a simple pleasure he and his wife enjoyed: making love on their screened porch during thunderstorms. A mother told me she really got to know her daughter when they began to take regular walks together. My friend Ethel created a memorable home-on-the-range night one summer by putting on old cowboy music in the backyard, roasting hot dogs and marshmallows, and having the kids sleep outside in a tent. Believe me, the kids (and grown-ups!) had at least as much, if not more, fun than if we had planned a major, in-the-woods campout.

Another *Simple Living* reader wondered what caused people's souls to flicker alive. For her, it was watching goldfish breathe, thinking about what it is like to be a fish. Other times it is cooking dinner for friends, starting with the dessert, taking time, letting the process between people shape its own design around food courses. No rush. Watching snow fall. Painting. Hiking out to the ocean. Being loved.

Take Time to Nurture

Much of what is missing in a hurried life is the simple act of nurturing. We're too busy to nurture ourselves and definitely too busy to nurture those around us. Often we get so caught up in our own drive to succeed and accomplish that we neglect our human relationships—and it is these relationships that can give us the most depth and meaning. Nurture is like nourishment—we all need it to survive. Nurture is taking care. Nurturing takes time. In order to nurture other people, we need to be fully present and, better yet, fully real. When we let down our guard, we can get closer to people, and thus, we can move into a relationship of deeper care.

I love this little Zen story that I ran across one time. It says so well what nurturing is all about.

I once heard a story about a visit to heaven and hell. In both places, the visitor saw many people seated at a table on which many delicious foods were laid out. Chopsticks over a meter long were tied to their right hands, while their left hands were tied to their chairs. In hell, however much they stretched out their arms, the chopsticks were too long for them to get food into their mouths. They grew impatient and got their hands and chopsticks tangled with one another. The delicacies were scattered here and there. In heaven, on the other hand, people happily used the long chopsticks to pick out someone else's favorite food and feed it to him, and in turn they were being fed by others. They all enjoyed their meal in harmony.

In a book titled *The Couple's Comfort Book*, author Jennifer Louden lists lots of ways that couples can care for each other. You can translate any of these ideas into caring for your friends, children, and other family members. Louden mentions things like simply accepting your partner for one whole day without judging or preaching. Or each week nurture according to a letter of the alphabet. For example, in the first week you might bring your partner apple pie, and so on.

Nurturing also means taking time to check in with those you care about. In our busy lives, this seemingly simple gesture is easy to push to the sidelines. Let people you live with know what's going on with you every day, and ask what's going on with them. Since simple living is about being real, this check-in ought to be done in a heartfelt way.

You can nurture other people only when your own life is open. I heard a very touching story once about a woman who was moving into a house that she would be sharing with new housemates. She didn't know either of the housemates; she was exhausted from the move and was very stressed and anxious because of this unknown situation. When she arrived, one of the housemates had the sensitivity to take the time to assess the newcomer's situation. The housemate went into the bathroom, poured a nice, hot bubble bath, laid out fluffy towels, lit a candle, and pointed the way. What a simple yet totally nurturing gift. My friend Candace knew I had been going through a very stressful situation and was open enough in her own life to see that I could use a little nurturing. She called me and said she was looking for a good masseuse for herself, and could I recommend someone? I gave her the name of my favorite one, silently thinking how wonderful it would be to go there. I returned home one night and there, taped to my door, was a note from Candace telling me that one session at my masseuse was ready and paid for—all I had to do was call for an appointment. What a shame when we are too busy to give these kinds of gifts to others.

Sometimes I can tell that my kids need special "nurture nights." I pour each one a bubble bath, bring candles into the room, turn the lights low, and then serve them special "finger food" while they sit in the bubbles. We came up with the idea of almonds covered with honey as this special bathtime snack. We serve them on a silver-plated tray and set them down on a small table next to the tub. Often the kids do this for each other. I bring their pajamas into the room so all is ready when they get out of the tub.

Rituals to Enhance Simple Pleasures

My friend Jane hosts an annual garden party for her longtime friends. We sit around all afternoon in her beautiful garden eating, drinking wine, laughing hysterically, and catching up on our lives. This 10-year ritual has become an absolute highlight of everyone's summer. Samuel Johnson summed up why this kind of connection is so important: "A man, sir, must keep his friendships in constant repair."

Rituals can be any size, any shape, but the focus is the same—a regular, repetitive action of some sort is an announcement that this relationship is special. I heard about one couple who sets aside a regular time to sit with one another on the couch. They bring with them a box of tissues, and each partner talks about whatever is important to him or her. The other one agrees to listen without judging. This simple ritual keeps these people emotionally close and is a signal to them both that they are important enough for this special time.

> *A friend is a person with whom I may be sincere. Before him, I may think aloud.*
>
> —RALPH WALDO EMERSON

I like this idea from *The Couple's Comfort Book:* "When you anticipate an upcoming busy time at work, fill a few postcards or greeting cards with words of love, stamp them, and keep them handy to mail to your lover at work when you feel the need to connect but don't have time for it." You can extend this simple ritual to sending cards to your children and friends as well.

My kids and I started a Friday night ritual. Friday nights are the end of busy weeks, and everybody usually likes to zone out. On these nights we rent old movies and make homemade pizza. This is one night when I allow eating in front of the TV. Our simple pleasure is coming up with interesting toppings for

Off the Grid

by Kirk S. Nevin

I am fascinated by the revelations experienced by Kathleen McCarty ("Fireflies," Opinion Commentary, July 2) during a recent power outage at her Baltimore home.

Ms. McCarty and her son delighted in the secrets of the technologically imposed darkness: not just magical fireflies, but such wonders as urban silence, crescent moonsets, and the long-forgotten comforts of family and neighborhood companionship.

Perhaps Ms. McCarty would not be too surprised to learn that some other not-too-distant neighbors have chosen and "unplugged" lifestyle, not just for an hour a day, but for every delightful hour of every wonderful day.

Our family has chosen to live "off the grid." When we built our home 20 years ago, stone by stone and board by board, we left out a few minor items: wiring, plumbing, lighting. No TV, no hair dryer, no bathroom, no washing machine.

Why choose this lifestyle?

The reasons would fill a book (which I hope to have the time to write some day), but let me just list a few of the more obvious examples of the benefits of our chosen lifestyle.

The single greatest benefit is that our kids were raised without television. No violence, no commercialism, no video games. They read, they climbed trees, they swam, they traveled with us . . . in short, they grew up as healthy young animals, which is what they are.

Another obvious benefit is economic. We have no monthly gas and electric bill. Also, the lack of wiring and plumbing considerably reduced the cost of constructing our house. We built an outhouse in the woods, got a couple of wood-burning stoves (one heats, one cooks), built a hot water heater from junkyard scrap, and bought a few kerosene lamps. We were home.

Our second daughter was born upstairs in the west bedroom. One of those black March nights, bitter cold, softly snowing. Three candles flickering, the fire crackling in the stove, the black kettle hissing. She was born gently, calmly. I carefully washed her in a tub of warm water and placed her on her mother's breast. She is, at 17, a calm and self-assured young lady.

Our outhouse is quite cozy, with windows facing west and south into the ever-changing woods. Every trip, whether first thing in the morning or last at night, gives one an opportunity to appreciate the weather of the moment. A soft pre-dawn mist, a brilliant starry night, a slippery path through the snow . . . each necessary journey to the outhouse fills the lungs and the heart with the beauty of that particular moment.

Our evening meal begins with a walk to the garden. This day was typical: We picked a quart of red raspberries and a pint of blueberries. That was our salad. We stir-fried a zucchini, an onion, a green pepper, some beans, a tomato, a few carrots, and a chunk of tofu. Put it on brown rice in a pretty ceramic bowl (made by our elder daughter) and ate with chopsticks. You can have your microwave.

For six months of the year we sleep on a screened porch in the woods, on the floor, on a thin foam pad. Last midnight's thunderstorm was a miracle: the faraway rumblings, then the hot hurried winds and first huge drops breaking on the screens into a million tiny droplets of life. We laughed, and we made love to the beat of nature's greatest sound and light show.

Art? Try the texture of our fieldstone, or the patterns in a blue-jay feather, or the seed pattern of a sunflower. Check out the pink blush on a rugosa rose hip or the dawn light on a riffle in the stream.

Music? Sit with me in the garden. We'll listen for the dusk hour to our macho mockingbird as he salutes this domain from the topmost branch of our tallest white oak tree. Listen to the doves on a hot afternoon. Listen to the bullfrog woo his mate at midnight. Listen to the warm spring wind in the April blooming orchard.

Come, be with us. Any day, any night. Each moment is truly a miracle, but this can only be so if we humans are willing to slow down, to turn off the lights, to be silent, to listen, to see, to wonder.

I believe we humans have a place on this fragile planet, but it must be that place chosen by our Mother Earth: as but one of many millions of miraculous forms of life, each depending on all the others.

Yes, Ms. McCarty, revel in the fireflies. And live calmly, so that they may revel in you as well.

Kirk is a *Simple Living* subscriber who originally wrote this piece for the *Baltimore Sun*.

the pizza, choosing a zone-out movie to rent, and snuggling on the couch for half the night. Sometimes we sit under a comforter after our pizza is finished.

Finding Pleasure in Everyday Life

Sue Bender wrote a whole book on the subject of finding meaning in everyday life. It is titled *Everyday Sacred*. Her book illustrates how, with awareness, we can find pleasure and delight in the typically overlooked moments of our lives. She writes: "Like the monk going out with his empty bowl, I set out to see what each day offered." She also wrote: "I wanted to see with fresh eyes. What might have been there all along that I had not been able to see? What had I taken for granted?"

Simple pleasures are about finding joy and delight in everyday things and everyday occurrences. Finding these pleasures is like walking along with children who are constantly enthralled with things adults no longer see. I remember spending time at a family camp one year with my kids. Groups of children kept hovering around a particular tree. Finally the adults moseyed over to see what was going on. A mother woodpecker was flying in and out as if feeding a baby in the hole in the tree. We couldn't see. Every day the kids would gather. Finally the baby got large enough to pop its head out of the hole. Then we all got to watch as the mother fed the little baby. It was a sight to remember. Had the camp been for adults only, there is a good chance none of us would ever have enjoyed this delightful encounter with nature. We would have been too busy in our adult lives to notice the tree. It took the awe and curiosity of children to wake us up.

You can take pleasure in simple chores, such as folding laundry. Think of each person who wears the item and what he or she means to you. I find it difficult to fold a kid's pair of overalls without feeling a little wave of love. In *Slowing Down in a Speeded Up World,* author Adair Lara collected ideas from lots of people about how they find pleasure in everyday life. Sometimes it helps to remind ourselves to slow down and see the world with new eyes. Other people's stories can inspire us. One woman wrote in that she found delight in shoveling snow, sometimes at 2:00 A.M. when the rest of the world was asleep, sometimes in the afternoon when the birds were chirping. The writer knew she could hire a snowplow, but that would have deprived her of this sensual pleasure. Another wrote in that he painted and refinished hardwood floors for a living. After he finished a job, he would lie down on the new floor and think about what might happen there. He wrote: "People will live and work and talk together; they'll argue and maybe fall in love."

Another one wrote in that she steps out on the porch in the morning, drinking coffee and watching people. While doing this, she asks herself whether what she is doing today will contribute to what is important in her life. If not, why is she doing it?

I also try to remember to turn everyday annoyances into simple pleasures whenever I can. If someone leaves her slippers on the living room floor, I like the feeling much better when I think of the slippers as signs that someone I love lives with me rather than getting angry that they weren't put away. When my sister's dog's hair gets on my car seat, I get annoyed but then quickly remind myself that I love having my sister around and the dog is part of her life.

One of my favorite stories in *Simple Living* was written by a retirement-age woman who wanted to get rid of a lot of the possessions that filled her large suburban home, so she could move to a small place by the ocean. (See story on page 362.) Rather than get frustrated by all of the things and by the tedious process of unloading, she stopped and thought about some of the special items and what they meant to her. She remembered a particular bowl that she and her beloved late husband had purchased together in a junk store many years before. She thought about all of the family dinners that were served on the now too-huge dining room table. She took simple pleasure in the act of letting go.

My friend Teryl lives on an arterial that is regularly used by a fairly steady stream of cars. Once I asked her if that bothered her. Most (not all) times it didn't. She said every time she heard a car or a person walking by, she remembered that she was surrounded by other human beings, and that was comforting to her. Another simple pleasure derived from the mundane or even distasteful.

Simple Activities and Dates

Many times we want to go out to do something fun but can't think past the usual get-dressed-up-and-spend-a-fortune kind of night or dinner and a movie. These dilemmas are the same whether you are going out with a friend, a partner, or discovering a new date. Here are a few ideas to spark your imagination.

Active Simple Pleasures

Active dates (with friends, partners, or potential partners) can set the stage for more authenticity because often they take us out of the realm of the usual status-quo. Sometimes you are pushed more toward your physical limits during physical activity, and this push brings out a part of you and your partner that you would not see in a totally comfortable, predictable environment. Also, active dates usually take place in the great outdoors, and the associated ambiance can deepen the pleasurable moment.

One of my sister Karen's favorite first dates was a day spent skate-skiing (like cross-country skiing). They left at 10 A.M. on a Saturday morning, skied until lunch, then had a picnic outside. This was the start of a long-term friendship.

By engaging in these not-so-typical activities, you can discover something in common and form a bond. If this is a date with someone new, you also can discover a bit about what kind of person you are with. Karen could tell from this first date that her friend was competitive yet still considerate. He had skate-skied before; and although she was a downhill skier, this was her first time skate-skiing. Naturally, she couldn't keep up. She noticed he was a little on edge because he wanted to go faster, but he didn't push her, leave her in the dust, or put her down for not keeping up. She would not have seen any of these qualities sitting over dinner or watching a movie.

The afternoon also gave the new friends plenty of time to talk and get to know each other. They were not distracted by a lot of noise; they had only their own voices interrupting the peaceful gliding through the quiet snow. And they got exercise in the process.

> *Imagination is the highest kite*
>
> *one can fly.*
>
> —LAUREN BACALL

When you're both (or all) in the mood for physical activity, here are a few inexpensive, fun options. You can do these day or evening. Try bowling, ice skating, or roller skating. Remember city parks have free admission. Play tennis at a public court. Play miniature golf. Play a short round of regular golf. Go for a bike ride. Follow with a picnic. Or ride your bikes to a specific event, such as a musical concert. Many cities have bicycle clubs that offer maps of good bike trails. Many park offices offer the same. I have a friend who went on a memorable moonlight bike ride. They started out in the late afternoon, and by the time they got to their destination, it was getting late. Nature saved the day. The moon lit their way back home.

Something else about active get-togethers—a little spontaneity can be a great thing. Remember the part in the movie *It's a Wonderful Life*, when Jimmy Stewart asked his date on the spur of the moment to go up to a mountain, throw off their shoes, and run around? The stuffy date gave him a strange look, as if he were out of his mind. Jimmy said something like "Oh, forget it." They didn't go out again and Jimmy married someone else.

How about walking around your neighborhood? If you'd like a change of pace, walk around a new neighborhood. Walk to a movie theater, day or evening. I've done this many times. It gives you time to talk and avoids parking hassles at the theater. If you think you live too far, try driving halfway or choosing a route that has a little café or coffeehouse that you could stop in on the way. Join up with a Volksport group. (These organizations sponsor group walks in city and rural areas, check your local phone book.) Walk along the beach. Stop and admire the sunset. Remember, sunsets offer unbeatable simple, sensual pleasure at no charge.

Day or evening, go for a hike in a city park or mountain area. Who says hikes have to be in the daytime? If it's at night, pack your flashlight, some food, and a red-checkered tablecloth. Spread it over a log for some good-natured dinner when you reach the lake. Extra bonus? Rub each other's feet.

Take a swim together. A friend and I went for a walk near a lake one summer evening and dove in. Absolutely free and absolutely fun. We were the only ones there, the stars were out, and the moon shone on the water. Sure beat the heck out of a high-spending, frenzied evening.

Rent a boat. Look under "boat rentals" in the phone book or call local universities that are near water. Often they rent boats. Pack a meal, pull up to a shore, and enjoy! For those musically inclined, take along a guitar and serenade your friend. Trust me, this will be memorable.

Nonactive Simple Pleasures

Go to a café that has regular groups meeting to discuss politics, events, and philosophy. Café talking is a growing trend in many urban areas, especially those with a vibrant café life. For the cost of a latte or hot chocolate, you can be part of a wonderful conversation. Or go to a quieter café that has board games, such as checkers and chess. This gives you the opportunity to do something that is nearly free (you do need to buy a beverage) and can be a lot of fun. One evening my kids and I went to a local bakery/coffeehouse and played Scrabble. We could have played at home, but we were in the mood for the energy of other people and chocolate cake too.

Many theaters that put on stage plays have discount seating a few minutes before the play starts. While it involves some risk (you may not get to see the production!), it is a cheaper way to see performances.

Go to an evening church service. Go to your own church, or check out a new one. Often these evening programs include beautiful music, dim lighting, and lots of candles. Who could ask for a more serene and sensual atmosphere? Don't like the religion idea? Churches can still be a good, low-cost place to go because they often offer free musical events and discussions.

If you want to go out for a traditional evening of dinner and a movie, try doing it for less. Most major cities have at least one movie theater that shows current films for $2. These same cities often have Cheap Eats–style books that offer lists of restaurants that feed you for less.

Picnics can be delightful ways to spend easy, flowing time together. Start off with flying a kite. Do they always have to take place in the daytime, in a park? What about a picnic on a rooftop on a Saturday night? It's wintertime? Get your fireplace going, bring out a bottle of wine, add tidbits and nibbling food, spread out a blanket or some pillows, and relax.

Here are some ideas that were sent to *Simple Living* by readers.

❖ Go stargazing and bring along some wine.

❖ Take a dance class together.

❖ Hang out at a comfortable bookstore, then go for coffee or tea.

❖ Have a private wine-and-cheese party. Buy a few bottles of wine, make baked Brie: Wrap a good-size wedge of Brie cheese with store-bought crescent-roll dough. Bake according to directions on the roll package.

❖ Take a nap together in a large patch of sunshine.

❖ Take a convertible for a test-drive—you don't have to buy it!

❖ Have a film festival—rent two or three movies of the same genre.

❖ Usher at a theater. Most performances, from student productions to grand operas, need ushers. Call the box office to inquire about signing up. It's a free way to see shows.

❖ Large book chain stores often have authors and performers who make personal appearances. This can be a festive evening out and a chance to meet your favorite author.

❖ Many libraries have regular film series. No charge for classic and recent films. You also can simply visit the library with your friend, showing each other your favorite books, discovering new ones, and maybe borrowing a CD or video to take home.

❖ Concerts in the park are a summertime activity, and city parks often offer early-evening and weekend concert series from pop to jazz. It's a nice place to take a picnic.

❖ Ride the local ferry, trolley, or bus to the end of the line. Great opportunities for people watching and maybe a little picnic before the trip back.

❖ Tickets to the local art museums or galleries are $3 to $5 for opening shows. Hors d'oeuvres usually are served at these opening nights.

- ❖ Large bookstores offer music in their coffee bars on weekends for free.

- ❖ Local arts festivals usually include evening concerts.

- ❖ Watch a meteor shower with the astronomical society.

- ❖ Volunteer together. Read to seniors, the blind, or children. Provide inside/outside chore cleanup for seniors. Share special talents in a nursing home—music, craft, photos.

- ❖ Join local outdoor groups such as the Mountaineers, Audubon Society, and Sierra Club. They offer hikes, birdwatching expeditions, canoe trips, and cross-country ski trips in winter.

- ❖ Demo cooking classes are advertised in newspapers. Go to one and then cook dinner together.

- ❖ Write and recite haiku together. Read the poems out loud.

- ❖ Borrow a friend's hot tub or rent one and watch the planets.

- ❖ Attend public lectures, workshops, seminars, talks, and forums that are advertised in newspapers and religious newsletters.

Romance

Just because you're out on a date doesn't mean you need to switch back to high, impersonal gear. You can continue enjoying simple pleasures as you get to know a potential new friend. This concept became abundantly clear to me on my first date after my divorce. Because I had been married, I hadn't dated for years before this and didn't know what to expect. My date, who also had been recently divorced, didn't know what the heck modern dating entailed either. So we went out on a literal whirlwind of activities one night that cost a small fortune in energy and money. It was as if we felt we had to be entertained all evening.

I returned home from the date exhausted. I thought to myself, if this is dating, I think I'd better sign up for convent life. Here I'd been writing in my *Simple Living* newsletter about enjoying the simple pleasures of life, letting nature do the entertaining, finding a balance between activity and quiet time, and

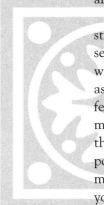

not spending a lot of money in the process. Then I date like this? Something was wrong with the picture, but I wasn't exactly sure what. I didn't know what people did on dates or how I could date in alignment with my values.

I talked about this to my friend Taso, who was also single. He had experienced the same dilemma. How could we get to know our dates in a more relaxed, less expensive way? We brainstormed and wrote a column called "Creative Dating" for *Simple Living*. We were not alone. Some columns resonate with people, some don't. This one did. People kept writing in with more ideas. I tried a few of the ideas during my dates and they worked! I felt better, the date felt better, and no one had to mortgage the house to pay for an evening out. I also discovered I could get to know my dates on a deeper level when we didn't feel the need to entertain or be entertained constantly.

Remember once again that living simply, in my opinion, is about living with balance. Does this mean I never go out to a more-or-less upscale restaurant or I never go someplace where you buy tickets for the evening? No! It means most of the time, I like lower-key dates, but it doesn't mean I'm some low-key zealot who will never do anything out of my sphere. It also doesn't mean that I rail on about these ideas to dates. I don't think extreme anything is a good thing. Creative dating simply means that you come up with interesting alternatives to expensive (financially and emotionally) nights on the town, and you do it with charm and balance.

Remember, dating is the one shopping expedition you can embark on and still live simply. Consider it the mall of life. You are trying out your dates to see if there is a fit. If not, try the next one. Find out now, while dating, whether the two of you have similar money and time values. I've known just as many couples break up over time issues as they do over money issues. One feels the need for more packed schedules and intense activity, and the other is more of a homebody. One likes to save money, and the other never heard of the concept. You know the stories. Creative dating gives you the perfect opportunity to live out your values and discover whether your date feels even remotely the same. Think of what happens if you don't date in alignment with your values. You present a false self to the person. How will you figure out whether your date and you are an honest match?

Besides the choice of activities, there are other ways to live out your simple living values while dating. What you wear, what you drive, and how you manage your money say a lot about you. Do you feel the need to race to the clothing store before your Saturday night date and get a new outfit to impress the person? What does this say about you and the kind of date you chose? (Does this mean you have to show up in rags and not give a hoot what you look like?

Quit it! Stop the extreme stuff. Balance, balance, balance.) Living out your balanced values means you want to look appropriate and decent, but if you feel your regular decent and appropriate is not enough, you ought to question your motivation for spending just to impress a date. Why isn't the usual you enough, and what will happen when you uncover the usual you?

Here's another simple living point, beautifully played out in the dating arena. Simple living is also about living a more authentic life. Living authentically means being who you are. How often do we choose careers, cars, clothes, houses, and the rest in order to impress other people? This doesn't mean we get no personal pleasure out of some of these things, but we ought to seriously question whether we would go as far as we sometimes do if it is just about meeting our own needs. Simple living means slowly uncovering these layers and exposing to the world the more authentic you . . . the one you were when you were, say, 10 years old, before you got distracted by commercial life.

> *Every morning we have twenty-four brand new hours to live.*
>
> —THICH NHAT HANH

If a value is presenting yourself to the world in a more authentic way, and if a value is living within your means and not being in debt, then why are you making car payments just so it looks to the world like you have a lot of money? Check this stuff out in you, and check it out in your dates. It might look appealing and "successful" if your date drives up in an expensive car, but if you look under the surface and find that the car is purchased on credit and the person doesn't have a dime in savings, you might question your date's values. (Remember, this is a shopping expedition. Shop with a critical eye.)

There are other important things to check out when dating. What kind of a life does this person lead? As my friend Taso got deeper into simple living, he also became more spiritual and more concerned with the world around him. He began to look for these values in his dates. Women who arranged their lives to have time to do volunteer work became very attractive to him. Women who were on some sort of spiritual journey became interesting. This was a far cry from the women he dated in his earlier, presimplicity days. Back then his criteria was whether she looked good, dressed well, and was fun. It is no surprise to Taso now why none of those relationships was satisfying in the long run. Now he has far fewer dates because his criteria have become more demanding, but those dates he does have are more authentic and satisfying in the long run.

Taso is able to distinguish these points only because he began the process of uncovering his own layers and has gotten to know himself in a more authentic way. He got to know himself by slowing down the pace of his own life and taking the time to look within. In his presimplicity days, he would go from one relationship, one date to the next, at lightning speed, with no breaks in between. One relationship would end and very shortly thereafter, he'd be on to the next. No time for introspection. Finally he stopped and made a long-term date with himself. He realized that he needed to get to know himself on a deeper level before he could possibly connect with a soulmate. He stayed home on Saturday nights and read philosophical books. He meditated. He cried when he thought of some of his old behavior. He spent no time blaming past dates—he spent it all looking within himself. This took guts and courage for someone who had been afraid to spend a Saturday night alone. I could relate to Taso's story completely. I think the longest time I ever went in premarriage days without a relationship (not even just a date) was three days. Unbelievable. How can we expect to get to know our dates if we never take the time to get to know ourselves?

When you emerge from a soul-searching journey, you will be a more authentic you. You will leave behind your need to impress in a material and verbal way. You'll be able to talk to your date from your heart. You'll be able to open up and be more vulnerable because you won't have the need to hide behind a facade so much. This doesn't mean you'll spill your soul out on the first date (balance, balance, balance); it means that your conversation will reflect who you really are rather than who you are trying to be. You know how some people like to impress you immediately with high-brow, analytical diatribes about politics or books? Then you feel insecure because you aren't able to jump to the challenge? Is an analytical diatribe about the real person? Heck, no. It's a mask of insecurity. We all have worn these masks to one degree or another, and they all provide a wonderful device to maintain distance. There is a big difference in having interesting back-and-forth discussions about politics and books versus that high-energy, one-sided diatribe. Then there are the dates who joke and tell stories half the night. Jokes and laughing are absolutely wonderful, but not for hours on end. An authentic date is a mix of fun and heartfelt talking between the two of you.

Another way to be authentic is by being honest about your likes and dislikes in a calm, nonjudgmental way. If your date has a plan for a wild and frenzied evening and you are not in the mood for this level of activity, being authentic means you gently say that you're more in the mood for something less busy. Being real is also important at the end of a date. When I first began this after-divorce dating, I didn't know how or when to end dates. I felt that they couldn't start until, say, 7:00 in the evening and had to last until all hours just because that's how I thought dates were supposed to be. I'd get tired earlier, but still I'd freeze a smile on my face and press on. Being authentic means saying how you feel and checking in with your date to see how he or she feels. Very possibly you both feel the same way, yet you feel the need to impress or keep up, and you both wind up behaving in a way that is not comfortable for either of you.

Simplicity means treating each other with respect. When you live more authentically, and when you have time and space in your life to really care about people as human beings, you'll naturally want to treat others in a respectful way. Neither of you will treat the other as an object. Traditionally we've blamed men, for example, for treating women as, say, sex objects. But women have treated men as "success" or money objects. While lamenting the shallowness of this behavior, we've encouraged it at the same time. If women don't want to be treated as sex objects, then why do they run to the store before Saturday night dates to buy certain outfits and load up with makeup? (Balance, balance, balance. Makeup is fine, a decent outfit is fine . . . but there are limits.) And if men don't want to be treated as success or money objects, why do they show up in cars they cannot afford?

Once again, moderation is the key. There is no question that success is sexy and that physical appearance is important. But stop and ask yourself what success, for example, really means. In my opinion, success means the person is living the kind of life she or he really enjoys and finds fulfilling. This could be at any financial level. What material things they have are paid for; they are not in debt (except maybe a reasonable mortgage or if the debt involves some well-thought-out financial plan); they have control over their finances (remember—all income levels); they earn enough to support whatever lifestyle they find comfortable; they have savings; they have time for work, time for themselves, and time for others; they generally like what they do for a living; they have mutually supportive relationships with people of both sexes; they take responsibility for their own actions; and they are generally, though not always, pleased with life.

These people know they are not perfect and know how to be real when they feel sad. They can be vulnerable. They give and receive help freely. They have the time and space to care about other people. When things don't go the right way for them, they know how to stop, take inventory, and start over. As for their physical appearance, they take care of themselves and are attractive. That doesn't mean drop-dead, movie-magazine gorgeous. It means their demeanor and choice of clothing shows they are someone with substance who is kind, honest, and interesting. If they don't have all of the above mastered, I like it that they are at least on the road like the rest of us. That kind of success, in my opinion, is sexy as all get out.

What's your version of success? Spend time thinking about this. It will make

147

a vast difference in how you live your life and in the qualities that you will look for in potential partners.

One last thing. Once you have gotten to know yourself and start living out your own values and begin dating in alignment with those values, don't give up on your dates too quickly. If it is an obvious no-match, then don't waste time. On the other hand, if the person seems like a basically good person who is worth spending time with but doesn't subscribe to all of your philosophies, ask yourself whether there could be any meeting of the minds and whether you could possibly influence him or her in some way. If you're hard-nosed about your ideas, people probably will get turned off. But if you show them by quiet example how enjoyable simplicity can be, maybe a little will rub off on them. A good partnership is a merger of two basically healthy people who influence each other in a positive way.

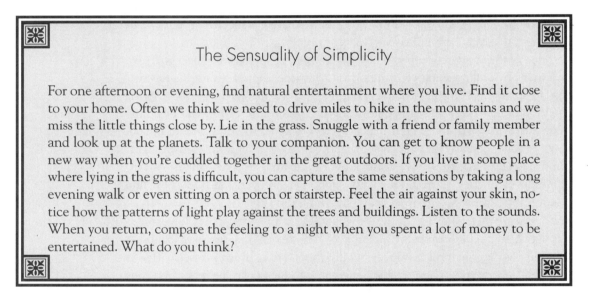

The Sensuality of Simplicity

For one afternoon or evening, find natural entertainment where you live. Find it close to your home. Often we think we need to drive miles to hike in the mountains and we miss the little things close by. Lie in the grass. Snuggle with a friend or family member and look up at the planets. Talk to your companion. You can get to know people in a new way when you're cuddled together in the great outdoors. If you live in some place where lying in the grass is difficult, you can capture the same sensations by taking a long evening walk or even sitting on a porch or stairstep. Feel the air against your skin, notice how the patterns of light play against the trees and buildings. Listen to the sounds. When you return, compare the feeling to a night when you spent a lot of money to be entertained. What do you think?

A POTPOURRI OF SENSUAL DELIGHTS IN THE CARIBBEAN

Some people dream of escaping the rat race and moving to a tropical island; others pack up and do it. A few of them find places with names most of us have never heard of, such as Vieques, Puerto Rico, a place one transplant describes as the island that time forgot. An island that is so sleepy that most people on mainland Puerto Rico don't recall when the last time was they were there.

Vieques is the kind of place that boasts a bakery in the little town of Esperanza that sells the most delicious, fresh Puerto Rican bread . . . but the bakery opens only when the proprietor feels like opening it. You can be lucky and happen by then. Otherwise you come back later. To get from one end of town to the other, you drive carefully on the one, narrow, winding main road that curves through lush jungle and alongside the ocean. You drive carefully because cars are no more plentiful than the wild horses that graze nonchalantly by the side of the road. There is not room for both. And there is not one stoplight on Vieques, anywhere.

Gail Burchard is one of the dreamers who packed up and left her mainstream life to come to this tropical island. She was a flight attendant in the 1960s, a job that frequently brought her to the Caribbean islands. She met her husband on St. Thomas. Already a seasoned adventurer, he had been around the world eight times by the time they met. "He was doing all the things I wanted to do but hadn't," Gail says. He owned a charter boat business on St. Thomas. Gail signed on. Two children and 12 years later, the couple divorced, and Gail found herself back in her hometown of Gloucester, Massachusetts. She was a nurse, leading a civilized life, and yearning again for adventure. She remembered visiting Vieques with her husband and decided to return with her two children. They lived on Vieques for a year, and Gail remembers the freedom. "It was the realization that I didn't have to live with all the 'shoulds' in my life: the clothes I wore, how I behaved, how much money I had. We lived in a little house with a tin roof and I didn't have to please anybody."

After a year, the family returned to Massachusetts and Gail began plotting her dream. She spent nights at her job as a nurse in the Emergency Room making lists of things she loved to do: physical, hands-on tasks, arts and crafts, causes. She would build a retreat for women seeking adventure and a place where they could go to refresh themselves and get rejuvenated. "I wanted to fill women with the spirit of 'yes, you can,' " Gail says.

She returned to Vieques and found her land: an affordable five acres of rich jungle in the countryside, totally undeveloped. She had no telephone, didn't speak Spanish, and says the road leading to her driveway was only paved last

Gail Burchard enjoys life in the tropics.

year. She also had no building experience. Undaunted, she decided to build her dream home by bartering. She offered a place to put up a tent on a tropical island, plus food, in exchange for helping to build New Dawn. The students came. The first year was spent framing and the second doing electrical and plumbing. They used *Sunset How To* books to learn the skills. "When there is no one to do the work, you just figure it out," Gail says. "I learned from my husband how to make things happen. By that time I wasn't afraid to tackle anything. . . . I had enough self-confidence to know it would work.

"If you have enough desire and limited funds or resources, you can make things happen."

By the time her children were in college, New Dawn was finished. The focus has changed from a women's retreat to a retreat for anyone wanting to get away.

New Dawn is a potpourri of sensual delights that are nearly impossible to convey without being there. It's the way in, curving up the dirt driveway through a veritable produce display of trees bearing every fruited delight: banana, mango, star fruit, cashew, passion fruit, guava, key lime, papaya, plaintain, lemon, and coconut. It's the huge wrap-around deck that is filled with hammocks of all sizes and shapes where you can loll in the tropical breezes. It's the outdoor, solar-heated shower where you and nature stand together, sprayed by warm water on a balmy afternoon. No need for an indoor shower—it's warm every single day on Vieques. With an indoor shower you wouldn't be able to look up at the palms, pink-flowered orchid trees, red-petaled flamboyants and hibiscus, all swaying overhead. Nor would you share the space with 10-foot bougainvillea bushes that dip their flowered branches into the roofless shower stalls. This botanical splendor provides more than ambiance; it ensures a thoroughly private cleansing experience.

New Dawn's sensual delights extend into the evenings. Before the sun goes down, you can look out over the rolling hills of Vieques and see all the way to the tropical ocean. You can see as far as the island of St. Croix, 40 miles away. And when dusk falls and the air cools, the jungle comes alive with a symphony led by the coqui, a thumbnail-size frog native only to Puerto Rico. The coqui joins with crickets, cicadas, and other nocturnal life and creates a delightful, earthy melody of chirping, trilling, whistling, and buzzing. No sirens, speeding cars, or urban cacophony.

"I value the openness of time and space here," Gail says. "You don't have to make so many decisions, because there aren't so many choices. You don't have to worry about what you will do tonight. And the pace is so relaxed that you don't get upset when the people in the car ahead of you have stopped to talk to someone in the middle of the road. It's part of the life here.

"Nature is an equalizer. Without all of the extraneous, unnatural things that are man-made, you get away from that whole realm of competition that you find in the city. Following your heart is important, and Vieques takes up quite a piece of mine."

❖ ❖ ❖ ❖ ❖ ❖ ❖ ❖ ❖ ❖ ❖ ❖ ❖ ❖ ❖

Resources

The Couple's Comfort Book by Jennifer Louden (New York: HarperCollins, 1994)
In our busy world, it's often hard to stay connected, let alone committed. The book explores the special bond between couples and what can be done to keep the flame alive when so many forces seem set on squelching it.

Everyday Sacred by Sue Bender (New York: HarperCollins, 1995)
Subtitled "A Woman's Journey Home," the book is filled with stories and human experiences that teach about depth and meaning even in the most banal activity. Uses the metaphor of the monk's empty bowl that must be refilled every day as a way to look at life for what it can give and what our part is in filling it.

Gracious Living in a New World by Alexandra Stoddard (New York: William Morrow & Co., 1996)
The hectic world provides both the cause and the cure for what can be a more harmonious life if we know how to harness it. Simple strategies on turning erratic activity into gracious living.

Heart Centered Marriage by Sue Patton Thoele (Berkeley, CA: Conari Press, 1996)
Discusses ways to avoid pain and misery in a relationship as well as ways to turn conflict into discovery and greater passion. In the process love and marriage as mystery and a sacred relationship is encouraged.

Home Sweeter Home, Creating a Haven of Simplicity and Spirit by Jann Mitchell (Hillsboro, OR: Beyond Word Publishing, 1996)
Finding happiness in our homes and in ourselves. Offers tips on turning the modern home into a repository of nurturing, spiritual, and healing ways.

Living Beautifully Together by Alexandra Stoddard (New York: Avon Books, 1989)
Not just a relationship book but ways to stay sane, fruitful, and soulful to your surrounding world—friends, family, and the general world. Discussion on parenting included.

Romance on a Shoestring by Colleen Cramer (Seattle: Shoestring Publishers, 1995)
Offers interesting, regional (Northwest) suggestions, but the ideas can be adapted anywhere.

Simple Abundance, a Daybook of Comfort and Joy by Sarah Ban Breathnach (New York: Warner Books, 1995)
Spiritual insights on a daily basis. The 366 essays blend old-fashioned wisdom with New Age inspiration intended to turn life into a daily source of awe and majesty. Even the dull can be turned into gold by the adept practitioner.

Slowing Down in a Speeded Up World by Adair Lara (Berkeley, CA: Conari Press, 1994)
Ways to slow down the thunderbird race and what to do with the sudden new bubble of time that you have. Filled with stories of people who have slowed down and lived to tell about it.

True Love—How to Make Your Relationship Sweeter, Deeper and More Passionate by Daphne Rose Kingma (Berkeley, CA: Conari Press, 1994)
What to do to make the stale relationship into something worth writing home about. Includes tips on having fun with your partner, how to be romantic if you haven't been in a long time, and finding more passion in your bond.

6
Virtues

In the beginning, love, in the end,
love, in the middle, we have to
cultivate virtues.

—SWAMI CHIDVILASANANDA

he essence of simplicity is living from the core of your being. We all have an inner core in there somewhere, sometimes more buried, sometimes more accessible. When we project to the world who we really are—our highest and best self—our lives naturally become more serene and simplified. We can name this essence—our soul, our inner being, our highest and truest self. And we can name the outward emanations of that essence—our virtues. Sometimes it helps to put labels on things because doing so gives us a framework. Michelangelo was once asked about the process of creating a great sculpture. He answered that all he did was cut away what was not the sculpture. Our highest self is in there, waiting.

When we practice living virtues such as honesty, respect, love, and compassion, we draw those same virtues back to us. When we are disrespectful to people or react emotionally with anger and impatience, our lives feel out of control. Living our virtues gives us the tools we need to lead a good life. We no longer need to complicate our lives by looking for answers outside ourselves. And we don't need to spend time wondering whom we said what to or how to act around certain people. We know we've done our best in all situations, so we don't fret that we "should have" or "could have." All of this wondering and fretting takes up an enormous amount of energy that often results in a more outwardly chaotic life. We've all been there.

In the 5th century A.D., the philosopher Epictetus taught that a virtuous life leads to inner coherence and outward harmony. He wrote: "There is great relief in being morally consistent: The soul relaxes, and we can thus efficiently move forward in our endeavors, without hindrance." In modern-day terms, this means that when we consistently act from our highest place (virtues) we have a more relaxed life because we know we are doing our best. Indeed, Epictetus asks us to minimize the importance we would place on "external" choices, what we might call "lifestyle choices," and to concentrate instead on our inner moral code of behavior.

When we don't act from our inner moral code, we feel off balance inside. As Sharon Lebell writes in *The Art of Living*, "The inconsistent feeling that something is not right with our lives and the longing to be restored to our better selves will not go away."

The remedy is to live according to our virtues, and this will simplify our lives immensely. Epictetus wrote: "When your thoughts, words, and deeds form a seamless fabric, you streamline your efforts and thus eliminate worry and dread. In this way, it is easier to seek goodness than to conduct yourself in a haphazard fashion or according to the feelings of the moment."

Virtues have been described as the essence of soulfulness. As Linda Kavelin Popov writes in *Sacred Moments: Daily Meditations on the Virtues:* "An act of love or justice, or creativity or any of our other virtues is essentially an expression of our spirituality." Linda also describes virtues as the gems hidden in the mine of the true self: "Unless we see them, name them and use them, they are lost to us, although they are always waiting, like treasures, to be found. But it takes some digging."

When Linda decided it was time to give a gift to the world, she sat down with her husband and brother and created her first book, titled *The Family Virtues Guide.* The trio combed through the world's religions and discovered common virtues, such as compassion, honesty, and generosity. They named 52 of these virtues, one for every week of the year, and created their book to be a guide for parents to teach virtues to children. The guide explains each virtue and discusses how to incorporate it into our lives.

Popov became my virtues mentor. I began teaching the virtues to my children and realized how important they were in my own life. Then I realized how living the virtues could simplify my life. Here are a few virtues that can simplify your life.

Contentment

Contentment is one of the hallmarks of a simple life. One of the most difficult aspects of being human is to curtail our insatiable desire for *more*. We spend the majority of our waking hours wanting something and striving to get it. As soon as we get one thing, we're off wanting another. It could be tangibles, such as a new car, new house, new sweater, new job. It could be intangibles, such as more love, more perfect children, more this and more that. Whatever it is, we are rarely satisfied. One of my favorite quotes is "True wealth comes not from having more but in wanting less."

So true, but so elusive. So elusive that an entire book has been written about the subject, titled *How to Want What You Have*, by Timothy Miller. Miller says that to want what you have is to think, act, and feel as if ordinary existence is sacred. Aldous Huxley said in his 1945 book *The Perennial Philosophy*, "A person's single most important task is to discover the divinity of ordinary things, ordinary lives, and ordinary minds."

Focusing on the virtue of contentment can help us *begin* to learn to appreciate what is right in front of us. Every single person I have interviewed for my newsletter, *Simple Living*, told me that once they began to simplify their lives, they also began to appreciate what was right in front of them. They needed and wanted less entertainment. One woman who had moved to the country told me, "Look out the window. It's beautiful. Absolutely beautiful. We have time to watch the hawks dive, I can watch the rainbows forming and the clouds drifting. . . . I can do that for just five minutes, and it can totally change my outlook for the day, even if I've been working really hard." Another couple stopped spending a fortune on nighttime entertainment and found more satisfaction in taking a small picnic to a river to watch the sun go down.

When we stop running on automatic pilot, we begin to notice that there is a world of wonder right at our feet. We find just a bit more contentment in small things. We become aware of our desires.

It's important to remember something about contentment. Being content doesn't mean giving up hope of things to come in the future; it doesn't mean stopping your growth; it doesn't mean becoming apathetic and giving up. It does mean focusing more on what is at hand. Instead of living for the future (I'll be happy as soon as I get my new car; I'll be happy as soon as my kids are in college; I'll be happy as soon as I find a new lover; I'll be happy as soon as I get the promotion . . .), being content means enjoying today. You can plan for the future and have hope in the future, but remember fully to enjoy and live in the present while you're at it.

Popov quotes from Thich Nhat Han in *Sacred Moments:* "We use hope to believe something better will happen in the future, that we will arrive at peace, or the Kingdom of God. Hope becomes a kind of obstacle. If you can refrain from hoping, you can bring yourself entirely into the present moment and discover the joy that is already here."

Order

Order is another hallmark of the simple life. Think about how much easier it is when you can find what you're looking for or when your bookkeeping is up to date. And how smoothly your life runs when your schedule (work and social) feels orderly. When we take on too much, we feel chaotic, rushed, and stressed.

Popov said she stopped labeling herself "scattered" when she realized that she had the virtue of order within her. Now she says her home and office are incredibly orderly and beautiful. It took her three days, for example, to decide what she wanted on her mantel. She wanted one special artifact rather than the hodgepodge of things that sat there before. She removed a lot of furniture and opened up a lot of space.

Order means not owning more than you can properly use, care for, and store easily. When we accumulate too much stuff, we don't know where to put it. Some of us even buy larger houses or remodel kitchens just to enable us to store more and more gadgets. The more we take on, the harder it becomes to find things, the more time we have to spend figuring out where to put our stuff, and the more energy we need to invest in cleaning and rearranging it all. Am I guilty of this? You bet. Does my life become a bit easier and easier the more I get rid of? You bet.

Think about how order relates to beauty. I recall a time when the home decorating fad was to mix and match all sorts of patterns. Supposedly, this gave your house sort of an eclectic look. What it really did was make people restless with so many things competing for attention all at once. Then think about the beauty of a more serene environment. Japanese houses are known for this. You feel restful when you walk in. And think about the beauty of, say, a single rose in a beautiful vase. Why do we need a tabletop of artifacts and what-nots jammed on there like crowds at a Christmas sale? Have I been guilty of this too? Absolutely. But more and more I find that less and less is better, so long as nothing is too extreme.

All the people with children are surely jumping up and down at this paragraph. "Who is she kidding anyway? A serene environment with kids?"

Let's back up. Order and serenity don't mean we all ought to go live in a monastery with only a wooden bed and chair in our rooms (although sometimes this idea does seem appealing). I personally like a reasonable amount of "lived-in" mess. When everything is perfect and tidy, I feel as if I shouldn't be there, and I certainly shouldn't relax too much. Other people feel more comfortable with nothing out of place and very little in the room. We each need to find our own level.

For me, the balance is having a lived-in level of comfort plus serenity. Both are possible with or without kids. First, kids don't need every kind of toy imaginable, and those they do have can be stored in an orderly way. This will teach them the value of being able to find what they are looking for without turning the house upside down. Plus, kids can't possibly play with everything all of the time. Just like grown-ups, we can't play with or use everything all of the time. We go crazy with too many choices. A little open space on a child's toy shelf is a beautiful thing. And when kids take out their toys, they don't need to leave them all over the house. Whatever happened to the rule of play with one toy at a time? Put one back before taking out another.

With or without kids, we don't need to overdecorate our houses, either. In fact, the less adult stuff families with children have to worry about, the easier their lives will be. I for one spend enough time trying to get the kids to pick up their things that I sure as heck don't want to spend any more time than necessary picking up my own. So the less I own, the better. I can still have a lived-in, comfortable house with far fewer gizmos. For instance, if the newspaper is lying around, that's fine with me so long as it gets picked up reasonably soon. If a pair of shoes is lying in the middle of the room, I know someone I love has been there and that makes me feel good. I smile when I find my son's paper airplanes lying in corners and my daughter's half-finished art projects sitting next to a stack of crayons on the floor. These kinds of things give a house a feeling of love and warmth; a thousand knickknacks and gadgets give it a feeling of chaos and confusion. Go through your house and keep only the things you really love and that give you a sense of pleasure. Make a commitment to create beauty in your environment.

You also can create order by having your papers, tools, gadgets, and checkbook organized. None of this can happen if you have too many of these things, or if you have scheduled your life so tightly that you don't have time to keep up with your checkbook and filing. This is the kind of order that brings peace into our lives.

Truthfulness

Being truthful (in a gentle, caring way) is one of the easiest ways to simplify your life. Think of Shakespeare's classic phrase: "Oh what a tangled web we weave." What this means is that when we are not truthful, we need to spend a lot of energy trying to remember what we said to whom. Think about the stress involved when you have an affair and lie to your partner. How simple your life would be if you didn't operate a dual life.

Truthfulness means being honest about your feelings and being real about who you are. Being honest about your feelings doesn't mean running around telling everyone your darkest thoughts or telling people a lot of negative things about them (what's the point?); it means being who you are. It means living from your essence—your core—and not putting on an act in order to impress others. I remember I finally felt that I'd reached a true level of acceptance of myself when I could admit to people that my favorite old show on television was *I Love Lucy*. *I Love Lucy* has absolutely no intellectual stimulation and few redeeming qualities, except that it is total airheaded, relaxing fun. I no longer felt that I had to impress others with my intelligence or dazzle them with intellectual interests I had or didn't have. I also abandoned a law career to return to my longtime love of writing. I no longer cared if people thought I was nifty because I was or wasn't a lawyer.

Truthfulness also means relating to others in a gentle and real way. If you like somebody, what a wonderful gift to tell him or her. If you are feeling sad, how comforting to be real and be accepted by someone who cares rather than putting on a false face and smiling like a cheerleader. Being real in this way takes a lot less energy. Putting on false fronts, having affairs, or telling lies keeps us filled with inner turmoil. The heart of simplicity is having inner peace, and we can be peaceful only when we are truthful and real.

Joy

Joy is similar to contentment, but different. If we have joy in our hearts, our lives can be much simpler because we won't need so much outside stimulation to keep us going. I began thinking about this virtue when I watched waiters and waitresses, for example. Doesn't matter if it's in an expensive, upscale restaurant or a roadside diner. Some of these people are crabby and tight-lipped. You can tell they're in the job for some miserable reason. Maybe it's all they're qualified to do. Maybe they're going to school and the hours are flexible. But they don't want to be there and it shows. Then you look at other people in the same job. They are joyful. Doesn't matter what job they have; these people have an inner joy that radiates and makes everyone else feel good. They're not the least bit embarrassed at being a waiter or waitress. They do the best job they can no matter what the job. I went to a public place one day during holiday season. I was happy to see a janitor pushing around his cleaning cart wearing a Santa Claus hat. He stopped and chatted with children and smiled at everyone. What a delight! Contrast this to someone who hates being a janitor and can't wait to do something else. I'd rather see and be around a joyful janitor any day than a downtrodden rocket scientist.

This same theory applies to our own lives. In the book, *Chop Wood, Carry Water*, the theme is to find joy in mundane chores such as chopping wood and carrying water. We have to clean toilets, we need to wash dishes, we need to do laundry, we need to weed our yards, so we may as well do these chores with a joyful attitude. What's the point of doing them with a snarling attitude when they have to get done anyway? Don't start thinking I'm some joyful zealot who sings while cleaning the toilet. Don't think I never get crabby doing mundane chores. But do think that I am constantly looking for new and creative ways to enjoy these things I have to do anyway.

Joy is what you make it.

Many of us have lost our sense of joy because we've become jaded by advertising that encourages us to find joy outside of ourselves. When our entire existence is spent pursuing one external stimulus after the other, we lose our ability to find joy where we are, in everyday existence. And it's not only advertising that encourages us to buy things to be happy. Our entire culture tells us we need to keep striving to reach the top where we will finally be happy. The theory is that we won't be truly happy until we get to wherever that "top" is.

In a book titled *Finding Joy*, author Charlotte Davis Kasl tells us that finding joy is about changing our attitudes. Chapter titles are illustrative, such as: "You Can Be Late and Upset or You Can Simply Be Late." Not that she's telling us to be rude and late all of the time, but rather, when we are occasion-

> *Joy gives us wings! In times of joy our strength is more vital, our intellect keener, and our understanding less clouded. We seem better able to cope with the world and to find our sphere of influence.*
>
> —'ABDU'L-BAHA',
> QUOTED IN LINDA KAVELIN POPOV'S
> *THE FAMILY VIRTUES GUIDE*

ally late, we can change our attitudes. When you're stuck in traffic and there isn't a thing you can do, you may as well change your attitude and lighten up. Getting wound up hardly simplifies your life. You're irritated, your irritation infects those around you, and this attitude may well land you in the hands of your friendly ulcer doctor.

Another chapter in *Finding Joy* is titled "If Someone's Throwing Garbage Out the Window, Move." Charlotte got this theme from a psychologist friend who told her she couldn't stop the garbage from falling out of the window, but she sure could step out of the way. Our alternative is to, what, sue these people? Lighten up, lighten up, lighten up. Lightening up makes our ordinary moments more interesting. Life becomes eminently simpler when we lighten up. We're not embroiled in battles within ourselves, and we're not embroiled in battles with others. This doesn't mean that we go out and erase all boundaries of decent behavior and let everything slide. It means finding balance. You can go so far in being "right" that you'll "right" yourself into a corner with no friends. You also can let everyone walk all over you. Neither is a good option. Maintain your boundaries with a joyful attitude, and once in a while, it doesn't hurt to soften up a bit.

Patience

All good things come to those who wait. We've all heard this phrase, and nowhere is it more true than as a slogan for the simple life. Probably the number-one reason why most people are in debt, for example, is lack of patience. They must have everything *right now*. Doesn't matter if they have the money right now, a credit card will suffice. Next thing they know they are in debt up to you-know-where and wondering how it all happened.

A little patience pays off. We don't need everything we see right now. We can live just fine without it. I've been in both positions. Usually I don't live on credit and actually abhor it, because debt means I need to keep working whether I'm in the mood or not. Nevertheless, during one period I got into the instant gratification mode of credit card spending. When I saw something I wanted, I whipped out the plastic. I accumulated more than my share of junk; much of it now lies buried in my basement. Now I'm back to my usual way of buying something only when I have the money. No matter how much my voice of desire stomps up and down and screams and yells, I don't give in because I don't want to be in debt. So I wait. If it is something that important, I will still want it when I have the cash. If it is not important, it will wash out

Acts of Loving Kindness

by Marilyn Meyer

When my daughter Molly was six, her friend Teru prepared to run away by packing most of her clothes in small plastic bags. Molly advised Teru that she herself had considered running away once but then realized, "Where would I go? I can't cross streets. What would I eat? I'd just starve, so I decided not to." But when Teru refused Molly's wise counsel, Molly ran downstairs to request emergency intervention from Teru's mother. "Becky, Teru won't listen to me. She's still running away. I think she needs a grown-up."

Ours is a violent world and our children are bombarded daily by the press, television, movies, and certainly video games with visual examples of humanity's inhumanity to animals, plants, our waters, soil, and one another. In the introduction to *Kids' Random Acts of Kindness*, psychologist Dawna Markova asks, "What can we do that will foster their open-hearted hopefulness, engage their need to collaborate? What if instead of condemning the darkness, we turn our children toward the light . . . What if we show them ways they can connect, reach out, weave themselves into the web of relationships that is called community?"

In Hebrew there is no word for charity, but there are several expressions for acts of kindness. *Mitzvot* are the mandated acts—respecting your parents, grandparents, and children, giving food to the poor, caring for orphans, widows, and strangers. *Tzedakah* are the righteous acts we model for our children by donating food and clothing, inviting others to share our holiday dinner, and also such virtues as education, hard work, honesty, and thrift. *Gimelut hasidim*, acts of loving kindness, are the little things, the unsolicited gestures that are gifts of love and empathy. *Tkun olam* (repair of the earth) are the acts as small as picking up Styrofoam litter, as large as saving rain forests and negotiating peace in Bosnia.

One does not have to be a Talmudic scholar of Jewish law to model acts of kindness.

Each one of us is a teacher; we instruct by what we do rather than by what we say. We teach our children how to care not only by giving them pet guinea pigs to raise but by loving and caring for our own elderly parents.

Society can pass on generosity of spirit to future generations only through deeds. Many of these acts are deliberate, not merely *random* acts of kindness. Children may not understand check writing, but they do comprehend what it means to box their own toys and donate them to the less fortunate. For many years my children have assisted me in a citywide toy drive. One of my daughter Genevieve's warmest memories of junior high was the day members of her eighth-grade class made lunches, then packed them into brown bags and distributed them to homeless individuals.

with the tide of other desire-infested refuse and I won't even remember what it was. I have never had to consult a psychiatrist because I couldn't buy something I wanted on the spot.

> *If there is a sin against life, it consists perhaps not so much in despairing of life as in hoping for another life and in eluding the implacable grandeur of this life.*
>
> —ALBERT CAMUS

As for money, patience definitely pays off in the long run. Not only do you stay out of debt, but you accumulate a nest egg through patience as well. When you put a little money aside every month, it will grow into a big pot in a few years. But it takes patience to persevere. You need to be willing to put off a few things today in order to have more comfort tomorrow.

Patience also means waiting for life and not expecting it to happen in an instant. This virtue becomes more and more difficult to incorporate into our lives the more technical the world becomes. With fax machines, E-mail, pagers, and cell phones, we expect to be able to connect with each other instantly. We get upset if we can't. Yikes! Let's give ourselves a break, puhleez! What if we don't feel like being contacted instantly? I belong to this group. Simple living has taught me that I don't need to go with the flow just because the world is. I am modern enough that I have an answering machine, but that's as far as I want to go, thank you very much. My kids and I eat dinner by candlelight most nights, and we don't answer the phone then. I've been to people's houses where they do answer the phone during dinner (and I used to be one of those). I will admit to feeling, well, not-so-special when my hosts hop up from the table to answer every confounded ring.

Patience also means trusting. You know how some people call you a zillion times before you get back to them? They think if they don't keep after you, what they want will not happen. A little quiet waiting is good for the soul and shows others that you trust they will come through for you. Patience also means trusting in yourself and having the courage to keep going when you don't feel like it. I'm sure not one of us has sailed through school with no difficult periods. It would be easier to quit and goof off. Patience is what carries us through—knowing we are building for something in the future.

I am constantly struck by the patience and determination of people I interview for *Simple Living*. They have an idea of the kind of life they want to lead and are not deterred by the glittering sideshow of commercialism. They're willing to forgo certain material luxuries in exchange for simplicity.

They're willing to make things or do repairs themselves in exchange for instant repair or an instant new item. Patience pays off for these people by giving them a life that is more serene and fulfilling.

Assertiveness and Tact

The two virtues of assertiveness and tact complement one another and, when practiced, can make your personal life much easier. Assertiveness means saying what you think and how you feel, and tact means saying these things in a gentle, nonoffensive way. We get into more trouble in relationships by not being direct or by being tactless and hurting people's feelings. Sometimes we attempt to control other people to give us what we want through criticism or verbal assault. If we call on the virtues of assertiveness and tact, instead of trying to control the other person to meet our needs, we make a simple, positive request. For example, if your partner seems to be away from you for more hours than you'd like, you could say, "I need to have regular time with you to just be together." This delivers a much more effective message than "You don't care about me," or "obviously I don't mean anything to you . . ."

When we are tactless, we embroil ourselves in angry or unfulfilled relationships. We express ourselves without stopping to think about how our words will affect other people. We can hardly simplify our lives when we're not getting along with people who are important to us. And when we are not assertive, nobody knows what we want or need, so we go around with long faces wondering why people aren't cooperating. When I was younger, if I was angry at say, a boyfriend, and he would ask me what was wrong, I would snort and say, "Oh, nothing. Just go away." Then, of course, I'd be upset that he didn't do whatever I thought he ought to be doing. I didn't have the nerve to tell him what I wanted. And it does take nerve to tell people how we're feeling. We're always afraid we'll hurt their feelings, or they won't understand, or they'll be angry, whatever. Over the years I've learned that it's worth it to get past my fear and say how I'm feeling. If I do so in a tactful way, I can expect a tactful response and we can begin the process of solving whatever issue we have. There is no hope of solving issues without tact and assertiveness. When little problems lay unresolved, they ultimately erupt like volcanoes and the relationship suffers enormously. An embroiled life is hardly a simple one.

It is difficult to be assertive when we are not in the habit of being honest and real about who we are. If we constantly project ourselves to the world as either the cheerleader or strong, has-it-all-together type, for example, it is much more difficult to be assertive when we need help or comfort. Projecting our real image to the world takes confidence. We need to feel like our ideas and opinions are valuable. It also takes confidence to be tactful. When we're buried in our problems or our lives are chaotic, we don't have the time, energy, or awareness to stop and think about how the other person may be feeling before we open our mouths.

Tactful assertiveness is a valuable behavior to model to our children. Without assertiveness, they won't have the nerve to stand up and tell their peers that something doesn't feel right. They might see other kids picking on someone and say nothing. They might be encouraged to smoke or drink and not have the nerve to say no. We need to remember that our children won't learn these virtues unless we practice them ourselves.

Creativity

By far the most common virtue I've encountered in the people I've interviewed for this book is creativity. I have been impressed by the creative things they have done in order to design fulfilling lives for themselves and their families. I began to take note of this after I worked on Chapter 11, "Housing." I was amazed at what these people created in order to have more affordable housing. All of them turned their backs on the status quo and took a look at entirely new options that made more sense to them. They really had to have their eyes open to new ideas and solutions. What a far cry from passively going with the flow because everyone else is doing it, whether it feels right to you or not.

When my friend Taso and I wrote the first column on dating for *Simple Living,* I instantly called it creative dating. This was because it takes creativity to come up with a date that is interesting and inexpensive. Readers sent in more creative dating ideas and, once again, I was excited to see the level of innovation. It was the same with people I interviewed for Chapter 4, "Work." Not one settled for business-as-usual if it didn't feel right.

Creativity means opening your box, tearing down the sides, and stretching out to discover new ways of looking at and doing things that will improve your life. The less buried you are in debt, overcommitted time, and junk, the more freed up you are to think of innovative solutions. What a delight to discover these new paths, and what a way to keep our energy renewed.

Creativity also can take hard work. I am reminded of that truth when I think of a statement by Red Smith, quoted in *Sacred Moments:* "Writing is easy. All you do is sit staring at the blank piece of paper until the drops of blood form on your forehead." As with all other virtues, often the highest way is not initially the easiest. Stepping out of a box takes energy. I remember a man who taught log house building told me that his students often complained of the hard work involved in learning this skill and in doing the actual building. He reminded them: "You think this is hard work? I think hard work is paying a mortgage for 30 years."

When we apply creative solutions to our own lives, we also are freed up to think of how we can help others creatively. Probably the most heartwarming example of this kind of creativity is Mother Teresa. She saw a need and filled it. Once we attain this level of creative simplicity, inner peace is just within reach.

The Sensuality of Simplicity

Create sacred time and space for yourself. Find or make a restful, beautiful corner in your house. You don't need a whole room; any corner that can be quiet will do. Put some comfortable pillows on the floor, perhaps include a little table where you can have a scented candle and maybe a flower. Let the aroma and the quiet surround you. Feel your skin on the soft fabric of the pillow. Take a few deep breaths, and sit quietly for 20 minutes. Think about a virtue you need to call on for something that is going on in your life. A routine of reverence is an important personal discipline that is very life giving.

FOR ASHLEY HUTCHINSON, GIVING IS THE SAME AS RECEIVING

Ashley Hutchinson left for Calcutta, India, with bags packed full of her lofty ideals; she was going to give of herself to the poor. When she arrived, she wrote to friends that "Everything you could ever imagine cannot prepare you for what I am now living." She gave to the poor and returned with something new: spiritual richness.

Hutchinson was following a lifelong dream to work with Mother Teresa at the home for the dying in Calcutta. She first wrote to Mother Teresa in 1975 to ask if she could work with her. "I had felt a calling," Hutchinson says. "Every time I'd see a picture of her or hear about her, a part of me wanted to touch her life. So one day I sat down at the typewriter and addressed it to Calcutta, India, hoping she would get the letter." Mother Teresa answered Hutchinson's letter, but it wasn't until 15 years later that the American with high ideals was ready to go. "The calling was so strong, I knew if I didn't go to Calcutta I couldn't live with myself," she says.

During those 15 years, Hutchinson raised her two sons, went through a divorce, and lived a life she describes as a normal one based on acquiring and working. Four years ago something changed in her. "I started not to want a car and I wasn't so concerned with clothes," she says. "When this process started people would say, 'Get real, in the 20th century you can't live without a car, VISA, and CD player.' But I *was* doing it! I felt so free and happy! It was a spiritual preparation for going to India."

Hutchinson's desire became a magnet. Soon people came to her with information about India and offers of help. One day her son went to a bookstore in the United States to find information on Calcutta for his mother, and a man offered her the use of his apartment there. She was also given eight boxes of donated medical supplies to take with her. Her trip became reality.

"I met Mother Teresa," Hutchinson says. "There is an aura about her . . . a peacefulness . . . her eyes are ageless and full of light." Every day Hutchinson went to work in the clinic—a large cement room with cots low to the floor and filled with the sick and dying people of Calcutta. She saw poverty and disease that she'd never imagined. She washed the feet of lepers. She learned she could love anyone.

Hutchinson was told by people who had gone before her that she would be changed when she returned and, indeed, she was. "It is how I view everything . . . especially the surplus and stockpiling we've been taught to do. Now I feel suffocated by all of this stuff. I buy one or two bandages now instead of a box full. I want to share more now. In Calcutta, no matter how little people have, they want to share with you. I admired a bracelet a young man was wearing as we rode the bus. He said he would be honored if I had it. An elderly couple who had two tangerines sat next to me one time and offered me one. There is no 'this is mine'; they are honored if you would share with them."

Hutchinson says she found stress in Calcutta, but of a very different nature from the stress many people live with in the United States. "In the U.S., we have big 'time' stress. We put ourselves in a horrible time stress here. In Calcutta, life is far less stressful even if you don't have material things."

Yet, she says, people in Calcutta want to come to America because they see us on TV. "They want to make money and buy things. We have convinced them that you're happy if you have things. They don't know we have stress, unemployment, and homelessness," she says.

Hutchinson returned when her daughter-in-law was ready to deliver her baby. She was prepared to combine her life in Calcutta with life in the United States, but it is a difficult transition, she says. "I returned with a feeling that I am grateful for what I have, but it is difficult. When I was in Calcutta, I had only two sets of clothing. Each day we would come home and wash one outfit in a bucket of water while we wore the other one. How would that work here at a job? Coming to work every day with the same outfit? People don't accept that."

Ashley Hutchinson says she learned a lot from working with Mother Teresa.

Still, Hutchinson lives without a car. She rides the bus or walks and is thankful she doesn't have car payments, gas, upkeep, or insurance. The few times she needs a car, she rents one. "It takes longer to get around on the bus," she says, "but I have learned to relax and think about what life is all about instead of getting so caught up in the routine of work and home, work and home. Walking helps me to be more peaceful. Walking to work, for example, allows me to center my thoughts."

Making a journey like this is very personal for each person, Hutchinson says. "No one can say it is better there than here, but I made up my mind not to judge. I learned a lot there about spiritual richness and about slowing down. I used to take high blood pressure pills and don't need them anymore. And I was a worrywart. I wanted everything everybody else had. I was jealous.

"Going to India confirmed that what I had been doing was right for me," she says. "People tell me I am crazy for wanting to go back to the filth and disease, but I found that when I helped the people, the giving was the same as receiving. I get filled so much.

"In our society, we believe that if you give something away you lose it, but I've learned that you gain. It is a feeling of contentment and happiness that you get. And it is not out of guilt that I want to simplify my life here or return to work in Calcutta. I don't think starving myself here would help the people in India. It is because I can honestly say with all my heart that I don't want the affluence that I used to have. There is a new richness for me. People in Calcutta would open their house and never feel put out no matter what time of day it was. This is their richness, to have people to share it with. I could not walk down a village road any morning without people asking me to tea.

"They recognize the oneness that makes us all the same. That invisible essence we all have inside of us."

What is the meaning of life for Ashley Hutchinson? "To always be thankful and grateful and content with what I have and to know what really makes me happy is the feeling of peace that comes with sharing what I do have. And to live according to what I need, not what I want."

❖ ❖ ❖ ❖ ❖ ❖ ❖ ❖ ❖ ❖ ❖ ❖ ❖ ❖ ❖ ❖

Resources

The Family Virtues Guide by Linda Kavelin Popov, John Kavelin, and Dan Popov (New York: Penguin, 1997)
Describes 52 virtues, one for each week of the year. Written for parents to teach virtues to their children. Includes discussion questions.

Epictetus: The Art of Living: The Classic Manual on Virtue, Happiness, and Effectiveness by Sharon Lebell (HarperSanFrancisco, 1994)
A new interpretation. Epictetus was born a slave and became a philosopher in about A.D. 55. He shares with us 93 instructions that show the way to happiness, fulfillment, and tranquillity, no matter what our circumstances happen to be.

Finding Joy, 101 Ways to Free Your Spirit and Dance with Life by Charlotte Davis Kasl, Ph.D. (New York: HarperCollins, 1994)
Based on the premise that many if not most answers lie within, the book contains 101 suggestions to a more developed life. The boundary between the outer and inner worlds is not a large river separating two countries, but a thin line with a two-way flow. The keys to balancing the two worlds are in the use of joy, awe, and reverence for life.

How to Want What You Have by Timothy Miller, Ph.D. (New York: Henry Holt & Co., 1995)
Compassion, attention, and gratitude are central cores to a fruitful, serene existence. Selfishness bankrupts the soul and contributes to a mean, unenlightened life. By using tenets from Eastern philosophy, Miller shows that we are richer than we think we are and how taming desire can lead to freedom and soul enrichment.

Sacred Moments, Daily Meditations on the Virtues by Linda Kavelin Popov (New York: Penguin, 1996)
Provides a list of topics ("Virtue of Love," "Virtue of Humility," etc.) As they relate to daily meditation and reflection. Quotes, brief stories, anecdotes from a welter of sources help to explain and diagnose each virtue. Borrows heavily from a variety of world religions.

7
Families

Teach a child to choose the right path,
and when he is older he will remain
upon it.

—PROVERBS 22:6

I learned about simple living and children from my own mom. She always had time for her kids, no matter what. She kept her life open enough that I never felt as if she were trying to "fit me in" to her busy schedule—she taught me the value of letting kids simply "be" with flowing, unstructured time. Because her own life wasn't crammed, she was able to have unlimited patience for her children.

Value Your Family Time

My own children were my impetus for wanting to simplify my life. I had them in the busy, get-ahead, me-first, must-look-important-and-successful 1980s, when so many women, me included, struggled with our identities. I wondered how I could merge the 1950s values that my mom lived with my 1980s and '90s life.

When my kids got older and began connecting with friends, I saw children thrown into the same frenzy and busy schedules as the adults—day care from morning till night, soccer on Monday, gymnastics on Tuesday, chess club on Wednesday, this on Thursday, and that on Friday. Not to mention more of the same on Saturday. I was exhausted thinking about it. Oftentimes when parents experience a loss of leisure as a result of their own speeded-up lives, they inadvertently put more pressure on their children for rapid achievement. They do this by overprogramming them. *Time* magazine once described this sad phenomenon: "If parents see parenting largely as an investment of their precious time, they may end up viewing children as objects to be improved rather than individuals to be nurtured at their own pace."

One week I brought my kids with me to attend a health seminar in a retreat center in the country. The simple living turning point for me was when I watched my children and a few others spend one entire afternoon rolling rocks down a hill to see whose rock could go farthest. A whole afternoon! I thought, This is the job of childhood—free-flowing, unstructured time so kids can create, think, ponder, dilly dally, and invent. When I returned to the city I was immediately caught up in the city frenzy. "Oh, gosh, if I don't enroll my kids in ballet and karate right now they'll start losing out. All the other kids are starting now so I'd better hurry." On and on.

Then I remembered the rock incident. I was torn. The city was so full of seductive activities of all kinds, each one guaranteed somehow to make my kids more successful, interesting, well-rounded, athletic, intelligent. Most other city kids were doing this, and I didn't want mine to be left out. What to do . . . what to do?

After much soul searching, I opted for conscious balance. Conscious balance means that I am fully aware of my motivations for making choices. If the choice is based on insecurity, I look hard at the insecurity. A typical insecurity is this: If I don't enroll my kids in everything under the sun right now, they'll lose the race because all the other kids are doing it. I decided that although many of the activities were enriching, it was just as important to have calm, unscheduled, unstructured time. We could still have a few enriching activities but nothing that would interfere in our family life.

> *Allow children to be happy in their own way, for what better way will they ever find?*
>
> —Dr. Samuel Johnson

We schedule activities after school rather than after dinner. Sometimes we agree to schedule an activity on one night a week after dinner, but no more. (Weekends are more flexible.) This is because it is a value to me to have a relaxed, peaceful dinner at night with the kids where we come together, with

Mothering as a Spiritual Path
by Melissa West

I sat on a back porch with my mother and daughter in Montgomery, Alabama, one humid southern evening last summer and realized that just one breath, one heartbeat ago, I was in my young daughter's place, sitting with my own mother and grandmother in the damp and fragrant heat. In yet just another breath, another heartbeat, I realized as well, I would be in my mother's place, rocking with my own daughter and granddaughter. How quickly time passes. How quickly the chance to practice open-hearted parenting slips through our hands. How precious this brief time we are given with our children truly is. Ask yourself: "If I were to go through one typical day with my children with this tender, bittersweet awareness of the fleetness and fragility of time in my heart, how would it change my life as a parent?"

candles on the table, and center ourselves. We can talk about the day and share our lives with each other. We can't do that when we are on the run. In order to maintain the focus on a centered family, I also don't schedule adult activities on certain evenings either. It doesn't matter whether I can get a baby-sitter to stay home with the kids while I zoom out the door. I tried it a couple of times and realized this is not the kind of life I want for myself or my children. To me, it's just as disruptive seeing other family members in a frenzy as it is to be in one yourself. What kind of message am I giving my children if I'm too busy to value our family time, or if I'm always on the run? Once in a while when something important comes up, fine. But as a regular or semiregular thing? Nope, it conflicts with my larger value. This doesn't mean I never enjoy adult activities—it means that I schedule them *around* my family time rather than fitting my kids into available open spots in the schedule. Maybe everyone in your family can decide that, say, every Wednesday or Thursday night is do-your-own-thing night. If so, then don't schedule anything on the other nights. Everyone will need to make choices, but the result will be a more calm, centered family life.

I remembered when I was a kid, I never felt like I was hauled around from one frenzied activity to the next, and I appreciated it. I appreciated being able to be alone in my room, or making up little inventions on the kitchen table, or hanging out aimlessly with my friends. Why did I want to give my kids anything less than what I appreciated? Certainly there are exceptions, but those are exceptions rather than the rule. I have had to say no to all sorts of enticing opportunities for both child and adult activities, but the choice has been made consciously, and I am happy about it.

There is another aspect of giving time to your children. A study by the Addiction Research Foundation in Toronto, Canada, which examined connections between family life and smoking, heaving drinking, and drug use, found that youths who feel relationships within the family are important and who spend time with their families were much less likely to engage in drug use and other problem behaviors.

Sometimes busy parents opt for the "quality time" rationale as a way to spend this important time with children. They do this by making appointments with their kids. "Making an appointment is one way to relate to your child," says a UCLA anthropologist, "but it's pretty desiccated. You've got to hang around with your kids." "Yet," *Time* magazine reported, "hanging-around time is the first thing to go. The very culture of children, of freedom and fantasy and kids teaching kids to play jacks, is collapsing under the weight of hectic family schedules."

Be a Role Model

Besides making conscious choices for your family, you also need to be a good role model. Every rule that applies to simplifying your own life applies to simplifying your life with children. The overriding principle is this: *Practice what you preach.* Naturally, we parents can't teach our children any of these concepts if we aren't modeling them ourselves. If we are living in debt, for example, how can we teach our children to live within their means? If we are rushing through our days on automatic, how can we share with our children the joys of living consciously and with purpose?

In addition to practicing what you preach, it is equally important to remember to practice and preach in a joyful way. If we look at simplicity as deprivation, then we can hardly expect our children to be excited about the prospect. But if we simplify our lives in a positive way, children will see that simplicity is joyful and rewarding. One way to present simplicity in a positive way is to remember to present your day-to-day decisions as a choice rather than deprivation. The scheduling issue is one example, and how you spend money is another. Think about this: If every time your kids want you to buy something, and your answer is always "We can't afford it," then the logic is that simplifying is deprivation, and as soon as we get more money we will buy all these things.

When our answer is presented as a conscious choice, then children (and adults) can understand that this particular choice is simply a step toward a better, more balanced life.

Here is one money example from my own life: When I needed to replace my car, I decided to buy a good, solid used one for $2,500. One day while driving, my kids asked me why I didn't drive a newer, fancier car. I replied: "Well, we could go buy a nicer car, yes. But that will mean that I'll need to work longer hours to pay for the car, and that means I won't be able to be with you as much. What do you think, should we go out and buy a new car?" Had I hung my head and answered the new car question with "Oh, gosh, I wish we could have a new car, but Mommy just can't afford it," I would be providing a negative role model for simplicity. The fact is, I *could* afford a new car, just like anybody else who wants to get into debt or use up all their savings. But I have made a conscious choice not to do either of the above. I prefer the freedom to work less and hang around my kids more over the temporary thrill of driving around in a shinier arrangement of metal. The more I spend, the more I need to work to earn the money. Now my kids understand that there is a trade-off for every purchase we make. They also understand that they are more important than things.

How we spend our money tells a lot about what we value. In his book *Shattering the Two Income Myth*, author Andy Dappen says having enough is vastly different from having it all, for it involves making choices and establishing new priorities. He says: "Do you want to make money and impress people with your corner office, $50,000 Mercedes, 4500-square-foot-house, tailored suits, swimming pool, Sun Valley–acquired tan . . . ? If these are your goals, tuck your kids into daycare, drink your milk of magnesia, and stop simpering about 60-hour work weeks. You've made your choice."

> *Nothing has a stronger influence psychologically on their environment, and especially on their children, than the unlived life of the parents.*
>
> —C. G. JUNG

The following are some of the major areas in which you can make a concerted effort to simplify your life with children.

Money

When it comes to money, in addition to living joyfully within your means, the best way to teach good money practices to children is this: *Seize the moment.* You don't need to wait for a class titled Living Simply with Children to come to town before teaching children these values. Use the myriad of daily events in your own life as your classroom. Here is a recent example from my house. For my daughter's 10th birthday, she received a check from a relative for $25. I used this opportunity as a "teachable moment." She was very excited to rush out to the clothing store and spend the entire check on the latest duds. She had every right to do whatever she wanted, since the money was hers, not mine. Nevertheless, I decided to attempt a short but important lesson in money management.

My daughter already knew the principle of saving, because I always suggest that she and my son save a portion of any money they get. Each has a savings account. It has always been fairly easy for them to save because usually they don't have a particular item in mind that they want to run out and buy. But this time was different. My daughter really wanted these clothes. When I suggested she save part of this check, her response was: "I'll save part of it *after* we go to the store. I want to see what clothes I want to buy first."

Whoops! I explained to my daughter that if she took the entire $25 into the store, she would surely spend the whole amount because, no doubt, she would find plenty of clothes that she "just had to have." Then I explained the concept of *pay yourself first.* (When you receive money, whether it is from earnings, a windfall, or what-have-you, put a portion of the money into a savings account first before you spend a nickel.) In this way you can begin to build a nest egg or savings account. I explained this concept in 10-year-old kid terms, but still, my daughter wanted to look around at the store first. Undaunted, I pressed on. I thought to myself what an important lesson this was for her to learn and what a perfect opportunity this was to teach it. My persistence paid off, and my daughter finally agreed to save $5 of the $25 *before* she ever set foot in the store.

Another teachable moment arrived days later. One of my daughter's friends had just gotten a pair of shoes that my daughter "had to have." She wanted me to buy them for her, as the other girl's mother had done. "Nope," I said. "I would have gotten them for you if you needed new shoes, but since I just bought you a pair of summer shoes and you have other shoes that fit just fine, I won't buy more." My daughter pressed on. She decided that she would spend her savings on the shoes. I used this opportunity to teach the meaning of desire. I told her how I understood perfectly well what it's like to desperately want something and how adults (me included) often blindly follow our desires and wind up with houses full of junk and empty bank accounts. I told her she could use her savings to buy the shoes if she waited 10 days. If the desire was still there, she could spend her savings. I also asked her to remember that in a few years, she would most likely want or need a large-ticket item and wouldn't have the money for it if she kept spending $10 here, $25 there out of her savings. Ultimately she forgot about the shoes.

My son used to pester me regularly to buy little gizmos from coin-operated gizmo machines at the stores. Finally he realized that I was not going to spend my money on more junk, so he began taking his own quarters and nickels to the store, "just in case." After a few times having to spend his own money on this stuff, the novelty wore off, and so did the pestering. On the other hand, once in a while I'll indulge just for the spirit of the moment. Once he and I were in a pottery store and happened to see small, wonderful-smelling scented candles. He wanted one. I let him pick one out. We enjoyed it together.

This is the next important money rule: *Teach balance*. Simple living does not mean always saying no and never having luxuries. If you pinch too many pennies your children will resent you. Once this happens, you won't be able to teach your children to be resourceful. You can get so caught up in saving and budgeting that you forget money is for fun as well as paying bills and planning for the future. When your children are in the grocery store with you and want a bag of potato chips or cookies that aren't on your list, go ahead and buy the darned things once in a while. Sometimes it's fine to buy extras for no good reason. Sometimes it's fine to splurge on larger items. The key is to maintain balance and don't go into debt getting these things. (Remember, most consumer debt is a combination of many smaller purchases.) To maintain balance, we need to go through the day with awareness, and have our larger goal of balance and freedom in mind as we cruise through the stores.

I also know that children don't need to cost a fortune. Often we buy our children more toys and things than they need out of guilt or because we want to buy them things "we never had." Certainly children need toys and clothes, but they don't need roomfuls. They need our time more than anything. We need to look at our motivation for spending. Overspending is often a symbol for guilt, insecurity, power, or independence. Do we want to teach our children that spending is a way to get our needs met? Remember that hugs, kisses, and time spent playing or listening are free. Find other, more productive and healthy ways to unload your guilt or to feel loved or secure.

More Money Rules

Set up a savings account now for yourself and your children. You don't need to wait until you have $500 or $5,000 to start a savings account. Your children can start with $1 out of a $2 allowance. Whatever amount you choose, be sure to explain why it is good to save and why it is important to put the money away. For further information on the power of saving and how you can earn money through compound interest, refer to Chapter 2. Share those compound interest charts with your children, or take your children to meet your local banker, who can show them the tables. My friend Barbara was able to retire from her job at age 44 because her dad shared these tables with her while she was in her teens. Barbara may never have had a clue about this had her dad not shared the charts with her. In fact, most people I talk to who are living in debt tell me that their parents never sat down and told them any of these principles.

Discuss the difference between wants and needs. As a general, not absolute, rule, I buy each of my kids one pair of new shoes twice a year—one for summer, one for winter. Those are shoes they "need." When they want other shoes throughout the year and their original shoes have not worn out, I point out to them that those are shoes they "want." I will pay for the "needs"; they must use their savings to pay for their "wants." This rule applies to most any purchase. Another example is this: Your child may *need* a pair of jeans and may *want* a pair of designer jeans. You could offer to pay the cost of regular jeans, and he or she can pick up the rest.

You also can use these "desires" as a way to teach the value of saving. If your children simply "must have" certain luxury items, use this opportunity to teach goal setting. They will learn to save for a goal. They can realize their goal even faster by doing extra work around the house.

One mother, as chronicled by author Linda Barbanel in *From Piggy Bank to Credit Card,* dealt with desire this way: Whenever her young son came to her begging for the latest toy he had seen in a magazine or elsewhere, she had him cut out or draw a picture of the item. They put the picture in an envelope. She allowed him to place only five pictures in the envelope. If he came to her wanting a sixth item, he had to remove one so at all times only five were in the envelope. This lesson taught the boy the value of prioritizing. When birthday or holiday time came, her son could choose one item from the envelope.

Have your child learn to pay for extras. When my son wanted to join the Lego Builders Club for $7, I told him I'd pay for half and half could come from his savings. He felt fine about this option. When my daughter wanted to go to a school camp that cost $75, I told her I would pay for half and she could earn half by doing extra chores around the house. We worked out a plan ahead of time. She met her goal. This teaches kids that they can't have everything they want and that you, the parent, aren't an endless money machine. This also forces them to make choices about what is important and what is not. You and your children should create a list of extra jobs and the amount you will pay ahead of time. Then when your child wants another pair of designer jeans or an extra activity, you simply point to the extra job list. But remember to maintain balance. Sometimes it is just fine to splurge on yourself and your children, as long as you maintain balance. You can maintain balance by being conscious about your overall budget and life plans.

Allowances. There are two main schools of thought on allowances. One is to pay children an allowance for doing chores. The other is to pay an allowance for the sake of teaching money management. To help determine which option to choose, think about your goal in giving an allowance. Is it to teach money management or to teach the value of work? Because both ideas have merit, it makes sense to choose the plan that fits your goals.

By paying children for chores done, you teach them that they need to work in order to earn money. In adult life, we all know that if we don't work, we don't have any money. You need to be clear which chores earn what amounts of money. Then if the chore is not finished by allowance time, you and your child know ahead of time how much money will be subtracted from the allowance.

The second theory is that kids should do regular household chores simply because they are members of the family, not in order to earn money. Adults don't get paid for household chores—they do it because they are contributing to the smooth operation of the home. If children don't do their chores, they should lose privileges, not money. Under this theory, the only time you dock an allowance is for serious transgressions, such as drug or alcohol abuse.

Whichever method you choose, a regular allowance is an excellent way to teach kids money management. The allowance should be given at the same time each week and for the same amount each week. The amount should increase as the kids grow. Parents need to be vigilant to pay the allowance and not wait until the child asks first. After all, we wouldn't want to have to ask our bosses for our paychecks.

Most money experts advise starting an allowance at ages six or seven. The amount of the allowance should be large enough so the kids have some money for play and some for saving and possibly giving. Determine the amount by talking with your children about what they feel they need and why, and what you think is reasonable and within the family budget.

The amount of allowance you give should be negotiated clearly ahead of time. How much do you expect your child to cover with the allowance? For instance, I know one 12-year-old girl who is given a weekly $10 allowance. She had to pay for all of her clothing from that money. When she wanted some-

179

thing special, she saved her money. Other kids get perhaps $2 a week. They aren't expected to pay for any essentials with their money. Some kids are expected to do basic chores for an allowance, such as keep their room neat, make the bed, help clear the table. For this, they get a bare-bones allowance. Any extra chores are listed on a board and earn a specific amount of money. Sunday night can be pay night when the kids bring their lists of chores completed and together you add up the amount they earned. You need to sit down with your children and, based on their maturity level, decide how many of their own expenses they should be expected to cover.

One mother with four sons taped a list of chores to the refrigerator. All chores were assigned. At the end of the week, she paid the kids in quarters. Then they checked the list. For each chore that wasn't done, they'd give back a quarter. No scolding. After a while, the mother wasn't getting many quarters. She began the system when each child turned two. They received $1 a week. The two-year-old had four chores: picking up toys, saying "please," saying "thank you," and saying nightly prayers. If he forgot just once during the week, it cost him a quarter. Each child had his own logbook. At the end of the year, they would sit down together and check the books. The one who paid the fewest number of quarters would receive a $1 raise. If anyone had outside activities or spent the night with a friend, he had to pay his brother a quarter to do his chores for him.

You also need to spell out, together, how much should be saved of the allowance and how much is for discretionary spending. The saved amount needs to go immediately into a separate pot or bank account. Some people think the saved amount needs to come totally from the allowance, and others like to match whatever the child saved with more funds. Still others agree to pay "interest" on whatever the child saves. (For instance, pay 10 cents for every $2 saved.)

Some families think that an allowance should be used to teach kids the value of giving as well. Their agreement is that the child will not only save money but also will put away an amount for giving. I know a single mom living on a very limited income who agreed with her son that he would set aside 25 cents per week for giving. At the end of the year (holiday time) Mom and son decide where the money will go. In order for your child to really appreciate the value of giving, it is best to have her or him decide where the money will be donated.

Special circumstances. Linda Barbanel related a story about a family whose VCR broke. They called a family meeting to decide what to do about it. The family decided that since everyone used the VCR and it was a luxury item, all members of the family, including teenage kids, should chip in proportionately to buy another one.

I know of another family whose children decided they wanted a Nintendo. The kids pooled their allowance money for months in order to buy it. Amy Dacyczyn, author of *The Tightwad Gazette*, related a story about special circumstances. One family could not get their children to turn off the lights when not in use. All of their sermons on saving electricity and money went out the door. Finally they told the kids that the electric bill was theirs to pay. Guess what? Lights were out.

Chores. Whether chores are tied to an allowance or not, they need to be done. It is not always easy to get kids to do chores without constant battling. The best way to allocate chores is to have a family meeting where you lay out the list of chores and discuss who should do them and when. Make sure everyone knows what the consequences are for not doing a chore, and when and how everyone is expected to perform the chore. When all parties have a say in creating the plan, there is more likelihood of follow through. One mother of three children created a lottery system. She wrote three after-dinner chores on three identical pieces of paper: Wash. Dry. Free (no chore). She folded the papers and put them in a bowl. After dinner, the kids picked from the bowl and did that chore.

You can try a chore wheel approach created by Amy Dacyczyn. Amy, mother of six kids (four old enough for chores), cut out 3- and 4-inch circles from cardboard. She marked these into fourths, and wrote a child's name on each section of the larger wheel. On the inside wheel (also marked into fourths), she wrote four chores: dishes helper, set table, clear table, cook helper. She drew arrows indicating the turning direction. She attached the two wheels with two buttons sewn together with thread. (A brass fastener works fine if you have one.) The dinner-helper job follows the dishwasher-helper job because the next night's meal is planned while the dishes are washed. The child can help choose the meal he'll help prepare the next day. Amy feels it is important to involve the children in helping plan and prepare the meals because it is one more job they can take over completely when they're old enough. When the kids are old enough to do adult-type chores, both parents and children can be added to the wheel evenly. They can still work together doing the chores because it makes it more fun. Plus, doing chores together creates an ideal time to bond.

It's easier to simplify when you are surrounded by like-minded people. I got a call from a reporter in Orange County, California, one time. She asked me how on earth parents could simplify their lives with children when all around them are affluent, high-spending people. This is an honest problem. While we want to raise our children to have their own code of behavior and set of values, we also don't want to put them in the position of being obviously different from their peers. If they choose to be "different" on their own, fine, but it should not be forced on children too young to have a say in the matter. Thus, if your child attends school with children wearing the latest designer fashions, you need to think twice before sending him or her out the door in thrift-store clothes. What to do?

The most extreme answer is to move or change schools. If you don't want to move or if it is simply not reasonable for the moment, you could look into changing to a less "showy" school.

You also can stay in the same neighborhood and school and have a positive talk with your children about how far you will go in order to help them "fit in." You could agree, for example, to spend a given amount on clothes, and anything over that will come from your child's allowance money. This might be a good time to use the method of giving the child a larger weekly allowance that is used to cover the entire clothing budget. You may be amazed to see how your child uses his or her imagination to create ensembles. The same applies to toys and entertainment. You could agree to pay up to a certain amount, and the rest comes from their allowance.

Involve children in real-life budgeting. At ages 8 and 10, I decided my kids could actually be a help to me in the grocery store. I make out a shopping list (sometimes with their help), and when we get to the store, I ask them to go find the best deal in, say, mayonnaise. They have learned to read prices and compare. Now, rather than begging for more and more or whining to leave, grocery shopping can be a game to get the best deals in food. You also could explain ahead of time to the kids how much money you have to spend at the store. The game would be to see how much you can buy within that budget. This also forces everybody to decide between the extra bag of chips or a staple item.

When your children are old enough, you can have them help you pay household bills. The money will come from your account, but the kids could sit down and look at your checkbook balance and the amount of bills and decide what bill gets paid when.

Outside employment. Some families get kids working as young as 11 (paper route), and others have kids work only in summer so as not to take away from schoolwork. My friends Mary and Ron had all three of their kids working in grocery stores, flower shops, and delivering newspapers as soon as they were able. This plan accomplished more than simply getting the kids to contribute to the family coffers—it taught them to be responsible with money as they grew up. You will need to decide what works for your schedule and budget.

Some families need their children to contribute to college or private school. If this is so, sit down with your children to decide how much they will be expected to contribute and how that can be accomplished. You could also help your child to begin a business. You can buy a package called The Busine$$ Kit (from Business Kid$ in Coral Gables, FL, 1-800-282-KIDS). This is a guide to starting and running small businesses. Included are booklets on organizing, marketing, and management. Also included is a simple guide to writing a business plan and a handbook to help parents coach. Better yet, go to your library and get books on starting a business.

Mistakes teach kids about money. Let your kids make mistakes about money. This is how they learn to manage it. If they feel the pain of not having enough money at the end of the week when they want to use it for the weekend, for example, do not advance them any money. Make the fact that you will not advance money clear ahead of time. They need to plan and budget throughout the week. Linda Barbanel suggests that parents share their own stories about how they made blunders about overspending. (We all have these stories!) An excellent book for young children (grades K–3) about this concept is titled *The Peanut Butter and Jelly Book,* by Adam Eisenson. The book is about Harry the Gorilla, who spends all of his money on a new baseball glove that he sees in a store window. (The usual scenario—we never think we "need" the item until we see it in a store.) Harry succumbs to temptation and buys the glove. At the end of the week, Harry is very hungry and has no money left with which to buy food.

One mother complained that her college-age daughter had gotten a large traffic ticket and dental bill and could not pay either. The girl had nothing left from her allowance. Should the mother bail out the daughter? Yes, parents should help their children with emergencies. They should pay for medical bills only if they agreed to do so ahead of time and if the amount of allowance is not sufficient to cover these costs. But traffic tickets are the product of irresponsibility. Parents of kids of all ages should explain ahead of time what they will pay for and what they will not pay for. If parents constantly bail out their children, the children will never learn to budget and save.

Advertising and Consumption

Advertising is probably the single most potent factor in creating little consumers out of your kids (adults too). All of your practicing and preaching about the joys of a simple life will go right out the window if you don't become savvy to advertising and share that knowledge with your children. No doubt you've read the statistics: TV carries, on average, 30,000 ads aimed at kids per year. The average kid watches six hours of TV per day. About 40 million preteens and early teens, from ages 5 to 14, buy nearly $17 billion worth of food, clothing, drinks, toys, and videos and influence another $165 billion in sales annually, according to consumer experts. Kids have plenty of pressure to consume, and for many, their social scene and consumption are intertwined. Kids no longer hang out playing ball in the nearby empty field; they hang out at the mall.

This is only the obvious onslaught. Here is some information that is not so obvious and, thus, far more disturbing: Your kids are subjected to advertising at school and in the movies as well. As school budgets are slashed, school administrators have turned to corporate America for financial help. On the outside, this looks like a wonderful partnership. On closer inspection, however, many of these corporations are using their captive audience (students) as a way to reap profit. For instance, one company sponsors a high school news program that forces students to watch commercials about the corporation daily. Consumers' Union reported in 1990 that 20 million school students a year use corporate-sponsored curricula designed to serve a company or industry. Here are a few examples from *Sojourners* magazine:

❖ One company co-opted more than 12,000 schools nationwide to force their Channel One program on students. The contract stipulates that students must watch two minutes of advertisements a day in return for free video equipment and a flashy news show.

❖ A cosmetic company's "Hot Looks, Cool Style" program targets 1 million teenage girls in home economics classes. Ostensibly to help self-esteem, the poster-size guide suggests activities called "Good Hair Day/Bad Hair Day" and "Hair Necessities," in which students list the three products they would "have to have" on a desert island. The guide, sent to 29,000 teachers, features styling tips and an ad for the company's hair products for teens.

❖ An oil company sponsors the "Energy Cube" program for high school physics students that entirely omits issues of fuel efficiency, alternatives to fossil fuels, and global warming. It does, however, include a game that challenges students to reverse the warming of a hypothetical planet. The "correct" answer is not to reduce fossil fuel use but rather to turn up the air conditioning.

❖ Another oil company video, *Polystyrene Plastics and the Environment*, purports to counter "hasty conclusions about what is good or not good for the environment." The news anchor claims on the video that plastics are the "ideal materials" to produce, recycle, burn, or just toss in landfills. This oil company is a major plastics manufacturer.

❖ A record company cloaked a national promotion for a pop singer's song as a history lesson plan. The singer encourages students and teachers to use the song as a way to kick off a class discussion. What began as a promotional effort to distribute cassette tapes of the song to over 4 million junior and senior high school students rocketed to nationwide acclaim.

My experience with my own children is similar. Their elementary school, in partnership with a major soup company, encouraged students to turn in that company's soup labels. The more labels turned in, the more library materials the school received. It would be one thing if the company earmarked a percentage of its profits to be used to donate materials to schools; it is quite another to encourage consumption of its product as a way to give books to schools. A motivational book and tape company sent around a flyer to schools about self-esteem. Parents could send away for a free booklet on building self-esteem. I thought, "Why not," and sent for it. After receiving the booklet—what do you know—I got an evening call from a company telemarketer wanting to set up a home visit with me to go over the "wonderful" line of products this company could offer me that would help build my child's self-esteem. I said no thanks and was angry that my children were being used as conduits for aggressive sales tactics.

Pay attention to what is going on at your children's school. Corporations are now writing lesson plans that are used to teach kids in school. *E Magazine* says: "One company that produces lesson plans for corporations effuses about the benefits of advertising to kids in school: 'Let XX systems bring your message to the classroom, where young people are forming attitudes that will last a lifetime . . .' Coming from school, all these materials carry an extra measure of credibility that gives your message added weight."

What can you do? Join with other parents to keep advertising out of public schools. Work with your PTA or school board to make sure teachers are not using corporate curricula. Teach your children about the ways of marketers; watch ads together and help them understand their purpose and method. Even if you don't have kids, you can work to ensure that local schools have the resources they need to resist the temptation of advertisers bearing "free" gifts.

Without your active involvement, schools will lose their independence and thus, their ability to turn out discriminating citizens.

You also can stop yourself from giving your child gifts because you feel guilty for not spending as much time as you'd like with your children. Gifts are no stand in for quality time, and when they are, it is no surprise that kids learn early to equate money with love. A 1995 study of parents and teenagers published in the journal *Developmental Psychology* notes that American culture encourages citizens to value money as well as family, community, and personal growth. "Yet . . . research suggests that these materialistic and pro-social values are rather inconsistent with each other," the study says. "It is this inconsistency that defines and frames the problems with materialism," said Tim Kasser, assistant professor of psychology at Knox College in Galesburg, Illinois, and coauthor of the study.

Kasser contends that people who are consumed by money and possessions generally are more depressed and anxious and prone to problems such as cheating and stealing. They're more self-involved and more likely to find themselves in shaky relationships.

"It gets them to ignore other important aspects of life like personal growth, loving, and helping others," Kasser said. "These are the things that are inherently meaningful and likely to bring happiness."

"Kids who cannot get a sense of belonging from family, school, or peers seek it in any form they can get it," said Cosby Steel Rogers, a professor of family and child development at Virginia Tech in Blacksburg, Virginia.

Kasser recommends giving kids a rationale for not buying certain items. He advises helping the child come to his or her own conclusion. He also advises showing the child that you value him or her above all else. "There are many ways to indulge a child and show that you love him or her; giving them things isn't going to be the best way," Kasser says. "I would ask myself as a parent what it was I really wanted when I was a kid. My bet would be that, thinking back, one will be more likely to say a hug than a pair of Nikes. Now, kids aren't always going to say that when they are kids, but my bet is it's the truth."

You also can order copies of a consumption activity booklet and game titled *The Real Deal: Playing the Buying Game,* published by the Federal Trade Commission and the National Association of Attorneys General. The 12-page booklet, which targets 10 to 13 year olds and is free, is designed to teach youngsters how to use information and make advertising work for them as well as how to make choices. One game in the booklet, geared to sports fans, is titled "Here's the Pitch." The cartoon character asks: Q: How did the baseball player convince kids to buy his brand of sneakers? A: He used his sales pitch. To order

How Is Your Family Life?

- ❖ Do we eat together as a family?
- ❖ Do we have family traditions that occur weekly, monthly, or annually that our children can look forward to?
- ❖ Do we let our kids experience cold, fatigue, adventure, injury, risk, challenge, experimentation, failure, frustration, discouragement?
- ❖ What kind of example are we as parents setting for our children? Do what I say, *not* what I do?
- ❖ When confronted by a choice of spending money or time on a material pursuit or on a family activity, do we choose the family?
- ❖ Is winning or getting an A the most important goal you set for your children?
- ❖ Do we teach our children that they have an obligation to the welfare of others?
- ❖ Do we give kids opportunities to grow by letting them manage their own money?
- ❖ Who is in control of our home—parents or television? (If we aren't taking the time to educate our children, the television will definitely be a factor in communicating ideas, morals, standards and lifestyles to our children.) Monitor television viewing.

Reprinted from *Simple Living*, no. 15, p. 11.

the *Real Deal* call the Federal Trade Commission at 1-800-769-7960 or send a postcard with your name and address to Federal Trade Commission, Real Deal, 6th and Pennsylvania Ave. NW, Room 403, Washington, D.C. 20580-0001.

What About the TV?

TV is the medium that delivers the most advertising to adults and children. So if you want to lessen the impact of advertising on your children (and yourself), it makes sense to turn the darned thing off or limit it. We've all read the studies that show that kids do better in school when they watch less TV. Kids are also more creative and imaginative and learn to entertain themselves when they watch less TV. Teachers report seeing significant changes in children's behavior in recent years. They say that kids have worse manners and social skills than in the past. We need to remember that TV is educational, especially the ads: They teach kids to be self-centered, impulsive, and addicted.

The most blatant example of how TV encourages consumerism is my tale of two Christmas seasons. During one season, my children had been in the habit of watching more TV. At that time I asked them what they wanted for Christmas. Both had huge lists of toys they "had to have" that they had seen on TV. The next year they rarely watched TV. I asked them what they wanted for Christmas. They had no idea. Think about how many of those gotta-have-it plastic toys we have all purchased for our kids that were exciting for maybe a month, only to be relegated to the back-of-the-closet toy graveyard forever after. What a waste of time, money, and resources.

When you do watch TV with your kids, discuss the ads you see. What are they selling? Do you really think it will make your life better if you have the item, as the ad seems to say? *Talk to your children.* When my children see an ad, we discuss the deceptive nature of advertising. And what about the messages we don't see on TV? Where on TV do you see ads promoting good nutrition or becoming a better citizen? The Center for the Study of Commercialism says that commercialism not only drains our wallets, but it creates an insatiable appetite for more and fosters feelings of envy, anxiety, and insecurity. We're not just teaching our kids to buy products; we're teaching them to buy the belief that they will be more attractive and have more friends if they use the product. I read somewhere about a boy who saw a certain toy advertised on TV and began to badger his dad to buy it for him. The dad reminded the boy that he already had the toy stuffed into a closet and he never used it! This was a good lesson in the power of advertising.

As with most big changes, it is not necessarily easy to turn off or limit the TV. If you are the type of vigilant parent who really and truly can monitor what your kids are watching and when, then you may be a good candidate for limiting the TV. One way to accomplish this is through scheduling. At the beginning of the week, sit down with your children and have them select the shows they want to see that week. The TV goes on only for those shows. Or you could watch TV on certain days only. Another option is to watch TV actively, not passively. Here is an example from the book, *What to Do After You Turn Off the TV*, by Frances Moore Lappe: "I don't like TV, but my children love it. To make it acceptable, I sometimes prepare headings on a large piece of paper, such as Mean Things People Do and Nice Things People Do, Girls Doing Interesting Things, Boys Doing Interesting Things, Healthy Foods or Junk Foods. My daughter makes checks under the heading each time it is appropriate. Sometimes we compare PBS to network TV."

If you think you would not be a good, long-term TV police officer, then it's easier to eliminate the thing altogether. One family waited until spring to eliminate the TV. They knew that in spring kids think more about being outside playing baseball, riding bikes, swimming, and engaging in after-school activities. During this busy time they wouldn't be as likely to miss the tube.

Another family, chronicled in *What to Do After You Turn Off the TV*, tried the cold-turkey approach with their older children, with these results:

> There was, perhaps, a month's worth of arguing. I listened to, responded to and ignored their pleas daily . . . And then something magical happened:
>
> They adjusted. I used to tell a friend that from that time on, coming home to my kids was like coming home to the Waltons. They talked together, they did their homework, they played board games and even practiced their music . . . uninterrupted by the captive fascination of the TV screen. It was lovely.
>
> Did they miss it? At first. But they soon discovered that "not having one" became a sign of distinction for them with their peers. They became more thoughtful. They liked being different.

An added benefit to less TV is, surprisingly enough, boredom. Keep reading! Boredom is especially good for children. Jerry Mander, who wrote *Four Arguments for the Elimination of Television*, said this:

> I am a member of the pre-TV generation. Until I was 14 or 15 we had no television. And I can still remember what it felt like to come home every day. First, I'd go look in the kitchen or refrigerator to see if there were any special snacks my mother left for me. I'd take care of those. Then, slowly becoming bored, I'd play with the dog for a bit. Here comes the boredom. Nothing to do.
>
> Slowly, I'd slip into a kind of boredom that seemed awful. An anxiety went with it, and a gnawing tension in the stomach. It was exceedingly unpleasant, so unpleasant that I would eventually decide to act—to do something. I'd call a friend, I'd go outdoors. I'd go play ball. I'd read. I would do something.
>
> Looking back, I view that time of boredom, of "nothing to do," as the pit out of which creative action springs. Taking all young people together, you could think of it as a kind of genetic pool of creativity. You got to the bottom of your feelings, you let things slip to their lowest ebb, and then you take charge of your life. Not wanting to stay in that place, you make an act. You experience yourself in movement, with ideas, in action.

Nowadays, however, at the onset of that uncomfortable feeling, kids usually reach for the TV switch. TV blots out both the anxiety and the creativity that might follow.

Empty spaces are especially beneficial for today's children whose lives often are as overly scheduled as their parents'. Many children are in busy day cares from the minute they rise in the morning until they return home at night just in time for dinner. Their summer vacations are no longer spent lazily fishing off the neighborhood pier or "hanging out" with their friends; now summertime is a frenzy of one day camp after another. There is very little time for children to simply "be." It is no wonder that these children (and parents) turn to the TV the minute things slow down . . . no one has any idea what to do with "space" anymore, so we fill it with the chatter and passivity of the tube. How could Thomas Edison have invented the light bulb and how could Marie Curie have been the first woman to receive the Nobel prize for her work in radioactivity if they had been running from one scheduled activity to the next and filling up their remaining open hours with the TV? They would have had no time to think, dream, create, and wonder. Our children need the same space in their lives.

Create Family Rituals

Another important way to center your life with children is to create family rituals. Rituals are small or large celebrations that make your family unique and special. Rituals also help to slow you down; they force you to say no to outside activities that interfere. Rituals bring order into our hectic lives. They are important because they give all members of a family a shared sense of belonging. Rituals help children and adults make sense of the world, making them less confused and more secure. It is our job as parents to bring some structure and guidance to our children's lives. Rituals can and should be inexpensive or free. The more of these you incorporate into your lives, the more you'll remind yourselves that you don't need to spend a fortune being entertained by others—you're quite capable of doing a better job on your own. Unfortunately, rituals are one of the first things to go when life gets too hectic.

A study of 100 households was conducted over an eight-year period by researchers from George Washington University Medical Center. The study showed that families that are highly committed to carrying out their rituals fare better emotionally and mentally. High-commitment families:

❖ Paid attention to the past and had a historical perspective of their family that endowed family life with meaning

❖ Strongly identified with an ethnic, religious, or community group and preserved this wider group attachment through the use of ritual

❖ Worked hard to preserve the family structure across the generations

❖ Truly enjoyed the hours when time was suspended as family members acted out roles from their family mythology; they looked forward to the special possessions, decorations, foods, and moods associated with various celebrations

Rituals can be traditional celebrations, such as birthdays, anniversaries, bar mitzvahs, baptisms, and holiday celebrations like Christmas and Passover. Rituals also can be smaller family customs, such as regular dinner hours, bedtime routines, and shared activities. A ritual can be as simple as designating every Wednesday "family night," where nobody schedules any outside activities on that evening. I know a couple who sets aside every Sunday afternoon for their family. They have two young boys. Every Sunday the boys look forward to their "choice day," when each boy gets to choose an activity to do with one parent. The parents rotate boys every Sunday so each child spends time alone with each parent.

You could designate every Friday night as "family night," where you rotate among family members who choose the activity. (Stay within an agreed-upon budget.) The person whose turn it is could choose a video to watch together, play a board game, go out for ice cream, go bowling. The list is endless. I know of other families who set aside certain nights for a favorite dinner. Saturday could be pizza night. The whole family gathers together to make a pizza. Or you could decide that is everyone's night off from cooking, and make it order-out pizza night. Every Tuesday could be spaghetti night. This gives all members of the family something to look forward to, and it makes it easier on the cook(s) because the regular food designation relieves the anxiety of standing in front of the refrigerator at 5:00 P.M. wondering what to cook for dinner.

I have a friend who came from a family of six kids. Every Friday night she looked forward to going with her dad and siblings to the library to choose books to read during the week. This ritual was not only special for the dad (who worked out of the house) and kids, but it also gave their stay-at-home mom a much-needed night to herself.

As recounted in the book *Chop Wood, Carry Water*, another family got tired

> *Children can be conceptualized as mirrors.*
>
> *If love is given to them, they return it.*
>
> *If none is given, they have none to return.*
>
> *Unconditional love is reflected*
>
> *unconditionally, and conditional love*
>
> *is returned conditionally.*
>
> —ROSS CAMPBELL, M.D.

of hectic breakfasts and decided to start the day together calmly. They ate breakfast together and found a short melody to sing in a round. They said: "It shapes a conscious moment in the ongoingness of time to say hello to the day."

Our favorite memories of childhood rituals are often the smaller, everyday happenings in our families. Did you have a special day where your family baked together? Evenings around the fireplace playing Monopoly? A special bedtime routine?

How about creating a family scrapbook? Once a month, take the scrapbook out and paste in collected items and photos. Create a family gallery. Put up a bulletin board in the hallway and have the kids choose their favorite art projects, crafts, writing projects, photos, or mementos to display. Designate once a month or so "gallery night" when the artwork is rotated.

To incorporate more serious rituals into your family, you could set aside "debate night" or "current events" night. You could have everyone choose an age-appropriate debate topic, such as "Should homework be abolished in schools? Why or why not?" Or pick a current events topic and ask an ethical question that is related. Make sure everyone follows the rules of etiquette: Listen to the other point of view without interrupting, no put-downs. This not only provides good entertainment, but it teaches kids the value of listening to both sides of an issue and respecting people even if their views are different from their own. Balance the seriousness of the evening by adding another tradition, such as sing-along time or ice cream time to follow the serious topic.

One way to provide your family with a sense of shared history is to adopt an old-fashioned storytelling ritual. You could create a regular, special time for members of your family to gather and talk about family stories. Loraine O'Connell wrote in the *Orlando Sentinel* about an advertising consultant who cherished these stories:

> "My father was a very stern, strict, hardworking man who put the fear of God in my brothers and me over ever being lazy," he recalls. In the conversations he had with his father, this man learned about the older man's experiences

during the Depression. As a result of those long talks, "I was able to overlook some of what I thought might be shortcomings," he said. "I was able to see how the Depression affected him, to realize just what a horror story that was."

His dad died 20 years ago, and the son has only memories of his father's stories. So he decided to go high tech with his mom, videotaping her as she reminisced about riding to first grade in a horse and buggy and other adventures in her rural Midwest life.

"We sat her down on a comfortable sofa in the living room and we'd go for one- or two-hour spells at a time," he said. "When she'd get tired, she'd say, 'That's enough, I've had it.'"

Most of us don't see our life stories as particularly interesting. Yet given a chance to talk about our experiences, we can learn as much about our lives as our listeners do, and can begin to understand how we've contributed to other people's lives.

Spirituality

The use of ritual is a wonderful way to bring spirituality into your family. You can refer to your religious or ethnic heritage to create rituals. Elizabeth Fishel, author of *I Swore I'd Never Do That!: Recognizing Family Patterns & Making Wise Parenting Choices*, recalls one mom she interviewed who had rebelled against the Orthodox Judaism of her own youth. But on the first few high holidays at which her children were old enough to understand what was going on, this mother had planned nothing special—and felt a surprising emptiness. She realized how much her children were not experiencing a spiritual awakening. Out of that feeling of loss, she organized a group of families to celebrate the holidays together and embrace religion again.

Some families read something spiritual after every meal. At times, I have set aside one night a week to have a virtues meeting, where my children and I pick out a virtue of the week, such as kindness, compassion, or honesty, and talk about how we can incorporate it into our lives during the following week. We read from *The Virtues Guide*, by Linda Kavelin Popov. We talk about real-life situations: What if you see a kid being picked on during recess? What does compassion look like? What if you're playing ball and the ball flies through the neighbor's window and the neighbor isn't home? What does honesty look like? In the winter, we have our meeting around the fireplace. Sometimes we add a little ritual of "letting go." If we have a trait, bad habit, or worry we'd like to let go of, we write it on a piece of paper and throw it to the flames.

I learned the value of prioritizing spirituality and rituals when I began to work with the virtues. I decided I wanted to have a time to talk about these with my children on a weekly basis and tried to fit it in wherever the schedule permitted. Naturally, the schedule rarely permitted a virtues meeting. More "pressing" or more exciting activities always came first. Finally someone suggested that in order to create a ritual, I needed to prioritize and set aside a specific time to have this virtues meeting. I needed to say no to outside activities that would interfere. Once I did this, we were able to have regular meetings.

You also can have family meditation time. Go to any spiritual or religious bookstore and find guided meditation tapes. Sometimes a guided meditation is easier for children to follow than, say, the insight style of meditation that I describe in Chapter 3. The point of this is to get your children accustomed to having quiet, reflective space in their lives.

However you incorporate spirituality into your family life, remember this important, number-one rule: If you don't have it inside you, it is difficult to teach or model it to your children. Far better for you to spend time nurturing your own higher self than to drop your kids off at some Sunday school while you go off to have coffee or run around the track. If you don't have love inside of you, it is impossible to give it to someone else. Your first job as a parent is to fill your spiritual cup so you have something extra to give. This concept is similar to the rule on airplanes that, in an emergency, parents should put the oxygen mask on themselves first before putting one on their children. This is so the parents remain alive and functioning in order to help the kids. Same thing applies to spirituality.

There are as many different definitions of spirituality as there are children. My own personal idea of spirituality is that it is a way to open up to know our higher selves. Depending on your personal beliefs, your higher self can be God or some higher universal truth or simply being the best human being you can be. Spirituality is important because the majority of our lives are spent on mundane, material pursuits such as paying bills, buying groceries, mowing the lawn, working at our jobs as accountants and waiters, helping children with homework so they can be accountants and waiters, and having dinner with our families and friends. The busier our material lives become, the less time we have to focus on the meaning of our lives and how to become better human beings. If we want our own children to have the ideal balance of spiritual and material, then we absolutely must model it ourselves.

It is helpful to learn about different kinds of spiritual paths, because most of them have ideals and beliefs that help people to connect to this "higher self."

You can join a formal church or religion, or you can learn and grow on your own by, say, meditating and reading spiritual books. You also can combine the two. For instance, you can be a Catholic and meditate. Find some kind of spiritual path to follow and stay on the path. Practice loving kindness meditation every day. It is described in Chapter 3.

You don't need to wait until you have reached some higher state of nirvana before you can teach your children. When I started on my own spiritual path, I took the kids right along with me. I had no idea where it would lead, but as I learned more, read more, thought about more, I talked about it with my children. I would tell them about one way of thinking and explain that it wasn't necessarily the only way. Some people believed it, some didn't, I would say. Then I would tell them about another way. I took them through an informal, ongoing, comparative religion class.

Once you begin delving into your own spirituality, there are many ways to share it with your children. For instance, one night at dinner my kids and I had a long talk about special people we could emulate, like Gandhi and Mother Teresa. We talked about how they structured their lives to have all of this goodness to give others. This is spirituality in action. A very important thing to remember about spirituality and children is this: Children *are* a spiritual path. The contemplative life on top of mountains or in retreat centers is a lofty thing, but if you think that is all there is to spirituality, you will be beyond frustrated when you have children. In the *Bhagavad Gita,* the Lord Krishna tells Arjuna: "I have already told you that, in this world, aspirants may find enlightenment by two different paths. For the contemplative is the path of knowledge; for the active is the path of selfless action. . . . You must perform every action sacramentally, and be free from all attachment to results. . . . Do your duty, always, but without attachment. . . . Desire for the fruits of work must never be your motive in working. Never give way to laziness, either. Perform every action with your heart fixed on the Lord."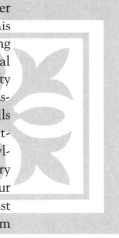

When you are thinking and growing spiritually, you also begin to see your children as spiritual beings who can teach you. For example, constant whining by a two-year-old can turn you into a tyrant, or it can awaken you to the virtue of patience. When your kids want to stop every few feet along the sidewalk to marvel at a new bug as you head for the store, you can get frustrated for not making better time, or you can be renewed with a sense of wonder. When you have cooked your twentieth meal of the week and you are sick of it, you can remember the virtues of service and love—you are showing your love by serving your children.

When you serve without attachment, you serve and love without the focus of a particular result. You learn to love your children as unique human beings, separate from you. Your job is not to turn them into miniature versions of yourself; rather, it is to help them become the best human beings they can become in their own right. Indeed, this selfless, goalless kind of love and serving is one of the highest tenets of a spiritual life. Give to others without the expectation of receiving something in return. Give simply because you love. What a gift to your children!

Create Community for Your Children

There's an African proverb that says: "It takes a village to raise a child." So true. Creating community (village) also simplifies your life. Once in a while I have had the need to hire sitters for my children, but not often. This is because I usually call a parent I know in the community and my child goes there to play. I do the same for them. No expense. No trouble. The kids have fun. The parents know the kids are in good hands. Nobody keeps track of hours.

Building community takes some effort, but it is worth it. Here is how I accomplished the endeavor. When my daughter started first grade, I decided to form a Brownie–Girl Scout troop for her. When my son was of age, I helped start an Indian Guide group for him. The reason was so they could get to know some of the other kids in their class and neighborhood, and I could get to know the parents. There were no existing troops. For my daughter, I went down the list of kids in her class and called all the parents to ask if they would like to help form the troop. For my son, I called friends in the neighborhood, and they called their friends. Years later the troops are going strong. Both groups were formed as co-ops, so all parents are involved. The families have gotten to know each other well and have even gone on vacations together. When my children want to play at one of these houses, I know exactly who the parents are. We can share parenting problems, and the kids have bonded with each other. Some parents and I have also formed smaller, after-school enrichment groups for our children. These activities keep us in frequent contact with each other.

Another way I get to know the parents is by volunteering in my children's classrooms. If your job does not allow you to be present during the day, you can volunteer on committees at night. If you home school your children, there are lots of activities home-schooling families can get involved in. Search out a home-schooling organization. If they don't offer enough camaraderie, form a group yourself from members of the organization.

Think of other ways to get to know your neighbors. Churches offer a wonderful avenue for you to join a community. And don't wait for your neighbors to invite you over. Everybody complains that neighborhoods aren't the same anymore. When was the last time you invited your neighbors to dinner? Create a round-robin potluck for your neighborhood. I know of an urban block of neighbors that convenes every Fourth of July for water fights and a potluck celebration. You can organize or join a neighborhood block, or building improvement group or block watch. Get to know a neighbor who was raised in a very different culture. The next time you are out mowing your lawn, mow a little extra on the neighbor's side. If you live in a high-rise, you have a captive audience right on your own floor. My friend Ethel was raised in the Bronx section of New York in the 1950s. She fondly remembers having friends all throughout her postwar high-rise apartment building. Since the mothers knew each other, the kids were safe going from floor to floor. The kind of safety and security offered by this kind of community cannot happen if you don't know who lives near you. Be creative in whichever kind of housing arrangement you have.

Our children need the safety and familiarity of neighbors and communities. If you are too busy to get involved with your neighbors, take a look at your calendar to see which activities you can let go of so you'll have more time for your community. This is one more opportunity for you to prioritize and make choices.

Children's Birthdays

My children have been to lavish, expensive birthday parties, and they have been to moderate birthday parties. One of their favorites was the most peaceful and inexpensive. Their friend was turning four. She had a summer birthday. The parents told her she could invite her two best friends, which were my two children. We all went to a saltwater beach that was about an hour's drive from home. Ahead of time, the parents created a treasure hunt. They made flags on sticks. Each flag had a number on it. They made treasure clues to be buried under each flag. Then they made three little "loot bags." The maps were made on arrival and the flags hidden while the kids played. Each child was given a bandanna and paper eye patch to look like a pirate. The map took them high and low through the sand, driftwood, and other beach-side paraphernalia to finally discover their buried "loot bag treasure." After the treasure hunt, we dined on simple, nourishing food and birthday cake. The rest of the day was spent creating sand castles, exploring, and inventing new treasure maps.

Children's birthday parties do not have to cost a fortune in either time or money. They don't even require unlimited imagination. Plenty of books in the library are full of ideas for creative birthday parties for children. You can re-create the pirate treasure hunt in your house for winter birthdays or in your backyard if you don't want to go to the beach. You can invite more kids and, depending on their ages, have more elaborate clues. For my son's eighth birth-day party, in the winter, we decided to hide each kid's loot bag in a different area of the house. My kids were responsible for creating the treasure maps and clues. Certain areas (my office, for example) were off limits. The rest was open to imagination. You can create minimysteries for kids to solve. You can create a real-life Clue game by choosing a "who-dunnit," in what room, and with what weapon. Then cook up clues to be handed out to the partygoers.

You could keep younger kids busy for the entire party with simple, silly games that cost nothing. Here are two examples:

❖ Shoe Swap for four-plus players. Everybody takes off his or her shoes and puts them in the middle of the circle. Each player must put on two differ-ent shoes (not her own and a different one for each foot). The fun starts when you look for your missing pair (worn by someone else), and you have to put your foot next to the missing pair. One foot will be on one side of the circle and the other somewhere else. Everybody gets tangled up and has a great time.

❖ A Great Wind Blows, for five or more players. Equipment: chairs arranged in a circle, one less than the number of players. Players take a seat except one who remains standing in the middle. The standing player says, for example, "A great wind blows for . . . everybody wearing glasses!" Immediately all players wearing glasses must jump out of their seats and try to get into another vacant seat. The player who made the call also scrambles to find an empty seat. Whoever is left standing with-out a seat makes the next call. Some examples: A great wind blows for . . . everyone wearing white socks . . . everybody who likes macaroni and cheese! . . . everybody who didn't floss their teeth last night!

You can do mini-relay races in a backyard or park. For four years, we cele-brated my daughter's summer birthday at a park. The kids always loved the doughnut game. You take a string and tie it between two trees or poles. Then hang round doughnuts (the kind with holes in the middle that look like life-savers) on shorter strings attached to the long string. Tie on as many dough-nuts as there are kids. Then have the kids line up in teams. They race to the doughnuts and try to eat the whole thing without touching it with their hands. Everybody wins because everybody eventually gets a doughnut!

There are hundreds of relay races you can play and hundreds of books filled with ideas for relay races. How about the belt game? Kids divide into two teams. Have identical equipment ready: a man's shirt with lots of buttons, a belt with holes, and grown-up pants. Each kid races to put the items on (buttoning and fastening everything) and takes them off before the next kid on the team arrives to repeat the process. No prizes necessary—just fun.

You can step away from traditional birthday parties by going camping. Last year, for my daughter's 10th birthday, four mothers and I took 10 kids camping for one night. With enough parental help, this can be a special treat for everyone. Don't forget the marshmallows, chocolate, and graham crackers for s'mores!

Take a step even closer to home by hosting a campout in your backyard. If your yard doesn't have space, maybe a relative or friend would let you borrow theirs. Set up tents and an outdoor firepit. Make your own firepit by using an upside-down metal garbage can lid or hibachi. Toast marshmallows, tell ghost stories, and sing camp songs just as if you were miles up in the mountains.

You can remember other values when planning children's birthdays. I know a family who hosts fun, at-home birthday parties for their children, but their invitations read: No gifts please; just your company. Please bring an item to be donated to the food bank. Their children somehow agree that they have enough toys—what they really want is simply the company of their friends.

It's also important to remember why party guests are with your child: to celebrate this special day together. For my son's birthday party last year, we covered the table with white paper. (You can get rolls of clean newsprint free from newspapers that can't use the end of rolls.) We put a cup of crayons next to each plate. When the kids sat down, we had them write what they like about my son. They could decorate their space however they wanted. This "tablecloth" served as a nice reminder for my son about how special he is, and it reminded the other kids that they are celebrating the birthday of someone special to them.

Helping Our Children to Become Better Human Beings

By placing less emphasis on material goods, you open the door to put more emphasis on becoming a better human being. In my family, I spend as much if not more time teaching my kids to be good human beings as I do with educational pursuits.

The Hebrew word *Tzedaka* means "justice." It is derived from the word

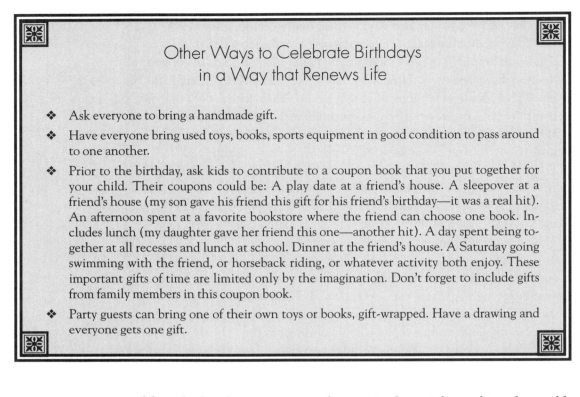

Other Ways to Celebrate Birthdays in a Way that Renews Life

❖ Ask everyone to bring a handmade gift.

❖ Have everyone bring used toys, books, sports equipment in good condition to pass around to one another.

❖ Prior to the birthday, ask kids to contribute to a coupon book that you put together for your child. Their coupons could be: A play date at a friend's house. A sleepover at a friend's house (my son gave his friend this gift for his friend's birthday—it was a real hit). An afternoon spent at a favorite bookstore where the friend can choose one book. Includes lunch (my daughter gave her friend this one—another hit). A day spent being together at all recesses and lunch at school. Dinner at the friend's house. A Saturday going swimming with the friend, or horseback riding, or whatever activity both enjoy. These important gifts of time are limited only by the imagination. Don't forget to include gifts from family members in this coupon book.

❖ Party guests can bring one of their own toys or books, gift-wrapped. Have a drawing and everyone gets one gift.

tzedeka, which refers to a person who acts justly or righteously in the world. The Jewish tradition teaches that we are partners in Creation and that part of our job in this life is to help repair the broken pieces in our world. The challenge to parents of all faiths is how to teach these values to children in meaningful ways. And the challenge is to model these values to our children.

One family created a "found money" system. They had their children decorate a box for the kitchen. Any money found on countertops, dresser tops, or in the washing machine went into the Tzedaka box. In addition, they donated money to the box when an event during the week warranted honor. "Making it through a tough exam, shooting a terrific goal, a birthday, recovery from a cold, or just celebrating the completion of another hectic week became a vehicle for sharing their good fortune," said Dale Schreiber, a mother of three who was quoted in *Parenting for Peace and Justice* newsletter, "Our children saw their contributions growing. One of them found $5.00 at the mall. It went into the Tzedaka box."

After sufficient time passed, the family decided to help a charitable organization near their home. The children sent the contribution along with a letter and received a nice reply that reminded them of their power to make a difference.

A Native American woman taught her children always to share what they had. Beulah Caldwell, a member of the *Parenting for Peace and Justice* advisory board, said her mother taught her to share food freely with strangers, to look after strangers, and to make them feel welcome in their home. She always taught that everything was to be shared. There was no emphasis on materialism or ownership. And she taught respect for all living things.

Acting "justly" also means to be aware of how we use our natural resources compared to the rest of the world and to be aware of our consumption and what our fair share of the earth's resources is. We can remind ourselves and our children that every day, in every town, thousands of links are made between citizens of the United States and of other countries—links that tie us together as one family, making us increasingly interdependent. Shoes are made in Brazil. Phone directories are keyed by keypunch operators in the Philippines. Bicycle shorts are made in Mexico. Bananas that we eat are from Somalia. Rubber on our sneakers is from Thailand, and our baseballs and gloves are made in Haiti. When we remember these links, we can act more responsibly when making consumption and life choices.

Stewardship is another word we can use to teach children to live their lives with concern for the world. One family keeps a "World Bank" container on their dinner table. Occasionally they invite the children to skip a dessert or snack and put 5 to 10 cents in the bank for hungry people overseas.

The family also has a "Shalom Box" on the dinner table in which they place any appeal letters they want to consider. Quarterly at dinner or a family meeting they read the appeals and ask the children which groups they should contribute to and how much. This serves as a learning experience about who needs help and what criteria they would use in deciding whom to help.

Although donating money is helpful, donating your time is even more compelling. You can teach your children (by example!) that giving up your own time or resources to help others in need is part of being a member of the community. There are many shelters and services in every city and town that feed the homeless, take care of the infirm, and help others in need. You and your children (depending on their ages) can tutor grade-school children, serve homeless families, and help out at nursing homes and hospitals. Call any church to get a listing of where you might donate your time and energy.

You also can encourage your children's school to instigate a volunteer program. My children's public school organized such a program a few years ago. They coordinated with a few charitable organizations, and all children were required to spend time working in some way that would contribute to the program chosen by their class. In Palo Alto, California, middle- and high-school students created a Youth Community Service Program. Students in grades 6 through 12 from four schools identified community needs, provided direct service to meet those needs, and involved their peers in community service. Undergraduate students from nearby Stanford University served as mentors and worked alongside the youth on service projects. For information, contact: Youth Community Services, East Palo Alto/Palo Alto, 25 Churchill Avenue, Palo Alto, CA 94306.

Students at Hockaday and St. Mark's Schools in Dallas, Texas, must go into the community in order to earn their diplomas and pass to the next grade. A student in each class becomes class representative and works with an adult Community Projects coordinator. The representatives learn leadership and organizational skills by speaking at school assemblies, recruiting participants for projects, and following up with peers. Contact: Community Service Coordinator, St. Mark's/ Hockaday Schools, 10600 Preston Road, Dallas, TX 75230.

You can find opportunities to help in many other ways. One of the first projects that my son's Indian Guide group did together was to build a playhouse. Our initial goal was to get our eight-year-olds working on a project that would help them to bond with each other. Then we took it a step further. We all decided to donate the house to a battered women's shelter. One of the moms found a lumber store to donate materials and a carpenter to donate his time. The boys were very proud when, after months of work, we finally loaded the finished playhouse on a truck to be taken to the shelter.

When your children are old enough, they can spend their summers volunteering. One way for both young adults and children to gain this hands-on experience is by joining a local, national, or worldwide helping program. There is nothing like firsthand experience to inspire children and young adults to live more simply. After one college student volunteered as an outreach worker to children living in housing projects, she said she really learned to ask herself "Do I really need this?" before making any purchase, even a pack of gum. She also wondered why so many people in the United States have so much, while others barely eat one meal a day. She hoped that her work as a volunteer would allow the children she worked with to enjoy their childhood a little more and empower them to hold high goals.

Another student spent a summer working in Calcutta, India, with Mother Teresa's Order of the Missionaries of Charity. He returned with a new outlook on service. He realized that service wasn't helping someone else, it was simply treating others as humans. He discovered that policies and legislation would do nothing until people acquired the sense of self-value and of valuing others.

For information on connecting with volunteer agencies, refer to the "Volunteering" section of the Resources at the end of this chapter.

The Sensuality of Simplicity

Nurture your children in a special way today. One Sunday morning I was tired and wanted to be pampered. Then I realized my kids probably felt the same way, so I made them special Beligan waffles with strawberries, put the plates on a tray covered with a linen cloth, and brought breakfast up to each of their rooms. They were absolutely delighted when they got to eat breakfast in bed and take as long as they wanted. Sometimes I'll pour them a special bubble bath in the evening, set up a little table by the bathtub, and bring in hot chocolate and honey-covered almonds as a treat.

THE AMIGOS PROGRAM

The Amigos program was started in 1965 to provide leadership development opportunities for young people, improved community health for the people of Latin America, and better cross-cultural understanding for people of both continents. After completing an extensive training program, high school and college-age participants are assigned to ongoing health projects in developing countries. Usually they live with families in small villages in remote areas and are supervised by more experienced volunteers.

Adri Kolff was 16 when she joined an Amigos program. She lived in a small village in Ecuador for one summer. When she returned to her home in the United States, she said she looked at everything with new eyes. "I learned to appreciate what I do have, and that you don't need all this stuff to be happy. The people in my village had great relationships within the family and happy lives even though their lives were sometimes hard. There is a strong bond between the families—they spend a lot of time together, they work together and care for each other."

Adri said that the families also shared a strong community bond. Some would even share a communal kitchen. One person might spontaneously cook for the whole family. Adri said it was difficult to know who had which children, because they all took care of each others' children.

"The people never expressed a need for more than they had," Adri said. "The only time I ever saw them raise money was for documents for a wedding

Adri Kolff says her life changed after volunteering.

. . . but basically money was a very insignificant thing in their lives."

Their houses simply met their needs, and no more. Each family owned maybe a couple of pots full of corn or cabbage, shelves with bags of rice and noodles, and a little fireplace in the corner of the room where they cooked their food; the bedroom was a wood bed with wool blankets, maybe a little table and maybe a little chair. They used a hanging stick to drape their clothes on. They always sat on the dirt floor to eat, and mealtime was when everyone came together. "They'd always give us more than they had," Adri said.

There was also little or no housework. They would get up with the sun at six or so, eat, and go to work in the fields. They washed their clothes on stones with a bar of soap, and Adri recalled this was not a problem because they had so few clothes to wash. The clothes would dry in the sun. When the children were 9 or 10, they would go to work with the parents . . . it was their way of life.

Because of this experience, Adri says she doesn't worry like she used to if she doesn't have something to do. "I'm satisfied just hanging around . . . I need a lot less. Sometimes I find myself feeling like I need something at the store, but I remember I really don't need so much stuff to entertain me anymore."

And she remembers the effect of the villagers not having a lot of things to worry about. "They didn't have a lot of superficial things to worry about like a vase that might break, or someone coming into their house and robbing them. Why would anyone steal something from people they considered their brothers and sisters?"

Adri's friend Lamont Glass has gone on three Amigos trips. Because of his experiences, he says he has a more relaxed way of looking at life now. He doesn't need a lot of material goods in his life. "I could see that had I not gone on the program, I would have been more interested in achieving something monetary," Lamont says. "If you've never lived without things you think you need it all. But when you see satisfied people who don't have 15 different shirts you realize you don't need it either. It is just a habit to want more than you need."

Lamont also says he has a more fatalistic view of life now. "If something bad or good happens to me I think oh, that's life, not it's not fair—I don't deserve this."

"I brought back a state of mind," Adri says. "I still have appointments, school, and things to worry about, but now I'm more relaxed. I prioritize what is important. I can step back and look at what I'm doing and take things as they come."

❖ ❖ ❖ ❖ ❖ ❖ ❖ ❖ ❖ ❖ ❖ ❖ ❖ ❖

Resources

Money

Kiplinger's Money-Smart Kids (And Parents, Too) by Janet Bodnar (Washington, D.C.: Kiplinger Books, 1995)
A guide for parents to teach their kids about all matters financial and how money actually works.

The Money Book (& Bank): A Smart Kid's Guide to Savvy Saving & Spending by Elaine Wyatt and Stan Hinden (Antioch, TN: Tambourine, 1991)
Hands-on introduction to managing money for kids four to 12 with tips on earning, budgeting, banking, spending, shopping, saving money, and family discussions on allowances. A bank with a transparent back and separate compartments for coins allows owners to watch their savings grow.

Money Doesn't Grow on Trees: A Parent's Guide to Raising Financially Responsible Children by Newale S. Godfrey (New York: Fireside Books, 1994)
Has helpful suggestions, especially on issues like allowances and helping children learn to save money.

Piggy Bank to Credit Card: Teach Your Children the Financial Facts of Life by Linda Barbanel (New York: Crown Trade Paperbacks, 1994)
Appropriate money lessons where author outlines the what money skills can best be learned from ages six through 18, articulating what goes on inside a kid's head at different ages; helpful to parents in deciding if your expectations fit your children's capabilities.

Media

Adbusters, with a circulation of 35,000, refuses real advertising. The Media Foundation, 1243 West Seventh Avenue, Vancouver, BC, Canada, V6H 1B7, 1-604-736-9401. World Wide Web site: http://hishi.cic.sfu.ca/adbusters.

Center for the Study of Commercialism, 1875 Connecticut Avenue NW, Washington, D.C. 20009-5728, 1-202-332-9110, fax 1-202-265-4954, www.cspinet.org

Four Arguments for the Elimination of Television by Jerry Mander (New York: William Morrow, 1978)
Thoughts on removing television from our lives and how to replace it with other more meaningful, enriching activities.

What to Do After You Turn Off the TV by Frances Moore Lappe and Family (New York: Ballantine Books, 1985)
Activities that can replace the time spent in front of the TV set, ranging from storytelling to baking cookies to playing games. Not only can this be a moral boost for attention-starved children, but it can bring families closer together.

Rituals

Family Customs and Traditions by Cynthia MacGregor (Minneapolis: Fairview Press, 1995)
Filled with real-life letters from families telling how they create customs and traditions for every day and holidays.

Festivals Together, a Guide to Multi-Cultural Celebrations by Sue Fitzjohn, Minda Weston, and Judy Large (Hudson, NY: Gryphon House, 1996)
Resource guide for celebrations and for observing special days according to tradition, based on many cultures. Stories, crafts, and recipes for sharing throughout the season.

How to Build a Storytelling Tradition in Your Family Robin Moore (Boston: Shambhala, 1991)
Guides parents and children in telling and listening to stories. Shows how to use storytelling skills to recover lost family memories and escape the tyranny of the clock in a quest for "quality time." Moore is a professional storyteller.

Birthdays

Co-op Games Manual by Jim Deacove (Perth, Ontario: Family Pastimes, 1974)
Seventy cooperative games and activities, mostly for younger players, aged 4 to 12.

Everybody Wins by Jeffrey Sobel (New York: Walker and Co., 1983)
Nearly 400 noncompetitive games for young children.

Everyone Wins! by Sambhava Luvmore and Josette Luvmore (Philadelphia: New Society Publishers, 1990)
Nicely indexed according to appropriate age level, activity level, group size, and location.

New Games for the Whole Family by Dale LeFevre (New York: Perigee, 1988)
An especially readable and lighthearted introduction to new games.

The Penny Whistle Birthday Party Book by Meredith Brokaw and Annie Gilbar (New York: Fireside Books, 1992)
According to the authors, almost every child they've ever talked to claims his or her best birthday parties were the ones held at home. "This doesn't mean spending a lot of money or planning a lavishly overproduced party, but rather spending your time and energy with your child. The dividends of this investment will last far beyond the actual party day." Overriding theme is that parties don't need to be expensive to be fun.

Volunteering

Books/Videos

Developing Caring Children by Kate McPherson
Tells how parents can model service, develop family service projects, and encourage and support community and school-based service learning programs. Contact: School Improvement Project, 2810 Comanche Drive, Mt. Vernon, WA 98273, 1-360-428-7614.

Ignite the Community Spirit, 300 Creative Ideas for Community Involvement by Joy Golliver
Filled with listings of programs and ideas for helping others. Contact: Ignite the Community Spirit, 500 W. Roy, W-107, Seattle, WA 98119, 1-206-283-4385.

Today's Heroes (video)
Documents the personal service experiences of four high-school students. Call: 1-202-457-0588.

Organizations

America's Charities, 12701 Fair Lakes Circle, Suite 370 Fairfax, VA 22033, 1-800-458-9505

Amigos, 1-800-231-7796

Earth Force, 1501 Wilson Boulevard, 12th floor, Arlington, VA 22209, 1-703-243-7400

National Youth Leadership Council for national service programs, 1-800-366-6952

Points of Light Foundation, 1737 H Street NW, Washington, DC 20006, 1-202-223-9186

Youth Volunteer Corps of America, 6310 Lamar Ave, Suite 125, Overland Park, KS 66202-4247, 1-913-432-YVCA

Miscellaneous

The Moral Child: Nurturing Children's Natural Moral Growth by William Damon (New York: Free Press, 1990)
Offers advice on the evolution and nurturance of kids' moral development, understanding, and appreciation, from babyhood until adolescence. Also discusses behavior as it relates to growth and maturity.

Raising a Responsible Child by Don Drinkmeyer (New York: Fireside Books, 1982)
Parenting book using the STEP method of development, updated to include such topics as stepparenting, the evolving nuclear family, AIDS, and dealing with learning disabilities.

Raising Kids with Just a Little Cash by Lisa Reid (Santa Fe, NM: Ferguson-Carol Publishers, 1996)
Book details how to get children from infancy to adulthood for a lot less money. Includes money-saving actions you can take to reduce the money you spend on raising children. Examples are birthdays, clothing, toys, entertainment.

Raising Self-Reliant Children in a Self-Indulgent World by H. Stephen Glenn and Jane Nelson (Rocklin, CA: Prima Publishing, 1989)
Using practical steps to teach children how to take care of themselves while learning important social skills.

Sharing Nature with Children by Joseph Bharat Cornell (Nevada City, CA: Ananda Publications, 1979)
Reflections on making nature be a part of our children's lives. Shares stories, anecdotes, and thoughts about integrating earth into our daily routine and how this is a soulful process.

8
Holidays

By scaling down your activities, you will have more time and peace of mind to enjoy the ones that remain.

—UNPLUG THE CHRISTMAS MACHINE

The holiday season is one of my favorite times of the year, and it is also a time most filled with paradoxes and mixed feelings. On one hand, it is magical: the tiny flickering lights, tissue-paper fairies hanging from golden threads, those long, dark nights illuminated by candle flame, excited children, gathering with people I care about, and a time to rekindle my spirituality. On the other hand, it's a time when we say we want to spend more time with our children and other loved ones, yet we're busier than ever, shopping, decorating, and attending parties. It's a time when many of us feel that our lives and our families aren't as "perfect" as others'. We think things should be more "perfect" at this time of year. We can experience stress and disappointment in the midst of all the festivities.

And holiday season is a time when the excesses of the privileged (me included) collide loudly with the scarcity of the unprivileged. This past season I left a department store after buying pajamas for my children. As I drove out of the parking lot, I saw a woman sitting on the curb, holding a sign asking for money. What really tugged at my heart was that there was a small child huddled up next to her. It was raining and cold and the little girl was covered in a worn, thin jacket with a hood. I was about ready to go off to the next store to pick up one more gift when I turned my car around. I offered to help.

How can we keep the magic of the holidays alive for ourselves and our families and also reach out to others who have no magic? How can we experience joy and revel in our gift exchanges while also being mindful that thousands of children are going hungry at this time of year? How can we get our shopping, decorating, and entertaining done and also have relaxed, flowing hours with our families and children? How can those who feel the void of not "measuring up" create an experience that is meaningful? We can do this by simplifying our holidays. A simplified holiday can be magical, joyful, and rewarding, and it frees a little more of our time, money, and energy to be available to our families, friends, and children, and also lets us reach out to help others. A simplified holiday also helps us to lower our out-of-proportion expectations and replace them with more realistic ones.

The holiday season, like anything else, is what we make it. It can be friend or foe, depending on how we host it. We can allow it to take us on wild spending sprees and keep us exhausted from overcommitted schedules, or we can look upon it as a friend, gently reminding us to think about what is important in our lives. If you sit awhile and listen, your holiday friend may remind you that this is a good time to start rearranging your life so it has more meaning. My friend Vicki Robin summed it up this way: "When you're leaving this earthly place, which would you rather be able to say: 'I have three cars in my garage,' or 'I've left the world a better place'?"

We can create holidays with deep meaning by looking past mainstream traditions and developing new customs for ourselves and our families. As with all other aspects of simplifying, going against the grain takes a little more creativity and energy, but the results are well worth it.

Call a Family Meeting

At the start of the holiday season, take time out with your family or circle of friends and decide what is important to you. If you are alone, take some time for yourself. To make this job easier, you might visualize a big umbrella over your head that signifies your values and feelings. For instance, one way to simplify the season is to think of it as an opportunity to help you and your family learn more about being together and about the gift of giving yourselves. If this is your umbrella of values, then the smaller, day-to-day decisions will come easier. What rituals could you do to bring your family closer together? How could you help others during this time?

If you are alone, what can you do during this time to further your values? If your family isn't close, what rituals can you create to take the emphasis off what you wish you had, to what is in alignment with who you are?

The holiday season is also the perfect time to rethink the love-equals-money myth. How can we express our love for each other without spending a lot of money? Nowhere is this love-and-money equation more prevalent than this time of year: "If he buys me an expensive sweater or piece of jewelry, then he *must* love me a lot." "She only spent $10 on my gift. . . . I guess I'm not that important to her." "My kids will be so disappointed if I don't buy XYZ toys."

Ever heard those lines churning through your head? When we stop to think about it, our entire holiday season, from gifts, to food, to decorations and entertainment, is now measured by money. All of a sudden we feel the need to spend money decorating and redecorating our houses at this time of year. All of a sudden we're supposed to turn into gourmet cooks. On and on.

What would happen to your holiday season if you changed the paradigm and decided that you were going to measure love by something other than money? And if you went a little further and recognized the value of deciding that going into debt was *not at all* a measure of love? Once you change your mind about the link between money and love, there are many ways you can create a joyful, rich holiday season.

Set a Holiday Budget

What budget is reasonable for us? I once talked to Amy Dacyczyn, author of the *Tightwad Gazette*, about her holiday budget. She and her husband agreed that they would only spend $10 on each other and try to come up with the most creative, ingenious way to buy fun and interesting things that fit their budget. Since they were both in agreement, neither was disappointed that one spent more than the other on holiday gifts. He loved a certain mystery writer, so one year she found a volume he didn't have at a used book store for $2. That left $8. His favorite jacket was in perfect condition except for a frayed collar. She made him a new collar. Her gifts entailed just as much love, if not more, than any expensive offerings she may have given her husband. She does the same for her extended family. One year she made a genealogy book for relatives. If she waits until the last minute, she gives homemade food items. One of my favorite food gifts from a relative was a big tin of homemade almond cookies.

You can do the same thing for children in modified form and set a limit on how much money you will spend on each child. Amy told me that every year, she and her husband tell the children they can make a Christmas list with items under $25 or $30 each. This is the budget for new toys. Throughout the year, Amy shops at garage sales and picks up miscellaneous gifts that she thinks the kids will like and stashes them until Christmas. Most of the time, the kids get more enjoyment out of the garage-sale purchases than the shiny new toys. One year she bought a child an entire cross-country ski outfit (skis and all) for $10 at a garage sale. Another child's favorite gift turned out to be a $2 computer game picked up at a pawnshop.

Remind yourselves that new is not necessarily better. More and more people at all income levels are doing their holiday shopping at secondhand stores—without apology. Sales have risen 20 percent every year since 1992 at one chain of used clothing and sporting good stores. Secondhand devotees see this kind of gift exchange as a way to save not only money but the environment as well. They see buying and selling used stuff as a good form of recycling.

You may or may not like the idea of giving used gifts. But whether you do or not, you still can create a family budget and stick to it. And you still can begin to rethink the myth that expensive gifts equal love. Whichever option you choose, the most important ingredient is that all of the gift exchangers in your family or circle of friends sit down and talk about the plan in advance. Decide on a gift limit that is comfortable for everyone. And to get away from the emphasis on gifts as the central focus, talk about past holidays and what each person recalls most fondly. My fondest memories, for example, are of hanging out with my grandma and watching her preparing the turkey in her blue-flowered dress and white cotton apron. I remember going with my cousins to that romantic midnight mass where the lights are turned low and everyone carries candles. I remember the smell of my grandma's house. I honestly don't remember more than a handful of presents I received in all of those childhood years. But I sure remember the Christmas dinners where our family served up as many horrible puns as turkey slices. We may all be surprised to hear what our own young children remember from one or two years ago.

We can talk about a homemade gift we'd like—nothing elaborate, maybe a book of photos or poems. Or maybe a memento from someone we love. My grandma used to love to play cards. After she died, as a Christmas present, my thoughtful aunt wrapped up one of her old decks of cards and gave it to me. I remember that gift vividly.

There are many reasons to remind yourself why expensive gifts really do not equate with love. One is this: Think about how many more hours you need to work in order to pay for these gifts. This is time away from those you love. Does it make sense to stress yourself and work a lot of additional hours just to "prove" your love on one day of the year? We still can show love and give each other thoughtful gifts in a myriad of other ways. When we spend less, we'll be able to show our love all year long because we won't be frantically spinning on the treadmill to pay off debt.

Keep It Simple

Along with the consumption-equals-love-theory comes holiday stress. Depression is rampant throughout the holiday season largely because our expectations have become so unreasonably high. Our gifts have to be more exotic year after year, our houses more perfect, our celebrations more intense, and our families in perfect harmony. What if we simply lower our expectations? If we get past the money-equals-love idea, we also can get past the "perfect" holiday idea. Keep the celebrations low key and comfortable. You want to create balance—a day that's not too much and not too little. This goal can be accomplished only if you and your family can accept less of everything. In exchange, you create a season that is harmonious, peaceful, and relaxing.

> *Love gives itself, it is not bought.*
>
> —Henry Wadsworth Longfellow

For instance, who says the house has to be perfectly clean? I personally like a little extra clutter during the holidays. And I feel more comfortable in someone else's house when I feel as if I can relax. Why do we think our places need to be different? Who said you have to serve a gourmet meal? Be serious. Would you rather get invited to someone's house where your hosts are relaxed and spend time with you, or where they are buried in the kitchen under a mound of exotic concoctions? Remember, people are the important ingredient.

There is something else about lowering your cleaning and decorating expectations. One aspect of simplicity is about being more authentic and showing your more real self to the world. What does it say if you generally live in a more "relaxed" way (polite way of saying not totally tidy) and then you scurry around like a maniac before guests arrive? If you are not a neatness fanatic, why are you pretending to be one when guests come over? I know about this syndrome because I have done it. Once I realized I liked to be a guest in a relaxed house, I slowly began to admit to the public that I had a more "relaxed" style of housekeeping. Now I scurry around some, but not as much. I scurry just enough to clean the bathroom and tidy up a bit, but I don't go overboard. Especially at holiday time, I don't need one more impossible standard to uphold.

I've also lowered my decorating expectations. My tree decorations are a conglomeration of items the kids have made throughout the years plus ornaments people have given us and an array of other miscellaneous goodies. Nothing matches, but it sure packs a lot of memories. Each year as we take out these ornaments we can reminisce about their origins. We hang a few lights around doorways, put some fresh greens on the mantel, add a few more candles on the table, and we're set.

In a book titled *Happy Holidays! Uplifting Advice About How to Avoid the Holiday Blues and Recapture the True Spirit of Christmas, Hanukkah, and New Year's,* author Dr. Wayne Dyer reminds us to recall the exuberance and joy we experienced as children and recapture the spirit as adults. Accept the holiday season and find delight in it. We can find delight only when we relax our must-be-perfect attitudes. So what if every detail doesn't get attended to? We'll feel better, and those around us will reap the results.

Here's how I handle Christmas day. When my house became the hub of Christmas celebrations for my extended family, I quickly decided that I was not going to slave alone all day in the kitchen cooking the "perfect" meal. I announced to everyone that from now on, Christmas dinner was potluck. I was met with a few groans and "how could you do that on Christmas" complaints, but I stood firm. Now I can host holiday dinners for 10 to 20 with less stress than I have on an ordinary night. I only have to cook one or two items, and I get to sit down to a lavish meal. When friends join my family, they also bring a dish or two. I'm not out a lot of money and I'm not out a lot of time. Neither is anyone else.

This potluck idea has other benefits as well. Sharing responsibilities takes the pressure off of one person to "do it right." It also invites a feeling of community. An interesting study was conducted in Barrow, Alaska, one year. There, where alcoholism and spouse abuse runs high, incidents of both become lower during the Christmas season. One reason is because Christmas in Barrow is a true community celebration. Everyone gets out of the house and involved in the very public festivities. Everyone participates in the preparations for those festivities. The emphasis is on the community celebration.

Create Easy Rituals

 Bet and Mike Kowalski have created holiday rituals that are simple and magical. They spread the emphasis of the season throughout the month of December and into January. On December 1 the Kowalskis and their three children decorate the house. They hang tissue-paper snowflakes and stars from the windows and ceilings, string angels from golden threads, and hang cedar boughs around the windows. They make an Advent wreath and put up an Advent calendar. In a corner of the room, they create an Advent garden where they display the special nativity scene that Bet made. Then they spread their collection of small votive candles throughout the house.

"We use the whole month to focus on the holiday season," Bet says. "It's a month to spend lots of time at home together. It's a month for nurturing and looking inward."

Each night they light a candle and read a Christmas story to their children. They sing Christmas carols throughout the season and reserve a day to make gingerbread houses. One evening the home-schooling group in their community holds a craft fair, which gives the children an opportunity to make gifts and ornaments. At home, all the family gets involved with making gifts for one another and extended family members. The children's handmade gifts may include a beautiful picture they painted for a grandparent, a tissue-paper transparency of the Nativity scene, or a little paper bug. "The more the parents get into the habit of making, not buying, the more the children will role-model. It becomes more of a lifestyle," says Bet.

Although most of the Kowalski gifts are handmade, a few are commercial. As many children do, Bet and Mike's children eagerly await finding surprises from Santa Claus under the tree on Christmas morning.

"I think it's important to have a day set aside for the children to feel special. Receiving gifts on Christmas morning is important for children, yet it's just as important to guide children in acknowledging all the wonder of the Christmas season," Bet says. "Our children have discovered much magic and wonder in Christmas legends we read during this time. Filling their lives with such stories feeds their souls and imaginations in a very positive way."

On December 21 the family celebrates the winter solstice. One year they built a fire outside; another year they put lots of votive candles around the house to symbolize the return of the sun. "It's a very magical time," they say. "We have a little story we read about the sun, and we sing a song. We go around a circle and each one takes a turn holding the candle and saying why they're thankful for the sun. It's a very simple way to acknowledge the sun coming back.

"Any family can do this kind of ritual. Light a lot of votive candles, turn off the lights, and say a few little verses, songs, or prayers . . . whatever spiritual background a family has. The idea is to bring the family together through rituals."

Another ritual is Christmas Eve. "We usually go for a walk that day, or a hike, then come back and prepare a finger-food meal together. We spread a blanket in front of the fire and eat together. Afterward, we have an ornament exchange when each person takes a turn handing out a handmade ornament. That night is so wonderful and is very important to our children."

The key to starting your own traditions is to begin with something very easy that feels right to your family. Create something that everyone can look forward to, and be flexible. Bet says: "Our traditions are not set in stone . . . they're still being formed as the children grow. If you have small children, start the first year by creating a new ritual. The next year they'll naturally want to participate."

At holiday time, the more you can make your home seem magical and nurturing, the more you can encourage the true spirit of the season. You can transform your house with simple handmade decorations and artifacts from nature. Let nature and your imagination do the job.

The authors of a book titled *Natural Christmas* advise getting to the heart of the holiday through the use of natural decorations. Their idea germinated in France, where they were stranded one winter with no ornaments, tinsel, or lights. They also had no electricity. They "shopped" in nature—foraging greenery from the forest, harvesting a little tree from the side of a stream, and decorating their house with candles and fruit. The authors advise shunning gold-sprayed garlands and turning your back on tinsel: "Nature is the goal," they say.

Add Richness to the Holiday

What other ways can we add richness to our holiday season, without spending a lot of money? When the authors of *Unplug the Christmas Machine* asked people what they wanted, the answer was more depth and meaning. It wasn't enough for people to just write out a check for a poor family at holiday time; it wasn't enough to drop off a toy at a collection site; they wanted to be filled with genuine compassion and a sense of connection to humanity. They were concerned at how self-centered their holidays had become, with worries about how their houses looked or what other people thought of them. They realized they weren't reaching out. They wanted to use the holiday season as a time to connect with ideas and experiences larger than themselves. The authors pointed out that a lot of us go through the holiday season without a clear sense of what we value. We plan our celebrations right down to what kind of cranberry sauce to serve, but we forget to ask ourselves why we are celebrating.

When we meet with our family or friends to discuss our favorite holiday memories and the money/love equation, we also should talk about what our

A Holiday Idea List

Ideas About Your Frame of Mind

❖ Make a list of all the things you dislike about the holidays, and allow yourself to get rid of most or all of them. This is your life: It is perfectly reasonable not to continue dealing with unnecessary, unpleasant things.

❖ The best thing you can do to feel good is to find a way to give to others: Talk with people who come to eat at a soup kitchen; visit someone who is sick or bereaved; take a few turkey sandwiches to the police or fire station; drive a house-bound friend or neighbor around the neighborhood to see the holiday decorations.

❖ You can decide what you want for yourself, your family, and your friends. Pick and choose what *you* want to do rather than focusing on what you believe *others* think you should do. Don't spend your holidays just fulfilling obligations.

❖ The efforts of many people make the holidays a success; you are not solely responsible.

❖ The way you celebrated last year (or the year before) need not determine the way you celebrate this year. Your "tradition" could be to celebrate the holidays in a variety of different ways over the years. Expectations are the greatest deterrent to happy holidays.

❖ You don't *have* to accept every invitation. Choose the events that you most *want* to attend.

❖ Save one day for yourself: don't schedule anything.

❖ The holidays need not be a time of competition as to the most expensive presents, the biggest tree, the most elaborate dinner, the most extensive decorations, and so on.

❖ If this is your first holiday after a divorce, death, or the end of relationship, leave town! Temporarily remove yourself from constant reminders of the past.

Written by Annie Morrissey, Director of Educational Services, Working Solutions, Inc., copyright 1995.

values mean to us at this time of year. If a value is spending quiet time at home with our children or family, then we need to accept fewer social engagements. If our value is reaching out to others, then we need to create a plan. For example, spend time calling churches in your area to volunteer for a helping program. How do we want to help others? Will it require money? If so, figure that into the overall holiday budget. If it means spending less on each other but accomplishes a goal of living a value, then it is not a sacrifice. Is a value wanting to get to know the neighbors? Spending less time shopping may free up the time needed to invite them over.

Lynn Willeford spent one Christmas volunteering with her family in Costa Rica. She and her husband, Blake, thought their middle-school-age son could use a break from peer pressure, and the family wanted something more than the usual hectic holiday season. Both had flexible careers, he as a carpenter and she as a freelance writer. They also own a movie theater in the small town in which they live, and found caretakers to operate it in their absence. The family planned ahead and worked hard from the beginning of the year and saved money so they could leave for two months. They signed on with a volunteer agency and went to work building roads, trails, and bridges in a rain forest preserve.* "That holiday trip was part of a two-month stay in Costa Rica," Lynn says. "We wanted our son Brook to experience living in another country where commercialism wasn't so rampant. There are so many commercial messages aimed at that age group."

Holiday season in Costa Rica is very focused on family and religion. The emphasis is on going to church, being with family, and having a feast, rather than frenzied shopping and decorating. "It wasn't about buying a lot of stuff to hide in the closet," Lynn remembers. "There were gifts, but the kids weren't all hyped up about it. People seemed to spend time making little things and being together. The whole season was far more low key than it is in America."

The Willefords lived with a group of volunteers and worked at projects that were directed by local people. Residents of the town of Santa Elena wanted to improve their local high school using self-generated funds. They decided to develop an old farm into an educational center for people visiting the local rain forest. The fees they would collect from trail users would go toward the high school improvement project.

The two-week volunteer work was finished just before Christmas, and the family stayed in Costa Rica throughout the rest of the season. They did their Christmas shopping in the little town. "It was interesting," Lynn says. "There was very little to buy and tempt you. We bought a string of twinkle lights at the hardware store, and our son wanted a machete to use back home at our house in the woods. We bought a couple of Spanish books. We got out of that whole shopping thing."

While the trip was very satisfying for the parents, Lynn says Brook was not totally pleased. He missed having a Christmas tree and some of the family's rituals. He missed Christmas cookies. Yet he says he gained an appreciation for

❖ ❖ ❖ ❖ ❖ ❖ ❖ ❖ ❖ ❖ ❖ ❖ ❖ ❖ ❖ ❖ ❖ ❖ ❖ ❖

*Contact Global Volunteers, 375 E. Little Canada Road, St. Paul, MN 55117-1628. With most volunteer agencies, people who wish to work must pay a fee to the agency that covers room, board, and round-trip transportation as well as fees that go toward operating local projects. Fees vary depending on the project and agency.

what Christmas means to people in other cultures, and he would do it again. Lynn says it was good for him to see how people could be happy at a much lower level of material comfort. He could see options that were fulfilling.

The family also got a glimpse of how a small, simple local economy works. When they stayed with a woman after the volunteer work, they could see exactly where their money went. They would give her money for food, and often she would go out and buy extras for them. She would return home with a blanket for their bed, and the Willefords knew that the money had gone to the blanket maker in town. When she bought them a reading light for their room, they knew the money went to the man who operated the one hardware store in town. When there was extra food, she would bring it to the family next door who was experiencing hardship. "You could see the effects of your money directly," Lynn says.

"For me, it was so relaxing not to have to do any of the things you normally do during the holidays," Lynn remembers. "It was very comforting. I'd recommend it even for people who are very attached to holiday traditions, because it sets you back a step so you can get perspective. You can look from afar to see what the holidays mean to you . . . if you've been racing around too much and lost the point of the season, you can rethink how you want to celebrate in the future. Or maybe you find that you really miss being with your sister or your aunts and uncles. Maybe you really miss having turkey dinner. You'll discover what you really care about and what you can let go of. I think it's good to be out of the country at least once."

Give Yourselves the Gift of Reflection

One of the best ways you can slow the hectic pace of the holidays and spread the anticipation and excitement over a period of time is by acknowledging the season of Advent, or *waiting*. In the Christian tradition, Advent begins on the fourth Sunday before Christmas and is the period of waiting for Christ to be born.

You don't need to follow any religious custom to ritualize this period of waiting. It's a terrific opportunity to clear your calendar and recall the value of patience. Think of time and waiting as a gift. Use this waiting time for daily reflection, both on the meaning of life and on the meaning of the holiday season. How much do we lose if we spend it partying, frantically shopping, and entertaining?

The inner preparation or "waiting" time usually begins around December 1. You can start the period by making or purchasing a "family candle." If you are alone, think about gathering with a friend or two. Choose a night early in the season and call it your Silent Night. (You can have one or more Silent Nights as you see fit.) Light your candle and have it be your only source of light. Have everyone sit around it. You can conduct your Silent Night in any number of ways and for any length of time that seems suitable to you. (For example, younger children can sit quietly for shorter periods of time than older children.) Here are some ideas from a book titled *A Gift of Time:*

❖ Meditate on different family members. Look at Mother, and ask how she could use help during this time. Look at Dad. Does he seem tired? What can we do to help him? How about brothers and sisters? Are they worried about anything? Can I offer to make her or his bed or prepare their lunch?

❖ Have a no-noise meditation. Have everyone sit quietly for five minutes of silence and look at familiar things in the room as if seeing them for the first time. Try to imagine how these things feel, taste, or smell. When the time is up, share what you have learned.

❖ Have a quiet listening meditation. Play favorite holiday songs, ring bells, listen to the crackling of the fire in the fireplace. Do each one slowly and allow time between each to fully savor each one.

❖ For couples, after the children have gone to bed, sit or lie on the floor in a darkened room with only a lighted candle nearby. Take a fresh look at the person beside you. Notice the shape of the face, the cut of hair, skin color, wrinkles, and blemishes. Spend a few minutes gazing into the other person's eyes and, as you do, remember the love you have for that person.

Or you can simply sit quietly and follow your breathing. Use this time to introduce yourself or your family to the power of silent meditation. Start with a short time of five minutes and work up to more time as it feels comfortable. After your silence, you could read an inspirational story or talk about how you can help yourselves and your neighbors, friends, and community during this time.

Another way you can ritualize this waiting period is by making an Advent wreath. You can make your wreath by gathering greens into a circle and placing four candles in the circle, with the fifth candle in the center. Many books in the library give instructions on making an Advent wreath. During the first week of Advent, for a little while each night, burn one candle. During the second week, choose a second candle to light along with the first one, and so on through the four weeks of the holiday. On Christmas Day, light the center candle.

In order to reflect during this time, you can turn each lighting into a small ceremony. Take this time for quiet and reflection. Talk about your values. Talk about the intangible gifts you will each give this week, such as sharing what you have to be thankful for, or telling family members or friends what you like about them. You could write these "gifts" on a piece of paper, wrap them up, and leave them beside a plate. Children can write on a paper star each week or day something they will give of themselves—help Mom, wash dishes, stop tormenting brother, put away toys without being asked. You also could write down one act of kindness that you performed or would like to perform each day or each week. You can include spiritual readings with the ceremony. Consider incorporating solstice celebrations by using the wreath to celebrate nature (greens) and the coming of light (candles).

You also can use this time to focus on how to be better human beings. Pick a virtue of the week, for example, and talk about how you can incorporate it into your lives. Compassion is a virtue. Find a reading on compassion, and then discuss ways you could practice compassion throughout the week. Two of my favorite books that explain the virtues are by Linda Kavelin Popov, *The Virtues Guide* and *Sacred Moments*. This time of reflection helps us to slow down the hectic pace of a commercialized holiday season and think about what is important to us.

Another way to symbolize the value of waiting is by making handmade gifts. It takes sweet, loving time to make a gift for someone you love. You can help your children understand this waiting concept by encouraging them to make gifts for family members or friends. They'll understand the joy of creating something, hiding it until gift-giving day, and then giving it to someone. Some projects take days or weeks to finish. There is much waiting involved.

Thomas Berger writes in *The Christmas Craft* book: "By occupying ourselves and our children in making these things, we create an atmosphere of preparation and expectation which fosters the spirit of Christmas in the soul of a child."

You can use an Advent calendar to talk about waiting. Commercial holiday hucksters remind us constantly that there are only 12, 11, 10 shopping days left, all in an effort to send us scurrying at an even faster pace to get everything done before the big day. Instead, create an Advent or waiting calendar that encourages a reflection of recognizing each other's good deeds, talking about what waiting means to us, and sharing examples of waiting. Get a piece of thin cardboard or white construction-type paper and draw a large house, church, synagogue, or other symbolic building with many doors and windows. If yours is a strictly earth-based tradition, you could make a forest scene and cut out little doors and windows in the trees and mountains. Make the sun your biggest and last door. Cut out three sides of each door and window so they open and close. On the inside of each door and window, write questions that are about waiting and patience. A few examples from the book *The Gift of Time* are: What do you think patience means? What do you think about when you are waiting? Describe someone you think is a patient person. Is it ever good to be impatient? If so, when? How is waiting a kind of loving? How can we grow to be better persons from waiting?

Create the calendar using your own secular or nonsecular beliefs. If you follow the Christian tradition, make 24 doors and windows, one to be opened every day from December 1 and ending December 24. If you follow the solstice tradition, have the calendar reflect the cycle of nature, and so on. Each day family members open one door and reflect on its question. And remember, you only need to make the calendar once. You can reuse it year after year.

Put Something Back

However you decide to create your holiday season, remember always to put back what you take away. For instance, if you and your family agree to spend less on gifts, be sure to add something better—more time together doing things you all enjoy, more effort into exercising compassion for each other and the world, more time spent celebrating nature. I read a wonderful nature story one time by Robert Fulghum, author of *Everything I Always Wanted to Know I Learned in Kindergarten*. Fulghum went for a hike way out in the back country of Utah one December and discovered, in the middle of nowhere, a decorated, live Christmas tree. It was a 12-foot-tall pine tree that was decorated with strings of popcorn, cranberries, dried fruit, and nuts. At the very top was a silver star with a tiny angel. Who did this? he wondered. Then he saw two sets of tracks—one large, one small—an adult and a child. These people carried all this stuff through the woods and decorated the tree with things birds and small animals might eat. When Fulghum returned two months later, the tree was undecorated. Fulghum was inspired by the imagination of this tribute to nature. What a wonderful way to add something better to our own holiday seasons!

Another family packs food, rents a cabin in the woods, and spends every holiday tracking animals. A busy photographer and his wife took one Christmas off from the usual family festivities and rented a remote bed-and-breakfast cottage. "Every year it was the same thing," he told me. "There were parties to

222

attend, gift exchanges . . . it gets to be extremely social. That one year we wanted a more peaceful, reflective time." They brought with them a small tree and decorated it with strings of popcorn and cranberries and little paper snowflakes that they cut. On Christmas day they opened the gifts they brought for each other, read, and made Christmas dinner together in the kitchen. The best part of that dinner was that they were able to prepare the meal in a mindful, leisurely way without outside distractions.

One year at holiday time, a couple I know had just moved to a new city. They wanted to reach out during the season, so they called a local church and offered to volunteer at a holiday dinner for homeless people. Rather than feeling lonely, they were instead renewed with a sense of compassion and selflessness. They also met new friends. A single man I know spent many holiday seasons lamenting that he didn't have his own family and didn't feel especially close to his parents. He felt left out and alone. Finally he decided to let go of his old expectations and look past himself. He began reaching out to his community and giving his time to those in need. He discovered that once he got involved in helping others, he felt better, and his holiday season took on new meaning. He continued to celebrate with his parents and still struggled with some of his old feelings, but he broadened his focus by incorporating new rituals into his season.

Learning from Ethnic Traditions

Kwanzaa

Some people take back the holidays by returning to their roots. Kwanzaa is an African American celebration of the seven days after Christmas. It is not a religious holiday; rather, it is a reaffirmation of African American culture through African rituals, traditions, and values. Kwanzaa was initiated in 1966 by Dr. Maulana Karenga, a professor of Pan-African and Black studies, as a way for Blacks to come together to celebrate their history and culture and focus on values that are beneficial to their development. Those values include collective work and responsibility (*ujima*), creativity (*kuumba*), faith (*imani*), and unity (*umoja*). Kwanzaa also includes principles such as self-determination (*kujichagulia*), purpose (*nia*), and cooperative economics (*ujamma*). Each day families prepare handmade gifts for people in their lives. The first day is devoted to the immediate family, followed by the extended family, neighbors, coworkers, and so on. A candelabra with seven candles sits on a straw mat in the home, surrounded by fruit to symbolize the adults in the family. One ear of corn is placed on the mat to represent each child. Each night of the weeklong celebration, a new candle is lit and the family shares juice from a special chalice.

Kimi Raburn was introduced to Kwanzaa in 1982. Over the years, she gradually incorporated more and more of the Kwanzaa principles into her family's Christmas celebration. "For me, Kwanzaa was an awareness-raising," Kimi says. "It made me more self-reflective. I said 'Wait a minute, I spend a lot of money on Christmas . . . I'm caught up in all that hype.' Now my Christmas is more simple and more meaningful, a return to the true spirit of Christmas, which is the birth of Christ, not running down to the mall."

Kimi says Dr. Karenga felt that part of his responsibility as a professor of Black studies was to discover lost rituals of African people. He journeyed to Africa and witnessed a ritual called *Kwanza* (Swahili for "first fruits"). Kwanza was a time to acknowledge the continuing harvest cycle—when it was successful, the people gathered to celebrate. Dr. Karenga also noticed a sense of unity brought on by the celebration and was impressed by the collective work, responsibility, cooperative economics, purpose, creativity, and faith of the people. He wanted African American people to experience this but wondered how, given that most Americans live in urban, not agricultural, areas.

Kimi Raburn prepares for Kwanzaa.

Dr. Karenga focused on seven of the principles he noticed and created a ritual that would fit into American lifestyles. He decided to incorporate Kwanza during holiday season, a time when African American people needed reaffirmation and inspiration. "Many African American people live in poverty," Kimi says, "and the holiday season isn't a good time for them because it has gotten so commercialized. Dr. Karenga wanted people to have a simple, more realistic, relevant celebration. Kwanzaa was born."

A series of events during Dr. Karenga's first Kwanza celebration led to the change of spelling. The American version is now spelled Kwanzaa.

Kwanzaa is not designed to take the place of Christmas or any other religious holiday. Thus, families who acknowledge Kwanzaa generally celebrate both Kwanzaa and whatever religious holiday they believe in. Kwanzaa simply changes the focus of a highly commercialized holiday and adds its own deeper, cultural rituals. "I get really offended when I see greeting card companies trying to make money from selling Kwanzaa cards," Kimi says. "Nobody wants to make money off of this . . . that's why Dr. Karenga created it."

Kimi says her family's Christmas celebration has deepened and simplified as a result of Kwanzaa. She has two children (ages 13 and 15) for whom she still buys Christmas gifts, but the gifts are fewer in number and less expensive. She has replaced the primary focus on money with a focus on giving and reflecting. Each year she and her children work at a Boys and Girls Club hosting a holiday party for needy children. "I didn't think about these kinds of values before I started celebrating Kwanzaa," she says. "Before I just accepted the usual way of observing Christmas. I wanted to make sure my kids had all the material things I didn't have. I was a very impulsive spender. Now I take a step back before I buy. Kwanzaa taught me to be more reflective and to not worry about keeping up with the Joneses. That just doesn't have substance. A friend of mine recalled the day he reached that same point. He told me, 'I can't hug my BMW.' What he needed was a hug from a friend."

Kimi says she believes African Americans are basically spiritual people who lost that quality as they assimilated other values and standards that are not African-based. "Experiencing Kwanzaa is like grounding people in a way they've never been grounded before."

Kwanzaa also has replaced the huge letdown that many people experience the day after Christmas, because Kwanzaa begins on December 26. "We're just gearing up then," Kimi says. And for her family, Kwanzaa doesn't end on January 1. "I carry the Kwanzaa principles with me 365 days a year. I'm a better person if I practice unity and creativity, for example, throughout the year. And my kids have a very good sense of who they are as a result of this daily practice. They have a high regard for others. I think practicing Kwanzaa on a regular basis is a way to continually reinforce these things for them."

Each year during the Kwanzaa celebration, Kimi's kids invite a new friend over to experience the ritual with them. "Without fail, every year those kids are so moved by our celebration they ask us to help them figure out how to bring it to their homes," Kimi says. "That's how Kwanzaa is spreading—each one teach one."

Latino Customs

Arturo Vargas was born in Mexico City and remembers that the emphasis in his family at holiday time was on friendship and affection rather than gifts.

"Giving presents to each other wasn't very strong," he says. "We felt it was an American thing. We might give one present to my mom and dad, but my dad especially didn't like it at all . . . he didn't feel it was necessary. He felt you could show love in other ways."

One way the Vargas family, and many other Mexican families, showed their love for each other was through the custom of *El Abraso de Navidad,* "the Christmas Hug." Everyone eagerly awaited the hour of midnight on Christmas Eve, when people would stop whatever they were doing and give each other hugs. "It was a very emotional time," Arturo remembers. People thought that Jesus was born at midnight on December 24, and the hug signified happiness over his birth. Sometimes they would place a statue of the infant Jesus in a shawl, swinging the shawl back and forth as if putting him to sleep.

"For Dad, Christmas was about being together and showing respect and love," Arturo says. "We never heard of Santa Claus."

Now that Arturo lives in America, he finds it more difficult to refrain from the gift giving, yet he indulges only his five-year-old-son and American-born wife. He carries on the tradition of showing affection for friends and loved ones. "Even for me, I'm not religious, but holiday time is at the end of the year, it's a time to see all of the people you care about and a time to get dressed up. It's an emotional time. We always make sure that our friends are taken care of and have a place to go."

Fulgencio Lazo is an artist who was born in Oaxaco, Mexico. He married an American, Erin Fanning, and together they have woven their cultures and personal interests into a meaningful holiday celebration. They live in the United States.

One year, on December 15, the couple celebrated the Latino custom of *Las Posadas* ("the inns"). It is a symbolic reenactment of the Holy Family's search for shelter. This festive celebration involves groups of adults and children dressing in costumes. They parade through the streets, stopping at houses along the way for hot beverages and doughnuts made of corn and honey. In Mexico, families usually begin celebrating *Las Posadas* on December 13 or 14 and continue every night until December 24.

Erin and Fulgencio decorated their house with *faroles* (tissue-paper lanterns) and made traditional *Las Posadas* food, such as ponche (fruit tea) and tamales. They started at a neighbor's house 10 blocks away and walked through the streets singing and carrying *faroles.* They gathered with 40 of their friends and neighbors. "We don't give out presents," Fulgencio says, "instead we give lots of food, drink, and music."

The couple shares a house with two of Fulgencio's brothers. For them holiday time is simply an extension of the way they conduct their lives throughout the rest of the year: giving of their time and love to friends, family, and community. Giving gifts is not important, and they do not exchange gifts with each other. "We have no tradition of giving gifts at holiday time in Oaxaca," Fulgencio says. When they do give gifts to other family members or friends, those gifts are always handmade by Erin and Fulgencio, such as papier-mâché masks, bowls, or decorative objects.

"Bringing people together and spending time together . . . that's the spirit of what we bring to the holidays. A lot of the spirit is being more tuned into the community by giving more of ourselves to people. It's not so much about giving material things," Erin says.

Erin and Fulgencio think it is best when people live out their daily values at holiday time. "People say the holidays are a time to bring families together, but a lot of time it's a kind of forced thing," she says. "If you live in the same area as your family and never see them except on Christmas, it doesn't make sense to force yourself to be with these people one day of the year." She finds that most Latino families place a lot of emphasis on spending time together throughout the year. "People think it's amazing that we share a house with Fulgencio's two brothers, but to us it would be abnormal if we didn't.

"In a lot of Latino cultures, family is not seen as oppressive but rather as a support system where you love each other. It's not all perfect, but in general, the ethic is that there will be unity. It's a way of providing support for each other and also so the children are raised in an intergenerational environment. We try to create that with our neighbors and friends here in the United States."

Hanukkah

Hanukkah celebrates the return of light and the promise of spring to come. Hanukkah commemorates the renewal and rededication of the temple in Jerusalem in the year 165 B.C. by Judah Maccabe. The celebration reminds Jewish people that devotion always requires renewal and rededication. During this holiday, people light a Menorah (candelabra) with eight candles, lighting one candle each night. The family gathers together and sings blessings and prayers. Often children are given one gift for each night of Hanukkah.

Marilyn Meyer is Jewish. She finds that when families are more observant, their Hanukkah celebrations are less commercial. As a conservative Jew, Marilyn says that Hanukkah is simplified by the mere fact that it is only one of nine major Jewish holidays observed throughout the year. Thus the emphasis on giving and celebrating is spread out rather than focused entirely on one day or one holiday. Marilyn says: "It's sometimes a bit embarrassing to be greeted by Gentile friends who ask how Hanukkah was, as if it were equivalent to a Christmas celebration."

Marilyn also observes Shabbat (the Sabbath) every Friday night. Shabbat is an ancient ritual dinner that welcomes 24 hours of nonwork. At Marilyn's house, dinner begins with everyone singing "Sholom Aleikhem," which means "peace unto you." "It's a song that welcomes the angels of peace and rest into your home," Marilyn says.

Because the dinner is a celebration, it involves several courses, including some traditional foods such as challah (twisted egg bread). No one eats until the bread is broken, and the bread is not broken until the close of a 10-minute ceremony of song and prayers (blessing for the Sabbath rest, sanctification of wine, hand-washing ceremony, and blessing of the children).

"Shabbat is based on the biblical law that commands us to rest on the seventh day," Marilyn says. "It is a holy ceremony where everything slows down. There are no interruptions during dinner—we don't answer the phone and we don't turn on the TV or music.

"I'm a single parent, and when you're a working single parent you don't slow down very much. It's important to me to slow down on Friday night and then observe the Sabbath until Saturday night. Instead of working during this period, we devote ourselves to family or nature and getting rest. I can choose to live a simple life for those 24 hours, and the fact that the Sabbath is an ancient ritual law helps me to keep it."

Because she incorporates so much of the spiritual aspect of Judaism into her family's daily life, Marilyn places much less emphasis on gift giving at Hanukkah. Marilyn says she gives her 10-year-old daughter one small gift per day, such as an art kit, a hat, or pair of earrings. "Faith fills in for the older kids," she says.

The tradition of giving gifts on Hanukkah goes back to medieval Germany, when children were given foil-covered chocolates. "The Hanukkah tradition escalated to where it parallels Christmas gift giving in many Jewish communities today," Marilyn says. "None of my children can go anywhere during this time without someone asking them what Santa is giving them. The potlatch of Christmas makes it more difficult for people with children to celebrate Hanukkah modestly."

Marilyn says her determination to remember the spiritual aspects of being Jewish has been worthwhile. Her oldest child, Ben, is 20. One year after he had gone away to college, Marilyn sat down to clean out her computer files. She discovered an essay that Ben had written many years before for an English class. In the essay, he talked about how proud he was to bring friends home to Shabbat dinners. At age 13, Marilyn's daughter Genevieve decided on her own to "adopt" a child by sending money to an overseas children's foundation on a regular basis. During last year's Hanukkah, Genevieve asked her mother if she could spend the money she had planned to use for a gift for her mother on a charitable donation instead. And Marilyn regularly donates to charity. "That makes me feel good," she says. "Paying bills doesn't. Donating comes from that spiritual sense of being raised to give."

Other Ways to Celebrate Ethnic Traditions

Many people open themselves up to community as a way to incorporate their heritage into the holiday season. A group of neighbors in one area opens their homes during a celebration they call Winter Revelry. Each house has a holiday theme, such as Kwanzaa, Hanukkah, or Christmas. Musicians gather and make music, children put on shows, and families serve traditional foods. A Jewish home features Jewish folk music and folktales. Another decorates with clouds of cotton hanging from the ceiling in a celestial celebration, featuring children's dance performances. The community feeling lasts far beyond holiday season.

You also can incorporate your ethnic traditions by cooking an ethnic dish or two for your holiday dinner. You could add a little background information to read at the table. By focusing more on your family's roots, you take yet another step away from commercialism, while adding more richness to your holiday.

Earth-Based Celebrations

Jacqueline Higgins-Rosebrook decided long ago to embrace pagan traditions and center her celebrations around the natural cycles of the earth. Although raised in a Christian family, Jacque celebrates winter solstice rather than Christmas. Winter solstice is celebrated on December 21, when light returns as the days grow longer again. The natural world begins to rejuvenate. Jacque celebrates the changing pattern of the natural world all throughout the year. There are dates to commemorate nearly every month. One example is summer solstice, celebrated on June 21. In February she celebrates a period midway between winter solstice and spring equinox. March 21 is spring equinox, another day to acknowledge new life and growth in the budding of the tree. October 31 is a time for letting go of the old and looking ahead to the new. It marks the end of the harvest season.

Every year on winter solstice, Jacque and a group of 20 or more friends gather to celebrate together. Because solstice is during a dark phase of the year, the group celebrates the power of the darkness. "This period allows for contemplative activity and time to acknowledge what darkness means to us," Jacque says.

Since most people in the group are artists (people involved in the theater, music, art, or writing), a few members gather early to plan each year's celebration. They set up the ceremony as a theater piece and include rituals such as sharing of food, calling on the elements of the natural world to help with the ceremony, and creating a sacred space by using a number of ritual elements.

Participants sit on the floor and there is one candle lit for each person in the room. After each person finishes talking about darkness, he or she blows out a candle. This ritual is repeated until the group sits in total darkness. Next they may do a guided meditation on some aspect of the solstice. As people are inspired, they relight a candle as a way to express the light returning.

The ceremony always includes children, who stay in the room until the lights are turned out. They go to a separate room and create an art project while the adults complete their darkness ceremony. They return with their completed project when it is time to relight the candles. One winter solstice the children made a collective painting using sparkling paints and passed out phosphorescent necklaces for all to wear. This symbolized bringing in the light. At the summer solstice ceremony, the children made and decorated kites. These were used to symbolize a letting-go of negative emotions and an offering of prayers at the end of that ceremony.

When the ceremony is finished, everyone shares food, stories, and fun. "Some of us don't see each other except at these ceremonies, so we share news of our families, children, and work," Jacque says.

Carin Wylette likes the eight-holiday-a-year celebrations that are associated with pagan traditions. "You get in tune with the natural world," she says. "And you don't put all of your eggs into one basket as we tend to do when focusing all of our celebrating on one day like Christmas." Carin often acknowledges one of the eight days by spending the day meditating. "My life feels more calm and centered that way."

Another family celebrates solstice by inviting friends and family to their house for dinner, and they decorate a solstice tree in the same way a Christmas tree is festooned. They put a pine and winter berry wreath on the front door and exchange gifts. While many of the outward trappings are similar to a Christmas celebration, theirs is about the change of seasons and the recycling and rebirth process that occurs.

You can combine elements of solstice with other holiday traditions in many ways. One family described how they integrate both into their Advent celebration:

> Our family celebrates Christmas. We love to celebrate and spend months making our presents because we love to create things and hate the commercialism. . . . We like to spend Advent bringing the true meaning of the season into our hearts. We sing, light candles, and enjoy the dark nights. We also lay a beautiful cloth over a small table. Each day of Advent the elves (we believe in magic around here) leave something small from the natural world on the table. The first week is small stones or other things from the mineral world, the second week from the plant world, the third from the animal world (shells, old nests, etc.), and the last week the elves bring in the nativity scene.
>
> This simple activity has taught our children more about the true meaning of the holidays than anything else we do. Christmas is one area where I feel our values have really made it through to our children. More than once they have said that the presents are not their favorite part of Christmas; they like the preparations.
>
> Patti Pitcher
>
> Seattle, Washington (Patti sent this letter to *Simple Living*)

You can celebrate solstice and the coming of winter as an opportunity to invite friends, neighbors, and/or coworkers to dinner, even if you have never socialized with them before. You can also call your local social services agency to invite a family or an individual to share your meal.

Inspire Your Children

If we want our children to find more meaning in the holidays than the latest toy, then we need to provide ways for them to get involved. It is not enough that they be passive observers to all of our celebrations. Involve the kids in your family meetings. Take their opinions seriously in deciding how to create a special holiday. A single mom I know gives her son a weekly allowance all year long. He spends part, saves part, and puts the last part into a pot to be given to a charity of his choice. Make giving even more personal by working with a church to find a family in need and go there in person to deliver your gift. You and your children can cook a meal to be delivered to someone who could use the help. In the book *Celebrating Christmas as If It Matters*,

Susan Schaeffer Macaulay remembers those experiences from her childhood in Switzerland.

Each year her family cooked a holiday dinner for someone in the village. Their mother would ask around to find a needy family. They had one roast dinner a year for their own family, but still, the mother would buy another one for the needy family. She put it in a box with other gifts, such as food and a plant. The family would hike through the snow to the needy family's house. Susan remembers one particular year:

> One year it must have been about a two-hour hike, way up into the mountains, on Christmas Eve day. We went to visit a little boy lying on a wooden bed who had been in the same room for nearly two years; he had a tubercular hip. The family had nothing. No running water, just potatoes and a bit of milk from their one cow. I shall always remember this little boy's eyes as we unpacked our things.

Another suggestion is from the *Alternate Celebrations Catalogue*:

> Last Christmas, we got together and gave a party for all of our children. The party was devised around the plan to have the children wrap their own toys to give to other children. We read to them from the Bible about what Jesus said about love and giving. . . . The children brought a tremendous amount of gifts that they wanted to give away: toys, books, clothing. When all the things were wrapped, we took the children and the gifts to the home of a family, fatherless, with 16 children. They understood that they were not taking these gifts to show that they were good boys and girls . . . they were humble, and I don't think that they will ever forget the experience.

Forget the Whole Thing

 If you have no religious ties to the holiday season and the whole thing seems totally out of hand, why not ignore it? Who says you have to turn this time into an event with deep meaning? Maybe your life is meaningful throughout the rest of the year. If so, what's the point of scrambling around to find meaning during one month of the year? Many people use the holiday season as their time to take a vacation and escape. Check into a cabin in the woods or a hotel in a tropical location and enjoy the peace and quiet. If you know this is what you would like to do next year, start saving now so your vacation doesn't cause you to go into debt. You also can check out in your own house. Use the time as a personal retreat and hole up with candles and books. Take off and go for a hike alone or with friends who feel the same as you do. Staying in town is more difficult, because often people will have trouble leaving you alone, since they assume everyone wants a "meaningful," involved holiday season. You can do it if you assure them (and yourself) that you have made a conscience choice to forgo all of the festivities. Make sure your choice is a positive one and not the result of underlying bitterness or anger. Making life choices based on negative emotions will hardly simplify your life.

If you decide to check out, first consider the impact this will have on people close to you, especially children. If you are a member of a family, make sure your kids are part of the decision and that you put back what you take away. For instance, if you want to ignore the commercialism of gifts and tinsel, add a cozy time in a cabin or other refuge. Perhaps agree to bring one gift each. If you are a grandparent, aunt, or uncle, make sure your checking out will not be hurtful to the children in your life. Children love tradition, and if your family has been in the habit of spending the holidays together, your presence may be more important than you think. Perhaps you could simplify in other areas, such as forgoing office parties and giving gifts only to your grandchildren, nieces, and nephews. And if you do elect to give gifts, they do not need to be elaborate. You also can simplify merely by acknowledging to yourself that you have no need to search for deep meaning during the holidays. You'll just enjoy whatever events you elect to partake in, remember the children in your life, and no more. That mind-set alone will free an enormous amount of your energy.

The Hope of the Holiday Season

For those who enjoy the magic and spirituality of holiday season, take this time to remind yourselves of your search for a greater meaning in human existence. By simplifying your expectations and schedules, you can free yourself to think about what is important. You can become reenchanted by visions of compassion, unselfish love, justice, and renewed spirit. You can take the time and space to dream and wish on stars. You can make out a new version of a wish list. What would it include? The intangibles of life such as health, nurturing family relationships, the well-being of children, ways to make our lives more meaningful? Rather than shopping frantically for the right gourmet cranberry sauce and the right sweater set and tool box, you can spend the same

Holiday Tips from *Simple Living* Readers

Homemade Chocolate

My husband and I make chocolate candy for the holidays. We make up gift baskets of chocolates, homemade jelly or cookies or bread, and a handmade item of wood. My husband's employer had been throwing away wooden packing crates and pallets until Michael laid claim to the wood. He makes 3-D wooden puzzles, Chinese puzzle boxes, breadboxes, mobiles, clocks, napkin rings, and holders for Chinese exercise balls. (The balls are air compressor ball bearings from the company trash.) While our gifts are time intensive, we are doing what we like to do rather than fighting crowds and spending large sums of money. Michael and I enjoy the time we spend together making candy. We play holiday music and talk and laugh.

Pamela   Pittsburgh, Pennsylvania

Candles and Liqueur on a Chilly Night

Six years ago I began simplifying the holiday season. I grow roses and herbs, and make potpourri and sachets as presents. I often give framed photos and handmade envelopes made with recycled *Victoria* magazine pages. I make jam, chutneys, and preserves all summer to give as Christmas gifts with fresh, homemade bread. My husband and I agree to one social event per week to attend during December. Since we have no children, we buy basic necessities for the children of all local migrant farm workers. Every evening of Advent, we light a candle, pour a little liqueur, and chat about our day as we read chapters to each other from *The Frugal Gourmet Celebrates Christmas*. Each year we select a fresh tree from a nearby tree farm and walk it home a mile. We get a lot of funny looks! For Christmas dinner, I plan a coordinated menu and then ask each guest to bring one thing. We get better each year at focusing on the sacred aspects and weeding out the commercial things.

Linda   Portland, Oregon

amount of time remembering how this is a season that ties us to something much larger than ourselves. And, it is hoped, we can remember to continue to lead a simple, rich, and grace-filled life all year long.

Gifts at Work

At work, we decided not to have "Secret Santa" where we spent too much money on trinkets. Instead, each person was required to give a gift of themselves. (For example, a tape of the recipient's favorite music, the accountant offered tax services, a good cook brought a box lunch of ethnic foods, two horse lovers went horseback riding.) We also adopted a homeless family and donated time, money, and household items.

Shirley   Alexandra, Virginia

A Spiritual New Year's Eve

Throughout my 20s, I lived through so many painful and heartbreaking New Year's celebrations—the usual hat and horn nightclub party scene. It seemed that even if I had a happy love relationship through the entire year, something would happen and I would end up alone, without a date, or, worse still, with a date I couldn't stand!

Then, years later in my 40s, during a divorce, I got the idea of spending New Year's on retreat at a local monastery in prayer and contemplation, as many of the religious do. It was during this particularly difficult time, when I knew that I would be facing divorce during the coming year, that I found myself on top of a hill in Carlsbad, California, gathering the strength and fortitude to face the coming year and its challenges. This turned out to be the best possible thing I could have done for myself.

Since that New Year's, I have spent two other New Year's at the same retreat center. However, now I have my own New Year's assessment of the last year and coming year at home. I go over my datebook and answer the following three questions: What happened during the year? What did I like about last year and want more of in the coming year? What didn't I like about last year and want less of in the coming year? Then I write down my outcome/goals for the coming year as well as action I will take to make those goals a reality. All this with time for prayer and meditation.

On New Year's Day, I try to take action, however small, on each goal and on every component I wish to have in the coming year. If I plan an exercise program, I go for a long walk; if I plan for more closeness with my children, I spend time that day with them; if I plan new writing projects, I begin one or more of the projects. This thoughtful and reflective celebration is extremely soul satisfying for me and seems to get the year off to a very solid and heartfelt start.

Kathleen   Joshua Tree, California

New Year's Eve. We get together with about 6 to 12 friends starting after dinner at whoever's house has the biggest living room. We try to make sure there are several children. We bring one delicious yet simple snack to share—marinated yard-long string beans, for example. Also one favorite alcoholic and nonalcoholic drink to share. The grown-ups sit and chat and the kids run around like crazy. At midnight we go outside, set off a few inexpensive and safe sparklers, bang pots and pans, and howl at the moon. Take the warm glow of good company with you into the New Year as you snuggle into your bed and sleep good dreams.

Valentine's Day. We've developed a tradition of exchanging word games with loving and sexy content along with a very extravagant chocolate dessert. This formula makes Valentine's Day relatively simple, but also great fun to find new twists on the words and desserts. Picking just one gift tradition and one food tradition has been a great boon for us.

Fourth of July. We go to see one of the megafireworks shows in our area. Our secret is that we bicycle there. No waiting in long lines of cars for hours to get in and out. It's free, fun, and festive, and pretty darned low stress.

Thanksgiving. We have a potluck feast and take turns hosting. The hosts provide one "meat" main dish (organically grown free-range turkey or wild salmon) and one vegetarian main dish. Everyone else brings something to drink and one food specialty to share. This can be something they feel "makes" the holiday for them, like candied yams or Jell-O salad, or an exotic new experiment. We feast like kings and queens, and the cost is low to everyone. We also do our own dishes so the hosts don't get stuck with a big pile. A typical menu has been something like: baked salmon, roasted root veggies with rosemary and garlic, wild greens salad with special dressing, curried pumpkin mushroom soup, couscous casserole, hot cider with fresh ginger, choice of beers, wines, and sparkling juice, cranberry-orange chutney, cornbread stuffing, homemade bread (still warm), lime Jell-O salad with shredded carrots and raisins, antipasto tray, creamed onions with sherry, sweet green peas, and three kinds of pie with ice cream. It's different and delicious yet traditional each year.

The best part is, we do all of this on Friday, not Thursday. Everyone gets to relax and/or shop and cook Thursday in a most leisurely way, and there is still the whole weekend to relax afterward. This also leaves time to give back to the community on Thanksgiving Day (Thursday). Part of our tradition is taking a long walk and picking up litter that day, baking extra pies for the local soup kitchen, helping deliver food baskets to the homebound. We always end up feeling both rested and blessed at the end of our four-day holiday.

Beckey and family   Seattle, Washington

The Sensuality of Simplicity

This year let nature and your imagination decorate your house. Go to your yard, a nearby park, or greenbelt area and collect branches, pine cones, flowers, or other natural items that have fallen to the ground. Bring them home and lay them out on the floor. Light some candles, and have your family or friends sit around in a circle. Take five or more minutes to sit quietly with eyes closed. Breathe deeply. After your quiet time, pass each natural item around and take all the time you need to touch it, smell it, turn it over in your hands. Is it prickly or smooth? How does it feel against your skin? What does its aroma remind you of? Think about where you will put each item in your house. Maybe you could create a little nature corner on a table. When the season changes, collect different natural items and repeat the process. Doing this will awaken you and your family to the cycle of nature.

HOW ONE COUPLE BECAME FINANCIALLY INDEPENDENT

One year on her wedding anniversary, Jacque Blix got the gift she wanted: a pair of $300 gold and amethyst earrings. The very next year she also got the gift she wanted: a tape course titled "Transforming Your Relationship with Money and Achieving Financial Independence," by Joe Dominguez of the New Road Map Foundation.

What changed during that year? Jacque and her husband, Dave Heitmiller, decided they wanted to simplify their lives so they could enjoy living more. "I didn't want to be a product manager for a big corporation for the rest of my life," Dave says. "I looked back to when we were kids. When do you ever hear kids say they want to be a product manager when they grow up?"

The couple met when both worked for corporations. "We wore suits every day," Jacque says, "and I had a whole set of those little ties. We had a new Audi 5000, a new Jeep Cherokee, we went skiing in Tahoe, went to Hawaii, put a hot tub on our deck, had a boat. We never thought about what we were doing."

Until Jacque decided she wanted to change gears and return to school. She was tired of the stress and wanted to do something more in line with her talents and values. "We had already realized we would be living on less money be-

Jacque Blix and Dave Heitmiller work in their community garden.

cause I wasn't working. Even when I found a teaching job, it wouldn't pay what even one of us was earning at the corporation."

They studied the New Road Map Foundation tape course. Next they joined a voluntary simplicity study circle. They decided to create a three-year plan that would allow them both to not work at paid jobs if they chose. "We decided really to tighten up and save as much as we could while Dave was still working," Jacque says. "We canceled the cable TV, looked carefully at our grocery spending, looked at every area of our lives bit by bit. We carried little notebooks with us to record what we spent."

They sold the second car after someone broke into it and stole the stereo. They realized if they kept the car they would have to get an alarm, continue with insurance, and spend even more money. They rarely used it anyway. They sold the boat they used only three times a year. The cost of moorage and upkeep weren't worth the little benefit they were getting.

"Our last major folly was to buy a 1,900-square-foot, three-bedroom-plus-den house for just the two of us," Jacque says. "We had thought about getting a condo but we had so much stuff to store we just couldn't fit it all in!"

They simplified their transportation. Dave began to take the bus to work, but Jacque still drove to school. "Then I got tired of paying for parking, so I started parking away from school on the street. Finally I decided I could ride my bike."

The couple became more environmentally aware and recognized how their use of resources impacted the world. They began to recycle and reuse.

Throughout the process, Jacque began to grapple with her inner transformation. "It was difficult to give up the security of a regular job," she says. "I was very proud of the fact that I had a good job and was able to support myself. It was part of my identity. It took me three years to work through that, and I have found it is really important to be around other people who are not living a nine-to-five life if you decide to make these kinds of changes. It lets you see you are all right for not doing what everyone else is doing."

Increasing the speed at which they saved money came easily to both Jacque and Dave because they already had strong savings instincts. A couple of life crises had thrown them into the turmoil of the faster-paced, high-spending life that they now see as an aberration. But even through that period, they managed to continue to save at a modest rate.

"We had been saving about 4 to 6 percent of our earnings," Dave says. "Looking back, we could have saved far more, but instead we bought hot tubs, cars, and toys."

Their first priority once they agreed on a three-year plan was to increase Dave's company savings plan to 16 percent, and they personally added in an extra $200 a month. Their savings went into Treasury bonds, IRAs, and a company savings plan.

They also could build savings quickly because they had never gotten themselves deep into consumer debt, other than a mortgage. They almost always paid off their credit card each month. When they decided to work toward financial independence, they didn't have to dig themselves out of debt first.

The couple's next goal was to rid themselves of their large house payments, so they sold the house, streamlined their belongings, and moved into a one-bedroom, 650-square-foot apartment. They later bought a 1,300-square-foot duplex townhouse.

"We want to have a more meaningful life," Dave says. "For me, a corporate-type job just wasn't cutting it. I'd worked for 24 years like that and I learned a great deal and gained a lot of self-confidence, but I never felt like the work I was doing had any purpose. I'd come to work and push papers around and go to meetings. It had little point other than bringing home a paycheck.

"The first question for me was: How do I get out of here? That was when we began our three-year plan."

It was almost three years to the day that the couple's plan of financial independence became a reality and Dave left his job. It helped that the company offered him a buy-out package. "I feel great," he says. "It took me about two to three months before I realized I was a lot less stressed out. When you work at a job like that you're not aware of how the stress gradually creeps up on you. Even going on a vacation feels good for a short time, but then you go right back into the cycle again.

"I feel a lot better now. My time is filled with activities that have a purpose . . . I can see the results. I've refined our budget even more, I spend time reading, writing, cycling. I became a Big Brother four years ago and really enjoy that, and I'm now getting involved in Habitat for Humanity. I would also like to do some tutoring."

With more free time, Dave's gifts have also become more personal. He gave his parents the gift of himself for Christmas. He agreed to spend one day a month doing chores and labor at their house. That has been so successful he plans to renew it again. "I would have had difficulty squeezing that in if I were still working.

"My identity is now a collage," he says. "I think I should have business cards printed up that say 'David A. Heitmiller, human being.' "*

❖ ❖ ❖ ❖ ❖ ❖ ❖ ❖ ❖ ❖ ❖ ❖ ❖ ❖

Resources

Christmas

Celebrating Christmas as If It Matters by David Lambert (Grand Rapids, MI: Zondervan Publishing House, 1992)
Filled with ideas for incorporating spirituality into your Christmas season.

A Foxfire Christmas: Appalachian Memories & Traditions by Eliot Wigginton (Chapel Hill: University of North Carolina Press, 1996)
Shares the rich history of Appalachia via recipes, stories, photographs, and memories by those who lived through many Christmas celebrations. A testament to local culture that can survive in a hectic world and how those traditions are kept alive by those who care for such cultures.

The Gift of Time, Family Celebrations for Advent, Christmas and Epiphany by Margaret Ehlen Miller (Ridgefield, CT: Morehouse, 1977)
Contains a collection of customs and activities related to these seasons. Along with prayers, stories, and exercises in meditation, suggests creative projects for the family to heighten the joy of sharing and family life.

Unplug the Christmas Machine by Jo Robinson and Jean Coppock Staeheli (New York: William Morrow & Co., 1982)
Authors interviewed scores of people for ideas on how to create a less stressful, more meaningful holiday season.

Hanukkah

The Hanukkah Book by Marilyn Burns (New York: Avon, 1994)
Tells young readers why and how Hanukkah is celebrated and delivers fun ways to observe and celebrate the holiday.

The Ugly Menorah by Marissa Moss (New York: Farrar, Straus & Giroux, 1996)
Rachel can't understand why Grandmother insists on using a menorah made of tin and wood. Then Grandmother explains that it is her most prized possession because her late husband made it from leftover scraps from a construction site during the Depression.

While the Candles Burn: Eight Stories for Hanukkah by Barbara Diamond Goldin and Elaine Greenstein (New York: Viking, 1996)
Reminds children why Hanukkah is observed. Each tale portrays one of the holiday's themes: religious freedom and commitment, faith, courage, charity, rededication, honoring women, lights, and miracles.

❖ ❖ ❖ ❖ ❖ ❖ ❖ ❖ ❖ ❖ ❖ ❖ ❖ ❖ ❖ ❖

*Dave and Jacque are the authors of a book titled *Getting a Life: Real Lives Transformed by Your Money or Your Life* (New York: Viking Penguin, 1997). It contains stories of people who made changes in their lives using the program in the book.

Kwanzaa

Books

Kwanzaa: A Family Affair by Mildred Pitts Walter (New York: Lothrop Lee & Shepard, 1995)
Explains the principles and symbols of this holiday originally started in America almost 30 years ago. Also shares how to have individual, unique Kwanzaa festivities.

Organizations

African American Cultural Center, 2560 W. 54th Street, Los Angeles, CA 90043, 1-213-299-6124. Publishes a booklet titled "Kwanzaa: Origin, Concepts, Practice." The booklet also includes a lengthy reading list on Kwanzaa studies.

IMIK Enterprises specializes in multicultural educational services, such as classroom experiences in African American experience, African American storytelling, and celebrating Kwanzaa. Contact: 1-800-468-IMIK (4645).

Pagan

Books

Celebrate the Earth: A Year of Holidays in the Pagan Tradition by Laurie Cabot and Jean Mills (New York: Delta, 1994)
Celebrates the eight holidays in the Pagan tradition. Includes earth magic, recipes, menus, and updates on ancient activities.

Organizations

Pagan Family Alliance, P.O. Box 30806, Seattle, WA 98103-0806. National center for people wanting to support paganism.

Miscellaneous

Festivals, Family and Food by Diana Carey and Judy Large. (Hudson, NY: Anthroposophic Press, 1982)
For people who wish to relate to the seasons and, at the same time, to each other. Ideas for festivals for all seasons of the year, including songs, food, games, crafts, growing things.

The Nature Corner: Celebrating the Year's Cycle with Seasonal Tableau by M. V. Leeuwen (Beltsville, MD: Gryphon House, 1990)
Seasonal nature tables using simple materials are a way to make young children aware of the changing cycles of the year. Includes ideas, patterns, and materials list.

Consumer Rights, The Buying and Selling of American Holidays by Leigh Eric Schmidt (Princeton, NJ: Princeton University Press, 1995)
Reexamines the story of holidays in the United States, showing that commercial appropriations of the holidays were actually as religious in form as they were secular. Book captures the blessings and ballyhoo of American holiday observances.

9

Cooking and Nutrition

At a dinner table, when asked by his friend Emerson which dish he preferred, Henry Thoreau replied nonchalantly, "The nearest."

—HELEN NEARING
SIMPLE FOOD FOR THE GOOD LIFE

Simple living is very much about slowing down and living sensually—smelling, touching, tasting, and seeing our way through life. Cooking offers the perfect opportunity to bring this sensuality alive by fully engaging all of our senses.

The word "epicurean" most often refers to having luxurious tastes in eating. Epicurus was a Greek philosopher who taught that the highest good in the world is pleasure. We may or may not agree about what constitutes the highest good, but we certainly can bring pleasure into our lives via our kitchens. We can indulge in this delight whether we like to cook or not. After all, we need to cook because we need to eat, so we may as well reap some enjoyment in the process.

For those who fear that sensual cooking means spending lots of time, rest easy. Sensual cooking simply means being fully present and mindful as we chop, stir, and mix. Rather than thinking about running to the bank or reworking in your head the report you gave your boss yesterday, you are instead really feeling the gritty skin of a potato as you scrub it, you're running the tips of your fingers over the soft, plump roundness of a tomato and watching the juices drip out when it is cut, or you are smelling and tasting all of the flavors and textures as you stir your spaghetti sauce.

Cooking can be an act of love and delight, or it can be yet another exercise in racing through life on automatic pilot—never stopping for a moment to notice, feel, or taste. Cooking performed as an act of love brings us renewed energy and vigor—cooking performed on auto pilot is draining. When we cook in a hands-on, no-rush style, we are forced to *stop, taste, feel, smell, see, and experience* our food. Isn't this what life is all about? Isn't this what is missing from a harried life? What senses do we need to drive through a hamburger stand or shove a plastic-wrapped microwave dinner into the microwave oven? Where is the joy and delight? The microwave oven supposedly has made things easier for us. In reality, it robs us of one more real life experience. In his book *Outlaw Cook*, John Thorne says:

> Microwave energy offers no equivalent experience to replace our intuitive understanding of heat; indeed, the body's inability to respond or protect itself means the cooking food must be locked away out of reach. Because microwaves cook food from the inside out, they are unable to provide us with any of radiant heat's familiar, helpful clues . . . what we never expected was that as kitchen experience in its entirety became progressively devalued, the aura that still clung to the stove would also necessarily fade. Unnoticed by us, the image of the chef before his range, sweat dripping down his face as hot fat shimmered in his sauté pan, was undergoing as radical a change for microwave users as the role of scullion had for us.

Thorne goes on to remind us that our love of convenience has created a generation of cooks who consider time spent in the kitchen wasted time. Welcome, he says, to a work-free way of cooking: "To live, after all, is to experience things, and every time we mince an onion, lower the flame under a simmering pot, shape the idea and substance of a meal, we actually gain rather than lose lived time. Such minutes are not only full and rich in themselves, but they brush a lasting patina of lived experience into our memory."

Viana La Place, author of *Unplugged Kitchen,* refers to cooking as an *embrace*. I love this metaphor. When I embrace someone special, I feel alive and in touch. I can embrace my cooking in the same way—I can hold an onion in my hands and begin peeling the paper layers off one at a time. I can open a little jar of dried basil and reap the harvest through my sense of smell. I can take the scent way into my nose and down my chest. I can rely on my senses to create meals rather than rigidly adhering to exact measurements and recipes. I can play with food as I put it together . . . hmmm, a little of this, a little of that, taste, taste, stir, stir. I can accept that some of my creations will not work and some will, and so what? And finally, I can think about who will eat this meal that I am cooking and who will receive the love that I put into it.

No matter what you are preparing, take a minute for yourself before you start to cook. Don't rush! Do some deep breathing, stretches, a two-minute meditation, maybe have a glass of wine. Remember, love is an ingredient. That is what simple living is all about—fully enjoying the little moments that are right in front of you. You don't need to go out to be entertained at fancy places; with a change of heart and a slower pace, you can find joy and delight right under your nose.

For all of you who have never experienced sensual delights in the kitchen, read the book *Like Water for Chocolate,* by Laura Esquivel. Perhaps you saw the movie by the same name. The book is a fictional tale about a Mexican woman who cooks for a large family. She puts her entire soul and being into her food in a way that hurried Westerners can never imagine. Cooking is literally a whole-body experience for her; it is not a chore that she does quickly in order to get on to the next activity. Cooking is an act of love: "Tita knew through her own flesh how fire transforms the elements, how a lump of corn flour is changed into a tortilla, how a soul that hasn't been warmed by the fire of love is lifeless, like a useless ball of corn flour."

> *Food should not be designed, it should be natural. Beautiful food is food that comes as close as possible to its natural state, that reflects the changing seasons.*
>
> —VIANA LA PLACE, *UNPLUGGED KITCHEN*

Whatever your forté, you can streamline your cooking routine by keeping it simple, nourishing, and inexpensive. In our harried, modern lives, most of us think that we don't have enough time to keep our cooking nourishing and inexpensive. After all, when we've been working at our high-stress, full-time paid jobs for eight or more hours a day, we simply don't have the time or energy to prepare nourishing meals. It is much easier to stop by the deli on the way home, eat out, or grab a frozen microwave entree. All of these choices are faster, but don't meet the other criteria: They have little nutritional value, and over time, they can cost a small fortune.

Diving into life and experiencing every small, delicious moment is part of living simply. If we are tired of racing through life on automatic, cooking can be one of our first forays back into sensual living.

Cooking Simply

Cooking simply is about eating and serving food in its natural, beautiful state. It is unfortunate that so many of us have accepted modern marketing's premise that it is somehow better to bury our asparagus in tons of cream sauce or open a box of stuff that no longer has any resemblance to what it was in its original state. We have accepted this way of "eating" to such an extent that many of us no longer like the taste of real food. We're used to concoctions that have been colored and "flavor enhanced," as if the natural thing doesn't have the proper flavors and color of its own. Children are a good barometer of this eating style. When children have been raised on processed food, it is nearly impossible to get them to accept the real thing. Check this out sometime. What are we doing to our own and our children's bodies?

Sauces and convoluted concoctions not only take a lot of time, money, and energy to prepare, but they can be far less healthy too. We've all had those days when we've spent hours in the kitchen preparing the perfect meal, only to have it gobbled up in minutes. Or we've worked so hard making a meal pleasing for everyone, only to have our children say "Yuk! I'm not eating this!"

Helen Nearing, who lived to the ripe age of 91, wrote several books about the homestead life she and her husband, Scott Nearing, enjoyed. Their most famous book is the one that chronicles their life, *Living the Good Life*. Helen also wrote a delightful cookbook called *Simple Food for the Good Life*. In it she told the story of a farm woman who spent her daylight hours preparing food for half a dozen farmhands and who one afternoon went quietly crazy: "As she was led to the wagon taking her to the looney house, she kept repeating: 'And they ate it all in twenty minutes. They ate it all in twenty minutes.' There were doubtless other ways this lady could have spent her life more happily and creatively."

We can stop thinking we need exotic creations at every meal. We can reprogram our taste buds actually to prefer simple food. I know this has happened to me. I used to think it was a real treat to go to a fancy gourmet

> *Unless we are incarcerated in a prison or in a hospital, where we are forced to take what we get, we can choose our nourishment. We can eat simple fresh food or we can eat store-bought fabrications.*
>
> —HELEN NEARING,
> SIMPLE FOOD FOR THE GOOD LIFE

French restaurant, for example. Now the thought of my food swimming in a lot of heavy sauce is not the least bit appealing. We can learn to appreciate the basic, simple food that looks and tastes like it came out of the ground. My tastes also have simplified with regard to drinks. I carry around a big water bottle and quench my thirst on that all day. I don't even want soda pop—water is free and tastes much better. Why do I want to put a bunch of caramel coloring and chemical mumbo jumbo in my body when I can give it something clean and fresh?

If you decide to switch to natural food, remember that it will take time to get used to the more subdued flavors. In time, your taste buds will come to prefer real to chemicals. It's one thing to sprinkle your carrots with a few natural herbs; it is quite another to hide them in butter and sauces. I've eaten my share of frozen, boxed, and other styles of processed food and walked away totally unsatisfied. There are no heavenly, natural smells, the food all shares the same chemical taste and texture, and I'm missing out on the whole array of sensual delights that wait for me when I work with real food.

We've all experienced the ultimate—there is nothing, I repeat nothing, like fresh-baked, whole-wheat bread. Yet we zoom through supermarkets throwing all manner of chemical-, preservative-, color-laden excuses for bread into our carts. Where are the heavenly smells in the supermarket from fresh produce and fresh, real bread? The foods of nature have a full, robust array of every flavor, color, and aroma imaginable. Simple cooking is about celebrating, not fooling with, what is right there. If you can't take the time to bake your own bread, then find a small, local bread baker. In the *Unplugged Kitchen* Viana La Place calls the makers of good foods artisans:

> *Until I was 12, I thought spaghetti came from a can, and that vegetables grew in the freezer. When I discovered that green beans grew in the ground, I thought it was a miracle.*
>
> —MOLLIE KATZEN, MOOSEWOOD COOKBOOK

> True artisanal foods reveal the hand of the maker, since they are crafted in a uniquely individual way. For example, a baker may bake black olive loaves, but each one will vary a bit in size or shape, be a bit bumpier from the dispersal of olives, or be less than perfectly rounded—a sign that human hands have been at work.

The touch of life is what makes the loaf of bread, the round of cheese eloquent and expressive—attributes that are unattainable in mass-produced foods.

After your taste-bud adjustment, you'll find that you spend far less time in the kitchen because you no longer will feel obliged to concoct all sorts of fancy ways to hide your food. You'll come to cherish the beauty of the fresh, real thing sitting on your plate.

Simple Food Is Healthy

Eating simply is not only easier, it is far healthier. One of the best things I ever did was take a year-long series of cooking classes from a Seventh-Day Adventist. I am not a Seventh-Day Adventist, but that doesn't matter. You don't need to be one either. Most Adventists are vegetarians; many are vegans. (Vegetarians eat dairy, but no meat; vegans eat no dairy or meat.) They eat a balanced, whole-food, diet. As a group, Adventists enjoy, on average, longer, healthier lives than mainstream Americans. Here are some statistics: Male Seventh-Day Adventists have an 8.9-year longer average life expectancy than does the general population, while female members have a 7.5-year longer average life expectancy. Seventh-Day Adventists have a lower incidence of breast, prostate, pancreatic, bladder, and ovarian cancers than does the general population. And Adventists do not believe that "aches and pains" are an inevitable part of the aging process, nor do they believe that senility or deterioration of mental faculties are inevitable. This is because they figured out the scheme early: Live according to the natural laws and you will be rewarded with health.

My Adventist cooking coach taught me to cut through all of the baloney out there about which additive is better in which food, or which fancy arrangement of food works better for this situation, or which precise measurement of which convoluted arrangement of vitamins is better for which body type. She taught me one basic, simple rule about food: *Eat the food in its closest state to the way it came out of the ground.* No fuss, no muss.

Remember that food loses more and more nutrients with each process it goes through. By the time most food has arrived in a beautifully designed, colorful box or can on a grocery store shelf, it has almost no vitamin content left. You are paying for a colorful box. You also are paying someone to process the food, add chemicals to it, design the box, and, very likely, advertise the product to get you to buy it. Not to mention, you are paying with your health. The more of this processed, puffed, colored, flavored, fumigated, sterilized, homogenized, hydrolyzed, bleached, defatted, degermed, texturized, fortified, dehydrated food you eat, the less healthy you will be. (Phew!) Your body needs the vital nutrients found only in real food.

Here is a perfect example of how we Americans complicate our lives with regard to food and health. We eat a refined-foods diet. These are foods that have had most of the nutrients whacked out of them and then the manufacturer puts back in chemical replacements. We eat white rice (totally processed and bleached), processed bread (the "whole-wheat" bread we buy in most stores has perhaps 10 percent whole wheat), puffed and bamboozled cereal, frozen vegetables, canned this, and boxed that. Then we get constipated because our bodies aren't getting any fiber, since the fiber has been processed out of the food we eat. So we add yet another chemical to our bodies to relieve constipation. Or, at best, we might add wheat germ to the top of our cereal in the morning in order to get fiber. Wheat germ and oat bran were the fad a few years ago. Stop and think about the logic of this way of eating and taking care of ourselves! All we need to do is eat real food that has all the original nutrients and fiber in it. Real food is cheaper by far, and we don't need to buy chemicals to unconstipate, nor do we need to buy expensive, processed wheat germ or oat bran. Wheat germ is the center of a grain of the whole-wheat berry. The manufacturers shoot the berry through some fancy process to remove the outer part of the berry, collect the germ, and sell it as some miracle health food! Same basic process for oat bran. All you need to do is eat the thing in its original state and you have a complete little package, just as nature intended it.

All of this sounds easy, but I can hear the groans. "I'm not going to start some organic garden in my backyard. Forget it." Never fear. Please refer to Chapter 13 for ideas on how you can sit on your you-know-what and still enjoy the bounty of garden-fresh produce. Or you can find natural, whole food (whole food is food in its whole, not processed, state) in most food co-ops. Some non–co-op-type grocery stores sell bulk whole food as well. You can shop at farmer's markets and roadside stands. This takes you out of the sterile environment of huge supermarkets and puts you in touch with real people who grow the food you eat—another sensual delight. While not as intimate, you can mail-order whole food as well. (See the Resources for the Goldmine Natural

> *What I love most is an abundance of simple food of perfect quality and staggering freshness, very simply and respectfully treated, tasting strongly of itself.*
>
> —Sybille Bedford,
> The Artist's & Writer's Cook Book

COOKING AND NUTRITION

Food Co.) You also can read labels on the prepared food that you buy. For instance, I cook with a lot of beans. If you can't buy dried, bulk beans, you can buy beans in a can. Read the label on the can. If all that's in there are beans and water, you're doing the best you can. If they've added colorants, mumbo-jumbo chemicals you can't pronounce, lots of salt, or their own vegetables and seasonings, or they've refried the beans in lard and who-knows-what-else, don't buy it.

Helen Nearing, who ate a healthful, whole-foods diet, relates her discovery about a box of frozen blueberry waffles that she found in the store one day. This is what was listed on the box label: sugar, cottonseed oil, salt, sodium carboxymethycellulose, silicon dioxide, citric acid, modified soy protein, artificial flavor and coloring, maltol, and blueberry solids.

Hold the phone! We are making the choice to put this stuff into our bodies! We are making the incredible choice actually to pay *more* for this horrific-sounding arrangement of chemicals than we would pay for the real thing!

Much of the food sold on grocery store shelves also has added preservatives. What the heck are we eating, anyway? Remember this important rule of nature when shopping for your food: *Eat only those foods that spoil, rot, or decay, and eat them before they do.* When you eat foods that spoil and decay, you are eating real, unadulterated food. That's what real food does: It spoils and decays and goes back into the earth for another round. That is *real,* not fortified, life.

By eating refined food, we're keeping ourselves on another kind of treadmill: We work harder at our jobs to pay the advertisers who entice us to buy their "easy foods" that cost more than the real foods and have fewer nutrients, so we can pay our doctors to keep us healthy because we haven't been giving our bodies the nutrients we need. In addition to the box and advertising, here is what else we are paying for when we eat processed food: In one year, the U.S. food industry used more than 90 million pounds of flavoring and flavor-enhancing additives. In addition, it used close to 800 million pounds of additives to improve the color, texture, and preservative qualities of food. From 2,500 to 3,000 food additives are now used in U.S. foods, including several leavening agents, 9 emulsifiers, 30 stabilizers and thickeners, 85 surfactants, 7 anticaking agents, 28 antioxidants, 44 suquestrants, perhaps 12 coloring materials, at least 8 acidulants, more than 30 chemical preservatives, and over 1,100 flavoring ingredients. New additives are introduced each year. America's bread industry used over 16 million pounds of chemicals a year, mostly leaveners, preservatives, and antisalin compounds. During one summer, a British scientist patented a new additive that would make bread taste like bread.

The Real-Food Diet

Believe me, there is no rocket science to creating a whole-foods diet. I happened to learn about this diet from the Adventists, who are vegetarian, and that is how I generally eat. You can eat meat and eat whole foods as well. Simply add meat to the dishes. If you are going to add meat, try to buy the organically grown kind. Most of the animals that turn into meat on grocery shelves are fed diets high in antibiotics, growth hormones, tranquilizers, and pesticides. After slaughter, the meat is injected with dyes and deodorants and irradiated. Most processed meats contain preservatives, stabilizers, plastic residue, and other harmful substances. This is what you are eating. Helen Nearing wrote that no one knows better than meat inspectors how much disease there is among animals slaughtered for food. She said: "A woman attended a banquet and ordered a vegetable plate. At her side sat a stranger who also chose a vegetable plate. 'You too are a vegetarian?' she asked him. 'No, madam,' he replied, 'I am a meat inspector.' "

You can have your own reasons for choosing a meat or meatless diet. There is no question, however, that a plant-based diet is the simplest, least expensive, and easiest way to eat.

You may wonder if a vegetarian diet can supply you with the proper nutrients. After all, Americans have been raised on the old pyramid-style of nutrition, with meat-based protein getting the most weight. The pyramid has since been revised to reflect newer thinking that Americans get too much protein, which in turn leads to degenerative disease such as cancer, heart disease, diabetes, and the like. (For more information on the link between food and disease, please refer to the Resources at the end of this chapter.)

The Senate Select Committee has recommended the following dietary goals:

1. Increase consumption of fruits and vegetables and whole grains.
2. Decrease consumption of refined and other processed sugars and foods high in such sugars.
3. Decrease consumption of foods high in total fat.
4. Decrease consumption of animal fat.
5. Substitute low-fat and nonfat milk for whole milk, and low-fat dairy products for high-fat products (an exception should be made for children).
6. Decrease consumption of butterfat, eggs, and other high-cholesterol sources.
7. Decrease consumption of salt and foods high in salt content.

Join the Slow Food Movement

by Jim Morrison

Appalled by the rise of fast food and the decline of culinary culture, a scrappy band of Italians fight back

At the beginning, it was just a playful tweaking, a good-humored philosophical shot at the ubiquitous burger, symbol of a minute-made and minute-mad world. McDonald's was poised to invade Rome's beautiful Piazza de Spagna at the base of the famed Spanish steps. Just the thought of it gave indigestion to food-and-wine writer Carlo Petrini and his fellow members of Arcigola, the Italian gastronomical society.

What better weapon, they thought, to battle fast food than "slow food"? So Petrini's pack formed the International Movement for the Defense of and the Right to Pleasure and issued a "Slow Food Manifesto"—the first salvo in the Slow Food War. "In our century, born and nurtured under the sign of Industrialization, the machine was invented and then turned into the role model of life. Speed became our shackles," the manifesto began. "We fall prey to the same virus: 'The Fast Life' that fractures our customs assails us even in our own homes, cages us, and feeds us 'fast food.' " The remedy? An "adequate portion of sure sensual pleasures, to be taken with slow and prolonged enjoyment"— beginning in the kitchen with the preparation of an elaborate meal, and ending at the table with fine wine and rambling conversation.

"It was just a game at first," says Petrini, a chance to remind people that food is perishable art, as pleasurable in its way as a sculpture by Michelangelo or a painting by Titian. Not mere nourishment to be wolfed down, but culture to be savored. The time had come, the group proclaimed, to get back to the two-hour lunch and the four-hour dinner.

But, ho-hum, McDonald's paid little heed, opening its restaurant in spite of the slow eaters' pleas in late 1986. With no competition nearby, it became one of the corporation's 10-highest volume locations worldwide. Nevertheless, Petrini discovered that his slow-food idea was catching. Calls poured in asking about the "movement." There was obviously an eager and growing following for the eat-a-lot-slowly philosophy.

"Slow food," says Petrini, "was in the air. We in Arcigola only made the idea concrete."

Formally founded at a Paris gathering in 1989, the Arcigola Slow Food Movement has become an international rallying point for the inevitable backlash against societal velocity and homogenized, industrial grub. Members meet for marathon meals and talk food, wine, culture, and philosophy. They organize wine tastings and classes about traditional cuisine. And they disdain the stressful fast life.

"Fast food is killing off the social aspect of food," Petrini says. "It strips people of their food wealth and culture."

The nonprofit movement has 40,000 members worldwide with supporters in more than 40 countries. The snail—slow, yet delectable—is its symbol.

Petrini has never heard of any reaction to the movement from McDonald's, or any of the other stopwatch chains. He says a McDonald's representative failed to show up for a debate arranged by a Paris radio station. Brad Trask, manager of international communications for McDonald's worldwide headquarters in Oak Brook, Illinois, says he is not familiar with the slow food movement. "But," he adds, "I don't think we'd want to go into any location and take away their food culture. We don't exactly go where we're not wanted."

Slow food, however, is primarily a state of mind, and Petrini is careful to point out that members are not gastronomic elitists. "Even eating a sandwich," Petrini says, "can be a slow food experience."

The group is well organized in Italy, but not in the rest of the world. There are roughly 600 supporters in the United States, but after an early flurry of activity, the movement there has fallen into disarray, Petrini says. He hopes that a worldwide newsletter now on the drawing boards will help bind the organization together globally. Eventually, he figures, strong chapters will coalesce in each country. There's no hurry.

Excerpted from *American Way*, the magazine of American Airlines. For more information on the slow food movement, contact Arcigola Slow Food Movement, Via Mendicita Istruita, 14, 12042 Bra (CN) ITALY.

Remember that good food is the best medicine. Fruits, grains, nuts, and vegetables are the body's finest building blocks. They contain all the nutrients necessary to make good blood.

I've taken a lot of cooking classes and read a lot of books about nutrition. None has made the process so simple as the Adventist plan. Here is how you can supply yourself and/or your family with a simple, nourishing, and inexpensive diet. First, treat your body with the utmost respect.

That means filling it with only the best, most natural food. The basic rules are:

1. Obtain as wide a variety of natural (whole, unrefined) foods as possible. This will give the body exposure to trace minerals and/or micronutrients whose benefits may not be fully understood yet. Eat a variety of vegetables, fruit, whole grains, tubers, and legumes each week. Eat two servings of raw vegetable salad and two more servings of raw or cooked green or yellow vegetables daily. Potatoes may be eaten daily. Eat beans or peas three times a week, sweet potatoes or squash twice weekly, and a member of the cabbage family (broccoli, Brussels sprouts, cauliflower, kale) three times a week.
2. Eat no refined foods, irritating foods, or fermented or aged products (cheese, vinegar, spiced pickles, etc.).
3. Eat only enough to satisfy hunger (not appetite) and to maintain an ideal weight.
4. Eat on time; nothing between meals. A lifestyle of regularity is strengthening to both mind and body. Have a set time for meals and sleep. Space meals at least five hours apart, and take them in the proper order, quantity-wise: breakfast, 50 percent; lunch, 40 percent; and supper (snack), 10 percent. Your digestive system needs a complete rest at times, just as you do!

Breakfast

Breakfast is one of the most important meals of the day. Your body needs fuel to get going. Each morning, cook a whole grain. The grain can be rolled oats, millet, cornmeal, barley, buckwheat, quinoa, and the like. Rotate them. I had never heard of many of these grains until the class. If you are the same, ask your local grocer, food co-op, or health food store for help. Or visit your library or bookstore for a book on whole grains. You'll also need large jars in which to store your grains and beans. Scrounge, buy, or otherwise gather about 10 or so.

I can hear the next round of groans. "Do you know what our mornings are like around this house? We're lucky if we can down a piece of cold toast before we have to race out the door. Get serious. Who has time to cook all this stuff?"

Answer: You do. There are a number of ways you can do this. One is to get yourself a crockpot. They were the rage in the 1960s, and you probably can pick one up at a garage sale or secondhand store very cheaply. The other option is to invest in a new one. At most they cost around $30. If that seems like a lot of

Timetable for Cooking Grains*

Barley ....60 minutes
Brown rice ....50 minutes
Buckwheat groats (Kasha) ....20 minutes
Couscous ....5–10 minutes
Cracked wheat (Bulgur) ....15–20 minutes
Millet ....30 minutes
Oats...10 minutes

*These figures are approximate and will vary with the volume of grain, the size of the flame, and the fit of the lid.

money, add up what you are paying to purchase those fancy box cereals that you eat every morning, or the cost of doughnuts and coffee at the local on-the-run store. The cost of cooking whole grains is pennies compared to the outrageous cost and outrageously empty nutrient content of those boxed cereals.

At night before bed, simply throw in water and the grain and turn on the crockpot. In the morning, voilà, you have a nourishing, inexpensive, and couldn't-be-faster breakfast. Put some fresh or frozen berries or other fruit on top. I always keep bags of berries in the freezer for times when no fresh fruit is available. If you are energetic, you can buy or pick berries in season and freeze them yourself. Otherwise, buy them in bags from the grocery store. Help yourself to a handful of nuts and seeds, and you have breakfast. You can choose from almonds, cashews, walnuts, and sesame or sunflower seeds. Buy these in bulk too. You can put milk on your cereal or not. If you want to stay away from dairy products, as the Adventists do, you can add soy or rice milk or use the juice from the fruit to add moisture.

Yes, you will need to get used to the taste of these grains. Most of us have been raised on puffed, fluffed, and fiddled-with box cereals and doughnuts. Whole foods are a new taste. I had the same experience. I can honestly say now that I much prefer the taste of my whole grain breakfast. I still don't eat the grain plain. I add blackberries or chopped apples, and it is absolutely delicious. The grain breakfast also stays with me for hours. I'm hungry in about 20 minutes after eating the cardboard-boxed cereal. You'll find that you snack less during the day when you have filled yourself with a nourishing grain breakfast. In fact, the Adventists think it is better not to snack, because our digestive systems need a rest. Whatever the reason, it's cheaper not to snack, and if you are concerned about weight, it's also better not to snack.

There are other ways to make your breakfast in less time. You can cook a pot or two of different grains early in the week and put it in the refrigerator. Then simply reheat a bowl in the morning. A grain with berries is the simplest way to feed yourself. If you want to add a little variety, you can make your own very easy muesli or granola. A recipe for easy, healthful granola is included here.

GRANOLA

8 cups rolled oats
$^2/_3$ cup sunflower seeds
1 cup nuts, chopped (almonds, pistachios, hazelnuts)
3 ripe bananas
$1^1/_4$ cup pitted dates
$^1/_2$ cup hot water
1 tablespoon vanilla

Mix together first three ingredients in large bowl. Whiz last four ingredients in food processor or blender. Stir into oat mixture. Spread on 2 cookie sheets. Bake at 200° F for 30 minutes. Stir. Bake 30 more minutes. Serve with apples.

Lunch/Dinner

As for lunch/dinner, I have not been able to follow the Adventist plan to its utmost. I cook the right food but at the wrong time. The Adventists believe that it's best to eat your biggest meal at around 2:00 in the afternoon. (Assuming you ate breakfast at around 7:00 A.M.) Again, this is because the body needs fuel during the day, not at night when most of us eat dinner and when the body is preparing to rest. The problem is that it is very difficult to eat dinner in midday in our culture. If you really want to follow this plan, you can accomplish it creatively by bringing your prepared-ahead dinner to work or, if you are an at-home parent, by having dinner ready as soon as the kids come home from school at around 3:00 or 4:00. I must confess, I have not been disciplined enough to accomplish this feat.

Nonetheless, I eat the right food. The general rule is eat beans three times a week and a combination of other simple foods the rest of the time. Beans are very inexpensive, very simple, and loaded with fiber, vitamins, and protein.

Endless creative recipes for beans are available. Check out your library or bookstore. I included two favorite bean recipes here. Because beans are heavy, you don't want to eat them every day. For a complete dinner, add brown rice, whole-grain bread, a green and yellow vegetable (a salad and carrots), and you are in business. Make at least one of your vegetables raw (salad or uncooked carrots). This classic "beans and rice" dish is what we in America often think of as "deprivation" food, to be eaten only when we can't afford steak or some fancy processed meal. Rearrange your thinking on this one. Beans and rice are one of the best things you can put into your body.

HAYSTACKS

BEANS

Cook pinto beans according to chart. Add chopped onion, salt, basil, marjoram, oregano, savory to taste. Boil 15 minutes. Blend in food processor or blender till smooth.

GUACAMOLE

$^1/_2$ cup raw cashews
$^1/_2$ cup water
1 clove garlic
2 ripe avocados
2 tablespoons lemon juice ($^1/_2$ lemon)

Blend the cashews and water till smooth. Then add the garlic and blend again. Finally, add the avocados and lemon juice.

TOMATO SAUCE

Soak handful of sundried tomatoes in water till softened. Add onion, basil, thyme, and salt to the tomatoes. Add handful of cashews. Heat.

Bake corn tortillas till hard. Break into chips. Put on plate. Layer the other ingredients on top: beans, guacamole, onions, tomatoes, olives, green peppers, lettuce (whatever is on hand!) and tomato sauce. Enjoy.

BLACK BEAN CHILI

(good for wok or large frying pan)

$^1/_2$ teaspoon cumin seeds
$^1/_8$ teaspoon cayenne
$^1/_2$ teaspoon paprika
1 medium onion
1 tablespoon olive oil
2–3 cloves garlic

1 teaspoon dry mustard
1 teaspoon chili powder
2 large tomatoes
2 tablespoons tomato paste (you can freeze leftover paste)
1/2 green or red pepper
3 cups cooked black beans
Plain yogurt (for topping)

Toast cumin seeds over medium heat in a dry pan till they pop (2–3 minutes). Add cayenne and paprika and cook 1 minute. Cook onions in water or oil to soften. Add garlic and cook 1–2 minutes longer. Add mustard, chili powder, tomatoes, tomato paste, and pepper. Simmer 15 minutes. Add cooked beans. Cook 15 minutes. Top with plain yogurt.

More groans from the audience. "Beans take hours and hours to cook. What, I'm supposed to come home from work at 6:00 P.M., put the beans on, and eat at midnight?"

Recall the crockpot. The night before you are to have a bean dish, throw the things in there with plenty of water and let them cook on low heat all night and all day. Or throw them in the pot right before leaving for work. A woman named Mary Bowman, who teaches cooking classes, has another trick she calls the Simple Beginnings method. In the beginning of the week, cook up a big pot of rice and a big pot of beans. Put them in the refrigerator. Then on your rice and/or bean days, simply take out the amount you need and add other fresh ingredients, depending on the season. "The secret," Mary says, "is to use really alive, fresh ingredients with your bean and rice dishes." She teaches her classes seasonally, because Mary, like the Adventists, believes that we need to nourish ourselves with fresh, local, seasonal produce.

Supper

If you eat your dinner in midday, you may or may not be hungry in the evening. If you are, eat something light, such as soup with crackers or fruit with toast.

Simplify Your Kitchen

❖ Get rid of all of your kitchen tools and junk that you don't use. Clean those drawers and shelves. The machines I use regularly are a food proces-

Timetable for Cooking Dried Beans*

Black beans	1½–2 hours
Black-eyed peas	1½ hours
Fava beans	2–3 hours
Garbanzo beans (Chickpeas)	2–3 hours
Kidney beans	1½–2 hours
Lentils	45 minutes
Lima beans	45 minutes–1½ hours
Navy and pea beans	1–1½ hours
Pinto beans	1½–2 hours
Small pink beans	1–1½ hours
Soybeans	3–3½ hours
Split peas	45 minutes
White beans (Cannellini)	1½–2 hours

*The fresher the beans, the faster they will cook.

sor, blender, and crockpot. On the other hand, sensual purists like Viana La Place use no automated machines whatsoever. She says of the food processor: "By placing so much distance between yourself and the raw materials, no learning takes place. You never come to understand the process on a gut level. And you are deprived of the primal pleasures of preparing food."

She adds: "A little pounding on the mortar might help you feel better and release some of the stresses of the day, not in an aggressive manner, but in a calming, rhythmical way. The color and scents will lift your spirits."

Whatever tools you decide to retain, have *what* you want *where* you want it. You can do this only if you have gotten rid of excess junk from your counters and shelves. And rethink just how many tools you really need. Question the amount of time it takes to clean and store all of these tools. If you're about to succumb to the latest ad about why your life will be easier as soon as you buy a fry-o-matic, think twice about your hard-earned money going out the door. Think about how *you* cook rather than listening to the TV chef tell you that a certain tool makes a certain gourmet job easier. If you make those gourmet items only twice a year, think about how you could use an existing tool to do the job. It might not appear as glamorous and easy as the tool shown on TV, but the up side is you are saving yourself money and you have one less item to clean and store. The American Friends Service Committee published a book titled *Taking Charge of Our Lives*. They suggest three things to consider before buying an appliance: *(1) Pare:* Can you get along with something simpler? Do you really need an electric can opener? *(2) Care:* Keep that knife sharpened and you won't be tempted to buy a new electric knife. *(3) Share:* If you need a large appliance, think of buying it in common with your neighbors.

❖ Learn how to cut vegetables. The simplest tool in your kitchen should be a high-quality chef's knife. Many people prefer the simplicity and hands-on experience of chopping with a good knife. If you know how to chop properly, you too may be able to get rid of your whizzing, buzzing gadgets. That indeed would be a simplified kitchen at its finest. Think about how much less time you spend cleaning and repairing a knife as compared to a machine. Think about how much less space you need to store it. All of those factors need to go into your equation.

❖ Know your ingredients. Know what is in season, for example. Better to buy local, fresh produce than produce grown in some faraway place that sits on a truck for days on its way to your grocery store. Remember, the longer food is out of the ground, the more nutrients it loses. If you stick with the same basic recipes, you will get a feel for what works with what.

❖ Learn your spice groups. That way, if you don't have a recipe, you'll know what goes well with what. For simple foods, you don't need a lot of fancy spices. Take 15 minutes to go through your spice cabinet. No doubt you have spices in there you haven't used since your grandmother came over on the prairie wagon. When you've purged the unused spices, you can organize in two ways: Arrange them in alphabetical order, or arrange them according to food types. For instance, if you like to cook ethnic foods, you can group your Italian spices together and your Asian spices together.

❖ Less is more. You don't need to put your entire kitchen into every dish.

❖ Pay attention to your weekly menu. Know ahead of time when to cook beans, for example.

❖ Prepare a weekly shopping list. One easy way to do this is to get out your recipes for the week and make five columns. Head the columns: Produce, Dairy, Dry, Meat/Tofu, Spices. Under each column write the item you need. A shopping list helps you organize yourself and avoid a lot of impulse buying at the grocery store.

❖ Develop four weeks of recipes and rotate your favorites. This eliminates the stress of standing in front of the refrigerator at 5:00 or 6:00 P.M., wondering what to cook for dinner. It also eliminates last-minute dashes to the high-priced corner deli.

❖ Keep dessert simple, if you serve it at all. Serve fresh fruit. After a while, you and your family might actually prefer this kind of dessert to the gooey, cream-filled kind. Anything is possible. (Remember balance! Will I turn down an occasional chocolate cake? Not a chance. Do I have chocolate cake regularly? No, thanks.)

❖ Clean as you go. Keep a tubful of soapy water ready as you cook. Wash and dry the knife immediately so it is ready for the next job. Clean the bowl right away.

❖ Substitute and use your imagination. The recipes included in this chapter are guidelines only. Use what is handy and don't sweat it.

Another way you can simplify your cooking routine is to join or start a cooking cooperative. Cooking cooperatives are comprised of people who share the cooking with one another. If there are three neighbors, you cook enough food to feed three people on, say, Monday night. On Tuesday, the second neighbor does the same, and on Wednesday, the third neighbor cooks. You don't need to eat together, but you can if you like. Or every Friday night might be cooperative night. You cook one Friday night, the second neighbor cooks the next Friday, and so on. Try a few variations with your neighbors.

Maintain Balance

As with all aspects of simplifying your life, remember to maintain balance. Yes, I eat healthful, whole foods most of the time. Does this mean I never indulge in a bag of chocolate chip cookies or potato chips? Heck no! I figure that if my main modus operandi is to cook healthful, whole foods, a bag of junk here and there is not the end of the world. If I am invited to someone's home and they serve processed food, I usually eat it. I don't make a big deal out of my eating habits or theirs. If someone wants to hear about my habits, I'll gladly share them. On the other hand, your balance is out of whack if your refrigerator and cupboards are usually filled with processed foods and snacks and you eat healthful foods only now and then.

Experience Mealtime

The importance of making meal preparation and eating sacred time is well illustrated by the following story: Once I went on a weekend vacation with another mom and her two kids. We all shared a cabin that had a kitchen. I was amazed when this mom began unpacking her food box. In addition to a chef's knife and real food, she had packed two candle holders and two candles. My, I thought, she really likes to make vacations special.

As it turned out, this is how her family ate dinner every night. With candles on the table. Every night. Not just when she and her husband decided to have a romantic meal alone. Not just at holidays. Every night. I learned my first lesson in meal ambience that night and brought the tradition home to my house.

If cooking and mealtime are to be priorities in your life, then most likely something else will have to go. Simple living gives you the option of saying no to extracurricular work and social obligations that will interfere with your cooking and eating period of the day. If you decide that the hours from, say, 5:00 to 7:00 P.M. are meal preparation and eating time, then you simply quit accepting invitations to be anywhere else but home during that time. (Remember to use the answering machine too.) Of course there are exceptions, but do your best to keep them exceptions.

Once you decide that this is going to be sacred time for you and your family, you'll develop a new attitude about cooking and can begin to chop, mix, play with, and eat real food. You'll also develop a new attitude about eating. If you cook simple foods, you won't need to spend a lot of time in the kitchen. Still, you can make your dinnertime special. Make your table beautiful with flowers or shells you've collected. Play music. Turn the lights low. You can do this every night! Cooking and eating can now become the sensual, joyful experiences that they deserve to be.

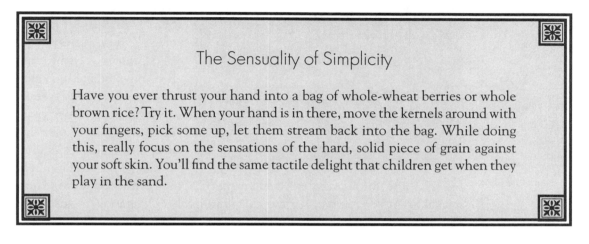

The Sensuality of Simplicity

Have you ever thrust your hand into a bag of whole-wheat berries or whole brown rice? Try it. When your hand is in there, move the kernels around with your fingers, pick some up, let them stream back into the bag. While doing this, really focus on the sensations of the hard, solid piece of grain against your soft skin. You'll find the same tactile delight that children get when they play in the sand.

JUST ENOUGH FOR THE CURTIS FAMILY

A religion? Not really. But a practical way of life is how Tim Curtis describes the teachings of Henry Thoreau and the transcendentalists. The quotes come easily to mind: "A man is rich in proportion to the things he can leave alone," Tim says, quoting from Thoreau. Tim apologizes for the men-only reference, but says the phrase means a lot to him and his wife, Chris.

Take a look around. There is just enough in the two-bedroom bungalow. Enough to be comfortable and cozy, but no more. Enough to invite a sense of serenity. A sanctuary. A place that invites you to calm down from the busy world. The Curtises say if you live in balance during the week, the weekend becomes dessert.

They describe their style of decorating as "floating." It is what graphic designers call "white space," meaning there is lots of room between and around things. In the living room, there is a couch, two chairs, two floor lamps, and three small tables, all gathered in the center of the room. The only knick-knacks are some books and a candlestick that Tim made. Not much more.

The dining room is the same. Clean lines, no clutter, just enough. There is

Tim and Chris Curtis and daughter, Nathalie, enjoy regular family meals together.

also a young daughter in the house, and for her, white space means not a lot of extra toys. Just enough to spark her imagination. "Let her fill in the blanks and create," the Curtises say.

A primary way the Curtises have created balance in their daily lives is their decision to make a ceremony out of the preparation and eating of dinner. While many families rarely see each other for dinner, Chris and Tim decided their dinner hour was to be a special time for creating, sitting, and sharing. The ceremony begins when Chris and Tim enter the kitchen and cook together. Meal preparation is a time of decompression. Chris usually manages the entree, and Tim makes the salad and whatever else is needed. Daughter Nathalie sets the table.

The family always plays music while they eat. Puccini, Bach, maybe an opera. They light the candles on the table. They talk. Nathalie knows the routine so well she often begins the conversation with "Well, what did you do in school today?" Then she answers her own question. They get to know each other. How was your day? What's going on? This hour is so special for the family that Tim says he wouldn't answer the phone if someone called to say the house was on fire. They want Nathalie to grow up with a feeling that families eat dinner together and everybody has a part in the process.

"Dinner is not something we rush through to go bowling," Tim says with a smile. "Dinner *is* our recreation. Ultimately, it comes down to choosing what is more important in your life. My job is teaching high school literature, and if you said to me, I'll triple your salary if you work until 7:00 P.M. each night, I'd say no. Absolutely. Time passes, Nathalie is growing up. It isn't worth it to me. This is my life."

A quote by W. S. Merwin comes to mind: "Those who work, as they say, for a living, are not to calculate how much they make an hour and then consider what they claim to own, remembering that there was a time when they made less per hour, and then consider that what they claim to own is perhaps all that remains of what they sold that many hours of their life for, and then try to imagine the hours coming again."

Life was busier before, and bigger. In the early 1980s, the Curtises were in their large-house phase. The phase with the big mortgage, big yard, big rooms, big house, big work. Chris calls the big house their fantasy house. A grand colonial with columns in front and a rambling yard. "We were pretty house proud," she recalls. In short time, however, the pride became an endless round of work. "I burned out on it because it was a tremendous amount of work to maintain," she says. "We both realized it became more of an obligation than we wanted."

The Curtises' yearlong teaching exchange in Denmark confirmed their feelings that they didn't need all the burdens of the big house. "When we got home," Chris remembers, "we knew we could get by with a lot smaller space and a lot fewer things."

There was no question they would sell when the Curtises discovered some boxes in their basement that contained clothes and household items that they had totally forgotten about during their year away. "That was a real awakening to me that most of the stuff I thought was important, we didn't even remember we had," Chris says.

It took about a year to sell the four-bedroom house for a two-bedroom-plus-den bungalow. It was a good move, they say. They relocated to a "cozy, manageable space." Their mortgage payment was cut in half, their house and yardwork cut immensely. In the big house, Tim would spend most of the day just mowing and edging the lawn. Now he goes out with his push mower and spends a few minutes. Housework? Vacuuming used to take one and a half to two hours. Now Tim says he can vacuum the whole house by plugging the vacuum into one outlet. Maybe half an hour. The couple devised a cleaning system so Tim is responsible for one set of chores and Chris the other. They agree it also helps to have fewer things around to clean. Tim recalls another favorite quote that describes the kind of simplicity they like. This one from Hemingway: "a clean, well-lighted place."

The Curtises both believe that the choices they make every day serve as models for their daughter. "We try to tangibly show Nathalie that we can have fun in simple ways that don't cost a lot of money, like making dinner."

❖ ❖ ❖ ❖ ❖ ❖ ❖ ❖ ❖ ❖ ❖ ❖ ❖ ❖ ❖

Resources

American Wholefoods Cuisine by Nikki and David Goldbeck (New York: Plume Books, 1983)
This book has been my recipe bible. Some recipes are simple, some not. Pick and choose which ones fit into simple cooking ideals. Includes whole-foods-philosophy and menus for international dinner parties.

Back to Eden by Jethro Kloss (Loma Linda, CA: Back to Eden Books Publishing, 1949, 1989)
The original bible (over 1,000 pages) on living in cooperation with nature's healing resources. Book skips nothing, and includes herbs, diseases, nutrition, food, natural treatments for ailments and much more.

Caring Kitchens by Gloria Lawson (Grimsby, Ontario: Caring Kitchens)
Be kind to animals, don't eat them, is theme of this recipe book. Adventist. Contact: Caring Kitchens, P.O. Box 123, Grimsby, Ontario L3M 4G3.

Cooking with Natural Foods as You Search for Abundant Health by Muriel Beltz (Hermosa, SD: Black Hills Health & Education Center, 1990)
Recipes, menus, and nutritional information based on Adventist program at Black Hills, South Dakota.

The Healthy Hunzas by J. I. Rodale (Emmaus, PA: Rodale Press, 1949)
The Hunzas are a people who seem to be less "civilized" than we, yet eclipse us dramatically in the pursuit of health and happiness. The Hunzas dwell on the northwestern border of India. The four reasons postulated for their health are: (1) Infants are reared at the breast; (2) the people live on the unsophisticated foods of nature: milk, eggs, grains, fruits, and vegetables; (3) they are essentially a teetotaling race; (4) their manner of life requires the vigorous exercise of their bodies.

Like Water for Chocolate by Laura Esquivel (New York: Doubleday, 1992)
Fictional tale about a Mexican woman who puts her entire being into her cooking in a soulful, sensual way.

New Start by Vernon Foster, M.D. (Santa Barbara, CA: Woodbridge Press, 1988)
Follows the health and lifestyle program at the Weimar Institute (Adventist) in California. Details eight essentials for maintaining and recovering health: how nature restores, sleep, nutrition, stress, lifestyle for preventing cancer and more.

Outlaw Cook by John Thorne (New York: Farrar, Straus and Giroux, 1992)
Author shows how learning to cook can be a voyage of self-discovery. *Outlaw Cook* is about having fun in the kitchen. Recipes are not always simple, but the theory is sound—enjoy yourself!

The Seventh Day Diet by Chris Rucker and Jan Hoffman, (New York: Random House, 1991)
Healthy cuisine based on Seventh Day Adventist philosophy.

Simple Food for the Good Life by Helen Nearing (Walpole, NH: Stillpoint Publishing, 1980)
Details Helen's philosophy about cooking simple, nutritious food. Includes recipes and thoughts.

Unplugged Kitchen, a Return to the Simple, Authentic Joys of Cooking by Viana La Place (New York: Morrow, 1996)
Move away from the fast-paced world of food processors, stainless steel measuring spoons, and dinner in a hurry and enter the sensual kitchen of Viana La Place. You'll rediscover the art of relying on your senses and hands rather than on machines to create simple but delicious food.

Vegetarian Express: Easy, Tasty and Healthy Menus in 28 Minutes (Or Less!) by Nava Atlas and Lillian Kayte (New York: Little, Brown, 1995)
Medley of quick, tasty, nutritional recipes.

Wellness to Fitness by Melvin Beltz, M.D. (Hermosa, SD: Black Hills Health & Education
      Center, 1991)
Another Adventist book, detailing the work done at their Black Hills Center. Follows
WELLNESS principles: water, exercise, limits (balance), life-giving air, nutrition, essential
rest, sunshine, spiritual dimension. Contact: Dr. Melvin Beltz, M.D., c/o Black Hills Health
& Education Center, Box 19, Hermosa, SD 57744.

Whole Foods for Whole People by Lucy Fuller (Harrisville, NY: MMI Press, 1986)
Adventist book on principles of nutrition and recipes.

10

Health and Exercise

There's no reason to give up
something I enjoy unless I get
something back that's even better. But
I find that when I give up certain
things that I might like, like
cheeseburgers, for example, I feel so
much better, those choices are
worth it.

—DEAN ORNISH, M.D.

The irony of our modern way of living and exercising was well put in a recent issue of *Business Week*. It is worth sharing: "We're the quirky civilization that rides elevators to the second floor and buys electronic stair steppers to condition our thighs. We drive to convenience stores and hurry back to our treadmills. Yes, we rely on machines to save us from working, then buy other machines to save our bodies from the terminal flab."

Take a look at nature sometime. When left to itself, everything flows and works in harmony with gentle, continual movements. When I was young, I used to hang out by a lake and watch the ducks. I wanted to be one; they seemed to have such a smooth, effortless life gliding along the water. No wasted energy, no staccato gyrations. Watch the effortlessness of birds flying south for the winter. They follow their deeply ingrained instincts and simply rise up into the sky. There are no hard edges in nature, and there is no extravagance.

There are cycles in nature. Not only do the birds instinctively know when to fly south, but the trees know when to shed their leaves, bears know when to hibernate, and salmon know when to swim upstream. Everything is in chaos when nature isn't allowed to function according to its own rhythms.

We are part of nature, yet we carry on in our daily lives as if we have no connection. We do as we please without a thought to what our own inner natures try to tell us. We spend enormous amounts of energy and money trying to outsmart nature in all ways, including how we treat our own bodies. We eat food that is so far removed from its natural state it ought to be called something other than food. We have natural gyms under our noses yet we think it's better to puff and sweat under a set of metal bars. Our bodies get tired and want a rest but we ignore them and pour down the coffee. On and on. We wonder why we're not as healthy and vibrant as we'd like and we wonder why we're stressed. We also wonder why we spend a fortune on medical care.

Who Is Healthy?

A group of people who live in northwest India do not know illness and stress and are incredibly physically fit. They also don't know a thing about treadmills and puffed and processed food. They are known as the Hunzas, and they follow nature simply because it is their way. It is worth taking a look at their lives. Author J. I. Rodale discovered these people in 1948 and was so impressed he wrote a book about them, titled *The Healthy Hunzas*.

They live in the mountains of northern India, not far from Tibet, and according to Rodale, "their pocket-handkerchief plots of land sustain them and there they flourish in hardihood and vigor, on into unusual longevity."

Rodale and others who have studied the Hunzas have been amazed that they stay so healthy when they are surrounded on all sides by peoples afflicted with all kinds of degenerative and pestilential diseases. An English physician who lived with the Hunzas for a time, Sir Robert McCarrison, said that he had never seen a case of appendicitis, colitis, cancer, fatigue, anxiety, or a cold. McCarrison wrote: "The powers of endurance of these people are extraordinary; to see a man of this race throw off his scanty garments, revealing a figure which would delight the eye of a Rodin, and plunge into a glacier-fed river in the middle of winter, as easily as most of us would take a tepid bath, is to realize that perfection of physique and great physical endurance are attainable on the simplest of foods, provided these be of the right kind."

McCarrison postulated four reasons for the Hunza's fabulous health:

1. Infants are reared as Nature intended them to be reared—at the breast. If this source of nourishment fails, they die; and at least they are spared the future gastro-intestinal miseries which so often have their origin in the first bottle.
2. The people live on the unsophisticated foods of Nature: milk, eggs, grains, fruits, and vegetables. I don't suppose that one in every thousand of them has ever seen a tinned salmon, a chocolate, or a patent infant food, nor that as much sugar is imported into their country in a year as is used in a moderately sized hotel of this city in a single day.
3. Their religion prohibits alcohol, and although they do not always lead in this respect a strictly religious life, nevertheless they are eminently a teetotalling race.
4. Their manner of life requires the vigorous exercise of their bodies.

McCarrison returned home and decided to conduct an experiment. He wondered whether rats could be endowed with health equal to that enjoyed by the Hunzas through feeding the rodents a similar diet. One group of rats was fed the Hunza diet. Another group was fed the poor diet of the southern India rice-eaters. A third group was fed the diet of the lower classes of England, containing white bread, margarine, sweetened tea, a little boiled milk, cabbage and potatoes, tinned meats and jam. The results were startling. McCarrison described the first group as being *hunzarized*. During the two-year study, there was no case of illness, no death from natural causes, no infantile mortality. "Both clinically and at post-mortem examination this stock has been shown to be remarkably free from disease," he wrote.

The second group of rats suffered from a wide variety of diseases involving every organ of the body, such as the nose, eyes, heart, stomach, lungs, bladder, kidneys, intestines, the blood, glands, nerves, and reproductive organs. In addition, they suffered from loss of hair, malformed and crooked spines, poor teeth, ulcers, and boils and became vicious and irritable.

The "English" rats also developed most of these troubles. They were nervous and apt to bite their attendants; they lived unhappily together, and by the 60th day of the experiment they began to kill and eat the weaker ones among them.

As for exercise, the Hunzas spend most of their time outdoors where they breathe in pure air. Rodale wrote:

This may sound elementary, but deep breathing is essential to optimum health. Many sedentary office workers have not taken a real deep breath in their entire lives. How the air gets into their lungs is one of the miracles of the workings of our bodies. A man who goes from office to trolley to home and does not compensate for it by taking long walks is bound to suffer physically because of this inaction and stagnation of air in the respiratory system.

The Hunzas do not take medicines, headache pills, or the like. They don't take nitroglycerine to keep their hearts from ceasing to function, because their hearts are strong. Nor do the Hunzas suffer from allergies. One Hunza wrote to Rodale that in Hunza everyone dies "by nature if he does not fall from mountains or by any other accident, otherwise, not before 80 or 85."

Rodale noticed more. They don't stop the flow of blood by wearing tight collars, corsets, or tight shoes. They don't get colds because the strength of their bodies is due to good nourishment and because their exposure to the elements and the rugged outdoor life has fortified their resistance. More studies were conducted. Were the Hunzas healthy because they are not city dwellers? Studies of city versus country dwellers in the rest of the world indicated that country dwellers were no healthier, mentally or physically. Were they healthy because they live at high altitudes? More studies indicated this was not the answer either.

The Hunzas are also very compatible with each other and intelligent. Divorce is rare, as is anger. They also take care of and look out for one another. Many studies have been conducted to show the correlation between good nutrition and intelligence. In one, a group of children malnourished at the beginning of the test showed a rise ranging from 10 to 18 IQ points after a period of years in which they were well nourished. The control group, well nourished throughout, showed no change in IQ. The Hunzas' food is grown by organic gardening methods. They put back into the soil what they take out and have rich, fertile soil in which to grow their food.

Rodale concludes: "We must live with Nature. We must develop a biologic rather than a chemic conception of our bodies. We must be people rather than test tubes. We must slowly begin the process of Hunzarizing our bodies."

Another group of closer-to-home people, the Seventh-Day Adventists, have also been studied intensely because they are well known for their vibrant health and longevity. The *Saturday Evening Post* once stated: "Probably no religious movement, ancient or modern, has put greater emphasis on diet and nutrition than the Seventh-Day Adventist Church." The Adventists follow a health and lifestyle plan that is similar to that of the Hunzas, adapted to Western culture. They eat a well-balanced diet, with emphasis on natural foods in season whenenver possible, they don't eat meat because of the animal fat and cholesterol, they stay away from alcohol and caffeine, and they do not eat refined foods because of the loss of vitamins and natural ingredients. Adventists also believe in regular exercise, and have a belief in something greater than themselves. Refer to Chapter 9 for a comparison of Adventist rates of disease with those of the general U.S. population.

The Simple Living Plan for Health

There are two aspects to the Simple Living health plan. One is to use nature to stay healthy by eating natural, healthful foods for nutrition and using the great outdoors as your gym, whenever possible. The second is to use nature as a doctor when you are sick, by using natural remedies. Both aspects tie in together, and both use the same parts of nature. The most important rule is this: *Cooperate with nature and you will be rewarded with health.*

What's the lesson here? Do we need to be an Adventist or Hunza to be healthy and vibrant? Nope. We have everything we need right under our own noses. If Dr. McCarrison could create a tribe of healthy rats in England by feeding them the Hunza diet, we ought to be able to repeat the diet in our own homes. We can adopt the Hunza or Adventist lifestyles without becoming them. We can eat as they do, and we can adapt our exercise to be a close approximation. If we live in the middle of the city, we certainly can't be running up and down mountainsides every day. But that doesn't mean we're stuck reading magazines or watching TV while working out on automatic stair-stepping machines either. There is another way. Welcome to the Simple Living plan for health and exercise.

Our bodies are not mysterious—everything boils down to simple anatomy and physiology. Our body mechanism, like nature, is very organized and follows a plan, just as the stars do in the sky. If you look at our cells under a microscope, you will see that they follow an organized plan. When we use natural remedies, we work *with* these laws rather than trying force things, as we do with overuse of drugs or machines.

It helps to know a little about how the body functions, just as it helps to breeze through an owner's manual for your car or home appliance before using it. Then you have a clue about why certain things happen. When they break down, at least you have some knowledge about what steps to take to fix it. In simple terms, the body is made of blood and lymph vessels, nerves, leukocytes, connective tissue, plasma proteins, biochemical mechanisms, and immune properties of living cells. When one of these guys breaks down, you need to find a remedy that assists, stimulates, and directs nature in her efforts to throw off an offending agent and utilize the body's own defense mechanisms. In other words, you want to do what you can to help your body fight its own battles. You can take pills to mask the battle and pretend it is not going on, or you can get in there and help win the war. When all you do is mask the battle, I hate to tell you, but the darned thing is still going on in there just the same. The only difference is you aren't so aware of it. The damage continues.

If you remember that the body is a part of nature and works according to a very organized plan, it is easier to remember that when the body gets sick, it also has an organized plan to get better, if we let it. This isn't to say that you should never go to a doctor. (One more time, balance, balance, balance—nothing extreme.) This is to say that when at all possible, use nature as your doctor and help your body do its natural thing to get well. If you have allowed your body to get too far out of whack by eating junk food and hanging out on the couch being a you-know-what kind of potato, then your body may not have the strength and resources to fight off impending enemies. This is all the more reason why you need to take stock of your lifestyle and make some changes.

If you have been treating your body as if you actually like and respect it, however, it will perform at top function for you in exchange. What better symbiotic relationship could you ask for, anyway? Your body is no different from a friend. If you are nice to your friend, your friend will be nice back. If you are a jerk, chances are your friend will either ignore you or be a jerk to you too. When your body is functioning properly, you may still get sick here and there, but you will be more likely to overcome the ailment without landing in the hospital. This is where you come in with natural remedies. You are showing up to help, not cover up.

When my daughter was a baby and I was breast-feeding her, I contracted mastitis. I had never had mastitis before (which is an inflammation of the breast) and was very frightened to notice a large lump in my breast, so I went to an emergency-type weekend clinic. They prescribed antibiotics for me. I filled the prescription, but my inner voice told me not to take the pills, especially since I was breast-feeding. I was concerned that the medication would get into my breast milk. I turned to a home remedy instead and was cured. The home remedy (hot castor oil packs) merely assisted my body to use its own defense mechanisms to get well.

Dr. Phillip Dow taught for many years at the Medical College of Georgia that normal physiological processes are basic to all healing and that no method, drug, or procedure could substitute for the process. He taught that the best that can be done by any external influence is to take away toxic substances, keep the field clean, provide necessary raw materials, remove all interfering influences, and wait for the body to activate its marvelous recuperative resources.

At the same school, Dr. Edgar Pund taught that the body's equipment is adequate to carry on needed processes of repair, and that even pain and fever are protective and healing in their objectives.

Mind-Body Healing

Another component to natural healing is the mind-body connection. Entire books have been written about this subject, with the most publicly known titled *Healing and the Mind,* by Bill Moyers. Moyers, a popular PBS television host, visited with a number of healing practitioners to talk about this correlation. The mind-body connection is evident in many ways. Cancer or AIDS patients with positive, don't-give-up attitudes live longer than those who do give up. Longtime spouses frequently die within six months of the death of their spouse, literally from a broken heart. Oftentimes people wait until a certain event has taken place before they are ready to die. One physician who had worked with Native Americans for 40 years said that very often they died when they decided to die. They would talk with their families and would be resolved about this. People who are depressed or who have just lost a loved one are more likely to have congestive heart failure and other illnesses. People who have more connection to their community have higher chances of recovery.

> *The greatest force in the human body is the natural drive of the body to heal itself—but that force is not independent of the belief system, which can translate expectations into physiological change.*
>
> —Dr. Norman Cousins

Most Westerners (me sometimes included) are too busy even to be aware of what our minds and bodies are quietly telling us. These busy Westerners include our traditional doctors, who have been trained in the "busy mode"—

that is, to treat the problem after it has occurred, and in the most expedient way possible. This route to recovery is: Don't pay attention to your body and mind until it's too late, then go in for a pill to fix it.

Luckily, more and more traditional doctors and hospitals are realizing that there is another way. John Kabat-Zinn, Ph.D., is founder and director of the Stress Reduction Clinic at the University of Massachusetts Medical Center and associate professor of medicine in the Division of Preventive and Behavioral Medicine at the University of Massachusetts Medical School. He is author of the book, *Full Catastrophe Living: Using the Wisdom of Your Body and Mind to Face Stress, Pain, and Illness*. He teaches people to get to know their minds and bodies through meditation exercises, which train them to focus in the present moment. In this way, people can work with pain and anxiety without medication. About the mind-body connection, he says: "As we begin looking at chronic illnesses like cancer and heart disease, which aren't infectious, we see more and more evidence that how we live our lives and, in fact, how we think and feel over a lifetime can influence the kinds of illnesses that we have."

California's West Oakland Health Center studied more than 100 people 55 and older. Those who performed meditation every day for three months had an overall drop in systolic pressure (the higher number in a blood pressure reading) that was 11 points greater than the drop in people who were simply counseled on lifestyle changes such as losing weight, cutting back on salt, exercising more, and drinking less alchohol. The meditators' diastolic pressure (the lower number) dropped by 6 points more than in the advice-only group.

Our relationship to others also can affect our health. Dean Ornish M.D., author of *Dr. Dean Ornish's Program for Reversing Heart Disease*, says: "People who feel isolated have three to five times the mortality, not only from cardiovascular disease, but from all causes, when compared to people who don't feel isolated."

Ornish says his own route to recovery from suicidal depression came when he finally recognized the role nature plays in healing:

> I began eating a vegetarian diet. I began doing yoga, and meditation, and exercise, and got glimpses of what it meant to feel at peace, and to realize that it came not from doing but undoing. When we work with the heart patients in our study, at the end of a yoga class or meditation, when they feel that same sense of peace and well-being, we point out that their sense of peace didn't come from getting something they were lacking, but, rather, that they simply quieted down enough to experience what they already have.

I've explained how to quiet yourself through meditation in Chapter 3. In fact, the whole point of the kind of meditation I explained, called insight meditation, is to be aware of how you are feeling and what you are thinking throughout the day. By doing so you'll be working in tandem with your body and treating it like a friend. Recall how wonderful it feels when someone really *listens* to you with their full attention; your body deserves the same.

Seven Rules of Natural Health

Here are the seven basic principles of using nature to stay healthy that I learned from the Adventists. They are all so straightforward, simple, and rational that I can't argue with them. Plus they are free.

Step 1: Pure air. Get outside every day, rain or shine, for fresh air. Learn to breathe deeply to take oxygen way into your body. Incorporate this step into your daily life; walk instead of driving to the store or go for a walk with a friend instead of meeting for coffee. Hang your clothes outside and get your exercise, save on electricity, and enjoy how fresh your clothes feel. Wear natural fibers that breathe (linen, wool, cotton, silk). Get out of the city whenever possible so you can breathe clean air. Keep the air circulating inside your house by opening the windows, even in winter, for at least an hour a day. Nearly every day I open all bedroom windows in the house to clear the air. If it is a cold day, I open them just for a short time; if it is warm, they stay open all day. I can really feel the difference when the windows haven't been opened. It is better to have cool air with oxygen than warm air that stifles. I also don't make my bed during the day because it is better to air out the sheets. Since I like to sleep in a neat bed, however, I make it at night before crawling in.

Step 2: Sunlight. My favorite! Remember to use all the available natural means of therapy and health maintenance. Sunlight is certainly one. Sunlight is the force that nourishes and energizes our bodies. It creates the environment necessary for our existence: oxygen and carbon dioxide. It regulates temperature and humidity at life-supporting levels. The body's daily requirement of vitamin D is about 400 units. Exposing your face to sunlight for just 15 minutes will give you more than your daily requirement. Vitamin D ensures straight and strong bones with the proper proportions of calcium and phosphorous. Certainly we are all aware of the dangers of too much sunlight, so take yours in moderation, and wear sunscreen and protective layers of clothing, but be sure to get a little each day whenever possible. You can read about all of the benefits of sunlight in a book titled *Sunlight Could Save Your Life*, by Dr. Zane R. Kime.

Step 3: Temperance. Don't indulge in any one thing. This doesn't just refer to alcohol; it refers to nearly everything. Temperance is one of the themes of this book, only I've called it balance. Think about it. Some people hear they ought to get exercise so they go out there and jog so much they get emaciated; jogging becomes their religion. Or they diet so much they become anorexic. They get into health foods to such extremes that they can't even go to anybody's house for dinner anymore. I learned about this idea when I first became enthralled with health food cooking. I cooked everything the healthy way— even a birthday cake for my brother. Everyone sat around the table politely eating teeny bits of my tasteless cake, looking up to see what everyone else was doing. They said things like "Oh, well . . . um . . . this is certainly . . . well . . . um . . . different!" I realized then and there that I needed to practice temperance. This doesn't mean you can't cook excellent-tasting healthful desserts. Indeed, since the birthday fiasco, I have come up with some good recipes. But it does mean that you need to lighten up and not go off in one extreme direction or another. Remember the rule: Moderation in what is good for you and abstinence from things that are not good.

Step 4: Rest. Your body and mind need rest in order to function. Get plenty of rest each night and take at least one day a week to devote to restful pursuits. As for the one day a week off, this is easy if you faithfully follow a religion, for most include a Sabbath. If you don't have rest built into your life via religion, do it without religion. Build it in yourself. Everybody needs a break from all kinds of work, both paid and unpaid. This is the day for families to go hiking or to relax around the house, or for people to hang out on the couch reading or doing some other restful or playful endeavor. If you are spiritual, this is also the day to spend thinking about spiritual matters and going to services, or reading something inspirational. If we ever want lives that are in balance, we must adhere to this rule. Otherwise we run ourselves ragged around the clock and drop from exhaustion during our two-week vacation. What kind of life is this?

Your digestive system also needs time to rest. Your system needs about five hours to digest food completely. Some health practitioners believe you should not eat between meals because if you do, your digestive system never has a chance to rest. The theory is that all systems and organs, whether you see them or not, need rest. In between meals you can drink all the water and herbal tea you want. After five hours, eat a huge dinner. Stuff yourself with hearty, natural food, as explained in Chapter 9. Take an hour to eat slowly and mindfully. Let your system rest again, feeding it only water and tea, or a light snack later in the evening.

You want to rest not only your internal organs but your whole body as well. You need at least eight hours of sleep. The math is easy. If you want to get up at 4:30 A.M., you need to go to bed at around 8:30 P.M. Here is the deal. Apparently you get better sleep every hour before midnight than you get after midnight. So this plan makes sense. All you need to do is try it for a while and see if you don't feel better.

In summary, whenever you get up, eat a huge breakfast, don't eat again for at least five or more hours, eat a huge dinner, and so on. Allow yourself at least eight hours of sleep. End of story. Once again you are using nature as your personal trainer and preventive doctor. It's free. What do you have to lose?

Step 5: Exercise. Exercising in fresh air takes poisons and wastes out of the body. Fresh air from exercising fills cells with oxygen. Stretch outside every morning and find an enjoyable form of exercise that fits naturally in your day, such as working in the garden, building a treehouse for your children, or walking or cycling to work. Jethro Kloss, the author of the age-old bible on natural living titled *Back to Eden,* faithfully went outside every morning, summer and winter (weather permitting), to do a certain number of jumping jacks. Afterward he would go into the kitchen for a glass of fresh orange or grapefruit juice. He began every day with fresh air, brisk exercise, and a nutritious drink. For parents, instead of putting your children on the school bus, walk them to school. It's a good way to get to know them as they share their day with you. Refer to the section in this chapter, Natural Exercise, for information about exercise.

Step 6: Water. Water is free or inexpensive, so use it liberally. Drink at least 8 to 10 glasses of water between meals to help purge your system. Drink the water 30 minutes to 1 hour before or 1 hour after meals to prevent dilution of stomach acids, which help proper digestion. I carry around an oversize water bottle with a built-in straw and sip from it throughout the day. Usually I refill it a number of times. When I do this I am well hydrated and not thirsty at mealtime. Use water not only to keep your body clean but as a tonic as well. Do this by taking a regular, warm shower and then, at the end, turning up the cold water. This wakes up your cells and keeps them functioning. I'm not saying this is easy, but when I do it, I am much healthier. Once I visited a retreat center that was near a mountain river. A man from Germany was also staying there, and we struck a friendship. I was amazed to see him jump into the icy river time after time and come out totally refreshed. I wanted to know his secret. He told me that he finished his showers with cold water every day. This man was absolutely vibrant. I tried the cold shower routine and found that I could go into cold lakes and rivers, too. I was more vibrant as well.

Water is also a perfect, natural cure-all for many ailments. When used by a doctor, it is called hydrotherapy. Here is an example of hydrotherapy in action. The next time you have a headache, keep the lid on your aspirin bottle. Headaches are caused by blood vessels swelling in the head. The pressure is what causes the pain. Put your feet in a bucket of the hottest water you can stand; this will cause a reflex reaction that causes the blood vessels in the head to narrow. Add a cold compress to the head, to aid the blood to flow to the extremities and away from the head—also promoting narrowing of the vessels. The hot foot bath compresses the vessels and the cold pack on the head sends the blood away. Hot draws blood to it, and cold sends blood away—a reflexive relationship.

Step 7: Nutrition. We are only as healthy as what we put into our bodies. According to current medical information, most of the degenerative diseases that plague modern America—heart problems, high blood pressure, certain cancers, and stroke—are primarily the result of improper diet. All cells and tissues in our bodies are formed by the food we eat. The best way to take care of our bodies is also the simplest and most inexpensive: *Eat food the way it comes out of the ground with nothing added and nothing removed.* These foods are grains, fruits, seeds, legumes, nuts, and vegetables. Eat a variety of these food groups every week. Eat two servings of raw vegetable salad and two more servings of raw or cooked green or yellow vegetables daily. Eat cooked beans or peas three times a week, sweet potatoes or squash twice weekly, and a member of the cabbage family (broccoli, Brussels sprouts, cauliflower, kale) three times a week. Try to make breakfast your heaviest meal and supper the lightest. Refer to Chapter 9 for more detailed information on food and cooking.

Other Ways to Use Nature as Your Doctor

Herbs

You can't get a more natural remedy than herbs. Natural healing devotees believe that the body possesses the inherent ability to protect, regulate, and heal itself. This ability is called the *vital force.* Herbs are an ideal way to restore this vital force because they are gentle and provide necessary trace elements, vitamins, and medicinal substances. Indeed, there is a plant for every illness. Herbs have been used since nearly the beginning of time and were the first medicine used by humans. Allopathic medicine (the more traditional type used today) is only about 500 years old. Jethro Kloss writes in *Back to Eden*, "The use of herbs in the written record actually dates back for several thousands of years B.C. The Chinese, Sumerians, and Egyptians all used plants for medicinal purposes. A Chinese book on herbs, dated around 2700 B.C., lists over 300 plants with their medicinal uses. In the Old Testament, several herbs are mentioned, including aloe."

Herbs grow nearly everywhere, and if they are not already growing, they are some of the easiest plants to cultivate. There is an herbal remedy for every disease you can think of. Determining the correct herbal remedy for your aches and pains takes more space than I can devote here, but I'll explain enough so you can go forward if the subject is of interest to you. Please refer to the Resources at the end of this chapter for books that detail the use of herbs as remedies.

You can take herbal remedies in a number of ways, as herb teas, tinctures, poultices, ointments and oils, and herb baths. The method you use depends on the ailment and the herb. For example, you can use stinging nettles and Swedish bitters in tea for hay fever and allergy. Drink agrimony, lady's mantle, or nettle tea for anemia. For swollen glands, you apply calendula as a wash or St. John's wort oil to the skin in the area of the gland. If you have gastric acid in the stomach, drink calamus root tea. If you can't sleep, you can mix the following herbs into a tea: cowslip, lavender, St. John's wort, hops cones, and valerian roots. Remember, these are examples. You'll want to get the correct proportions from a reputable herb book.

Some of these names may sound foreign to you; your local herbalist or health food store can provide information. You can read books or take classes on how to grow herbs yourself or how to find them growing in the wild. If taken properly and with knowledge, herbs cannot harm you in the way that traditional chemical medicines can; the worst thing that may happen is that they won't cure your ailment. As with any natural remedy, if you feel uncomfortable, it's best to see a traditional physician first to make sure you are not ignoring a more serious problem that is best treated with chemicals.

Home Remedies

If you haven't tried home remedies, you should. Home remedies are the kind our grandparents used to rely on. Over the years these terrific family "hand-

me-downs" landed on the back burner due to our modern overemphasis on consulting professionals for everything, thinking we can't possibly take care of anything ourselves. Recently they have become increasingly popular as more people consider a return to more natural, simpler styles of living. They are very easy, very simple, and, surprisingly, often very effective. They can save you the whopping expense of a doctor visit, and you feel pretty good about yourself when you use a home remedy that works. As with other natural remedies, the worst that can happen with a home remedy is that it won't work—but rarely does trying them out pose any danger. Some of the books listed in the Resources for this chapter provide ideas for home remedies. These remedies are some of the best examples of simple living in action because they help you to be more self-sufficient rather than relying on expensive professionals. Home remedies are best for nonacute conditions, such as acne, bee stings, colds, colic, headaches, indigestion, nausea, and warts, to name a few. Most home remedies utilize everyday items you find around the house or in the grocery store: hot water bottles (for colic), fresh ginger root (for heartburn and nausea), garlic cloves (for high cholesterol), oatmeal (for itchy skin), eucalyptus oil (for sinusitis), and fresh, easy-to-find herbs like hyssop (for sore throats).

Coping with Stress the Natural Way

Mindfulness—one of the themes of this chapter—is the most valuable way I know of to deal with stress. (For a full description of mindfulness and meditation, refer to Chapter 3.) When you are mindful, you get to know who you are and why you make the choices you do. Then you can better handle stress. Here is why: If you are truly honest with yourself and are aware of your strengths and weaknesses, you will know what options are better for you in your life. It is when we run around on automatic pilot that we get into trouble, which often leads to stress. For instance, reacting to life from your weaknesses is one part of the autopilot syndrome. We all have these weaknesses, believe me. There is a difference, however, between someone who is aware of his or her weakness and someone who isn't. Here is one example: When people act out of their weaknesses, they tend to overcommit themselves. (We've all been there, done that.) Overcommitment is a very common reason for stress. We take on more than our bodies and minds can handle, but our insecurities cause us to keep taking on more and more. Why? To make sure people notice us, so we feel accepted as part of a group, to feel important, or so we don't have to be alone with ourselves. If we are mindful, we can stop *before* committing to something and think deeply about our motivation. Some motivations are the result of our more healthy self and some the result of our weaker self.

Awareness also can help with worrying, another cause of stress. If you start to worry, sit for a meditation and take a look at your worry. What is it? Remember, worry is just thoughts and no more. A thought is nothing solid. When worry comes into your mind, simply label it "worry" and let it go. It'll come back again; when it does, tell yourself something like "Oh, there's that worry again," and let it go. Think of yourself as an observer—passively observe the worry thought. Then return to your breathing.

Natural Exercise

There are two ways to get exercise naturally. One is to get exercise during the normal course of your day, by walking or bicycling to work, walking to the store, mowing your lawn with a push mower, cleaning the house, and so on. The name for this type of exercise was coined by Randi Hacker, who wrote *How to Live Cheap, Green, and Happy*. She calls it the Earth Gym. The second way is to engage in more deliberate workouts, called mindful workouts. The difference between the usual deliberate workout and mindful exercise is the amount of mindfulness you bring to your exercise regime.

Mindful Workouts

Mindful workouts are an intimate way of looking at exercise. As Deepak Chopra, author of 49 books, including *Perfect Health*, says: "People discover the intimacy that nature has established between awareness and physiology. The body is not just a shell or walking life-support system. It is your self intimately clothed in matter. Getting back in touch with this intimacy is very reassuring and delightful, particularly for people who have given up on exercise and have become virtual strangers to their bodies."

The conventional way to exercise is to set some kind of goal for yourself and go at it to achieve that goal. For example, say your goal is to lose 10 pounds and maybe tighten your thigh muscles. You research some exercise ideas and decide the best way to achieve your goal is by running. The books say you should run at least three days a week for 20 minutes a time—whatever. And you also have a plan to increase your distance and time within a certain amount of days or weeks. Now you have a goal. So you strap on your Walkman and run for 20 minutes every Monday, Wednesday, and Friday. Some days you don't feel like it, but you push on anyway, and you continually increase your speed and distance. You push pretty rigorously because you want to lose these 10 pounds by June 1, and here it is, spring already. Often you are exhausted from this workout.

Mindful exercise is very different. It is about being friends with your body and listening to it. Listening to your body means setting goals that are in alignment with your body, not some outer-directed goal, and listening to and feeling your body and muscles as you exercise. When you have pushed it too far, your body will tell you, if you listen. You can't listen if you are one of these people with a Walkman on your head or a magazine or book sitting in front of you while you work out on the electronic treadmill. Mindful exercise is being fully present and aware during your workouts—it is another form of meditation. This way you are fully engrossed in the *process* of exercise, not simply some end goal. When exercise is simply goal oriented and no more, it makes sense that people try to distract themselves from the present moment by using Walkmans and magazines. When you need to distract yourself, your mental state is that the activity you are doing at that moment is distasteful, so you cover it by zoning out to music or reading. Think about it. Do you need a Walkman or magazine when you are doing something you love? No, you want to be fully present in the moment, soaking up every bit of what you are doing. It's no wonder that only 10 percent of Americans exercise regularly and the rest give up. When you're doing something distasteful simply for a goal, it's easy to give it up.

The program of mindful exercise is spelled out beautifully in a book titled *Body, Mind, and Sport,* by John Douillard. Douillard follows a form of health and mind-body connection that is taken from a system of preventive medicine and health care called Maharishi Ayurveda. Ayurveda dates back more than 5,000 years in India and comes from two Sanskrit root words: *Ayus* (life) and *Veda* (knowledge or science). Ayurveda is usually translated as "the science of life." Deepak Chopra, author of *Perfect Health*, says: "The guiding principle of Ayurveda is that the mind exerts the deepest influence on the body, and freedom from sickness depends upon contacting our own awareness, bringing it into balance, and then extending that balance to the body."

According to Ayurvedic texts, exercise has three main functions:

1. To rejuvenate the body and cultivate the mind.
2. To remove stress.
3. To develop mind-body coordination.

The first function, rejuvenating the body and cultivating the mind, means you should feel rejuvenated, not drained and exhausted, after a workout.

The second function is to remove stress. One study found that moderate exercise gives our immunities a boost. Serious athletes, however, such as marathon runners, may actually get more colds and infections than the average person. For example, Douillard discusses the runner Jim Fixx who wrote *The Complete Book of Running* in the 1970s. Fixx started out as an obese, sedentary drinker and smoker. Once he discovered running, he became obsessed. He would run 10 miles a day, rain or shine, no matter how he felt. He became addicted to running. Indeed, running ultimately killed him—he dropped dead after a 10-mile run. Fixx ignored his body signals of fatigue and exhaustion. Mindful exercise is about paying attention to your body.

The third function is developing mind-body coordination. When the mind and body are acting in unison, far greater things can happen than if the two work in opposition. When they are working together in harmony, we can experience the zone that athletes talk about, often called a runner's high. This is when the body and mind are working in effortless, perfect harmony. Mind-body coordination can't occur unless you are mindful while working with your body.

The mindful exercise program is about *enjoying the process* of exercise. This is much different from using exercise only to achieve a goal. If we don't make our workouts fun, then we're more likely to quit. If we truly enjoy each moment of our exercise, we will be far more likely to continue. If we continue and at the same time pay attention to our bodies, we will reach far higher states of fitness, both mental and physical, than if we stick to the traditional goal-oriented style of exercise.

There are a couple of ways you can connect your mind and body while exercising. One is simply to be aware of your body as you exercise. This means leaving the Walkman and magazines at home. When you exercise, pay full attention to everything your body is doing—your breathing, your calf muscles, your leg muscles, arm muscles, chest, and so forth. Note when your breathing is becoming more labored, note when your muscles begin to get sore. This is your body telling you to slow down. Just because you slow down when your body signals it is time doesn't mean you will never improve. It does mean that you will go with the flow of your body, so that when your body is ready to take on more, it will tell you. Then rise to the next level. The difference is that you are rising to new levels when your body tells you it is time, not when your head says it is time.

I am a classic case in point. Whenever I get gung-ho on some exercise program and do not listen to my body, sure enough, something breaks down and I ultimately quit. Running is one example. I tried running once and kept a very moderate pace and went a very moderate distance. I stayed with this for a while. All fine. My body was happy. Then I decided it was time to really push myself, so I ran faster and farther, without much gradual buildup. Sure enough, I got shin splints and had to quit. Same thing happened with swimming. Whenever I would push my laps to more "macho" levels, I'd get soreness in my legs and thighs and I'd quit until they got better. By then I'd be out of the swing of exercise. So I tried fast walking. I read an article about how it's good to walk a 12-minute mile. I love to walk anyway, and I have strong, long legs. So I pushed myself immediately to walk this 12-minute mile. More shin splints. I had to stop entirely. Had I listened to my body, I would have slowed down and not increased speed or distance until my body gave me the okay. Then I might have continued exercising all of that time. I would have built up gradually to a stronger level. Which is better? Now I pay attention.

As with meditation, remember to watch your breathing as you exercise, and breathe through your nose. The success of the mindful program is not how far you can run or how much weight you can lift, but rather with how little effort you can do it. Douillard likens this experience to the eye of a hurricane—the winds of the hurricane are strong and dynamic but inside is the calm, centered, peaceful eye. We can attain that calm, peaceful center through mindfulness. In return, our bodies will react with strength and vigor.

According to Douillard, here is why nose breathing is important to the mind-body connection:

> When you breathe through the nose, *prana* (Greek for breath), which is carried by oxygen, enters the nasal cavity. The air while in the nose is prepared for exchange in the lungs, but the prana is said to travel into the brain along the olfactory nerve, which transports a smell or scent from the nasal passage to the appropriate centers of the brain. The first stop for the prana is therefore in the brain, which when enlivened can coordinate with any or all parts of the body engaged in physical activity.

There is an art to nose breathing. Your goal is to breathe via the diaphragm, to get really deep breaths of air into your body. This will take practice, no doubt, but if you keep at it, the results are well worth it. The diaphragm is the membrane that separates the lungs from the visceral cavity. It works by a downward movement, which forces the stomach a little outward. If your stomach does not expand as you inhale, you are not breathing diaphragmatically. Without proper breathing, true health is impossible. Often people don't breathe properly because of mental strain. Diaphragmatic breathing can gradually overcome the tension. As Donald Walters says in his book *Yoga Postures for Higher Awareness*, "Proper breathing is, indeed, one of the most effective forms of psychotherapy."

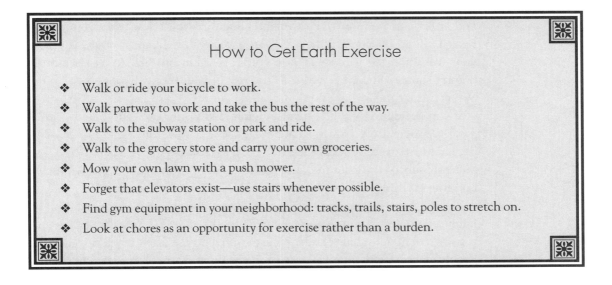

How to Get Earth Exercise

❖ Walk or ride your bicycle to work.

❖ Walk partway to work and take the bus the rest of the way.

❖ Walk to the subway station or park and ride.

❖ Walk to the grocery store and carry your own groceries.

❖ Mow your own lawn with a push mower.

❖ Forget that elevators exist—use stairs whenever possible.

❖ Find gym equipment in your neighborhood: tracks, trails, stairs, poles to stretch on.

❖ Look at chores as an opportunity for exercise rather than a burden.

Once you learn to breath diaphragmatically, begin your exercise program by combining breathing with a few simple yoga postures. Do these before your aerobic exercise. Yoga is, by definition, the union of body and mind. It emphasizes the breath and mind as you do the postures. In this way you begin to tune into your body. When your mind and body work together before you begin to exercise, you are more likely to enjoy your workout. Your entire system will be acting as one harmonious unit. You can get many books and videos at the library that explain basic yoga postures.

When your mind and body are working in unison, you'll find that your body becomes stronger and you experience more inner contentment. John Douillard says: The real challenge is not on the top of a mountain or the finish line of a race, it is within. To harness the potential of the mind and body to win any race or accomplish any goal while remaining inwardly calm, silent, and composed, to be restfully alert while running a marathon, climbing a mountain, putting for par, or even while in the deepest sleep, is the goal not only of the athlete but of humanity itself.

The Earth Gym

There are many reasons to use the Earth Gym, not the least of which is expense. Membership at a no-frills health club usually runs about $100 for initiation and $25 to $35 a month. Midrange clubs generally charge about $300 for initiation and $50 a month. High-end clubs may cost $500 to join and at least $75 a month. How many people do you know who have joined health clubs who are still active even a year later? In most cases, you lose your initiation fee when you stop going. In addition, $25 to $75 a month doesn't sound so bad, but add it to the rest of your monthly not-so-bad bills. What is the total?

If you decide to forgo the health club and buy your own equipment, you'll pay $400 to $800 for a rowing machine, $350 to $2,400 for a treadmill, $200 to $1,500 for an exercise bike, $200 to $2,000 for a stair-stepper, $200 to $700 for a cross-country ski machine, and $200 to $1,500 for a home gym (muscle-building machine).

These prices may or may not be an issue but for one slight problem. Rarely, rarely do people continue to use their machines over time. Think about everyone you know. I literally can't think of one person who uses their machine regularly. People always use them religiously in the beginning and then some life change takes place and the machines sit in the basement, taking up space. One obvious reason is that the darned things are boring as you know what. The only way to make them at all palatable is to do something else while you are on them—watch TV, read a book, whatever. But pay full, mindful attention to what you are doing? Not a chance. Who wants to pay attention to this kind of monotony?

There is another reason to use the Earth Gym rather than machines: balance and fresh air. You want to exercise as much of your body as possible—when you are on a stationary bike, you are not required to use the muscles necessary to balance. With an outdoor bike, you are using one set of leg muscles to push while muscles in the other leg do the balance work. Plus outside bicycling is more fun, you get fresh air, and thus, you're more likely to continue exercising for longer periods than on a stationary bike.

Covert Bailey, fitness guru and author of *Smart Exercise,* says even running requires more balance outdoors than in, because you have to zig and zag, jump over sticks and potholes and so on, none of which happens on a treadmill or indoor track.

Gym owner, professional trainer, and body builder Dan Potts says machines like ab trainers are good only for one thing: to teach you how to work your muscles in the right position. You can do that by going to a store that sells the machines and trying them out in the proper position, or taking a free tour at a gym and asking for a demonstration. Then you'll have the feel of how to align your body for that type of exercise. After that, they aren't worth it, he says. Potts says that in his pursuit of tight abs he uses just two exercises: weighted abdominal crunches (with the weight plate held behind the head) and knee lifts at an upright station. Potts says "Every single person who buys an ab machine wants to get fat off their waistline. And that's the last thing they need to do it." Potts suggests instead doing 50 crunches three times a week. "Sit down in front of your favorite couch, and put your feet up so your knees are at a right angle. Think of 60 percent of your back staying on the floor. Exhale as you come up, to get the air out of the diaphragm, and think 'low' to involve the bottom part of the muscle."

To get the knack of the muscles to use, Potts suggests standing up and trying to pull the belly button back into the spine. "Scrunch down on it and feel the muscles you're working." Potts says we can even work our abs just standing around. "Most people walk around with a pelvic tilt, with their back swayed and belly out. If they walked around with their belly in all day, most people wouldn't need to do crunches."

Potts says that often gym owners and trainers make exercise seem more complicated so people think it is more valuable. In fact, it is very simple to exercise and stay fit. "If you depend on all of these machines, what are you going to do without them?" he asks. He advises that clients not engage in anything they cannot continue for a lifetime. "Usually people have been at a certain flat-line place in their exercise and nutrition, so in their effort to change they become overzealous. They announce that they're quitting all red meat or all sugar and starting on an intense exercise program. It's better to be moderate in everything and make gradual lifestyle changes. All the pieces have to fit—your program needs to fit into your work life, your family life, and so on. You're not going to stick with something if you have to weigh your food every day for the rest of your life, or if you leave a gym and are sore and hungry."

Potts says people simply won't stick with a lot of complicated diets or exercise routines. "I tell them if they really want to simplify their health program, all they need to do is increase their physical activity by 50 percent and decrease the amount they eat by 20 percent. Look at all the food you regularly put on your plate and cut it back by 20 percent. You can lose weight by eating the same foods you are eating now. If you are doing no exercise, start walking three days a week for 20 minutes. Then your natural desire will take over and you'll increase when your body is ready."

Potts compares complicated health and fitness programs to shopping for CD or VCR players. "If the guy at the store tells you about all these bells and whistles and complicated electronics, you probably won't buy the thing. You'll walk out thinking 'All I want to do is listen to music!' "

The key to successful health and fitness programs is to make them as painless as possible. The best exercise is walking, and you can add a few squats, pushups, chin-ups, abdominal and upper-body exercises that you can do on your floor. If you do it slowly and painlessly, the fire will catch on. You need to go with your own flow.

Earth Gym Equipment

You will need a few items of equipment for the Earth Gym, but not much. Decent athletic shoes are first. This doesn't mean you need to run out and buy the most expensive ones on the market. The point is to find shoes that fit your particular feet. Look in *Consumer Reports* or reputable fitness magazines for detailed evaluations of the different shoes that are currently on the market.

You can get inexpensive home exercise equipment: a set of sturdy plastic steps or a floor mat can cost between $20 and $100. Hand weights can cost as little as $1 per pound and many people prefer them to the home gyms. Hand weights often isolate certain muscles better. Exercise videos may cost around $20 and may be found in the library. You can trade with friends if you get bored.

You can buy a secondhand bicycle and try bicycling to work or at least to your errands. My friend Jean doesn't want to bike all the way to work, so she bikes to a bus stop instead. That's certainly better than nothing. If you're just starting out, don't get sucked into some bike sales pitch about how you need a superdeluxe model. Get yourself a basic, secondhand bike from someone else who wanted to trade up for bells and whistles.

Joining the Earth Gym

To join the Earth Gym, begin by looking for opportunities everywhere. Use what is available: hills, grocery bags, stairs, mops, lawn mowers, sidewalks. For instance, if you have an errand, leave your car home and walk. I can hear the excuses: "I would walk but I don't have the time." Wait! You probably do have the time; you just don't know it. What about the time it takes you to shop for just the right gym clothes? How much time do you spend driving to the gym, sitting in traffic, looking for a parking space, working out, cleaning up, and driving home? Then there's TV time, rearranging clutter time, surfing the Internet time, and so on. Not to mention the extra time you spend at work earning money to pay for your gym membership.

Walking

Here are a few walking stories to get you inspired. Right after reading about the Earth Gym, I had scheduled two appointments in town one day. The first was to a doctor whose office was within two miles of town. I left the doctor, and as I headed into town where parking costs $3 and more per hour, I began to grumble about the cost of doing business in town. Then it suddenly occurred to me. Parking near the doctor's office was free. I could easily have left my car in the doctor's neighborhood and used the Earth Gym by walking briskly to and from my second appointment. With traffic and other downtown foolishness, I don't know that it would have taken me much longer to walk.

I lost weight one summer while walking to work. In college, I lived in an apartment that was about two or three miles from where I worked. I didn't want to pay the exorbitant rates to park my car all day, so I walked. It helped that I was always waiting until the last minute so I had to walk very briskly. Without trying or thinking about it or dieting that summer, I lost two pant sizes, felt great, and saved huge amounts of money that I would have had to spend to park.

My friends Chris and Tim live in the city because they like to walk to their errands. Although many of their city neighbors drive to the grocery store one mile away, Chris and Tim pull their red wagon to the store, fill it with food, and haul it home. They simply don't comprehend the logic of driving to errands, complaining of not getting enough exercise, driving to a gym to do exercise, and driving home. They were fair-weather walkers until they lived in Denmark for a year and saw people walking rain or shine. Now a rain jacket solves their weather problems.

What? No red wagon? How about carrying two bags of groceries in your arms? Think of the biceps! You may have to go to the store more often, but so what? How often were you going to the gym to use the upper-body machines?

Bicycle Commuting

My neighbor created a tandem bicycle to take his five-year-old daughter to preschool. After pedaling from his job he swings by his daughter's school and picks her up, and the two of them pedal home. In the morning the same routine is reversed. Every day, rain or shine, he commutes this way.

Commuting by bicycle has done a lot for my neighbor's life. First, he says, it saves a lot of money. At the most it costs him under $100 a year to keep his bike in good repair, and many years it costs nothing. He makes no payments, buys no oil, gas, or insurance, and never has to take it to the mechanic for costly engine work. Second, because he doesn't use gas, he doesn't contribute to pollution problems. Third, it reduces stress in his life because he can pedal the stress right out and because he's not sitting in endless traffic jams. Finally, he doesn't need to make exercise a separate part of his life since he keeps in shape during the natural course of his day.

"People can commute an hour by car and think nothing of it," he says, "so why not bike for an hour instead? There is nothing better than to get out of work and get on a bike. By the time I get home all my aggressions are out. I'm relaxed and I didn't have to deal with traffic because I take side roads."

He stays in excellent shape because he pedals approximately 3,000 miles per year during the regular course of his day.

Do Chores, Get Exercise

The word "chore" usually has a negative connotation. It did to me until I learned about the Earth Gym. Now (believe it or not) I think of chores as an opportunity to get exercise. Here is my story. One weekend I attended a family camp. All participants drew cards in the beginning that indicated which chore each would perform during the three-day camp. My job was to mop the floors of the lodge building. The lodge building was huge and the floors filthy because that was where everybody ate dinner.

Prior to learning about the Earth Gym, this task would have put me in a very crabby mood, because shoving one of those big, heavy, industrial mops and buckets around an enormous amount of floor space demanded a lot of energy. In fact, it seemed that I picked one of the hardest jobs.

Enter Earth Gym. I had grumbled for about five minutes when the light bulb went on as I began to sweat, push, pull, stretch, and lift. I was getting a free aerobic workout while going about my daily life! This is a true story. I suddenly became joyful and thankful that I had drawn that card!

I was thankful because I had been trying and trying to make it to a gym or an aerobics class. I just never seemed to get there. With the Earth Gym, I accomplished four things: (1) I saved money; (2) I saved time; (3) I got exercise; (4) I got a new attitude about chores. Chores are now an opportunity rather than a burden. Who would ever have thought it?

Take your chores outside too. If you have a lawn, it needs mowing. You could either pay someone to mow it for you while you are working out at the commercial gym (spending money twice—once for the lawn service, once for the gym membership), or you could mow it yourself. When I looked at my wimpy biceps muscles one day, I decided to sell the big gas-powered mower and buy a push mower instead. My sister thought I'd never be able to devote an hour a week to this chore. Then I reminded her of something. "Karen," I said, "when people join a gym, don't they go at least once, twice, three times a week for an hour or more each time?" The logic connected. Why couldn't I devote one hour a week to developing my upper body while getting a chore done while saving lots of money?

Modify this concept to fit your life. Maybe you can't imagine giving up your cleaning or yard service. How about cutting the service in half and using it, say, once a month rather than every two weeks? That way you'll save money and still get some workout. Who knows, eventually you may reap such benefits from the Earth Gym that you'll want to do all of the work yourself. I know one man who stays on top of housework by cleaning one room a day. Because he stays on top of the job, he only needs to spend 15 to 20 minutes per room per day. The bathroom one morning, a bedroom the next, and so on. Around and around he goes. I used to think this was an awful way to spend time, but look who is in shape and saving money.

Work Together

You can add variety and interest to your Earth Gym chore workout by sharing it with other people. Once I joined a barn-raising group that rotated around to members' houses to do whatever work was needed. We usually met one morning every other weekend and spent two or more hours working at one person's house. We did lots of yardwork, we scraped and painted the outside of garages, painted rooms, hauled junk to the dump, and performed odd jobs and repairs. True to form, I grumbled when I had to get out of bed on a weekend to go work at someone's house. But once I got there, I was with a group of interesting, energetic folks and I pushed, pulled, lifted, and stretched the entire time. And of course, I was helping to get a lot of work done that might otherwise sit undone for months or cost the householder vast amounts of money to hire out. Start your own version of this group. Maybe you could have a clean house rotation where you gather with one or more people to clean each other's houses. Now you have company, you're getting exercise, and you're saving money. What more could you ask for?

Create Your Own Gym

House and yardwork are terrific ways to keep your body limber and get work done at the same time. But unless you vacuum vigorously for 30 minutes with an elevated heart rate, you are not getting the aerobic part of exercise. (Any exercise program should combine 30 minutes of aerobic exercise, warm-up and cool-down periods, and stretching and toning.) Never fear, you can get aerobic exercise with the Earth Gym too. Recently I realized I was in need of a more focused workout than my weekly lawn mowing, cleaning, and walking. My weight was slowly creeping up to digits I had never seen before. I was getting nervous about this enlarged version of me. In a panic, I thought seriously about joining a commercial gym.

Then I remembered, once again, the Earth Gym. I looked around my neighborhood. There is a soccer field not more than two blocks from my house. Around the soccer field is a quarter-mile track made of soft earth. Across the street from the track is an old amphitheater. Nothing remains but a lot of high, steep stairs. Near that is a little set of rings and bars. Three minutes away was this entire gym, waiting for me. No charge, fresh air. No embarrassment that I didn't have the latest neon Lycra wear. I walked and ran around the track, climbed the stairs, hung from the bars, and did stretches.

I know a college professor who's only on-the-job exercise is walking around the front of the classroom and exercising his fingers with pencils and computers. But he likes to stay in shape and keep his life simple at the same time. He jogs after work around his neighborhood and has a rule never to take elevators. His Stairmaster is everywhere he can find it. What? You can't imagine climbing 20 flights of stairs? Then take this test. The next time you are in the commercial gym using the automatic stair machine, count the number of stairs you climb during your workout.

Remember the hint I mentioned earlier: If you can't figure out how to work the same muscles that you work on with gym equipment, sign up for a one-day visit to a gym and pay close attention to what your body is doing on each machine. Some gyms have trial memberships where you can become a member for a month or two. Others allow you to use the equipment as a drop-in where you can pay for the day or hour. Then figure out ways to emulate that workout in your house, place of work, or neighborhood. Try to think of which job or chore you do each day, or which ones you hire someone else to do for you, and think of which part of the body you could build by doing that work. The bicycle, Stairmaster, and stationary jogging machines are easy. Use the real thing! Get fresh air! The rest of the machines may require some imagination.

Create Your Own Vacation Spa

You also could turn a vacation spa idea into a boot camp vacation. People pay huge sums of money to attend week- (or more) long health spas. You could stay right at home and do the same with your friends and a personal trainer as a one-time consultant. With the trainer, devise a weeklong plan with exercise activities to do each day. Don't forget to add in healthful meals and some relaxation, such as a massage, and you have your own spa for nearly nothing.

Here are some ideas:

❖ Day 1: Try one: Walking, bicycling, yoga, rollerblading, and floor exercises with weights. (Your personal trainer can give you ideas for good floor exercises.) Agree that you will add an item of healthful food to your breakfast.

❖ Day 2: Walk a little farther, run, or use an aerobic dance tape in someone's living room. Do more floor-type exercises. Keep the healthful breakfast item and add a healthful lunch food.

❖ Day 3: Swim, row a boat, walk a little farther, and do a different set of floor exercises. Add a healthful item to your dinner.

❖ Day 4: Go for a bike ride in the mountains or regular roads, find a deserted stadium and use it as your Stairmaster, or alternate walking and jogging. Do more floor exercises. Now that you've added some healthful food to your diet, today you can make your two early meals your largest. Refer to chapter 9 for a discussion of healthful food.

❖ Day 5: Depending on your locale and weather, you could go cross-country skiing, bicycle on a trail you've been thinking about, or put on a weighted backpack and go for a hike. Do more floor exercises and try not snacking between meals. This will be easy if you eat two huge meals early in the day.

❖ Day 6: Take a rowboat out in a lake, go swimming, put on another dance aerobics tape, run, walk up and down deserted stadium stairs, go rollerblading, or take a longer bike ride. Add in your floor exercises and enjoy your healthy meal program.

❖ Day 7: Rest.

This program will get you into the habit of being healthy and fit. If you don't have a full week, set aside one weekend. By doing so you can also sample a lot of Earth Gym exercises. And the good news is you will spend very little money and get a lot of fresh air. If you live in a really cold climate, consider starting this private spa in the springtime. The purpose is simply to get you in the habit of exercising and taking care of yourself. It's hoped that you will feel so great after this week that you won't want to return to your couch potato lifestyle. And remember, the only way you will want to continue this is if you do these exercises and sports mindfully, with full awareness of your body. Don't push.

Exercise Is Preventive Maintenance

Simple living is about taking care of our bodies *before* they fall apart. This gives us not only a better life, but a cheaper one too. Fixing a broken body costs a lot of money. While exercise is no miracle cure, literally every study on earth tells us that it is one of the best methods of preventive maintenance, for both our mental and our physical well-being. Exercise helps our body systems to operate more efficiently, maintaining healthy organs and cells, increasing circulation, improving digestion, making us more mentally alert, and ensuring physical stamina. Exercise is also a terrific stress reducer. As John W. Farquhar states in *The American Way of Life Need Not Be Hazardous to Your Health*, research shows that people who increase their physical exercise are more likely to adopt other lifestyle habits that further lower cardiovascular risk. They are likely to eat less, cope more effectively with stress, and even quit an established smoking habit.

The Sensuality of Simplicity

Pick from one of the seven rules of natural health and try one today. At the very least, get outside in the fresh air for 15 minutes. Better yet, make this a 20-minute walk. As you are walking, focus on your feet touching the earth or pavement, focus on your arms swinging, and try to breathe out of your nose. Take in nice, deep breaths. Focus on your muscles—how do they feel? Pay attention and slow down or speed up as your muscles dictate. How do you feel after paying attention to your body?

THE SIMPLE PLEASURES AT EKONE RANCH

"There is nothing better for the inside of a child than the outside of a horse."

In the spring, Ekone Ranch begins to wake from its winter hiatus. The ground is warm enough to dig into. It is time to plant dahlias, tulips, and vegetables.

There is new life at Ekone now. Six new foals joined the menagerie of 35 horses, 5 bison, 3 llamas, dogs, cats, wild rabbits, pigeons, chickens, and turkeys. Soon the children will come. Children of all ages will ride the horses, run through the fields, play with the dogs and cats, help to build and repair, plant gardens, swing from the big rope that takes them out over the pond where they can plop in and swim.

The frog will be there too. The little green frog that lives in the bathroom and hops onto the edge of the tub to watch while you take a bath. When you're finished, it hops back into one of the potted plants that line the windowsill. It arrived voluntarily one day and never left.

Chris Coffman and Ray Mitchell at their ranch.

Ray Mitchell says it's the frog and the trees and the open space that perform all the miracles at Ekone, not he. Ray says he is simply a facilitator. "I open the door and allow it to happen."

What happens at Ekone Ranch is something that needs to be experienced. Maybe it's the long, winding, bumpy drive through miles of open space to get there. Maybe it's the magic of this ancient forest where Native Americans once lived. Ray knows they used to live in this sacred land because he finds arrowheads and artifacts when he is out working. Maybe it's the wide, wide expanse of open fields. Maybe it's the quiet. The calm. Maybe it's the songs at night; the frog symphony, the crickets with their soft, high chirp. The coyote's howl now and then way off on another hill.

Surely it's the nurturing that goes on here: the way Chris Coffman takes care of you. The way she cooks the solid, hearty meals. It must also be the music. The drums, stringed instruments, tambourines, rattles that everyone plays together at night. At night it must be the candles sitting everywhere. No glaring bulbs, just soft flickers. It's that sense of peace that needs to be experienced.

This is Ekone Ranch. Ekone means "land of the good spirit." Ray Mitchell and Chris Coffman live here. Throughout the years, they have been awed at the healing that goes on. Ray bought the original 160 acres 25 years ago. Chris joined him in 1988. Ray says he was tired of city life, the greed, the pace, the values. "I yearned for something else," he says. "I hunted for land with friends for two to three years before I found this." It was land that belonged to a friend's grandparents, but nobody had lived on it for 30 to 40 years. Ray decided to see if he liked the place, so he spent a night on the land and walked all around.

"I had a dream that this was the place for me and that I should buy it immediately," he says. "I wanted a place where I could raise horses and live in the country. I'd never used a chainsaw or heated with wood before I came here, but I yearned to see if there was a more sane life for me."

Ray learned to use a chainsaw and heat with wood. He learned to live in isolation because the nearest neighbor was six miles away. He began to feel overwhelmed. Had he done the right thing? Then one day he walked out of his cabin, stood on the porch, and opened himself up to the spirit of the land. He had a vision that he should never sell the land or look at it as a financial asset. Instead, he should use it to nurture children and preserve for generations to come.

"I went about my business with that vision locked into my being," Ray says. "If I wouldn't have had that kind of rock to rely on I couldn't have made it for the 25 years I've been here."

Ray worked hard to make his vision a reality. Over the years, friends helped him build the big lodge that serves as a central meeting place, housing for Chris and Ray, guest quarters, kitchen, tack room, storage, and herbal medicine room. As money came in, the lodge grew. Ray built stables and fences. He cleared land, built outhouses, a wood-fired hot tub, and guest cabin. Friends came and friends went. Then Chris arrived with her own herd of horses. She had been a midwife, a zookeeper, and was learning about herbal medicine. She also loved to ride. She stayed. They blended the herds.

Then the children came. Ray and Chris decided they would open their doors to summer camps for children where they could teach city kids to ride horses and give them fresh air to breathe. "Our cup was full and we wanted to share with others," Chris says. Now the summer camps swarm with children running, jumping, laughing, and singing from June to August. No TV to tie them down, no proper city blocks to fence them in, no microwave ovens, no rush.

"There's more to life than what you can make or stow away in your home," Ray says. "We try to stir that up in people. We're trying to protect an ecosystem here and share it with children of all ages."

Ray and Chris love to see the change in the children after they have been at Ekone for a two-week camp. They remember one boy who didn't even know how to look people in the eye when he came and who couldn't eat all sorts of foods. Ray and Chris worked with him.

"After a couple of days I said, 'Let's just get this straight,' " Ray remembers. "I told him all he needed to do was work hard, eat good food, get a good night's sleep, and do it all again the next day. I just don't have time for all this fancy fru-fru."

In two days the boy was eating everything in sight and feeling stronger. He didn't go home after the end of the two week-camp. He stayed for one and a half years.

"We're living close to the earth without a lot of needs beyond the things we need to keep things flowing and moving. The practical needs," Chris says. "We eat a good, healthy diet; we have firewood to keep us warm. It fills my heart and soul to hear the sound of a meadowlark in spring. None of these involve money, they are just the simple things in life that mean so much."

❖ ❖ ❖ ❖ ❖ ❖ ❖ ❖ ❖ ❖ ❖ ❖ ❖ ❖

Resources

Kids' Health

Natural Healthcare for Your Child by Phylis Austin, Agatha Thrash, M.D., and Calvin Thrash, M.D., M.P.H. (Sunfield, MI: Family Health Publications, 1990)
Discusses 125 ailments and natural ways to tackle them, including a symptom index for quick reference. Written in a style meant to be read by layfolks, the book lists each illness, followed by ways to treat it. Range of age: birth through teenage years.

Home Remedies

Home Remedies, What Works by Gale Maleskey and Brian Kaufman (Emmaus, PA: Rodale Press, 1995)
Compilation of 650 home remedies from the readers of *Prevention* magazine, including recipes for conquering headaches, cholesterol, and back pain. Each problem listed, from bee stings to

foot odor, is given several remedy choices, with a comparative discussion of each remedy's effectiveness.

More Natural Remedies by Phylis Austin, Agatha Thrash, M.D., and Calvin Thrash, M.D. (Seale, AZ: Thrash Publications, 1994)
Gives natural remedies for common ailments, such as cervicitis, lice, lupus, and ringworm. Designed as a reference book, the treatments advocated eschew drug therapies in favor of do-it-yourself concoctions, some of which have been around for centuries.

Health and Exercise

Body, Mind, and Sport by John Douillard (New York: Harmony Books, 1994)
Here is a sports-oriented look at exercise, at your body type, and at workouts that best suit your body. Use of graphs to explain how the body and mind work in relation to exercise. Also contains a discussion of nutrition and its importance to the body.

How to Live Cheap, Green, and Happy by Randi Hacker (Mechanicsburg, PA: Stackpole Books, 1994)
This is a fun guide on what to do to save money yet stay healthy in the process and not feel guilty about destroying the Earth.

Take Care of Yourself

Perfect Health by Deepak Chopra (New York: Harmony Books, 1991)
Here is a wide-ranging look at diet, stretching, and stress relievers to help balance the body and promote better health. Learning about your body and body type helps to arm you with knowledge about how to best take care of it. Also contains discussion of transcendental meditation and how it fits into a healthy routine.

Take Care of Yourself by Donal M. Vickery, M.D. and James F. Fries, M.D. (Reading, MA: Addison-Wesley, 1994)
Offers specific advice for many problems, such as common injuries, eye problems, skin concerns, and stress. Each problem then gets a home treatment as well as what a doctor's visit might bring. Intended for early reference.

Sleeping

Restful Sleep by Deepak Chopra (New York: Harmony Books, 1994)
Discusses the use of body postures, diet, exercise, and stress control to effectively counteract sleep disorders. Dreams and insomnia in children and the elderly are also covered, as are how certain body types are more prone to sleep problems than others.

Medicine and Health

A Challenging Second Opinion by John A. McDougall, M.D. (Clinton, NJ: New Win Publishing, 1985)
Takes a "contrarian" viewpoint on commonly diagnosed diseases such as cancer, heart disease, arthritis, and diabetes. Contains an explanation of each disease and the author's opinion about the remedies for it.

Mind/Body Connection

Healing and the Mind by Bill Moyers (New York: Doubleday, 1993)
Explains healing through a series of interviews with well-known personalities, including John Kabat-Zinn, David Eisenberg of Harvard, and Candace Pert of Rutgers University. The body is shown for the remarkable instrument that it is and how our understanding of it helps in its dealings with disease.

Herbs

Back to Eden by Jethro Kloss (Loma Linda, CA: Back to Eden Books, 1971)
Here is a comprehensive look at herbs and their effects on disease, foods, and "non-traditional" methods of dealing with illnesses. Effects of pollution and "adulterated" foods on the human body are offered as part of a general understanding of how the body works.

The Complete Medicinal Herbal by Penelope Ody (London: Dorling Kindersley, 1993)
Heavily illustrated book that begins with history of herbs and their uses in earlier medicine to their current uses as home remedies for a wide variety of problems, such as urinary disorders, leg and foot disorders, and nervous disorders. Reference section at the end of the book outlines major ailments and their remedies.

Health from God's Garden by Maria Treben (Rochester, VT: Healing Arts Press, 1988)
Companion to *Health Through God's Pharmacy*, this book explains common garden-variety herbs and how common ailments (cysts, frostbite, intenstinal problems, and so on) can be alleviated using them.

11

Housing

Finding your cottage is like Goldilocks finding the chair that is just right. It wraps around you in cozy fashion and all seems right with the world.

—MARIANNE AGNEW, QUOTED IN
THE COTTAGE BOOK, BY RICHARD SEXTON

When I first began delving into the topic of voluntary simplicity, I wondered how anyone could *really* simplify when the cost of housing is so high. Before you're even out of the gate, you've got either a staggering rent or whopping mortgage keeping you tied to the grindstone. What's the point of shaving off a few dollars here and a few more there on daily expenses when you're stuck paying $1,000, $2,000, and up just for a place to live?

Over the five years I've published *Simple Living,* I discovered dozens of innovative people who were able to simplify their lives by creating fabulous alternatives to traditional American housing. They decided to create models that fit their own unique lives rather than quietly following the dictates of the status quo.

As with all other aspects of simplifying, housing demands a very conscious choice: Either you'll follow the mainstream model of buying a sprawling house with a sprawling mortgage, which means you'll be tied to a job for at least 30 years, or you can say "Wait a minute, I'd rather be creative and look at entirely new options for myself and my family." This chapter is about those options.

Some will save you just a little money, some a lot. It all depends on how far afield you are willing to go. Whichever you choose, your first job is to toss out all of your preconceived notions of what a traditional house should be.

House Size

One of the easiest ways to afford a house is to have less of it. To accomplish this, build new on a small scale, buy small and remodel, or buy big and split the structure into units. Seriously question the amount of space you really need. The more space you have, the higher the cost. The higher the cost, the longer you'll have to work in order to pay for it. Don't forget the intangibles: You'll have to spend more time cleaning and caring for the place, and, without a doubt, you'll find more stuff to fill up a larger house. The water-seeks-its-own-level colloquialism is nowhere more right-on than in this scenario. It costs more money to buy the stuff, and more time and energy go into maintaining, storing, rearranging, and insuring all those new items you have purchased to fill your larger space. Also think of the personality and intimacy of your house. The larger the house, the more difficult it is to stamp your individual personality on it.

Chris and Tim Curtis (profiled on page 263) followed the traditional American dream like many of us do. They simply accepted the bigger is better program without ever taking a hard look at how that really and truly applied to their own lives. It was after the family lived in Denmark for a year on a teacher exchange that they realized they could live just fine with much less space.

The family had no qualms about their decision to sell and move to a small, two-bedroom bungalow in the same neighborhood. Their mortgage payments were cut in half. They took all of the profit from the large house and put it into the down payment on the much less expensive small house. In order to save on capital gains taxes they carefully documented every expense that went into fixing up the large house for its sale and in upgrading the small house.* Those expenses are deductible from capital gains. Despite the remaining tax bite, the Curtises say they still came out way ahead. Tim says he sleeps better at night now, without the worry about how he'll keep up the expensive mortgage payments.

Think about your own space. Walk around your house and take serious

❖ ❖ ❖ ❖ ❖ ❖ ❖ ❖ ❖ ❖ ❖ ❖ ❖ ❖ ❖ ❖ ❖ ❖ ❖ ❖

*Homeowners are charged a high tax penalty if they sell a more expensive house and move to a less expensive house before age 55—check the law.

inventory. What rooms do you *really* use regularly? Another couple, Bob and Jody Haug, profiled in Chapter 1, realized that most people tend to congregate around the dining room table, so why not make that the central focus of the room? Their main living area is one open room that includes kitchen, dining/living, and small work areas. In the middle of the room they built a large table with wrap-around padded seating. Bob says most people may as well cut off half their houses, since they never use that space anyway. The Haugs live in the 900-square-foot basement of their renovated 1880s house. They rent out the two upper floors.

The Haugs advise those considering a similar move to remember "you should only have space for the things you really need, so keep pruning away at the lower layers and keep the top stuff. To find out how it will work for you before taking the plunge, borrow a friend's RV and live in it for a week."

What about those new houses that are being built with family rooms *and* formal living rooms? How many times have you visited friends and actually sat in the living room? People congregate where there is life—most always in the family room. If you need a quiet space, carve out a special niche in a corner somewhere. I have a friend who lives in a house with a teenage boy and husband. She felt the need for a "feminine" corner where she could write letters and read. Instead of using the breakfast table area in the kitchen for its intended use, she created a cozy reading area for herself. The house already had a separate dining area. Don't pay a huge chunk of money to have a pristine living room sitting empty waiting for your monthly visitors.

Look around at the rest of your house. What is used regularly and what is wasted space? What items of furniture, appliances, and decor are there simply to fill up space in the extra rooms? What could you live just fine without?

Your next step is to get creative. No one wants to move from a spacious environment to a cramped little cubbyhole. Many architects and builders have thought about this issue and have come up with all sorts of appealing solutions. Lots of books will give you terrific ideas. Once you have gone through your house and eliminated the excess, you will have less to store. American architects are learning from the Japanese, for instance, to build storage areas under the floors, in the walls, and in the ceilings. That way you have more open space in the rest of the house.

Rather than having a house with separate guest rooms, you can build window seats that can double as beds for overnight guests. One woman I know likes to meditate. She built a special seat in her living room that has a quadruple use: meditation area, guest bed, living room couch, and storage space. (She built storage units under the area.) Build a dining room table with storage compartments underneath. If you're short on space and long on view, you can build open shelves in the kitchen, for instance, and place them along the window. You can build slatted shelves that double as dish drainers and place them over the sink. When you hand-wash dishes, simply put them upside down on these special shelves, and let them drip into the sink.

Think about bathrooms. Why is it families in the 1950s got by on one bathroom and all of a sudden now everybody in the house has to have a bathroom? I don't recall too many of my 1950s neighbors out jumping and dancing in the yard waiting for the toilet. Just how often are both or all toilets in use at the same time? Ten percent of the time? The percentage for the cost is sky high. If more than one toilet really seems warranted for your household, question whether each toilet needs to be in its own room. Can you put two in one bathroom and use a divider? Also question how often two or more people want desperately to occupy the shower at the same time. Staggering schedules would be much cheaper than having an extra shower.

According to architect George Suyama: "People need very little to live, and actually it would enhance their lives if they had less. We camouflage our lives so much."

If you live in an area with mild climate, think of the outside as part of your house. Noted 1920s-era Berkeley, California, architect Bernard Maybeck once said: "Hillside architecture is landscape gardening around a few rooms for use in case of rain." When I visited the Caribbean, I noticed that most of the houses had a deck that was bigger than the house. As with our unused, formal living rooms, people in this hot climate figured out that they rarely use the inside of a house anyway, so why spend the money on wasted space? I know of a house in California that is only 10 feet wide, but the entire glassed front opens onto a 50-by-50-foot yard.

Architect Ross Chapin, who specializes in designing small houses, says many big houses simply highlight the ego. "It's about the outer surface of life," he says, "spending phenomenal amounts of money on things that really don't mean that much. I look at finding what the deeper priorities are. If we design from the heart, we'll be less likely to celebrate a facade."

Chapin says small doesn't necessarily mean less expensive. It all depends on what materials you use and how many traditional finishing touches you require. You might consider building with solid, durable materials that will last, but use less of them. It's a huge waste of resources to build with cheap materials and then later tear the house down. For example, you could use good materials for the general structure, then save money on your kitchen by forgoing cabinetry. Some families opt to forego expensive cabinetry, and instead make creative use of open shelves. One woman designed her kitchen to have no upper cabinets. She hangs all of her pots and pans from the ceiling and built a slatted shelf above the sink for her cups and glasses to drain upside down. She has a couple of open shelves in one corner for her plates and bowls. Everything else is stored on shelves under the counter. A curtain of her favorite fabric hides the shelves.

If you'll be sharing your small house, you need to include places for everyone to have refuge. Chapin, who lives in a 1,200-square-foot house with his wife and daughter, built a 7-by-11-foot kid's cabin in the backyard. He says he is the one who uses it most often as a refuge. "That's one way to relieve the pressure cooker of close living," he says. Other options are to create niches and nooks within the house.

The $45,000 Small House

Leslie Ferril had just separated from her husband and had a baby and small child. She had very little money and no place to go. Leslie had been planning to join a cohousing group and had gotten to know the founding members. She and her husband had also acquired a collection of salvaged materials that they had planned to use to build a house someday.

"I was getting divorced and really needed a place to live," Leslie says. "I said, Okay, this is the budget and I'll have to build a house with what I have. When the money runs out, I'll stop building."

A $20,000 loan from Leslie's mother added to Leslie's $25,000 was all she needed. Leslie called her friends in the cohousing community to tell them she was ready to build. She enlisted the help of one member, a builder, and told him about her budget. Could he create a house for her family?

Evan Simmons, the builder-member, set to work. He already had an affinity for small, simple houses. "There are no secrets to building inexpensive houses," Evan says. "There are basically three items that add cost: (1) size, (2) complexity, and (3) expensive materials. It is pretty easy to make it simple. You build a box with a gabled roof. Every time you add a dormer or a new corner, you add cost. But because a box can look dull, you can do things to make it more interesting, like adding a gabled porch, making large overhangs, and using wood for the trim, windows, and shingles. Every decision I make is based on whether it is a good value. I don't value complicated houses.

"I love small spaces because we live in a world of finite resources of raw material, time, and money. A small, simple house results in a small mortgage payment. This way you have time and money left over to do other things in your life. It's not that hard to keep your mortgage under $500 per month. That's what I value."

Evan builds small and simple, yet he doesn't compromise on materials. He finds quality materials for low prices by salvaging and buying from the sources. He found shingles, for example, by buying directly from the mill. There he paid 40 cents per square foot instead of the usual $1. Leslie had already salvaged enough clear vertical-grained fir to trim all of the windows, doors, and stairway. The wood had fallen off a truck and Leslie was able to buy it at a salvage price. The trim makes the house look very gracious. She had also salvaged sinks, faucets, and a claw-foot bathtub. She bought tile from a garage sale. "I just kept my eyes open for deals," she says.

Leslie also saved money by streamlining the building process. She worked directly with Evan, rather than hiring a contractor who pays a subcontractor who pays laborers. "Find one person who is good and have him do the whole job," Evan says.

The house was finished within Leslie's budget. It measures 20 by 28 feet. The two children, now seven and four, sleep in the open half-loft upstairs, and Leslie sleeps in the bedroom on the main floor. There is one small bathroom. The rest of the house is an open floor plan. The floor is plywood, which Leslie finished by sponge painting. Friends helped her paint the outside of the house, and Leslie helped with small construction-related projects as she could. Two friends donated a couple days of framing, and Evan did all of the carpentry.

Leslie's mortgage payment is $150 per month. This allows her to work part time so she can be home with her children.

"Building this house took a lot of determination, but I didn't have a lot of options," Leslie says. "I just did it."

The Cost of Building

Builders and estimators use an index known as CSI (construction specific index) to determine the cost of house. You can use it to get an idea of where you can cut costs in your design. There are 16 divisions.

1. General conditions: 5–6 percent of total cost. These are expenses a contractor would normally incur in the construction process, such as deliveries, su-

pervising, portable bathrooms. You can cut these costs by doing the work yourself.

2. Sitework: 5–8 percent of total cost. The only way to keep this cost down is in the choice of your property. For example, if you buy property on a steep slope or with bad soil, your sitework costs will be higher.

3. Concrete and Foundation: 5–6 percent of total cost. Mobile homes avoid this cost.

4, 5. Masonry and Metals.

6. Wood and Plastic: Roughly 15–18 percent of total cost. (Finish carpentry is 3 percent, exterior finish is 6 percent, cabinets are 4–5 percent.) Includes framing, rough carpentry, finish carpentry, cabinets.

7. Thermal and Moisture Protection: 4–5 percent of total cost. Keeping water out and heat in. Includes roof and insulation.

8. Doors and Windows: 6–10 percent of total cost.

9. Finishes: 13–20 percent of total cost. Includes sheetrock, paint, ceramic tile, floor finishes, carpet, vinyl.

10. Specialties: 1–2 percent of total cost. Bathroom accessories, mirrors, shower doors.

11. Equipment: 2–3 percent of total cost. Appliances.

12, 13, 14. Miscellaneous: $1/2$ percent of total cost.

15. Mechanical: 5–8 percent of total cost. Includes plumbing, forced air heating.

16. Electrical: 4–6 percent of total cost.

Creative Real Estate Purchasing and Financing

Get to know local realtors and bankers. Now and then they have leads to properties available at low prices. One couple found a waterfront lot so inexpensive realtors had assumed there was something wrong with it. The absentee owner had inherited it, never visited, and didn't want to pay the taxes. Another family got a deal on a house that had been seized in a drug raid. One man bought a half-finished house from a local bank. The bank wanted what they had put into it: $20,000.

If you'd like to buy a house but don't have the down payment, check into zero-down programs. One is the Farm Home Loan Program that is reserved for those who cannot qualify for a standard mortgage. Each county determines income limits and qualifying areas. The mortgage is 30-year fixed, the interest rate based on the current Fannie Mae rate. Terry and John Mosely bought a house using the Farm Home Loan Program. Like most homes under the program, it is in a rural area. "We have to commute farther to jobs and it's long distance to everywhere," says Terry. But the fact that they paid nothing down made owning possible.

Before you enter into a zero-down program, be aware that the less money you put down on a house, the higher your monthly mortgage payments will be. Plus, you'll save on mortgage insurance if you put 20 percent down. You will hardly simplify your life if you are paying an astronomical amount of money every month for your mortgage. One way to offset this high mortgage is by renting out space in your house.

Creative Renting

Some people rent for years and have no interest in buying a house. They don't want the hassle and have figured out other ways to invest their money, or they don't believe that owning is a good investment for them. For many others, renting is not a good option, but they find it difficult to save money for a down payment on a house while at the same time paying high rent. You can apply your creative simple living thinking to renting and find yourself a decent environment for less. The most time-honored way to save money while renting is by sharing an apartment or house with others. This may not be your ultimate dream idea of living, but if you remember that it is temporary and helps you reach your long-term goals, then it might become more palatable. And who knows, you may enjoy communal living so much that it will figure into your more permanent plans.

It was election year when my friend Barbara Ahern came up with two basic creative rental options. I liked them so well I reprinted them here.

The Bob Dole Method

(During the Depression, the Doles were able to keep their family home by living in the basement and renting out the upper house.)

Put up with something most people find undesirable, such as crowded conditions, lack of amenities, living on a busy or noisy street, an inconvenient location, an ugly building, a poorly designed floor plan. Remember, this is most likely a temporary condition, while your savings build up. Putting up with inconvenience is much easier when you are young and resilient than it will be when you are older.

The Bill Clinton Method

(The Clintons look for jobs that include housing, such as a governor's mansion or the White House.)

Use your skills and services to defray housing costs. Do you love to garden? Be a groundskeeper. Do you love to cook? Cook for the rich and famous. Boating and fishing? Try living aboard. Marine biology? Manage an aquarium. Construction? Build a mother-in-law apartment for a homeowner in exchange for rent. Live in it while you are building. Or offer to do other repairs and carpentry work in exchange for rent. Child care? Try live-in nanny. Travel? Work in resorts where housing is supplied. Nursing? Be a companion for an elderly person. Wilderness? Try the park service. None of the above? Be a professional house-sitter or a live-in apartment manager.

Shared Housing

There are a number of variations of shared housing. One way is to buy a house larger than you need and rent out the rooms. The rent from your tenants helps pay your mortgage. The house is yours, the equity is yours, and the major upkeep is yours. Tenants come and go and are usually in a transitional phase in their lives. They rent your room only until they have enough saved to buy their own house or get their own apartment. Elena Daniels was 27 when she bought a four-bedroom, $180,000 house in a very popular urban area, not far from a university. She had worked hard and saved for years in order to come up with the down payment. Now she lives in one bedroom and rents all the others, including rooms she created in the basement. The rent pays her mortgage.

The other way to share a house is to form an intentional group that lives together more or less permanently. This is different from simply renting a room in order to save money to move on. Intentional groups choose this lifestyle and form "family" groups. Members can either rent or buy together, or one can own and the others can rent. Often the most successful forms of intentional shared housing are those in which members have equal ownership or where all members are equal renters and the owner lives elsewhere.

Dorothy McMahan, 64, had been married for 28 years and raised seven children when she turned to shared housing. When she first lived alone, she craved silence and privacy. Later, when she had her fill of silence, she sought a balance of privacy and companionship and answered an ad from an 88-year-old lady who wanted to share her house. "I learned a great deal from living with her," Dorothy says. "I learned that I do still need someone to care what happened to me during the day. I learned that by softening my boundaries and relaxing the need to judge other people's actions, I could live much more comfortably with myself. I learned that I could 'problem-solve' directly with the other person, when we both wanted to work things out. We listened to each other and found a mutually agreeable solution to all of our concerns."

Dorothy also found that by sharing a house, she could increase her income by cutting her outgo. By sharing housing, she cut her rent by one-third. In exchange, she gets a comfortable place to live, company, someone to share her joys, and access to a washer and dryer and other amenities.

You can find communal houses in nearly every state and city in the United States, and many internationally. (See the Resources at end of the chapter.) One of the most successful is called Prag House, which was formed in 1972 by a group of graduate students and professors. They bought an enormous, 16-bedroom mansion in a marginal neighborhood for $45,000. Although there has been some turnover of members over the years, for the most part the group has been phenomenally stable. Today there are 10 adults and 4 children. Some of the adults are couples, some are single. All adults own the house equally and share equally in the maintenance and repairs.

The house was in an advanced state of disrepair and had been sitting vacant for a year when the group found it. They were able to create additional bedrooms after hiring an architect to design living spaces from what had been "dead space." Over the years they have rehabilitated the place, the neighborhood has become very desirable, and the house is now worth over $1 million.

Soon after purchase, members realized they needed to protect the house so it would remain a communal household. In 1974 they formed a land trust as a non-profit corporation established to take the land and house out of the marketplace. The $5,000 down payment was considered a loan to the corporation that was paid back with interest. Now everyone pays a base of $430 a month, plus a percentage of take-home pay for home improvements. Couples also pay $430 each. That money pays for food, utilities, a share in the corporation, and upkeep and maintenance. As the group has gotten older, the house has improved. "Our values changed over the years and we didn't want to live in a hippie crash pad anymore," says Nick Licata, one of the early members. "We used the money to make slow improvements in our lifestyle, like buying new furniture for the living room, painting the exterior, and remodeling the kitchen."

Since the original house was purchased, the land trust has purchased several other communal properties, holding title to two houses and three farms.

When someone moves out, he or she does not take any equity. Licata says it can be difficult for many people to understand the concept that you own a portion of the property without equity. All of the equity remains in the land trust. This way the life of the communal house is not dependent on any one individual possibly moving out and taking equity. The group decided to keep the monthly payment low enough so that people could use their excess money to invest elsewhere, in other real property or in stocks and the like. The low payment also gives people the opportunity to invest in low-cost lifestyles, enabling them to work part time and pursue other interests. Interests range from working with peace groups to hang gliding. Professions include social workers, computer programmers, publisher, insurance agent, and Zen priest turned counselor.

The house provides a mix of public, semi-private, and private spaces. The living and dining rooms are used not only by house members but also for Democratic Party functions, meetings of peace groups, and the monthly Full-Moon Computer Programmer Nerds poker game. Licata says: "I love coming home and seeing people holding meetings in the house, using it to further their own dreams and their own attempts at community. And I love being able to share my ideas, to talk with the others, to escape the regimentation of living in a nuclear family."

Nick Licata and "family" gather on their front porch.

The group holds monthly household meetings. That's where any disagreements or household issues are worked out. They operate by consensus minus one in all areas except deciding whether to accept a new member. In that case everyone has veto power. They deal with the same issues any traditional family has: child rearing, money, television, who cooks what and when.

The presence of children at Prag House is also a plus. Those with children have built-in baby-sitters and other adults for the kids to relate to. The kids have someone to talk to other than their parents. Those without kids have the chance to be part of a child's life and enjoy the feeling of living in a family.

Licata finds that, in general, members are very conscious about their environment and of the trade-offs involved in living communally. "The basic rule is, you are not going to get your way. No one gets their way here . . . there is always compromise. People who get frustrated with having less control over their environment usually move on. For me, this is how I want to live."

Hailey Land, 42, his wife, Leanne Clarke, their daughter, Addie, 8, and two single adults paid $130,000 for an old, run-down, four-bedroom house in an urban neighborhood. They did not set theirs up as a land trust. Land likes the idea of communal living for a number of reasons: He has cut expenses so that his monthly house payment, taxes, insurance, and utilities is only $250, and he shares the responsibility for upkeep and beautification. What he likes best is the notion that he has bought into a family.

"There is a big difference in simply renting together versus creating a communal house," he says. "Living communally is like growing up with brothers and sisters. Even when you'd fight with your siblings, you knew you weren't going anywhere. That's very different from the attitude of moving on when you don't get along with someone for a period of time.

"To live together successfully you need an attitude of willingness to work with people and not run away from problems . . . you have to love one another in spite of the imperfections. For me, it's very appealing to love and relate to someone on a consciously committed level—you have bumps in relating to each other, but you also have this innate confidence that this too shall pass and there is a nice time around the corner. That's what makes the difference between just renting a room versus sharing your life with other committed adults."

Land also thinks it is very beneficial for his daughter to live with other caring adults. "I think it is important for a child to see adults having fun," he said. "So many kids grow up seeing adults tired and cranky. Here, we work real hard to find a niche that pleases us. I want Addie to look forward to what it means to be an adult."

Communal living has enabled all of the adults in the house to work part time. Hailey and Leanne make ceramic jewelry and sell it at a local farmer's market. Together they earn about $10,000 a year. The other two adults earn approximately $6,000 to $8,000 each, working as agents for other artists. They have the time to do most of their own household repairs, including putting on a new roof and painting the exterior. "Life is interesting," Hailey says. "I think you make it more interesting when you keep your eyes open and are flexible."

Cohousing

For those who like living in community but need more privacy than shared housing provides, cohousing offers a terrific option. Cohousing is a Danish institution, the old style of village given new life. Typically land is purchased as one piece, eliminating many fees and commissions, then split into shares among the members of the group. Cohousing provides the privacy of a single home coupled with the old-style neighborhood feeling of the 1950s. Everyone knows and looks after one another, and the children are safe to roam the property. Members share the dinner meal in a common house, sometimes every night, sometimes twice a week. They also take turns doing cooking and cleanup.

Houses are purchased or built individually, and all members also own a share of the common areas, including the common house. Tools and common area labor are shared. The houses often are smaller than traditional homes because the goal is to get everyone out of the house into the common areas . . . but not all of the time. Privacy is an important element, and members are free to retreat to their own homes any time they wish.

Cohousing groups take on as many forms as there are people. Some groups take out a large loan and build identical or similar-looking units all at once. These have the look of an apartment complex, but without roads going through the property. Others allow for individuals to build their own homes so long as they fit into basic common guidelines. Whatever the building style, most cohousing groups adhere to a common layout scheme: Houses are clustered in one area, cars and parking in another, and as large as possible segment of natural space is reserved. This allows children and adults the freedom of visiting back and forth without the intrusion of cars. This also provides for more neighborliness; instead of looking out your front window to see streets, cars, and your neighbor's garage, you see a winding pedestrian lane leading to your neighbor's front porch.

A down side of cohousing, like any communal arrangement, is that change is slow because most groups have a consensus style of government. Whenever anything new is on the agenda, groups usually have lengthy meetings and discussions in order to move forward. Sometimes, but not always, it can be more difficult to resell a property in a cohousing community, because most groups have strict rules about taking on new members. Prospective cohousers usually need to sit in on at least three meetings to understand the slow consensus process, and they must be interviewed by various members of the group. The process ensures that the new member fully understands the nature of cohousing and is someone who can fit into this style of living.

Therese Kunzi-Clark, 39, lives with her husband and two children in a cohousing community of 50 adults and 35 children. She grew up in a close-knit village of 700 people in Switzerland and longed for that closeness after she left as an adult. "All the parents were very involved in the village, helping each other out," she says. "The kids had the whole village to play around." When she first read about cohousing in a newspaper article, she knew it was for her. She had never felt so isolated as she did in the urban neighborhood in which she lived. "I was home with a baby," she remembers. "I kind of knew the neighbors next to me, but people were very private. Everybody was either in their house or car. In Switzerland we'd meet people we knew because we'd all be out walking to the store or the post office."

Therese was a founding member of her cohousing group and says it meets her expectations. Her children have other kids to play with, and she is relieved of the constant duty of making play dates for them. Her community is close to shopping and schools, and her children can walk to school, the store, and karate lessons. When she got a part-time job, a cohousing neighbor offered to get her kids ready for school in the morning. If she has a 30-minute errand, she can leave the kids with any number of cohousing families.

Cohousing is not necessarily a less expensive way to live for Therese, because her community took out a large loan in order to build the entire community at once. Her mortgage payments are similar to what she would pay in a single-family house. Yet she saves money on buying extras like lawnmowers, tools, and even sewing machines and kid's athletic equipment because these can be shared by community members. Although her own unit is of modest size, she is also part owner of a 5,000-square-foot common house and all of the land on which the community is built. The most lucrative advantage is the sense of community that cohousing offers.

Another way of accomplishing the aims of cohousing is for like-minded individuals to get together and buy houses in a given neighborhood. This was the route taken by N Street Cohousing in Davis, California. Started in 1979, N Street was almost an accident. One man, faced with the loss of his rental, decided to purchase it. Later a friend bought a neighboring house. Rather than a planned purchase for the purpose of cohousing, N Street was put together bit by bit. Residents knew they wanted to create a community, but not until 1988 did they decide to adopt the cohousing name and ideology. Like other collective housing groups, N Street values a nurturing environment, shared resources, diversity, and community responsibility. Advice from N Street is to look for an area of town that may not be the best area and take advantage of low-income housing.

Since most new cohousing communities are built in rural or semirural areas where land is available, people who like living in the city can come up with other ideas. More and more groups pool resources and purchase marginally maintained apartment buildings. They create common areas with existing space and operate essentially the same way that rural groups do.

Mother-in-Law Apartments

If you like your house and neighborhood and don't want to move or build a new house, think about maximizing space and dollars by building a mother-in-law apartment. "Mother-in-law" is simply a euphemism for a rental unit in your home. Traditionally, such a space was reserved for extended family members, but today they're rented out to the public just like any other apartment. Lots of people at varied life stages have mother-in-law apartments in their homes. First-time home buyers use the rental income to help pay their bills. Parents with children in college can trade their excess space for tuition money. Divorced people can stay in their existing homes by renting out a room or basement apartment. The American Association of Retired Persons (AARP) says that seniors are virtually unanimous in their desire to stay in their present home but often have trouble making ends meet. They can rent to younger people who can help with rent or household chores. And people can rent or share with a real mother-in-law. Extended families are slowly returning to vogue as people once again realize the benefits of multigenerational living. My friends Renee and John built their house with a separate living space for John's mother.

One architect/planner in California built an entire development of houses that include accessory apartments. He helped convince the city to allow the units because they are less disruptive than high-density apartment buildings. He was quoted in the *Washington Monthly* as saying: "It creates great diverse neighborhoods, and it adds enough density to support transit systems and local shops. If you work with small-lot, single-family homes, it avoids the condo landscape we seem to have fallen into. It tightens the feeling of the neighborhood."

Before embarking on this option, check your local building code. Some cities allow mother-in-law units, others do not. If yours doesn't, you could try lobbying for a change. You also should take note of whether the area in which you live is attractive to renters. Naturally, if you live near a college, you'll probably have them waiting in line. If you live way out in a rural area, you may have slim pickings. Talk to Realtors to get an idea.

Take a look at your basement or detached garage. Most basements are rarely used and filled with junk that you think you will use "someday." What a waste of space. You don't need a beautiful, light basement in order to turn yours into an apartment. White paint, light carpet, and good lighting can turn a dark, dingy basement into a spacious, attractive living space. Depending on your budget, you can turn the whole basement into an apartment, complete with bathroom and kitchen, or you can just rent out a room or two, add a bathroom, and share your kitchen. You can get good, used appliances and secondhand cabinetry. A little paint and imagination go a long way. Make sure the amount of money you put into your apartment is in line with the kind of rent you can expect to get in your neighborhood. There is no sense spending a lot of money on a top-of-the-line job if your neighborhood can bring in only marginal rent.

I have seen all sorts of permutations on the mother-in-law theme. Every variation nets income for the homeowner. Some have only half basements and offer tiny studios. Some have larger areas and build in two-bedroom apartments. One single mother lives with her son in a large older home that is divided in half on the upper, main, and basement floors. She lives in half the main floor and half the upper floor. The other half is a separate, full apartment. Yet another full apartment is in the basement. She also rents an extra room in her space to a housemate. Because of this additional income, she is able to work part time and be available for her son.

Another couple bought a rundown yet sturdy house in a good area and renovated it. Next, they turned the dark, unfinished basement into an appealing, light, one-bedroom apartment and moved in. The rent they collected from the upstairs tenants paid their mortgage. With the money they saved, they bought a little duplex and kept the original house. They moved into one unit of the duplex and rented out the other. Now they collect rents from a total of three units and pay nothing out of pocket.

If you have a detached garage, you can turn it into a cottage. I know a single woman who lives in one of these cottages and loves her special little place. A childless couple I know lived alone in a large house and decided to turn the basement into one apartment and the attic into another. All three units have separate entrances.

You also can buy a multiplex and live in one unit. Nicholas Corff figured out the housing angle early. In his 20s, he knew he didn't want to be chained to a job just to pay high mortgage, so he and two friends bought an old triplex. They renovated the building, and each friend lived in one unit. With the mortgage payment split in thirds, each person paid very little to live in a nice unit. They also had companionship when they wanted it.

> *We shape our buildings.*
>
> *Then our buildings shape us.*
>
> —WINSTON CHURCHILL

A few years later the friends moved on to new lives, and Nicholas bought the building. He was able to do so because he always saved a portion of his income. For years now, the rent he collects from the two units has paid his mortgage and Nicholas pays nothing. "One of the things I like about having this building is that you are not isolated," Nicholas says. "My wife and I interact with our tenants; there is always something going on. The sense of having people around is very satisfying and gives us a sense of security."

Types of Housing

Green Housing

There are two general types of "green housing." One is eco-housing, which typically uses recycled or reused materials in the structure of the house. Most often, the interior is created with recycled materials as well. The other is earth-based housing, which uses the earth as the basis for the structure of the house. Often people who choose this method become so enamored of using natural materials that they continue using them throughout the interior of the house.

Eco-Houses

Eco-housing architecture means using recycled or environmentally friendly products when building your house. There are many reasons to build in this way. One reason is to use the earth's resources more efficiently. The average wood-framed house uses 11,000 board feet of lumber. According to *Parade Magazine*, this is enough, stacked end to end, to top the Empire State Building and both World Trade Center towers combined. The other reason many people build green is because of chemical sensitivities or allergies. Unfortunately, many of the materials that promote energy efficiency (insulations and foams) or recycling (recycled plastics and rubber) contribute to indoor air-quality problems. *E Magazine* says: "This makes many of the super-insulated eco-homes built in the 1970s and early 1980s anathema to the chemically sensitive."

Examples of green architecture are building with recycled products and using solar energy and nontoxic materials. Recycled products can be as simple as salvaging an old door rather than buying a new one, to using recycled car windshield glass to make ceramic tile. In a model green home in Montana, builder Steven Loken used products such as a kitchen sink made of epoxy and granite dust (a by-product left when granite is quarried), carpet made from recycled plastic milk jugs, and insulation made from blown bits of cellulose derived from shredded newspaper. Loken used one-sixth of the wood required to frame a conventional house of the same size. The wood he used was either salvaged or "composite" lumber made from the chips of slender trees.

> *There is a certain magic to living in buildings with thick earth walls. It's hard to describe, but easy to notice. . . . it's almost as if I'm in some ancient building with centuries of its own secret stories to tell . . .*
>
> —DAVID EASTON,
> THE RAMMED EARTH HOUSE

The ideal green home would have as little impact as possible on its natural surroundings. Some of these options can save you money over the long range, but they can be very expensive initially. Solar hot water systems cost 10 times as much as conventional systems. Solar electricity costs five times what utility power costs. But when you buy a solar water heater, you are effectively buying 20 years' worth of fuel. If compact fluorescent lighting is carefully used along with an energy-efficient refrigerator, you will use one-fifth the electricity of conventional products. Conservation plus solar electricity yields the same costs as utility power without conservation. However, installing utility power can sometimes cost thousands of dollars; in such cases it may be cheaper to install a solar panel.

Green houses can be much more expensive than traditional homes. If you want natural carpeting, for example, the green choice is wool. Wool carpets are far costlier than synthetic ones. The Environmental or Healthy House of the Year on the cover of national home or decorating magazines will have as steep a price tag as any that get major-league attention. There also can be hidden hazards inherent in new technologies. For example, early efforts to use recycled newsprint as blown-in insulation failed to take into consideration the toxicity of the ink. That problem has been solved now, but with every new recycling effort come newly charted technological processes. No one knows for sure what will happen with the recycled plastics now being used in housing. It is also debatable whether a new product made by a "green" method is "greener" than one that is simply reused or less processed.

Earth-Based Housing

Earth-based houses are gaining popularity because the product used in the structure of the house is earth, which is an entirely inert and natural substance. Not much can compare to the cozy feeling of living in an earth house with its soft, rounded corners. One such homeowner, mentioned in the book *The Rammed Earth House*, by David Easton, said that walking into her rammed-earth house was like walking into her lover's outstretched arms.

Earth-based houses are generally of four types: rammed earth, cob, adobe, and straw bale. The first three use 100 percent earth in the structure of the house. Straw bale uses straw plus earth to cover the bales. Straw bale, rammed earth, and cob can be used in most climates, to varying degrees. Adobe is more adaptable to hot climates because adobe homes are constructed of earthen "bricks" that must dry before they are used. This requires several days even in the hot Southwest.

While a frame house generally requires sophisticated tools and solid carpentry experience, earth houses require only very basic tools, and the art can be learned in a weekend workshop. Once people learn the methods, often they feel so empowered that they begin searching for other innovative ways to complete the rest of the house for less, such as by salvaging materials. One 68-year-old woman attended a cob workshop and was so filled with renewed energy in her own power that she said: "For my whole life, all I've been able to do is host the potluck after the house was built. Now I can build it myself."

Earth houses can offer three advantages over traditional methods. One is a better indoor environment: They are quiet, since the earth absorbs noise in the house, and the air is clean. Nothing in the wall system contains chemicals, such as the formaldehyde present in many processed wood and insulating products used in traditional homes. Two, earth houses are more environmentally friendly, since you don't need to cut many trees. Three, the houses can bring people together, because friends and neighbors can help build. This is in stark contrast to traditional methods in which you hire contractors and other specialists to do the work for you and rarely get to know them.

Not all states' standard building codes cover the natural materials, so getting a permit to build with them can be a little more of a challenge than when using conventional materials, but it is certainly possible to do so. Building codes are set up for doing things the "usual" way, but they explicitly state that the codes are not meant to disallow other approaches. A separate chapter in the Uniform Building Code covers these alternative methods. In essence, it says that alternatives may be approved by the local building department if the plans are prepared and "stamped" by a registered engineer or architect, and if the local official determines that the plans are equal in safety to the "normal" approaches. Your plans must still meet earthquake and wind and snow-load safety considerations, and it still must be safe in the event of a fire. The tricky part can be convincing local officials that your approach is as good or better than the systems they are used to. The more experienced the officials are, generally, the easier it is for them to understand and accept the alternatives.

In some locales you can take another path to get an alternative structure approved. Some counties have adopted the Owner-Builder-Code, which allows owners to construct pretty much anything they want, even if it does not meet the standard code language. The trade-off is that there is a note on the title to the effect that the structure was not built to code, and the owner is required to notify renters and future buyers of this fact. This allows an owner to take whatever risk he or she is comfortable with and allows future dwellers to make the same conscious choice. If your county does not already have this option, you could lobby for its adoption.

Here are the basics of each method.

Straw Bale

Straw bales—yes, the compressed squares you see in farmer's fields—are used as the basis for straw bale houses. There are two ways to build with straw bales. One is to stack the bales like kid's building blocks into the shape of a house you want and use them as load-bearing walls. The second way is to build with traditional post-and-beam construction and use the bales only as insulation.

The most frequent questions put to straw bale experts have to do with fire, water, and mice. The plaster-covered bales easily pass a standard two-hour fire test. Trying to burn the tightly packed bales is like trying to burn a thick book: They simply char on the surface. Moisture is the only true threat to the straw, and with simple but thoughtful detailing, such as at the floor or around windows, it is not a problem. The walls are covered inside with plaster and outside with stucco. That, combined with the lack of anything edible in the bale, means that mice are no more likely to inhabit these walls than they would standard wood-stud walls.

Straw bale is adaptable to all climates because the bales are the insulation, and they breathe. The straw acts as a huge air-to-air heat exchanger retaining warmth while allowing air to pass slowly through.

Cost. Straw houses can be built any size and finished with any variety of materials; thus, prices can range from inexpensive to prohibitive. Owners can do much of the labor themselves and save significant amounts of money. You can bale a 1,400-square-foot house in two days by calling on 20 friends and neighbors (and supplying pizza and beer). One owner built his 1,300-square-foot straw bale house for $22 per square foot. The total cost of the house was $29,000, which includes all interior and exterior finishes.

Rammed Earth

Rammed-earth houses look similar to straw bale houses, except that the walls are more square. This is because rammed-earth houses begin with a "form." The outer walls of the house are laid out by building a foundation or marking a line in the dirt. Next form panels are constructed into which the dirt is rammed. The panels, placed anywhere along the building line, are filled with layers of moist soil and compacted until the form is full. After it is full, the panels are disassembled and moved to the next spot on the building line. Completed sections are closed off with end board. This process is continued all around the foundation until completed.

Cost. Rammed-earth construction costs are similar to all other forms of construction. If you build small and simple, you save money and energy. Also, rammed earth, like most earth dwellings, is far more energy efficient over the long haul. Almost all earth houses are a more sustainable way to build, because, in general, they use fewer resources and last longer than traditional building methods.

Adobe

Adobe houses, like all earth houses, are sculpted and thus can have a more intimate, sensual appeal than traditional frame buildings. They are also very

The Straw Bale Retirement House

Nancy Simmerman, 60, built a straw bale retirement house. She learned of the method after taking a permaculture workshop, which taught her about creating a lifestyle that is more gentle to humans, wildlife, and the earth. It made sense to her to recycle straw into a house. "Straw bale building doesn't eliminate the use of wood," she says, "but you use a lot less wood and use it more selectively, such as for beautiful wood floors."

Nancy enrolled in an intensive straw bale building course, then hired carpenters to erect the post-and-beam frame, and slowly built much of the rest of her house alone in order to save money on labor. She used funds from the sale of her previous house to fund her new one. She has no mortgage. Nancy built her house with an eye toward retirement; she was mindful of keeping future costs down and was attracted to straw bale because it is much less expensive to heat and is easier to maintain. Straw bale avoids constant repainting because the color is in the stucco and never blisters. Nancy also plans to continue growing most of her food in a self-sustaining garden that feeds her, plus provides extra to sell at farmer's markets. "I haven't bought fruits or vegetables for four years," she says. "What I don't grow, I don't eat. I don't miss buying things like bananas that are trucked for miles, because the fresh food I grow is so satisfying." Her house includes a pantry and root cellar and is wheelchair accessible.

"I've been a commercial photographer for years," Nancy says. "I've been on the road a lot, and now I want to stay home and turn to spinning and growing things. Maybe even open a bed and breakfast. My way of figuring out my life direction is to throw a lot of things on the table and then take a look at what I enjoy and what pays."

"green," in that they are made of readily available, on-site materials. Adobe is made from a mixture of clay and straw. The mixture is taken right out of the ground and shaped into molds that form bricks. The bricks are approximately 18 feet wide by 3 to 4 inches deep and 2 feet long. Each brick weighs approximately 25 to 30 pounds. There is no framing required to build an adobe house—it is made entirely of the clay/straw bricks.

Adobe is most suitable in hot, dry desert climates for three primary reasons:

❖ The bricks must dry in the sun for about a month before building.

❖ Adobe gradually erodes in rain. (With normal maintenance, and when adobe houses are built in suitable climates, they can last for many years—

it is not uncommon, for example, to find 400-year-old haciendas in Mexico that are standing as strong as ever.)

❖ The walls absorb the sun during the day, keeping the house cool, and then gradually emit the heat into the house as the air cools in the evening.

Cost. Traditionally, adobe houses were made on-site by owners. This made them very inexpensive because people used their own earth as the primary building material and did the labor themselves. As people move away from this kind of self-reliance, however, more and more homeowners purchase premade adobe bricks that are constructed off-site and delivered. This, plus any labor costs, brings the price of an adobe house within a range similar to other kinds of construction.

Cob

The word "cob" comes from an old English root meaning "lump" or "rounded mass." In cob building, hands and feet are used to form lumps of earth mixed with sand and straw. Cob, like other forms of solid earth building, stays cool in summer and warm in winter if it has good solar input. Cob's resistance to rain and cold makes it adaptable to both cold wet climates and dry desert conditions. Cob is the most labor intensive of all the earth methods because it is made of solid earth—there is no insulating material inside as in straw bale construction, and there are no forms as in rammed earth. The clay is mixed and kneaded just as if you were making a loaf of bread. Because the form is so labor intensive, cob houses are usually very small in size.

Cob houses have been around for centuries in England and now command very high prices. According to the Cob Cottage Company, the ancient technology doesn't contribute to deforestation, pollution, or mining, nor does it depend on manufactured material or power tools.

Cost. Cob building can be the least expensive of all the earth methods because it uses no forms, ramming, cement, or rectilinear bricks. Cob houses are built by sculpting, using only earth. You can make a cob house as thick as you wish and in any form you like. The down side of cob, however, is that the process, though an ancient one, is not widely accepted in the United States. Many building codes do not allow for it. Before embarking on a cob project, you'll need to check codes in your area.

The $4,000 Cob House

Brigitte Adams, a 36-year-old single mother with limited income, built her house for a total cost of $4,000. She had recently divorced, had no building skills, and was in the midst of traditional postdivorce insecurity when she discovered the art of cob building. She attended a cob workshop and says that within three hours, she knew she could build her own house. She had a total of $4,000 to her name and wanted to be able to stay home with her four-and-a-half-year-old-daughter. "I needed something that wouldn't drain me financially," Brigitte says. She knew if she chose the traditional, more expensive housing path, she'd have to put her daughter in day care, something she was very opposed to doing.

"It was a wonderful experience," she says of the building process. "In fact, it was a pivotal experience in my life. It made me feel like I could conquer obstacles that many people would be set back by."

The $4,000 was spent mostly on the roof and that only because Brigitte says at the time she built, she didn't know how to scavenge materials. The only help she received was in the carpentry, such as the roof, building kitchen counters, and wooden gables.

Brigitte's house is two stories and 450 square feet. It is built on a portion of her parents' 23 acres. Upstairs is the sleeping loft, and downstairs is one main room with living and dining areas and a large kitchen. She uses an outside composting toilet and has no electricity inside. For house heat and cooking, she uses both a woodstove and propane cooktop. She uses top-quality oil lamps for lighting. One day she may add electricity, but for now, she says she enjoys the nonelectric quiet. Brigitte says the house was the result of "lots of good fortune." A neighbor who was remodeling donated her sink and bathtub. Various friends donated 22 windows. A friend who is a master craftsman donated tiles for the counters and kitchen floor. "Everybody seemed to have something," she says. "It's a patchwork quilt of friends represented in the house."

Brigitte says cob is "dirt cheap" because you use available dirt to build. Even her floor

Brigitte Adams and daughter, Elyse, in their cob home.

(except for the tile kitchen) is adobe, made of sifted dirt, sifted sand, and shredded straw, mixed together into an earth plaster. To make the floor more linoleumlike, you can add linseed oil, and paint can be added for color. Brigitte says she likes the floors because there is nothing between her and mother earth. It mops and cleans like any other floor.

Though very labor intensive, cob is easy to use. Brigitte and daughter, Elyse, did all of the cob work themselves. "She stomped up little batches of cob and added it to the house," Brigitte says. "Her creative process is attached to the house too. That's why it is a very special house for us."

The project took from May to September, with mother and daughter working about four to six hours a day. The work is extremely physical and aerobic, and also very therapeutic because the houses are shaped, rather than built. Working with cob is similar to sculpting with clay. All of the walls are curved and gently rounded.

"I not only wanted to work within my budget, but I also wanted a house that would be very aesthetically pleasing to me," Brigitte says. "It was very urgently appealing to build out of the earth . . . it is spiritual."

Now, with no house payments, Brigitte is able to live comfortably on approximately $300 per month. She earns money playing the flute, doing art jobs, and a little office paperwork. "It's such a freeing option," she says. "It seems overwhelming at first. When I started, I had no background in building. On a scale of 1 to 10 in spatial awareness, I was a 1. I couldn't hammer a nail straight. But building with cob is such a natural process. Anyone can do it, and because of the low cost, it's within anyone's budget. My daughter and I did 90 percent of the work ourselves. You need to be very determined and stubborn, but you can do it. It helped that I had the factor of necessity pushing me.

"There is something about curved spaces that opens everyone's heart," Brigitte says. "People come to visit me as total strangers, and after a few minutes they're pouring out their hearts to me. I think it's partly due to the loving energy that goes into building with cob. You sculpt with your hands rather than using noisy machines . . . you can feel it. It's like a hug. The hug of a house that embraces you."

Recycled and Salvaged Materials

Pat and Marti Murphy claim to have built their home for $15 per square foot. "I knew how much I had to start with and what I had at the end," says Pat. They spent about $55,000 for land and materials to build their 2,400-square-foot home. A very pleasing place, the house looks lived in but doesn't reveal its low price tag. From oak floors, to brass knobs, to art deco stained glass, it's made of the best stuff around. Pat says the secret is to pay nothing or next to nothing for materials by finding houses that are being torn down and negotiating to remove what you want. Owners who want to put a new house where an old one is know they will have to pay to have the rubble hauled away. With dumping fees sky high, the salvager can pretty much name a price.

How to find a planned demolition before it's obvious and, therefore, too late? City newspapers have a classified section on buildings to be torn down and building departments have planned demolitions (which require permits) on file. Small Buy-and-Sell–type newspapers are good sources too. A metropolitan Sunday newspaper recently listed these items under Building Materials: bricks, 25 cents each; garage door, $50; carpet (new), $5.99 per square yard; insulated skylights, 4 by 4 feet; $99, 50 gallon electric water heater (new), $85; 8 by 8 foot hot tub (new), $2,000. Also look for listings for auctions and garage sales. Remodeling contractors hired by upscale homeowners to tear out kitchens, carpeting, doors, and windows often give away or sell the items at significant discounts. You can get old single-pane windows and turn them into double pane by adding on another sheet of glass. You can learn the art to this method by calling a window manufacturing company. One man got himself tongue-and-groove timber from an 1800s building that was being torn down. He bought a planer, ran the wood through, and had himself a stack of new-looking, old-growth lumber that he used to side his house. He paid nothing except his time. Call construction companies and salvage their no-longer-used plywood. Often they use it for forms and then throw it away. It's also possible to buy seconds or lower grades of just about anything. Top-quality oak flooring costs $3.80 per square foot retail. If a more knotty look is okay and you have a business tax license, number-3 grade is $1.25 per square foot. For 1,000 square feet the savings would be $2,550.

More and more stores are cropping up that buy and sell only second-use building materials. Check your local telephone directory and ask builders and lumber stores if they know of such businesses in your area.

There are lots of pros and cons to salvaging. The Murphys' $15-per-square-foot price, for example, doesn't include Pat's labor. "Things always take longer than you anticipate," says Pat, who found out the hard way what it's like to grind all the old nails out of oak flooring. But it worked for him. "It's kind of a hobby with me. I like the idea of reusing stuff."

Using recycled materials for your house is a terrific idea, as long as you are aware of two things: Your local building code may not allow such materials to be used in the structure of your house, and there can be hidden costs. For example, if you buy an old door, you will need to spend more money reframing so it will fit. If you are handy like Pat Murphy and enjoy this kind of work, your extra labor will be worthwhile. If you have to hire out all this work, you may be better off using new materials.

A man in Alabama determined that in one six-year period, the state tore down about 6,000 houses to make way for a highway and urban renewal. He calculated approximately 5,000 board feet of lumber in the average house, for a total of about 30 million board feet tossed into landfills. Unfortunately, this man discovered a stipulation in standard building codes that only new wood, grade-stamped for quality, could be used in home construction or repair. He was able to get the building code changed in his county. You need to check your local codes. You also may be able to use salvaged wood in the structure of your house if it has been regraded.

Living Off the Grid

I was so touched by a story sent to me by a *Simple Living* subscriber, Kirk Nevin, that I decided to look further into this concept of living off the grid. Kirk's story is reprinted on pages 136–137.

Living off the grid means that you supply your own power and water and do not depend on public utilities to keep your house functioning. There are both financial and ecological reasons for choosing this kind of lifestyle. The ecological reason is that harvesting energy from the sun, water, and wind uses less energy and creates less pollution than does energy provided by a public utility. While off-the-grid equipment is more expensive than traditional equipment initially, you will save over time because your energy costs will be lower; once you are up and running self-sufficiently, you'll have no monthly water, light, and electric bills to pay. Off-the-grid living is the most immediately cost efficient if you want to live in a remote area where it would cost more to run a power line to your property than to put together a power system of your own.

According to the Power Company in Seattle, Washington, an independent system is composed of four key elements:

1. Energy source comes from your surrounding natural assets. Examples are living near a river, the sun, wind, or, if your natural resources are limited, fuel.
2. Energy equipment. This is what you use to capitalize on your natural resource. Solar panels catch the sun's rays; a hydrogenerator utilizes the force of a river; a generator powered by propane, gas, or diesel uses those fuels.

3. Energy storage. Energy provided by your energy sources is stored in batteries. Two types of batteries can be used, lead acid and gel cell. The latter is a high-performance battery that requires less maintenance and lasts longer. With proper care lead batteries can be expected to last 3 to 5 years; gel batteries, 8 to 10 years.

4. Energy transferral. Energy is most commonly transformed with an inverter, which converts the battery's DC energy to AC to power equipment, appliances, and lighting. An inverter is a quiet piece of equipment that runs solely on the energy of the batteries and can be used instead of a fuel-powered generator if the batteries are being fully charged by solar, wind, or hydrogenerators.

The ideal, totally independent system runs purely on the energy of the sun (solar) and requires no fuel. Such a system can be highly cost effective, produces no pollution, and wastes no natural resources. (Some people with complete solar systems even have solar ovens.) Sometimes fuel is required to power a generator. Some appliances, such as a refrigerator, demand a lot of energy and are usually powered by a generator or are manufactured to use with propane.

Off the Grid in Nevada

 Bert and Patti Reslock live off the grid in northern Nevada on a 12-acre parcel. Their two-story home is earth-bermed on the north and sits in a bowl with a beautiful valley for their front yard. This creative use of the natural landscape allowed optimum performance from the secluded home's solar array, while giving up neither power nor creature comfort.

By day a solar electric system automatically tracks the sun, silently storing power that Bert and Patti, their six kids, and friends consume. Inverters provide 120-volt electricity. Backup power, if necessary, is provided by a woodstove and a propane generator set.

"We designed the house to show a family can live 'off-the-grid' and not be cave people to do it," says Bert. "At the peak of winter, we were snowed in for eight consecutive days with four- and five-foot snowdrifts, and 10 people in the house. But we were never without household power."

"We've undergone minimum lifestyle changes since we moved in," he says. "We turn off the electricity when we're not using it and often gauge our appliance usage based on the time of day. But we're not without all the normal household amenities: microwave, dishwasher, 120-volt refrigerator, curling irons, hair dryer, coffeemaker, garbage disposal, stereo, computer . . . we're not unlike any other home in America."*

Buy a Tear Down, Move It, and Fix It Up

The $53,000 Moved House

The lowest price I ever heard of for a house was $1. Can't beat this one. Betty Martin, a chiropractor and single mother, needed housing that wouldn't cost a fortune. She got wind of a house that was going to be torn down to make way for a fire station. The price was $1.

"The project looked manageable to me," she says. "I couldn't imagine designing and building from scratch because I didn't have any experience. I decided I was ready for this."

Betty decided to take on the challenge. Her land was two blocks away. She paid $13,000 to move the house and build a foundation. She spent an additional $40,000 replacing windows, installing new plumbing and electrical systems, putting in insulation, moving walls, replacing drywall, and completely remodeling the kitchen. She hired a consultant designer/builder to give her good ideas on remodeling and negotiating materials prices. "This helped a lot," she says, "because I didn't have a clue where to start."

The finished house is 850 square feet and includes a bedroom and studio upstairs and an open living room/kitchen area downstairs. Her mortgage of $500 per month includes $15,000 that she borrowed for other purposes.

While moving and rebuilding a tear-down is a good option for some people, it is not always easy to find the houses. Look in want-ad sections of newspapers, check your local building department for permits to tear down houses, and contact your state for a list of surplus homes that result from plans for highway or other public construction. You also can call house-moving companies for referrals. Sometimes they get calls from homeowners who want to know what to do with their surplus place. The factors that determine the cost of moving a house are house size, type of building material, and type of terrain over which you will transport the house. Brick houses are harder to move, as are two-story houses and those with large chimneys. The distance from your

*Story printed with permission of Trace Engineering, 5916 195 NE, Arlington, WA 98223.

331

property to the house is not as much of a cost determinant as is the presence of power lines along the way. If your house is one story and can fit under the lines, you will save significantly. The most basic factor is the cost of loading and unloading the house.

"I'm very happy with the house," Betty says, "because the space suits us now. Plus, I didn't feel prepared to start from scratch. I needed to go with something I could see myself tackling."

Manufactured Houses and Mobile Homes

My preconceived opinions about mobile home life went right out the window when I visited an old friend in Anchorage, Alaska, who lives in one. Peggy is a single woman in her 40s who owns a small barbershop. She lives in a single-wide, no-frills mobile home in a mobile home park just outside of town. Peggy's inexpensive, long-ago-paid-for home has allowed her to live a full, rich, and unencumbered life. While others with far more elaborate houses spend work weeks paying the mortgage and weekends maintaining the place, Peggy is off traveling the world for long stretches at a time, or kayaking, hiking, and enjoying life on weekends.

Another inexpensive option is manufactured housing. Manufactured homes are built in a factory and shipped to the home site as virtually complete homes or in sections. You've probably seen these homes, usually in two halves, as they are hauled down the freeway on flatbed trucks. Since 1976, all manufactured homes must be built to standards enforced by the U.S. Department of Housing and Urban Development (HUD). The average sales price (across the United States) of a 1,140-square-foot manufactured home in 1995 was $23,700. The average price for a 1,905-square-foot, site-built home in the same year was $119,025. (Both prices exclude land.) There are nearly as many manufactured house designs as there are on-site designs.

A nationwide survey of 24,000 manufactured home residents, which appeared in the *Journal of Housing* (November/December 1990), showed that most residents plan to stay in their homes indefinitely or to move to another manufactured home. The most repeated benefits named in responses were low maintenance, affordability, and the efficient use of space. The survey showed that more than 70 percent of new buyers are under 60, with an average age of 45 years.

Log Houses

Log houses can be inexpensive and make ecological sense if you live in area where logs are plentiful. Log houses save the waste involved in the traditional manufacturing process because the logs are not cut into pieces. Built correctly, log houses can be energy efficient because of the thickness of the walls. Whether they are more energy efficient than other methods is debatable. You can save money on energy and on labor and materials because you don't need to buy insulation, sheetrock, and framing, and you don't need to pay a skilled person to do your building.

There are two ways to build a log house, the expensive way or the inexpensive way. As with anything else, the inexpensive way takes a little energy and creativity, but the end result can be freedom from a 30-year mortgage. If you think you don't have the energy for the creative way, consider this equation: Paying off a 30-year mortgage is much more difficult than building a log house. You need to work for 30 years to pay off a 30-year mortgage. You need to work maybe a couple of months to build a log house the inexpensive way.

The most *inexpensive* way to build a log house is this: Avoid lumberyards at all costs and get your logs as close to the source as possible; use simple, used hand tools that can fit into the trunk of your car; and do not make the number-one mistake: delusions of grandeur. This means do not make your log or any other type of house bigger or more elaborate than you need. You'll get in too deep. Add on later if you want.

The most efficient way to build a log house is to use the logs you would tear down anyway to make room for a house on your property. If you don't have heavily wooded property and still want a log house, you can save by getting your logs close to the source (the woods). Many professional loggers have access to land and timber, and you can purchase logs directly from them. This is so because property owners call them when they want trees cut to make room for their non-log homes. Work out deals with the property owners and loggers. To find loggers, try visiting areas in which logging is plentiful and ask around, or put up a sandwich board, offering to buy logs.

When you pick your logs, pick ones that are straight as possible with a one-inch taper for every 10 feet of log. Most timber from the same forest has approximately the same taper. For this reason it is better to cut all of your logs from the same area.

You'll need to use wood that is acceptable to government standards, and you should check building codes in your area before planning your log house.

You can build a log house to live in or use several to achieve economic freedom. One way to achieve economic freedom is to start by building one log house the inexpensive way, live in it, then sell it for a profit. Get a down payment and carry the mortgage. Use the down payment to build a second log house, which you will live in, sell it, and build a third. While building, you can live inexpensively elsewhere. Continue until you have say, eight log houses. Carry your own mortgage on each one and you will have monthly income for life. Not only are you *not* tied to a 30-year mortgage, but you're a step further: You are financially independent.

You don't want to do all of this labor building log houses? Since log house building does not require elaborate carpentry or construction skills, almost anybody can build one. Therefore, you can go out and find laborers to do the work for you. Pay them $10 per hour and even offer an incentive of a trip to Hawaii or somewhere if they get the job done on time. Before quibbling about the cost of a trip to Hawaii for say, five laborers, think of the profit you are making and the work you are not doing.

Living Inexpensively on the Water

The $16,000 Houseboat

A divorce and midlife crisis got Gary Lewis, 43, thinking about what was important in his life. He was busy working to pay his $1,425 mortgage, health club membership, cable TV subscription, cellular phone, and other "necessities." Gary also had a small pontoon houseboat that he used on weekends. One day it dawned on him that he could live just fine on the boat and dump the house, mortgage, and maintenance. Now he and his dog, Phoenix, live on the boat and Gary pays only a $265 monthly moorage fee, which includes water and electricity. He is the only "live-aboard" in a 15-boat marina on a river.

Six years later, he has no regrets. Sometimes he misses having a bathtub, but nothing more. Gary paid $16,000 for the 18-year-old houseboat and spends very little in time and money for upkeep. "It's very manageable," he says. "My other house was 1,800 square feet and I felt like I just couldn't keep up with it. Now I spend maybe two to three hours a month painting, putting in new carpet, or caulking. Every two to four years I spend about $800 to paint the bottom of the pontoon."

Gary's boat is one room and 200 square feet. The room is divided by a curtain—the back half for Gary's bedroom, the front for kitchen and living. The front room also includes a steering wheel, so Gary can take off when the mood strikes him. He heads off to explore little out-of-the-way sloughs for weekends.

"Most of my acquaintances think I've lost my marbles," Gary says. " 'How are you going to live like this?' they ask. "But I wake up in my houseboat hearing ducks quacking, not my neighbor's lawn mower. I see blue herons flying instead of the side of my neighbor's house. When it's time to clean house there's 200 square feet to worry about instead of 2,000.

"A life of pursuing the things that have always interested me, but for which I've never made time, now awaits. Writing, bicycle touring, volunteering to help natural disaster victims, possibly a stab at being a musician, and just having more time to visit with friends and family are some of my dreams. Would I go back to living on the land? Never. It's too peaceful here."

The Two-Story Family Houseboat

Inexpensive houseboat living can work for families too. Nancy and Russ Adams and their two children, ages 7 and 10, have lived in a two-story pontoon-style houseboat for four years. The futon in the living area doubles as a bed at night for Nancy and Russ, and their two boys sleep upstairs. The boat is 42-feet long and approximately 8-feet wide.

The Adamses bought their boat for $6,000 as a bank repossession and spent an additional $13,000 to $14,000 gutting, refurbishing, and adding a second story. They wanted it to look like a home, not a boat, and added wallpaper and custom kitchen cabinets. A woodburning stove heats the entire boat. There is more work to be done, but the family waits until they have the money to do the projects.

Their original plan was to remain living in their duplex in a bedroom community and fix the boat to resell. But as their neighborhood began to feel more and more unsafe, the family decided to move onto the houseboat permanently. Although it was initially difficult for the children to leave their friends behind, the transition went fairly smoothly. Nancy says the family loves living on the boat and has no plans to return to traditional housing. "We're so busy with sports and volunteer work that a house with a yard and upkeep just wouldn't work," Nancy says. "Plus, it's like being on vacation every day here. It's very relaxing and much quieter."

The kids have learned to live with the unique rules of living on the water. No running on the dock, and they must wear life jackets whenever they are outside the house. The family keeps a collection of life jackets handy for visiting friends. Often in the evenings they like to sit outside on the balcony, stargazing or watching the wildlife.

"Last week our youngest son spent the night at a friend's house," Nancy said. "The house is huge, like a mansion. I overheard him telling his brother that his friend had a really nice house. Then I heard our oldest son say, 'Yeah, but we have a really nice house too.'"

You can find pontoon-style houseboats by searching marinas or checking houseboat rental companies for used rentals.

Living on a Sailboat

Barbara and Steve Roberts, ages 36 and 37, have lived on sailboats since their marriage and continued living on them even after having three children. The family, which now includes daughters Frances, age 2, Laura, age 11 months, and son, Charlie, age 5, lives on a Cal 36 sailboat moored in Seattle. The couple met when each lived on a separate boat. Soon after Steve got an offer to sail around the world. Barbara figured that was the last she'd ever see of him. When the owner of the boat died unexpectedly in South America, Steve needed to gather a crew in order to return the boat home to the man's widow. He called Barbara.

"We learned a lot about each other on that trip," she says. "We *had* to communicate, and we were together during the most trying times. You picture sailing as lying around on the bow in your bikini in warm weather, but in reality, that's only 10 percent of sailing. The rest is cold, hard work."

The couple returned to port and married. They got a good deal on a 22-foot boat, fixed it up, and moved aboard. They had their first two children while living on that boat. When Steve, who has worked on boats his whole life, came across the hull of a Roberts 25, he made a trade for the 22-foot boat. He and Barbara built the interior. Finally they moved once again to the 1967-built Cal 36. They paid just under $30,000 and added another $10,000 to bring it up to live-aboard code. They took out a mortgage to finance the cost.

Despite the tight quarters, Barbara says she likes living on a boat for a number of reasons. First are the intangibles. "I like feeling the boat rock, and I love to hear the wind whistling through the halyards. And we're all forced to get along, which I like. My brother-in-law once asked us what we do when we're angry at each other and there are no big doors to slam," Barbara remembers. "Steve and I looked at each other and said very matter-of-factly, 'Well, of course you just have to talk it out!'

"We learned how to communicate on the South America trip. We learned how to deal with problems right away because we lived in such tight quarters. When someone is having a problem, you're

Barbara and Steve Roberts and their children, Charlie, Frannie, and Laura, in front of their sailboat home.

forced to get it out immediately and face it. The kids have learned to do the same thing."

They also like living on the boat because they're more ready to take a 'round-the-world cruise. "If we were to move off the boat and get a house, we'd get bogged down with all of our stuff and probably never leave," Barbara says. "Our goal is to leave on a cruise in about five years. Then Charlie will be old enough to pull watch, they'll all be swimmers, and we'll have our mortgage paid off."

When the five-year-old questions why they live on a boat, Barbara and Steve have ready answers. "We tell him that if we lived in a house, we wouldn't be able to afford a boat too, and then we couldn't sail. He loves to sail. We also remind him that the only way we could afford a house would be to live far away from Steve's work. Then they wouldn't be able to see as much of Daddy because he'd be spending so much time commuting. When we explain these choices, he always agrees that we should stay on the boat."

The family pays $280 for a 40-foot slip at a 150-boat marina in the city. Their electricity and propane are extra. They use blocked ice in an icebox for food refrigeration. They use a Port-a-Potty and take showers at the marina. The kids use a 16-gallon food bin filled with water for their bathtub.

All three kids sleep in the main cabin of the boat, and Barbara and Steve sleep in the V-berth in the bow. At 8:00 P.M., lights are off for the kids, and the parents read in their berth, which is separated by a small door.

The couple is very creative in making storage and play space for the kids. First, they buy very little because there is no place to put it. "I can walk through a store and say 'oh, that's nice' and walk right out," Barbara says.

When they buy toys for the kids, they choose the type that requires imagination. They set up a wooden train layout in the rear berth, toy airplanes hang from the ceiling, and the kids store their clothes in three cloth storage bins that Barbara made. Barbara also built a wooden fold-up table and covered "porch" area in the cockpit. Extra clothes, toys, and seasonal items are stored at Steve's parents' house, an hour-and-a-half drive away. They rotate the toys. Rather than store photo albums, Barbara cut out pictures of family members and mounted them collage-style in a frame on the wall. They built a swing and hang it from the boom. In the summer, they put a blow-up swimming pool on the bow for the kids. The entire boat is rimmed with a net-style fence.

"The kids don't get bored here," Barbara says. "I look at our yard as the whole of Seattle. There are a zillion parks, there's the zoo, the aquarium, science center. And what is really important is that our kids don't fight. All of us are forced to get along because our space is so small. Steve and I feel getting along is an important value."

The kids are also very good at following rules. They know never to leave the cockpit of the boat without an adult, and they know they must always put each toy or item of clothing away before taking out the next one. "There's no room and no choice," Barbara says. The boat is kept so tidy that when the family wants to go on one of their frequent short cruises, they can leave the dock in less than 15 minutes. Their motto is to keep everything as simple as possible.

Only in wintertime, when it rains for days at a time and is difficult to take the kids out, does Barbara feel the pressure of living in such a small space. Yet she still doesn't wish she were in a house. "When I married Steve I knew I was going to live on a boat," she says. "It's all a mind-set. To me it's not too small because you learn to adjust. And we have little money, but money is not going to kill our happy family life. The way I look at it is we don't have that stress of having to pay for a $2,000 mortgage."

Live in a Less Expensive Town

 Barbara Amorso, 44, and Michael Palmer, 55, moved from a Philadelphia suburb to Livingston, Montana, a town of 7,000. She traded a $30,000 a year job and he a $25-an-hour union job for $6 and $7.25 an hour. They bought a three-bedroom house for $96,000 and wouldn't return to their busy former lives for anything.

"We came here on vacation and decided to come back to live," Barbara says. "Living here is like looking back to how things used to be."

Barbara remembers taking the streetcar alone into Philadelphia when she was a young girl of 12 and remembers how those kinds of freedoms were eroded for her own children. She had two grown children and wanted the last one, age 16, to enjoy a few years of that same sense of lack of restraint. Now their daughter can walk home from the one movie theater in town at 11:00 at night. "I don't have to worry about it," Barbara says. "We wanted our last child to be raised without fear of the world. Kids can't be kids anymore."

Their daughter was also ready for the move. She appreciates that in a high school of 400, she knows 375 of the kids.

Barbara says there is very little stress living in a small town because life is easier. Her work isn't so pressured now. "Here, if someone asks me for a report, they'll give me a week to get it done. Then they say thank you. In the city, everything had to be done immediately." Barbara goes home for lunch and sits on her deck watching the birds.

There is no stress from driving and parking either. It's an easy walk to the small downtown section that is five blocks from their home, and Barbara rides her bike to work.

A typical evening is casual and relaxed. "Last evening Mike and I were watching TV, and two neighbors came over for a visit. Tonight another friend is coming for dinner. We go to bed now at 9:30 because we want to. In the city we went to bed at 9:30 because we were exhausted."

The only difficult aspect of the change is Barbara's family. She had lived her entire life in Philadelphia and left behind her parents, cousins, aunts, and uncles. "I miss my family, but I find that I get very anxious when I go to visit them because I'm not used to the stress of getting around in a city anymore," she says. "Here there's no looking over your shoulder, and here you know everyone at the store. That's very comforting."

Wanda Urbanska and Frank Levering liked their move to a small town so much they wrote a guide book for others considering making the change. The couple left busy Los Angeles and moved to a town of 7,000 in the Blue Ridge Mountains. They also left professional careers and friends who said Wanda and Frank would "turn to mush" if they left. Instead, their careers blossomed, they connected with their new community, and they couldn't be happier.

They say the most significant reason for moving to a small town is the desire for community and for real-life interaction with genuine people whom you come to know over time. In their book, they cited a study by Duke University that indicated that residents of so-called hostile cities (cities in which people exhibit high levels of cynical mistrust, anger, and aggression) are more likely to suffer fatal coronary heart disease and death from other causes than do those living in more pleasant places.

Some find a move to a small town positive, and others more negative. Much depends on the small town's the location and political climate. Before making a move, do thorough research in these areas and visit more than once to get a feel for the true costs and general "people climate." In some small towns housing can be very inexpensive; in others there are hidden costs, such as high fuel bills in places where winters are longer. One Canadian woman who moved from a major city to a small town ultimately returned to the city. She discovered that the farm folk didn't take to some of her more New Age ideas and that there wasn't enough for her children to do.

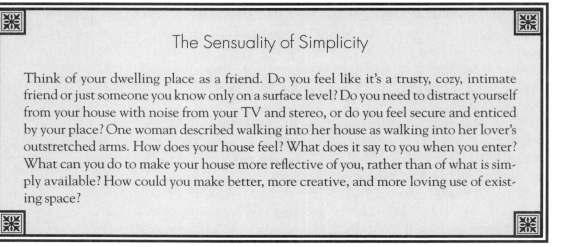

The Sensuality of Simplicity

Think of your dwelling place as a friend. Do you feel like it's a trusty, cozy, intimate friend or just someone you know only on a surface level? Do you need to distract yourself from your house with noise from your TV and stereo, or do you feel secure and enticed by your place? One woman described walking into her house as walking into her lover's outstretched arms. How does your house feel? What does it say to you when you enter? What can you do to make your house more reflective of you, rather than of what is simply available? How could you make better, more creative, and more loving use of existing space?

LAYING A HECTIC LIFE TO REST IN TAOS, NEW MEXICO

His fine-tailored business suits? She's thinking maybe she'll turn them into a quilt someday. A fitting reminder of a life they left behind.

Pass by the little earth-colored adobe houses, the Valdez and Gallina peaks, the mesas. Head toward the orange, blue, purple, and pink sky. The colors are everywhere, and they go on for miles and miles. So many miles of open light you can't see to the end. Couldn't possibly. Take a left and head down Hondo Seco Road. It is a narrow, winding, gravel road. Pass the horses, wind your way along the vast mesa where the Rio Grande has cut a spectacular gorge, and you begin to understand why author D. H. Lawrence said this was the most beautiful place he had ever encountered. And why Kay Giddens wants to lay their old, hectic life to rest in a quilt and hang it in their Taos, New Mexico, house.

Keep going along the little dirt road. Stop when you see the simple wooden sign that says LITTLE TREE BED AND BREAKFAST. Open your arms wide as possible, stretch every muscle, and take a deep breath. Smell the juniper. It grows everywhere. Sagebrush too. You can literally see for miles. There is no end to this vista. Kay and Charles Giddens open the door. "Welcome," they say. Charles Giddens did much of the building and all of the contracting himself. The thick adobe walls were made the authentic way: sand mixed with mud and bits of straw. There are warm tile floors,

Kay and Charles Giddens at their bed and breakfast, Little Tree.

a kiva in the corner, and hand-sculpted archways. And there are cats curled up seemingly everywhere. The couple has three: Willy, Miss Kitty, and Mr. Mudd. Step outside to the courtyard, benches, or garden, and enjoy the kind of quiet city dwellers have only in the middle of the night when the traffic slows. Traffic in this place amounts to a few cars here and there bumping down the gravel road, or bicyclists heading toward the little village of Arroyo Seco, or people out for a walk taking in those vistas.

The Giddenses built their dream bed and breakfast to look old in the pueblo style with giant *vigas* (log beams) and *latillas* (small sticks for the ceiling). Old Mexican tile was used for the common areas. The house is built in an L-shape with portals (porches) running across the back facing an adobe-walled courtyard. They found a Taos folk artist and expert adobe worker, Pablo Quintana, to help build. Charles knew he had succeeded in authenticity when a local Hispanic man came up before the house was finished and asked if they were redoing that old house.

This is a long drive, a far cry, from their old life in Dallas, where Charles was a trial lawyer and Kay a paralegal and former social worker. Charles remembers when the shift began. One day he asked Kay what all those people were doing bringing their problems to him for. "That's your job!" Kay announced. "Then it's time to change my job!" Charles said.

"I was also tired of the big city . . . it was so crowded with everybody always in competition . . . I'm tired of competing and knew there was more to life. I knew I had to change direction. I was 45 or 46 at the time."

"We had just gone in lock-step doing what we had to do, without ever thinking about what we wanted in life," Kay says. "It was a long process . . . that feeling of dissatisfaction. Unfortunately, most people don't think they have any options. It was a long, hard process for us, and we did a lot of talking."

The Giddenses had visited Taos often during weekends away from Dallas. For 10 years they escaped like this and for years they hated to return home. They also loved staying at bed and breakfasts. Finally they decided it really was time to move on to a new phase of their lives. They bought an acre in the Taos countryside and set to work building a bed and breakfast of their own. They went to a seminar offered by the Professional Association of Innkeepers, where they learned about finances, reservations, food service, handling the public. Their dream was becoming reality.

"We really hadn't saved money during all of our working years," Kay says. "We have six kids and it took what we had just to get by. Then after we made the decision to change direction, Charles settled a fairly substantial case and we decided we'd better invest it in our new life or we'd spend it."

By then the kids were moving on to lives of their own, but the Giddenses wished they had started earlier so the kids could have grown up in the country.

Charles gradually phased his practice out by not accepting new clients. "I wanted to do something that I felt good about and enjoyed . . . and that certainly wasn't battling with people," he says. Although he had never built anything before and never thought of himself as a handyman, he stayed in Taos more and more and built their house. They didn't want to have a mortgage on it, so they did the work in stages. It took about 18 months to finish construction. Charles and Kay did all of the finish work and completed it on Charles's birthday, December 24, 1991. They had their first guests the next day, on Christmas. Those guests loved it so much they moved within the year from Atlanta to Taos, bringing their business with them.

Kay furnished and decorated the four guestrooms with antique and eclectic furniture she had collected over the years. She's made a quilt for each room. Together she and Charles make a hearty breakfast for guests in the morning, and a jar of homemade cookies waits for visitors in every room.

"When people ask me if I miss practicing law, I say no, I'd rather clean toilets," Charles says, "and as a matter of fact, that's just what I'm doing!"

At night, look up at the sky. The stars are so clear you can see the Milky Way. By day you'll hear the chirps of magpies, piñon jays, and mountain bluebirds. At sunset and at night you can hear the yips of coyotes from arroyos nearby.

The Giddenses' day begins at 6:30 A.M. when they get up to start coffee and breakfast, light the fire, and visit with guests. They both like to cook. "Kay told me if I could read I could cook," Charles says. "So I learned how to cook." Breakfast lasts until 9:00 or 10:00 A.M., and then they clean the kitchen. Rooms are cleaned next. They recently hired an employee to help out. Midday they do grocery shopping, errands, take the linens to the laundry service in town, and garden. Charles likes vegetable gardening and Kay likes flower gardening. Evening is for relaxing together or with friends. The house is designed so the Giddenses have their own private quarters. Although they love the hospitality, this allows them the privacy they also need.

"This is not a sedentary job like working in an office," Charles says, "so I'll always make it a point to stop during the day and sit and relax for a while. Mr. Mudd will come in and want me to pet him. That relaxes me."

"This has been better than we expected," Kay says, "but you need to really enjoy people and create a balance of time for yourself in this job. We have truly met some marvelous people and have formed relationships with some of our regular guests. In fact, we've watched two separate guests go through the same process as we did and move here.

"We earn a lot less money now than we did in Dallas, but we find that we need a lot less here," Kay says. "We don't wear the suits and expensive clothes anymore . . . there's nowhere to wear them. We don't have that burning need to take vacations and breaks so often because we feel so much more relaxed now. We don't need the expensive cars and other things you buy when you're advancing a career or keeping up with the Joneses. And we save a lot of money by not going out to be entertained like we used to. In Dallas we went out for the nightlife and spent a lot of our money to make life bearable. Now we don't need to do that; we can create our own entertainment. We also save money by fixing things ourselves. We used to hire everything out."

"I never realized how stressed I was until I got out here," Charles remembers. "I was very serious about my practice and my clients and always trying to do the best job I could. That's stressful."

"When he started coming to Taos to work on this house," Kay says, "he would return to Dallas and even *look* different. Then 48 to 72 hours back in the city and you'd see the stress creeping up on him again. I don't think either of us realized just how badly it affected him."

"We work long hours, but it's worth it, and it's a different kind of long day," the Giddenses say. To maintain balance, they give each other a day off every week, and they take long weekends away when time permits. They'll work longer vacations into the schedule too. But now when they take a break, it is without that urgency, that need to unwind. Sometimes if there are no check-ins arriving, they'll go hiking or cross-country skiing for the afternoon. And other days? They'll load a basket with a bottle of wine, crusty bread, and a little cheese and take off to sit on the Rio Grande plateau, watching the blues, purples, pinks, golds, and oranges coloring the sky.

Kay smiles. "I sit and look at the mesa and that takes care of me."

❖ ❖ ❖ ❖ ❖ ❖ ❖ ❖ ❖ ❖ ❖ ❖ ❖ ❖ ❖

Resources

Small Houses and Spaces

Books

The Cottage Book by Richard Sexton (San Francisco: Chronicle Books, 1989)
A tribute to the small house via photographs and drawings. The book provides inspiration, interior design, renovation, and landscape ideas to show how the cottage house might be a valuable and worthwhile alternative to more standard homes.

Designing for Small Homes by Dylan Landis (Glen Cove, NY: PBC International, 1996)
Landis, a contributing editor to *Metropolitan Home, American HomeStyle,* and *Gardening* magazines, grew up in a one-bedroom apartment.

Small Spaces by Azby Brown (New York: Kondasha International, 1993)
Thinking small and minimal, an international perspective on converting tiny spaces into livable homes. From kitchens to basements to offices, no space is missed. Extensive photography and drawings.

Tiny Houses by Lester R. Walker (New York: Overlook Press, 1987)
One person's shack is another person's home in this overview of diminutive homes that range from townhomes to tool sheds converted into real living spaces. Whether it's a canvas house or a tent, the philosophy of putting more into less remains the same. Dozens of "diminutive" homes (complete with drawings, photos, and etchings) are shown and discussed as alternatives to the standard-sized house. The range and diversity of these tiny homes is immense—from townhouses to ice-fishing shanties.

a Hom4Me is a 225-square-foot house that is designed with add-on modules to build as money permits. Write: a Hom4Me, 387 Merrow Road, Tolland, CT 06084, 1-860-875-1426

"Redefining a Dream" MacLean's, July 16, 1990. Discusses the search for more affordable housing in Canada. Includes discussion of the Grow Home, a townhouse that is 1,000-square-feet long and 14-feet wide and can be built in most Canadian cities for construction and labor costs of $40,000 (1990 prices).

"San Francisco Solutions" Architectural Review (November 1993). Describes the work of innovative San Francisco architect Donald MacDonald and his individual plywood sleeping pods for urban homeless and a simple prototype starter home, using simple building technology.

Buy with No Money Down or Low Cost

Books

How to Buy a House with No Money Down by Martin M. Schenkman and Warren Borosun (New York: John Wiley & Sons, 1989)
Alternative financing to house purchases made by two real-estate specialists. Especially intended for first-time buyers.

How to Buy Land Cheap by Edward Preston (New York: Gordon Press, 1991)
Description of numerous ways to find good purchasing details on land, including getting repossessed properties and other alternative means to finding cheap housing. Glossary of terms included to help readers through the arcane process of land transactions.

Build It Yourself

Be Your Own Architect by Gene B. Williams (Blue Ridge Summit, PA: Tab Books Division of McGraw-Hill, 1990)
Cut costs by designing your house to meet your needs. One of many how-to books on all aspects of house building and how you can do it by yourself.

The Self-Build Book by Jon Broome and Brian Richardson (White River Junction, VT: Chelsea Green Publishing, 1996)
Complete listing on building your own wood-frame house, from start to finish. Drawings, charts, photos, diagrams, and every manner of explanation is offered to show you how it's properly done and why so many do it on their own today.

Miscellaneous

The Greenloan Program, Residential Lending Services for Building a Sustainable and Affordable Society. They help you explore financing options for "green" housing. Hallmark Mortgage, 2505 Cedarwood Avenue, #5, Bellingham, WA 98225, 1-360-738-1520, E-Mail: hallmark@nas.com.

Manufactured Housing Institute, 2101 Wilson Boulevard, #610, Arlington, VA 22201, 1-703-558-0400, Fax: 1-703-558-0401, for low-cost alternative manufactured housing.

"National Partners in Homeownership" program offered by the federal government for low-cost housing and ownership for women and minorities. Contact the local Housing and Urban Development Office or nonprofit Community Home Ownership Center in your area for more information. The Seattle branch is 1-206-587-5641 or 1-800-317-2918.

Real Goods Institute offers year-round classes in Strawbale Construction, Sustainable Building and Eco Design, Solar Electric Systems, Country Property and Homestead Development, Home Retrofitting for Energy Efficiency, Do-It-Yourself Hydro Systems, and Developing Your Own Water Systems, from Financing to Finishing Your New House. Call Real Goods at 1-800-762-7325.

Whole Earth Review offers abundant information on housing, 1-415-332-1716.

Green, Solar, and Off-the-Grid Housing

Books

Green Shift by John Farmer (Oxford, England: Butterworth-Heinemann, 1996)
Written by a British architect, the book discusses historical and current attempts at balancing human housing needs with environmental concerns. It covers the various architectural movements in the past and why the "green shift" is now a common concern among many architects and builders.

The Independent Home by Michael Potts (White River Junction, VT: Chelsea Green Publishing, 1993)
A compendium of information on getting off the grid and how to live a comfortable, sustainable yet self-reliant style. It explains the process of how energy is obtained, distributed, and brought into the home; how to utilize existing resources and save money in the process; and what the future holds for energy development. Filled with real-life stories of people who live off the grid. Also explains how the systems work and why off-the-grid living makes sense.

The Natural House Book by David Pearson (New York: Fireside Books, 1989)
Discusses building homes that blend into and are comfortable with the environment. Contains extensive examples of current homes from the world over that show how houses can fit harmoniously with mother nature while providing comfort and joy.

Solar Living Source Book by John Schaeffer and the Real Goods Staff (White River Junction, VT: Chelsea Green Publishing, 1996)
Complete digest for the solar-power buff. Everything from harvesting energy to using better and more economically and ecologically efficient light bulbs. Includes a listing of books and prices for products shown in its pages.

Resources

Books for Sustainable Living catalog from Chelsea Green Publishing, 205 Gates-Briggs Building White River, VT 05001, 1-802-295-6300, Fax: 1-802-295-6444

Center for Resourceful Building Technology, P.O. Box 3866, Missoula, MT 59806, 1-406-549-7678

EnviResource, The Environmental Home and Building Center, 1-800-281-9785. Has resource list of free materials, and web site: http://www.eren.doe.gov. Materials are wide ranging and include information on insulation, lighting, energy saving, windows, wind energy, geothermal, solar thermal, and efficient air conditioning.

Environmental Building News, RR1, Box 161, Brattleboro, VT 05301, 1-802-257-7300. This is a very helpful bimonthly newsletter.

Guide to Resource Efficient Building Elements. Available for $25 plus $3 shipping and handling from the Center for Resourceful Building Technology, Dept. P., P.O. Box 100, Missoula, MT 59806. Also call the Energy Efficiency and Renewable Energy Clearinghouse at 1-800-363-3732.

Home Power magazine, P.O. Box 520, Ashland, OR 97520, 1-916-475-3179

IMEX, Industrial Materials Exchange offers industrial waste products and surplus material, some free, some for cost. In Seattle call 1-206-296-4899 or Fax: 1-206-296-3997. Call your city to ask if an IMEX is available.

The International Institute for Bau-biologie and Ecology, Box 387, Clearwater, FL 34617, 1-813-461-4371

The Journal of Light Construction, P.O. Box 686, Holmes, PA 19043. This is a monthly magazine with how-to articles on resource-efficient building.

National Green Pages published by Co-op America, 1612 K Street NW #600, Washington, DC 20006, 1-202-872-5307

Home Varieties

Books

Complete Guide to Building Log Homes by Monte Burch (NY: Sterling Publishing, 1990)
Discusses the joint method (logs cut to fit one another tightly) and how to do it all by yourself. Hundreds of illustrations supplement the text as you work your way through the actual process of building the functional log home.

The Rammed Earth House by David Easton (White River Junction, VT: Chelsea Green Publishing, 1996)
One of the oldest forms of building a house (commonly found in places like Africa and Asia), the rammed earth home uses a common ingredient found around the planet—dirt—as the mainstay of its construction. Photos and drawings show current examples and portray how a quality rammed earth house is built.

The Straw Bale House by Athena Swentzell Steen, Bill Steen, David Bainbridge, and David Eisenberg (White River Junction, VT: Chelsea Green Publishing, 1994)
Like *The Rammed Earth House*, this book offers a detailed explanation for building your own house from straw bales. Photos of models from the past and present supplement the text, as do many diagrams that show how the process is done and why it's a valid alternative.

Underground Houses by Rob Roy (New York: Sterling Publishing, 1994)
These homes take advantage of the ground not only as insulation but also to provide more "pleasing" aesthetics for those who wish to blend in more with the surrounding environment. Underground homes have been in existence for thousands of years, and the book has plenty of photos and drawings to explain the process of building one.

Resources

Cob Cottage Company, offers workshops and newsletter *The Cob Web*. Box 123, Cottage Grove, OR, 1-541-942-2005

Eco Construction Company, 7340 N. Moore Lane, Primeville, OR 97754, 1-541-447-5336

GreenFire Institute specializes in straw bale design and construction. www.balewolf.com, E-mail: wilbur.balewolf.com

The Natural Building Center, offers workshops. 2300 W. Alameda, #A5, Santa Fe, NM 87501, 1-505-471-5314; Order *A Holistic Home Building Guide* by Robert LaPort.

Out on Bale publishes *The Last Straw* newsletter, which is filled with articles and lots of resources, and offers workshops, P.O. Box 42000, Tucson, AZ 85733-2000, 1-520-882-3848

Small Towns

Moving to a Small Town by Wanda Urbanska and Frank Levering (New York: Simon & Schuster, 1996)
A planning guide for those who want to move to the country. While it goes over practical

matters (how to choose the right town, making sure it is "wired," and so on), it also covers important issues of living the simpler life in your new community.

Nature on View by Peggy Landers Rao and Jean Mahoney (New York: Weatherhill, 1993)
Features 28 American homes, urban and rural, that highlight the principles of Japanese design. Many photos and diagrams.

Places of the Soul by Christopher Day (New York: HarperCollins, 1990)
Architecture as if human beings really mattered. Or turning buildings and dwellings into places that feed the soul, not just as prepackaged structures that house the body.

Power of Place by Dolores Hayden (Cambridge, MA: MIT Press, 1995)
Architecture and landscape as reflection of human history and our attachment to "place." Where we live tells a lot about who we are as well as about our social and cultural standing. The author traces the history of how we shape our environment and how it shapes us.

The 100 Best Small Towns in America by Norman Crampton (Englewood, NJ: Prentice Hall, 1996)
A nationwide guide to the best in small town living.

Cohousing, Intentional and Communal Living

Books

Cohousing by Kathryn McCamant, Ellen Hertzman, and Charles Durrett (Berkeley, CA: Ten Speed Press, 1993)
Uses as its models intentional communities already in existence in northern Europe, especially the Scandinavian countries. Explains these communities, how they work, and how they were planned (using diagrams and drawings). Because the focus is on existing communities, the information offered leans on practical suggestions.

Intentional Communities Directory (Fellowship for Intentional Community and Communities Publications Cooperative, Rutledge, MO, 1990)
Source book that lists existing intentional communities across the United States and organizations and groups that support the concept. Also explains how these communities work and operate and offers practical advice on starting one.

New Households, New Housing edited by Karen Franck and Sherry Ahrentzen (New York: Van Nostrand Reinhold, 1991)
Nearly 80 percent of households created since 1980 have housed other than the traditional married couples with children. Three alternatives to traditional housing are examined: single-parent households, collective housing, and single-room occupancy housing. Examples from Europe are included.

Resources

Cerro Gordo Community has lots of resources on community living. Dorena Lake, Box 569, Cottage Grove, OR 97424

CoHousing Company, 1250 Addison #113, Berkeley, CA 94702, 1-510-549-9980

CoHousing Network. Membership is $20 a year and includes the magazine, *CoHousing*. P.O. Box 2584, Berkeley, CA 94702, 1-510-486-2656

Communities Magazine, 138-CR Twin Oaks Road, Lousia, VA 23093, 1-540-894-5126

Communities Magazine: Journal of Cooperative Living, Route 1, Box 155-M, Rutledge, MO

Eco Villages is a listing of international communities throughout the United States. Contact them at P.O. Box 11470, Bainbridge Island, WA 98110

Follow the Dirt Road: An Introduction to Intentional Communities in the 1990s is a video by Monique Gauthier, 1 Evergreen Court, Landenberg, PA 19350-9389.

Human Investment Project, Inc., 364 S. Railroad Avenue, San Mateo, CA 94401.
This organization builds group homes for all kinds of special groups and offers a wide range of resources and programs for lower income people.

National Shared Housing Resource Center, 321 E. 25th Street, Baltimore, MD 21218

Shared Housing, 155 E. Olive, Suite 6, P.O. Box 1457, Newport, OR 97365, 1-541-574-0551.
This is one of the few shared housing resource centers specializing in rural areas.

The Shared Housing Center, 3110 Live Oak Street, Dallas, TX 75204, 1-214-821-8510.
This program uses large numbers of volunteers to meet housing needs for families and seniors.

Shared Living Resource Center. 1-510-548-6608.

12
Clutter

*One day I had the sudden
realization: If I stopped buying things
right this moment, there is no way I
could ever use all I have now.*

—DON ASLETT, *CLUTTER'S LAST STAND*

I am not a naturally organized person. Therefore, the only way I can even remotely manage any of my mess is to have less of it. Even then I have problems, but at least I can *find* the problems. Usually.

The simple living lesson on clutter is this: If you don't like to clean, sort, and fool with stuff, have less of it. Very simple. It's the same basic principal as my work theory. If you don't like to work too much, don't spend so much money. Also very simple.

Henry David Thoreau once said that if he was dusting and came across an object in his path, he would toss the object rather than fool with it. I like this approach. This guy knew what he was talking about. Think about it. Our friend from Walden Pond had time to wander in nature, write books, and philosophize about life. What are the rest of us doing? Dusting; rearranging; insuring; shopping for stackable, color-coded storage units; renting storage space; buying houses with extra rooms and basements; worrying about our stuff; polishing; cleaning; repairing; selling at garage sales; and working overtime to buy our *clutter!*

We buy gadgets guaranteed to make our lives easier, and what happens? They make our life easier once or maybe twice a year and then they make our life miserable because we have to do something with them. We feel too guilty to throw them out because we paid good money for these shiny gizmos. Try these on for size: A special electric dealie that makes hamburger patties for $39.95. Come on. How much trouble is it to shape hamburger into a circle and cook the darned thing in a frying or broiling pan? Unless you own a hamburger stand, how many nights a year do you make hamburger patties? A special screwdriver with at least 35 changeable heads, top-quality for $24.95. I actually bought one of these thinking it would turn everyone in the house into a functioning carpenter. What a joke. Unless you are a cabinetmaker for a living, how often would you ever have a need for anything but the two basic kinds of screwdrivers? Nevertheless, the thing was too expensive and too nifty-looking to throw out.

Pasta machines. Absolutely. In this day and age, everyone has time to make homemade pasta. Who are we kidding? I don't care how great the stuff tastes. When was the last time you used yours? Electric can openers. In my humble opinion, these have always been the paragon of a life gone junk bad. This is one item I never could understand. Hold all phones everywhere—we can't open cans with a hand crank? We can't? I'm going to guess the person who invented the thing probably did it as a joke and never really expected anyone to buy one. Exercise machines. Just about everyone I know has at least one sitting somewhere in their house collecting you-know-what. (The answer is not "Sweat dripping off the exerciser." It is a word that starts with a *d* and ends with a *t*.) They go hog-wild and use them all the time at first, thinking soon they will look like those people on the cover of exercise videos. And there is always a very good reason why these people will be different. They really need this stair-climber, rower, ski machine, or treadmill. Honest. Unlike everyone else, they *will* use theirs. Decorating accessories. I once saw a pair of totally artsy-looking elephant candlesticks that I knew would make my life 1,000 percent better. They were made in India but I bought them here at home. They would make my house look more international. They were $40. Now they sit on a basement shelf because they take up too much room on the table. I can't part with them because they cost $40. I like my 25 cent junk sale candle holders better anyway. They are much less obtrusive.

No question, clutter has become a fact of American life. It extends into every corner of every activity we ever even considered embarking on. Take sports. For crying out loud, I went to an upscale outdoor equipment place the other day and wanted to turn into a couch potato immediately. Now you can't go anywhere or do anything outdoors without mortgaging your house first. The latest in family hiking gear is a special baby hiking backpack with an awning over it and a window in the awning to keep your baby dry while hiking. Please! Whatever happened to a jacket with a hood? Except for the people who get sucked into this contraption, the rest of us know exactly what will happen to the backpack with the awning. The family will use it two or three times and, before they know it, the baby will be too big to fit under the awning. Voilà! The basement!

There is clutter food. You buy a whole jar of a specialty spice for one ethnic dinner. I know about this because I've been hauling around a good number of these for so many years that I bet if I looked inside the jar, I'd lose 10 years off my life. Or gourmet specialty items that go into only one recipe, and you buy a whole container.

> *In order to seek one's own direction, one must simplify the mechanics of ordinary, everyday life.*
>
> —PLATO

There are cluttered closets. I once watched a video about organizing your home and was pretty amazed. Let's see. Organize your blouses and shirts. Not so easy. First organize them into patterns. Then colors. Then seasons. Then dressy or casual. You can imagine how many shirts and blouses we're talking about if there are entire groupings of each category. Organize your shoes into high heels, medium heels, no heels. This means there are lots of shoes in each group. Then into shoe colors and, finally, into dressy or casual. Organize your belts into the kind that hang and the kind that don't hang. Organize your handbags into color and whether they are casual or dressy or evening. Organize your sweaters into color piles. All the white ones here, the blue ones there, and so on. Then there's jewelry. Take an entire drawer and organize it into piles of earrings, piles of necklaces, piles of bracelets, watches for this occasion and that occasion, pins, this and that. And those are just the pieces you don't wear regularly. Put the ones you do wear regularly in a separate jewelry box that sits on top of a dresser.

I kept thinking, if this person just got rid of three-fourths of the stuff, organizing would be a snap! Who wants to spend that much time worrying about stuff? Holy mackerel! Exactly how many sweaters, purses, blouses, shirts, and belts does one person need anyway? What have our lives become? We have gotten so out of hand that there are people who earn a full-time living as professional organizers! There are specialty stores that sell nothing but storage contraptions. We'd be putting an entire industry out of business if we simply got rid of our stuff.

You get the picture. My own personal junk saga is travel mementos. I'm not sure why I bought some of these. I think it was to prove to other people that I was a sophisticated, interesting world traveler and if they had any sense, they'd hang around me because of this. So now I have five miniature porcelain tea sets from China that I couldn't leave that country without. After a while I got tired of showing these to people as an introduction to my speech on how I'd been to China and you haven't. Now every time I have to dust the darned things I get in a bad mood. They are a pain in the neck. At least I could have stopped at one!

Then there are my travel slides. Once I went to Hawaii and fell in love with Hawaiian sunsets. I was also just learning photography. I took scads of "creative" pictures of sunsets. Sunsets with palm trees in front of them. Sunsets with catamarans sailing by. Sunsets over the water. Sunsets with hula dancers. Sunsets behind mountains, behind fields, behind thatched roofs. Then I came home loaded with all these slides I didn't know what to do with. So I called a group of friends over to watch my Hawaiian slide show. I'm surprised I have any friends left. I never saw so many people sleeping all at the same time in the same room in my life. That was the last time. I've been schlepping shoe boxes of those and other prove-I-went-there slides around for years and haven't looked at them since Nixon was in office. I keep thinking "someday I will sort them."

Don Aslett, the king of clutter control, described out-of-control clutteritis in his book, *Clutter's Last Stand*. Is this you? He says you may have a serious junk problem if you do things like live in fear that someone you respect may someday open your closets, or if you have to think about how to cross a room. There's more. Do you hide the tangled contents of a messy drawer by laying a couple of neatly folded things over the top? Do you have an unquenchable desire to paw through a moving neighbor's garage before the trash truck comes?

Getting Rid of Clutter

Ready to get rid of your clutter? There are several ways to withdraw from your junk. (It's no coincidence that these are probably the same words drug counselors use for their clients.) You don't need a doctorate in nuclear physics to get rid of junk and then organize what is left. I've read books that tell you to make elaborate charts and storage patterns and go through some detailed process to figure out what to keep and what to store and on and on. I've decided it's easier being buried by clutter than following those schemes. Instead, try the simple living simple method.

The Cleaning/Organizing Neurosis Rule

If you're the type who likes to get in and get things done, set aside a Saturday or weekend and go through your entire house. If you can handle only 10 minutes at a time, set a timer and get to work. If you need to reward yourself after

10 or 30 minutes, do it. Don't make a big deal out of whatever cleaning or organizing neurosis you have. Just get the job done in whatever amount of time you want to give to this project. If you are a 10-minute person, set aside 10 minutes a day until the job is done. Whatever method you choose, stick with it until you are finished and I guarantee you will feel terrific.

The Drawer-by-Drawer, Shelf-by-Shelf Rule

If you look at your entire house as one unit of junk, you'll never do anything because the job is too overwhelming. Take it one drawer at a time. Start anywhere. Pick one room and work around in a circle until you've gone through the entire house. Take each room shelf by shelf, drawer by drawer.

Pull all of the junk out of that drawer or off that shelf. As you take each piece out, form groups on the counter, table, or floor. Say you pick your entryway closet first. Put all the hats in a pile, all the gloves in a pile, all the boots in a pile, all the kids' coats in a pile, the grown-ups' coats in a pile, and so on. As you take each item out, sort it by putting it in the proper pile. Once everything is out of the closet and in sorted piles, return items back to the closet according to groups. Make containers for the small items, such as gloves. Group the jackets together, and so on. (First get rid of excess items; keep reading for tips.)

Head on into the next closet. I went through my linen section once and was surprised to find sheets in there I didn't even know I had. Now I keep only two sets of sheets for each bed. One flannel winter set and one cotton summer set. The summer sheets are pure white and the winter are plain rose. That way the sheet pattern will not go out of style. Plain colored sheets also make for a more restful sleep, in my opinion. The same goes for towels. How many towels do we need, anyway? It's nice to have open space in cupboards and closets. When they are packed to the ceiling, I feel burdened and overwhelmed.

Before you put anything back on a shelf or into a drawer, get rid of what you don't use first. Here's how.

The One-Year Rule

If you haven't used the item in the last year, get rid of it. I used to think this one-year rule only applied to clothes—if you haven't worn it in a year, it's out the door. But now I know it applies to *every* kitchen gadget, medicine cabinet resident, tablecloth, pair of socks, towel, item to be mended, miscellaneous tool, home decor item, and exercise object. I've kept kids' items in a "to be mended" pile for so long my kids have outgrown them.

Unless you are the type who loves turning the lids of old frozen juice cans into, say, exotic jewelry or wheels for a toy, these things have to go. This rule very much applies to those on the simple living path. They start thinking they can save money if they hang on to anything and everything because these things can be turned into some other thing. They may get around to one in 100 such projects; more likely than not, they get around to none of these projects. What they do get around to is a visit to their therapists because they are so filled with guilt for not doing the projects that will save all that money.

Be serious with yourself. Either you're the type who loves transforming odd objects or you are not. I am not. I am more concerned with the level of junk that accumulates in my house. I discovered two potato peelers in a kitchen drawer. When was the last time I peeled potatoes in tandem?

The maybe-I'll-use-it-someday rationale is a seductive one. I think, "What if one peeler breaks? Then I'll have to waste money buying another one." Or "What if I have a dinner party one day and feature mashed potatoes? I'll want the help but no one will be able to help me." These are excellent rationales, I have to give myself credit. But here's what happens when I let the rationalizations rule. My drawer gets so thick with objects I literally can't even open it sometimes. This is no joke. I have had to yank and use unmentionable language on more than one occasion trying to open the drawer to find one peeler. The reason is not because I have two potato peelers. It's because I have two or three of everything, including the tops only to tea strainers. I save them because I just know I'll locate the other half someday. Everything in that drawer has its own heartbreaking story that convinces me it needs to stay. Sort of like stray cats or something.

You, like me, need to start somewhere. You also need to get ruthless. Can you imagine a kitchen drawer with only one layer of tools? Can you imagine seeing every tool when you open the drawer? Not having to rummage for anything? Can you imagine a whole house where you knew what was in there? You would actually know where to go look for everything and you wouldn't find surprises lurking on the backs of shelves and buried in drawers? Yogis in India can have their nirvana from higher consciousness. My nirvana is a drawer that I can open smoothly and see a few nicely arranged contents sitting all in one layer. And where I have in my house only what I actually use. This doesn't mean I don't have a few beautiful things that are there just for the ambience or memory, but those things are very carefully selected. Let's move on to the next rule to figure out what "ambience" paraphernalia to keep.

Layer-by-Layer or Imagine-a-Fire Rule

I learned about this from *Simple Living* reader Jody Haug. The layer-by-layer rule applies to things that you missed during your drawer and shelf attack. Often these are decorating items and knickknacks that are sitting on tables and elsewhere. You know what I'm talking about—all those items you bought that were guaranteed to impress your friends. The ones you hoped your friends would see in your house and say, "Wow, I didn't know you went to decorating school! You didn't? Gosh, I'd never believe it." Or "Gee, you have an artistic touch. I love the way you do your home."

Go through your house one layer at a time. The first time through you'll remove the really obvious items, like the fur toilet seat cover that you've had since 1968 when they were in style. Now that it is home to organisms smaller than the eye can see, it obviously should go first. Go through your entire house like this. The first time through you'll pick out things you've been considering dumping anyway: the easy stuff. Wait a few weeks or whatever seems comfortable and do it again. Now go through with a more critical eye. Take a hard look at each memento and ask yourself what it really means to you. Why is it there? How much effort is required to maintain it? Maintenance includes dusting. Remember, one item alone is no big deal; a houseful of these objects becomes a very big deal.

The other thing to do is take a broad, sweeping view of an entire room. What does it look like? Do you feel relaxed and peaceful, or anxious? I'm all for having some things around in a room. The Shaker look (absolutely the bare essentials and no more) is fine for Shakers. But there are extremes. While I like some things out on display, I don't like walking into a room where every shelf and windowsill is packed with knickknacks. I don't feel rested. I also don't feel rested if it's too spare. Then I feel like I shouldn't relax. Consider your own style and comfort level, but take note of how you feel in your room. Take note of how you feel in other people's rooms. This "big picture" will help you to decide what to toss and what to keep. If the big picture doesn't do it, the imaginary fire will. Imagine your house is on fire. What will you take? Does this help?

The Three-Pile Rule

Connie Cox and Chris Evatt came up with this rule in their book *Simply Organized!* One drawer at a time, pile things on the floor. Make three piles. One is the love and use pile. These are the things you feel good about and use often.

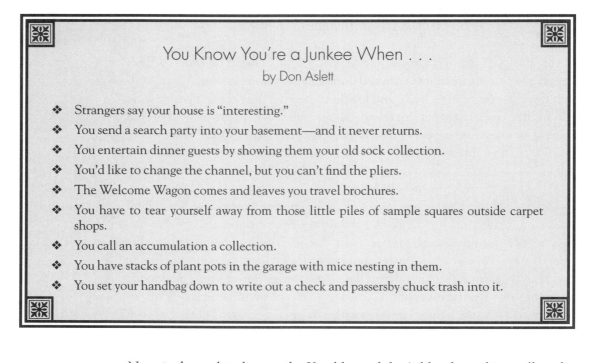

You Know You're a Junkee When . . .
by Don Aslett

❖ Strangers say your house is "interesting."

❖ You send a search party into your basement—and it never returns.

❖ You entertain dinner guests by showing them your old sock collection.

❖ You'd like to change the channel, but you can't find the pliers.

❖ The Welcome Wagon comes and leaves you travel brochures.

❖ You have to tear yourself away from those little piles of sample squares outside carpet shops.

❖ You call an accumulation a collection.

❖ You have stacks of plant pots in the garage with mice nesting in them.

❖ You set your handbag down to write out a check and passersby chuck trash into it.

Next is the ambivalence pile. You like and don't like these things all at the same time. You rarely use them, but guilt or pack-rat rationalizations cause you to hang on. Finally, the discard pile. You never use these things and are willing to get rid of them. Connie and Chris advise that parents make signs saying "I love it," "I don't know," and "Out" for their children to use when doing the same activity.

Now clean the area thoroughly. You'll feel much better returning your "loved" things to a clean place. Next, remove the discard pile and distribute accordingly: garbage, recycling, and charity. The stuff from the ambivalent pile goes into a taped and dated box in the basement. Keep reading.

The Taped-and-Dated-Box Rule

I read about this rule in Elaine St. James's book, *Simplify Your Life*. She heard it somewhere else. It's a great rule. This is for all of the items you intellectually know you neither need nor want, but for some emotional reason, you aren't ready to part with. Put them in a box and label the box for six months or one year hence. Mark the date on your calendar. If you haven't had reason to open the box during that time, call the charity truck to come to your house on that date. If this is too ruthless for you, try putting the stuff in a box in the garage without sealing or even closing it. You'll pass through every now and then and take a peek at the contents. Some you will feel you still can't live without the things in the box and some not. I'll admit, I've done the open-box-in-the-garage version of this rule and have taken out one or two things. But that's it.

If you were to walk through my house now, you'd see general mess from kids and living, but not a lot of knickknacks (except the five miniature Chinese tea sets, to name a few). There are newspapers around, other reading material, kids' art projects, kids' half-finished science projects, kids' half-finished miscellaneous projects, in-progress kids' games, and piles of papers indicating adult projects and plans. With all of this, I don't have much room for knickknacks.

Think hard about this rule. Recall the times you have been away from home for any length of time on vacation or whatever. Just how much time did you spend thinking about how you missed your "things"?

The Rental Storage Unit

The rental storage unit is the most outrageous outgrowth of clutteritis: actually paying money to store stuff you never even see. Often people rent these places thinking they'll just use them temporarily until they get around to sorting their stuff. As the months drag on and the items become less important, it becomes easier to keep writing out a monthly check than go to the storage unit and do something about it.

If you are one of these people, hasten to your storage unit and do a ruthless-beyond-ruthless purging. Do a purging like the world has never seen. What on earth could be in there that you actually need? If you need it so badly, why aren't you using it? If after your ruthless purging there is still an item remaining, then get rid of stuff in your house to make room for this thing. At least you won't be spending your hard-earned money to rent a place to keep it. You think it's not much money you are spending, maybe $55 a month. Take a seat and add up the total you've spent since you got the unit. Say you've had the unit one year: $55 \times 12 = \$660$. There is absolutely no reason on earth to have a rental storage unit unless you are moving overseas for a year, or it is somehow connected to your business and it makes money for you. Maybe you store and refinish old furniture in there and turn around and sell it. Only you know if this unit is making you money. If not, buy some beer and pizza for your friends and ask them to help you one Saturday. Often purging is much easier when you have friends with you. They're not attached to your stuff the way you are; as a result, they can be very ruthless.

Keeping Free of Clutter

New Items

When you are in a store and get the urge to buy some gadget or other, ask yourself what it really will mean over the long haul. You will need to do something with this item. You will need to put it somewhere, you will need to clean it, repair it, and so on. Get ruthless in the store. Better yet, don't buy the item until you go home for a while and think about it. Take a look at your shelves and cabinets and see if there really is room for one more thing. Do you want one more thing? Is there another, simpler, less-expensive way to do the job this gizmo is purported to do? Will something you already have do the job? Maybe not in the same sleek, slick way, but will it work? How many of these chop-o-matics have you purchased in the past that are now collecting you know what. If you can't remember, take a tour through your closets and cabinets.

Personal Inventory

Sit quietly for a while. Think about this. How much of your time is spent on the following: (a) Working to buy a houseful of stuff; (b) working to earn money to pay to insure your houseful of stuff; (c) cleaning, rearranging, storing, and maintaining your stuff?

You may need a pen and paper. How much do you earn per hour at your job? Say you earn $15 per hour. Take taxes and deductions out. Your take-home pay is maybe $12 per hour. Say you bought a veg-o-matic speed chopper for $24. You just spent two hours of your life buying this item. Say you "had-to-have" a Stairmaster for $500. Divide $12 into $500 to figure out how many hours it took you to buy the Stairmaster. I'll tell you. About 42 hours of your life. Do you like your job? (Just thought I'd ask.)

I learned about this way of looking at junk from Joe Dominguez and Vicki Robin, who wrote the book *Your Money or Your Life*. Most of us never consider that we are devoting the precious hours of our lives to the pursuit of not happiness but junk. Add a few more hours into your calculation for cleaning, insuring, maintaining, and repairing these items. Add up all the items together and get yourself a sum total. If you want to get serious about this, take one room at a time and add up what you think you spent on everything in there. Don't forget the little stuff because it adds up quickly. Do you still want to spend your life this way? If so, carry on. If not, think very hard the next time you are in a store. Probably there is another way to accomplish whatever the chop-o-matic promises to do.

While you are thinking in the chair, here is another question. Are you working in a job you'd rather leave but can't because you have indebted yourself to installment payments, payments on maintenance and repair, and on trying to impress others?

Before you get up, try a couple more thoughts on for size. Did you ever stop to think that our stuff creates errands? I've never heard anyone say they just loved to do errands. Never. Yet a big reason for errands is our stuff—in the buying, maintaining, repairing, or storing. (You have to buy or find storage compartments for your stuff—one more errand.) If you don't like errands, don't buy stuff.

The other thing to consider is this: psychic energy. You know how some people you are around seem to inspire you and fill you with good energy and others seem to sap your energy? Same goes with stuff. Is some of your clutter draining your psychic energy? Have you been hauling around some memento for years because you thought you should, but you really don't want it? This is a drain on energy. It might be a subtle drain, but it's a drain nevertheless. Add up all these little subtle drains and you have quite a flooding problem. Imagine how free you will feel if you don't have all of this stuff weighing on you like a ball and chain.

Equilibrium

"Equilibrium" means that things are balanced. It applies to clutter in a big way. Once you complete your search-and-destroy mission in your house, keep things in equilibrium by never bringing in more than you take out. Take your hall closet, for example. After you have simplified and organized it, do not, I repeat, do

We never buy more than we need

We never need more than we use

We never use more than

it takes to get by

Til we learn to need less.

—OLD CHINESE SAYING

not buy anything new in that department until you remove the same number of things as you plan to bring in. Why do you need another jacket or hat anyway? Think of each space (closets, shelves, drawers) as finite. Nothing else will fit in them. Period. If you take this rule to heart, it will stop you in your tracks before you go out and buy more stuff. This way you'll have to do some soul searching about why you need one more jacket, one more kitchen appliance, one more item of outdoor gear, one more tablecloth ("Oh, but this one is *so*

The Richness of Simplicity

by Ann Hyman

The buzzword for what I am doing is downsizing. I am moving from a large space to a small space, from a two-story house in one of the established neighborhoods of Jacksonville, Florida—quiet streets, tall old shade trees, high ceilings, storage space, kitchen and baths that sprawl spaciously—to a small beach cottage on Anastasia Island, near St. Augustine. We built the cottage more than 20 years ago as a weekend getaway. Skeptical friends say, "Don't do it. A weekend house is not a home. What about your things?"

Things.

Oh, yes. Things. They are the rub, sure enough.

When the time came that my mother should have moved out of the house where we all grew up, she wouldn't hear of it. She said she couldn't leave because of her things.

What would she do with her things? At the time I thought, Things! She's in bondage to her things. So now it's my turn, I reflect, and I'm in bondage to my things—and here's the funny part, some of them are the same things.

There is the dining room furniture, for instance.

After my mother died, when we were closing her house, I wondered whether I wanted the dining room furniture. Yes, my husband said . . .

My husband was right, of course. The table held too many memories, too many years of memories to let it go. And now I look at it again, almost 20 years later, and it is heavier still with memories . . .

So memory and history blend, turn to glue, stick our things fast to our affections or our sense of duty to the past, to our real or imagined obligations to our ancestors and origins. Eventually, sure enough, we're in bondage to our things.

I have a wonderful stoneware bowl that I found years ago in a junk shop in Hartsfield, Georgia. When I spied that heavy old bowl in the shop, grimy and fly-specked, I saw, in my imagination, a country woman beating biscuits in it. It didn't seem right for her bowl—something from the heart of her family—to be stacked with a lot of worthless gimcracks in the back of a junk shop.

I redeemed the bowl for a couple of dollars. A good soaking and a run through the dishwasher took care of the grime and fly specks. It's perfect for potato salad or holding a summer day's harvest when the tomato plants are at peak. As I write, it is full of ripe temple oranges, just the size of baseballs and almost the weight, their pebbly hides shining and pure gold.

When I look at that bowl, I know the season by its content—and I see me exploring a dark, cluttered shop near Hartsfield, Georgia, on a particular autumn afternoon . . . oh, yes, that bowl has a history underneath its pitted glaze.

Of course, bowls and the like aren't really a problem when it's time to downsize.

It's your father's rolltop and the piano that are the problem. It's Granny's bed and Auntie's good china, your mother's good china, and your mother-in-law's good china, makes four sets of good china that are a problem.

So, that's easy enough. Simplify.

Isn't that what we are always taught?

Right.

Simplify.

It's good advice, but those who teach us these things don't often have good china and rolltop desks that need to be sheltered until the kids outgrow sleeping on futons in far-away lofts. They have already simplified, chucked the good china, and we don't hear much of their kids. What we hear from them is advice—simplify.

Okay.

I do it.

I simplify.

I throw away. I give away. I pack away. I leave that downright historic dining room table and all those sets of good china for my son and his wife and child. We'll see how it works out, we say to one another. Nothing permanent. Nothing legal. Not yet. We'll try it for the winter.

We'll see.

It's spring.

The windows are open, and I sleep in the sound of the ocean, suspended in it, aware of it even when I am asleep. I think it is like the sound of breathing.

At night, when it's clear, I sit on the deck. I do this all through the winter, even when it is very cold, and I look up and realize that I haven't seen the stars in years, not really, and I haven't given the moon much more than a passing glance.

I have not looked up often enough, and when I have, there were trees and houses everywhere and all that city light leaking into the night. The lights are beginning to sneak up on the cottage too. I remember, 20 years ago, sitting on the deck in the middle of the Milky Way. No more. But what is there is there, and I am in it again.

The names of the constellations begin to come back to me, as if I am recalling the names of old friends at a college reunion. Orion, his belt pointing the way to Canis Major and Sirius, the brightest of all stars. Taurus. Gemini. Little Lepus. The sweet Pleiades.

One night my granddaughter, barely three, and I climb to the crow's nest of the deck. We are wrapped in an old quilt against the wind off the ocean, and our mission is to see the first star. We watch the sky for almost an hour after sundown, chatting comfortably about all we see and whatever else crosses our minds. Finally we spot the first faint twinkle through the thin curtain of buttermilk clouds between heaven and earth.

"There it is," I say.

"I want to say it," Jessica says.

"You say it," I agree.

"Twinkle, twinkle little star, how I wonder what you are, up above the world so high, like a diamond in the sky," she says.

"Awesome," I say.

I had not even known she knew the verse.

"Awesome," she agrees.

And it is. Awesome, all awesome, Granny and baby, earth and ocean, sky, poetry, ritual in that quiet hour waiting for the first star.

No one is more prone than I to depend on television specials and the science section of the news magazines to acquire information about the universe. It's easy to get too busy to look up. I depend on astronomers to tell me about the Big Bang and the galaxies, the black holes and the white dwarfs—I can't see them for myself. I must take someone else's word for what is there.

There is a scene in *Huckleberry Finn* in which Jim and Huck sit on the edge of their raft as it floats down the Mississippi and look up at the stars and wonder where they came from, how they got there, whether they're put there by purpose or whether they just happened. Huck believes they just happened. But Jim's got another idea. He says the moon laid 'em. And Huck reckons that might be true—he's seen frogs lay that many eggs in a sitting.

We marvel at the Aztec calendar and the precision of the rings at Stonehenge at measuring the movement of the planet. We scratch our heads and wonder how the ancients figured it all out without computers.

It's simple. They watched. They were just as smart as we are, and they looked up at the stars for years and years and years until they began to discern the patterns of the stars and planets and their movements.

The Aztecs and the people who built Stonehenge had their names for the stars, other names than the names I have begun to pass on by the simple act of pointing to that galactic cluster of stars on Taurus's shoulder and telling Jessica "Pleiades. The Seven Sisters."

"Pleiades," she repeats.

Awesome.

Downsizing? I think not. I have by no means moved from a large space to a small space. On the contrary.

beauuutiful . . ."), one more sweater, or one more tool. People who don't follow the equilibrium rule are the ones who rent storage units. They took in more than they took out and now they are paying for it in more ways than one.

Consider the Impact of Your Gifts

If you decide you don't like clutter, what makes you think you ought to give it to someone else as a gift? Unless the person specifically asks for a certain item of clutter and you can't talk her or him out of it, don't buy gadgets and gizmos for gifts. Often these turn into the biggest clutter guilt-producers of all—we all have doilies, doodads, and dealies that were given to us by aunt this and uncle that, and we can't part with them because of the psychic attachment. We don't want them, don't use them, but can't dump them either. When you give a gift of clutter, you are giving a gift of guilt. Better to buy something the person absolutely needs or some kind of service or entertainment gift. You can give gift certificates to the movies, to a restaurant, to a hotel for a fun night away, to a sporting event or a concert, or even make a payment toward a big trip the person may be planning. If you want something less expensive and more personal, give a gift of your time. Offer to cook dinner for someone, offer to take a child rollerblading or bicycle riding, offer to clean someone's garage, mow a lawn, weed a garden, repair a broken item, on and on. A group of you can go in on one service gift. This past holiday season my brother and my parents joined with me to buy dog training lessons for my sister's new dog. Why did she need three guaranteed-for-the-back-of-the-closet gizmos from us? Answer: She didn't. My brother and sister did the same for my birthday. My old bathrobe was ready to head south, so they joined together and bought me a new one. This is something I can really use and was very thankful for.

Think Twice About Garage Sales

Holy mackerel. I can hear them railing now. This is a book about simple living and she's telling us *not* to go to garage sales? I realize I am stepping on very holy ground, but I will proceed anyway. I think of garage sales, thrift stores, flea markets, and the rest as I think of credit cards. If you are disciplined, they can be terrific. If you are not, they can be a huge problem. Here is the thing about garage sales. The prices are usually incredibly low. You can get gadgets and gizmos for practically nothing. Very tempting. Only one thing wrong with this picture: Unless you go to garage sales with a firm shopping list of exactly what you are looking for and stick to that list, you almost always come home with armfuls of stuff that will very shortly turn into sale items on your own garage sale table. How can you pass up a chop-o-matic for $3? Remember the problem? The chop-o-matic will clutter your house. It alone is not the problem. The problem is all of the chop-o-matic's cousins, aunts, uncles, friends, and neighbors. Chop-o-matics never live alone. Ever.

The simple living theory is not limited to running around getting good deals. It is also about owning less so you have less to worry about and you can have the time and freedom to do other things besides fool with your things. A chop-o-matic requires fooling with, whether you bought it for $3 or $24.99.

Accept Some Mess

I probably can't say it too many times so I'll repeat it: Simple living is not about being perfect, and it is not about living in deprivation. Since it isn't about being perfect, accept that your house probably always will have its share of mess. A certain amount of mess says that real people live there and they have real interests. When you have children I hope you have some mess. A few science projects lying around are an indication that creative little minds are at work. You may not see these things in home decorating magazines, but they are what real life is about. You also might think about this: The less useless clutter you buy for yourself, the more money you will have left over to spend on science projects and stimulating things for yourself and your kids. Don Aslett shared this sad vignette of clutteritis gone bad in *Clutter's Last Stand:*

> Don't be like the father who had four antique guns—not one-of-a-kind collector's items, but respectable pieces worth about $5,000 each. When his daughter reached college age, the family was pinched for cash and could see no way to pay $5,000 per year to see their vibrant and musically talented daughter fulfill her education and her dream. She never did, and the father kept those old guns around in a rack until he died. Then the kids divided them up, sold them, bought cars and couches, and partied. His daughter could have been a living inspiration for all his posterity; his guns ended up valueless. I know people who buy silver saddles and snowmobiles before putting braces on their children's crooked teeth. Fascination with trinkets passes, but a self-conscious child is cheated for fifty years.

The nice thing about getting rid of excess clutter is that now you will have the room for signs of real life. A plastic or porcelain figurine in a corner is not life in action in the same way that newspapers and projects are.

As for deprivation, simple living is not about living in some austere, totally functional place. I'll always have art on the walls, pictures of people here and there, and flowers on the table. The important thing is to know when enough is enough. Things stand out much better when you have fewer of them.

Organize What Is Left

Once you feel as if you are fairly close to having what you need in your house, being organized makes your life simpler. Here is how:

Rule 1

Put like things together. Remember the hall closet scenario I painted awhile back in this chapter? Hats with hats. Boots with boots. Remember, you take everything out of the closet or drawer and put it on the floor or counter. Put like with like. Get yourself some free boxes and put them on your shelf for all the hats, for example. If your shelf is open to public view, you may want to invest in or decorate a little nicer box. The point is not to go out and spend a fortune buying the perfect storage item but to create a reasonable area that will corral like with like. Since hats tend to fall off shelves and get lost or disorganized, they are a perfect candidate for a box. Same with gloves.

The like-with-like rule applies literally to every single area of your house. When you store like with like, you can find your stuff. All camping equipment, for example, should be in one big box. Then, when you are ready to go camping, you don't need to run around the house in a frenzy trying to find the pocket knife and tin cup. All travel paraphernalia should be in a box: travel alarm, money belt, and so on. I put these on a shelf next to my maps and travel books. You can put them in any closet you like so long as they are all together.

When you organize your clothes closet, yes, you should put shirts together and sweaters together. But it's hoped that you have far fewer of them than in my earlier example. Once I switched to this method in my closet, my dressing time became much shorter. I know exactly what I have.

In your kitchen, group not only your tools but food as well. All knives together and all measuring utensils together; also, all soup cans together, all cereal together, all tomato sauce together. Now you'll know at a quick glance what you have when you are heading to the store. You won't come home with the sixth can of tomato sauce because you didn't think you had any. Also if you regularly pack lunches, put all the lunch paraphernalia together. I have a box filled with Tupperware sandwich containers and juice bottles. This sits right next to the lunch boxes.

You might take inventory of the number of plates, silverware, and glasses you have in your kitchen. If you are a household of three, for example, why do you have servings for 16 in your kitchen? Yes, yes, I know all about dinner parties. I put my extra plates, cups, and silverware in a separate place. This way my frequently used kitchen cabinets aren't cluttered with things I use infrequently. Having fewer dishes and cups at my handy disposal also keeps me on top of dishwashing. Most of us aren't going to do this, but for illustration, consider the more extreme version: What if each person in your family had one cup, one plate, one bowl, one fork, one spoon, and one knife? Period. You would never have dirty dishes piling up. People would have to wash their bowl if they wanted to use it again. Now what do they do? Grab another one off the shelf, and another, and another, and soon you have a sink or dishwasher full of dirty dishes. I've thought about the one-bowl, one-plate method, but in the meantime, fewer plates and fewer bowls are a good step in the right direction.

You also should put the most frequently used items within reach and less frequently used items higher up. Think about spices. This sounds incredibly picky, but when I had my spices arranged in alphabetical order, I found things in record time. Then they got out of order, and I had to paw, poke, and sort to find anything. In general, when things are orderly, your life becomes easier because you spend less time fretting over and digging for the item you need.

In my basement, I keep all of my gift items together in a box and on adjoining shelves. I always reuse wrap and bows so this kind of storage is useful to me. In the same area, I keep all other seasonal decorations together. All the Easter table decorations are in a bag, and the same goes for other holiday paraphernalia. I know exactly where to go to find these things at the proper time. I have no need to go out and spend money buying new decorations each year.

Your basement is also a good place to keep old tax records. They should be in covered, same-size banker's boxes, and each should be labeled with the tax year. Before you rush out and buy banker's boxes at the store, stop in at neighborhood print shops first. They get reams and reams of paper delivered in these boxes nearly every day and are happy to find a home for them. So what if the boxes aren't perfectly white? Tape a piece of paper over them for your label. You can use these boxes to store your sewing, mending, and everything else you can think of. They can be your travel box, miscellaneous sporting goods box, Easter box, and camping box. They are all of uniform size with lids and are absolutely free. Otherwise you'll spend a small fortune at some specialty storage or department store for essentially the same thing in different materials.

Another organizing trick I use that has been a superb help is my household out basket. Before this I had outgoing mail somewhere, library books somewhere else, borrowed items elsewhere—and you get the picture. A mess. Now everything that is to leave the house, no matter where, goes in the out basket. It is right next to the front door and very easy to see on my way out the door. Once again, like is with like. In this case everything that goes out of the house is alike.

Rule 2

Use all spaces well. Use those plastic hanging shoe holders and hang them on the inside of a door. Store all kinds of things other than shoes in them. Think about gloves, scarves, socks, folding umbrellas, and so on.

Rule 3

As you go through your house organizing, keep a shopping list for things you'll need to get organized. For instance, those plastic shoe holders and other kinds of storage compartments are the perfect thing to find at a garage sale.

Rule 4

Label your boxes. It makes for a neater-looking and more orderly house if you put all of your stored items in same size banker's boxes with lids. Stack them on shelves and label the side you see: "Camping," "Travel," "Sewing," and so on. Think twice before stacking these boxes two deep where you can't see the label on the box. If you need to double stack, you probably have too much stuff, and it's time for another ruthless tour through your house.

Rule 5

Miscellaneous items. Here's a phone message idea. Instead of writing on the backs of envelopes and bits of paper lying around when you need to take a message, get a small notebook and keep it by the phone. If you have more than one phone, put a notebook by each phone. This way you never lose messages. You also can get a clipboard and clip to the board a pile of the plain back side of recycled paper. Keep it by the phone in the same way. The point is to keep your phone message papers together.

Simple Living in Nepal

Helen Sherpa is a New Zealand native who met her Nepali husband while both were studying in New Zealand. They now have three young children and live in Kathmandu, Nepal. They have also lived in the United States.

"In Nepal," Helen says, "we have need-based shopping. It never occurs to people to buy products they don't need because there is no advertising, no sales, no junk mail, and no credit cards. Also in Nepal, because people walk to the neighborhood store, they buy only what they can carry home, and then make do.

"In the United States we are constantly being bombarded with things we never thought we needed, and we all wind up getting drawn into this whole buy-buy sort of thing."

Helen believes that despite the bombardment, we do have choices in America. In order to make our lives ultimately simpler and richer in nonmonetary ways, we need to exercise those choices every day.

Instead of buying Heinz catsup and contributing to that company president's salary of $75 million a year (see *Time* magazine, May 4, 1992), we can buy a local brand or make our own. Instead of contributing to the Reebok Shoe Corporation president's annual salary of $2 million a year, we can choose to bring our old sneakers to the neighborhood shoe repair shop.

By doing this, we not only save ourselves from buying a second pair of $100 designer sneakers, but we're putting our hard-earned money into the pockets of someone who could use the money and who we can get to know. Since we haven't spent as much, we don't need to work as much.

We can also shop at cooperatives, where we can, as part owner, have a say in how the business is run. Instead of putting the profits into one pocket at the top, the money can be circulated back into the community.

Helen Sherpa compares life in the United States and Nepal.

"I think we have to make sacrifices," Helen says. "My mother always supported the local vegetable market rather than the big supermarket because she wanted to see that family make a living.

"The question is whether you're saving money by shopping at a large store so you can buy your daughter a fifth Barbie doll," she says. "Most people aren't saving money for survival things."

Helen believes these choices reflect social justice issues: where we spend our money, whom we employ, whether we get rich at someone else's expense, or whether we make a modest income.

There is also an ecological issue that is equated with loss of connection. In Nepal, Helen says, you don't see waste because people use things until the life of that item is over and then they find other uses for it. They don't just discard items the way Westerners do, she says.

"For example, you have a tailor repair your garment. By doing this, you are generating a job for the tailor and you're not wasting resources and polluting the environment. In the West, we give our things to charity . . . out of sight, out of mind, and as result we generate huge quantities of waste."

Helen believes credit unions and building societies are two more ways to retain power over our lives and money. In a credit union, the profits don't all go to a few at the top but are used to keep the credit union functioning. And in New Zealand, people use building societies, which operate essentially the same way. In Nepal, families pool their money and labor to build modest housing.

"People in America are so surprised to see that people in other cultures like Nepal are monetarily poor yet happy. They can't imagine how these people could be happy since they equate happiness with money," Helen says.

"We know that a millionaire's health problems and marital problems don't go away just because that person has a million dollars, yet we keep thinking money is the answer. We need to look for happiness in life from nonmaterial things . . . not what we have or can afford, but be happy wherever we fall on the economic spectrum, from the most poverty-stricken farmer in Nepal to the wealthiest person in America."

❖ ❖ ❖ ❖ ❖ ❖ ❖ ❖ ❖ ❖ ❖ ❖ ❖ ❖

Resources

Get your name off catalog and junk mail lists by writing to: Mail Preference Service, Direct Mail Marketing Association, P.O. Box 9008, Farmingdale, NY 11735-9008.

Clutter Free by Don Aslett (Pocatello, ID: Marsh Creek Press, 1995)
Helpful hints on uncluttering the clutter from the battle lines of real life as well as testimonials from those who have improved their junk-infested environments. Discusses how to tell the difference between junk and nonjunk and what rules to apply when shopping and then storing the goods bought.

Clutter Control by Jeff Campbell (New York: Dell, 1992)
Methods for keeping a house clean and organized and reducing unnecessary time-eating events to a minimum, such as buying stamps in bulk rather than going back to the post office each time to buy stamps. Discussion also on "psychology" of clutter.

Don't Be a Slave to Housework by Pam McClellan (Cincinnati, OH: Betterway Books, 1995)
Housekeeping doesn't have to be the "housemother's" role but can include the entire family—kids and spouses can help. Author offers ways to turn cleaning and chores into a fun, family activity that also can teach important lessons of cooperation and pride in one's living space. Checklists included.

Guide to Eliminating Clutter from Your Life compiled by Susan Wright (New York: Carol Publishing Group, 1991)
Uses specific questions to tackle the mind-set behind clutter and messy disorganization. Whether home or business, the cluttered existence can invade and infect one's life. Organizing and getting rid of unused junk is a way to open up one's life to more meaningful activity. Includes summaries to offer helpful reminders.

How to Avoid Housework by Paula Jhung (New York: Simon & Schuster, 1995)
Focusing on the house as the center of the cluttered world, Jhung uses the concept of "antihousework" to keep the modern home clean and spiffy. Discusses ways to clean up one's home for unexpected visitors, coping with pets in the house, and what to do about messy plants.

Make Your House Do the Housework by Don Aslett and Laura Aslett Simons (Cincinnati, OH: Betterway Books, 1995)
Hints on using thoughtfulness in building the house to cut down on cleaning, such as using fewer tiles in the bathroom or building cabinets that reach the ceiling rather than shorter ones that collect dust. Shows how better placement of furniture can help cut down on maintenance.

Not for Packrats Only by Don Aslett (New York: Penguin Books, 1991)
Using cartoons, drawings, and hilarity, Aslett shows the clutter monster that lives in every home and steps to keep him at bay, including developing a cold heart for clutter hot spots, the best time and place to start cleaning, dealing with clutter codependents, and how to stay on the dejunked bandwagon permanently.

The Non-Toxic Home by Debra Lynn Dadd (Los Angeles: Jeremy P. Tarcher, 1986)
Covers everything you've ever wanted to know about cleaning and maintaining your home without chemicals. Surprisingly enough, the book says, making a nontoxic home for your family is less expensive than living with the chemicals that now surround you.

Organize Your Family by Ronni Eisenberg with Kate Kelly (New York: Hyperion, 1993)
Compendium of information on making family life less hectic and more enjoyable. Discusses specific steps, such as creating a family calendar of events and how to use it, practical tips on holiday planning, and mastering space management for ease of storage and use.

Organize Your Home by Ronni Eisenberg with Kate Kelly (New York: Hyperion, 1994)
Establishing rules for keeping house, garage, and basement neat and spiffy. Suggestions for planning a grocery list, when to do the laundry, setting up a household filing system, organizing meals, and creating a household notebook to keep track of lists.

Organize Your Office by Ronni Eisenberg with Kate Kelly (New York: Hyperion, 1994)
Techniques for making office life smoother and more efficient. Offers suggestions on setting up a home office, organizing a briefcase, knowing how to avoid interruptions, and comparing the benefits of a paper versus electronic calendar. Also tips on filing and learning how and when to delegate.

CLUTTER

13
Gardening

There is life in the ground;
it goes into the seed;
and also, when it is stirred up,
goes into the person who stirs it.

—CHARLES DUDLEY WARNER

Essayist and naturalist John Burroughs (1837–1921) said very well why so many people like to get their hands in the dirt:

> Many persons know the luxury of a skin bath—a plunge in the pool or the wave unhampered by clothing. That is the simple life—direct and immediate contact with things, life with the false trappings torn away. To see the fire that warms you, or better yet, to cut the wood that feeds the fire that warms you; to see a spring where the water bubbles up that slakes your thirst, and to dip your pail into it . . . to be in direct and personal contact with the sources of your material life . . . to find the universal elements enough . . . to be thrilled by the stars and night, to be elated over a bird's nest or over a wild flower in Spring—these are some of the rewards of a simple life.

Shallow Pockets, Deep Soil

For those who love it, gardening is a source of passion and even spiritual nourishment. It offers a way to connect with the natural cycle of life—something many of us have insulated ourselves from as we work and live inside climate-controlled buildings day in and day out, working with high-tech machines and shuffling papers.

Even for those who don't love to garden, there is nothing like a patch of growing green life to awaken the senses and spirit. Either way, for those who love to garden and those who don't, there are ways to create beautiful landscapes or a yard full of fresh vegetables by spending less money and less time. With a little ingenuity, you can have a terrific yard for practically nothing. And for those, like me, who think of gardening as another room to clean, there are ways to have an attractive landscape that will require very little of your time.

Create a Beautiful Garden for Less

Clay Antineau loves to garden and loves to save time and money. He has created a beautiful, lush, sprawling garden for almost no money by salvaging nearly everything, including plants. At last count, he said he has 650 named plants, most of which he got for free.

Clay is a trained horticulturist with a bachelor's of science degree in horticulture; he's also got a master's and is a Ph.D. candidate in botany and horticulture. He got his salvaging experience on his first job as a nursery manager. "I became exposed to the vast waste produced by nurseries," he says. "The nurseries throw away hundreds of plants either because they aren't in bloom or they're wilted, stressed, or diseased. The nurseries don't want to sell these plants because they can't have a reputation of selling less than prime materials. As I began looking at other nurseries, I was dismayed by the amount of waste that I saw."

Some nurseries simply throw the plants into Dumpsters, others throw them onto compost heaps, and a few sell them at reduced prices. Clay has gotten plants by all three methods. It is not illegal to take items from Dumpsters unless posted. One year he found 400 primroses that had been thrown away. They were in perfect condition except that they had gone past the point of flowering. Those with flowers sold for 90 cents a pot. He salvaged over 100 of them, using some in his garden and giving others to neighbors. Then he decided to conduct an experiment to assess the value of discarded plants. He returned to the same store during the peak nursery season of March through July. Once a week he looked in the Dumpster and scrounged only what he could use in his garden. Then he checked the prices in the store. He netted four labeled clematis varieties (while some plants are thrown away simply because they have lost their label, for some reason these perfectly good plants were tossed with their labels), 200 tomato plants (which ultimately fed half the neighborhood), 42 deciduous shrubs in containers, 20 labeled rose hybrids that were out of flower, gladiolus corms, seed packets (end of season), houseplants, orchids, cactus plants, perfectly good dwarf conifers, annuals, ornamentals, all the vegetable starts he could want (some were too leggy, some had only five of six plants in the flat, some were overstocked), and hanging fuchsias that were perfectly good and in full flower. He also found a sprinkler, B-12 fertilizer, and 20 pounds of lawn fertilizer that had rips in the bags. Total retail value: $1,200.

"That was the start of my nursery salvaging," he says.

For those unwilling to look in Dumpsters, do not despair. You can still get throw-away plants for nothing or nearly nothing by getting to know your local nursery managers. Clay says literally all nurseries have throw-away plants. A few will refuse to give or sell them to you, but most will be happy to recoup at least a little of their loss. Always go to the manager or assistant manager and ask if they will sell or give you these plants. If you have to pay for them, you'll be able to bargain more effectively if you offer to buy a large quantity, since nurseries generally buy their plants in bulk. Clay says he always gets discounts of 80 to 90 percent. He has been able to revive all of the plants he has gotten this way. "All they need is to be put into the ground," he says.

Another way he saves money is buying gardening supplies and plants at the end of the season. The best time to buy equipment and fertilizer is right before the holiday season starts. The stores want to make room for their Christmas trees and sell garden supplies at substantial price reductions. Clay stocks up on fertilizer and other materials during this period. "There is never any reason to pay retail prices for gardening supplies," he says.

One item Clay pays full but low price for is compost. He believes composting is an essential part of creating a healthy, low-maintenance garden. He discovered a compost program through his city that sells excellent, sterile compost and has about six yards delivered to his house once a year. Check your city Solid Waste Utility to find out whether it sponsors such a program. Clay mixes 50 percent compost with 50 percent shredded bark. He says he spends most of his gardening effort spreading this mixture into his beds once a year during the winter months between December and March. The rest of the year, he says, his yard requires very little effort because sterile compost doesn't contain weeds. Since he replenishes it once a year, his weeds are kept to a minimum.

Clay Antieau's 11-Point Gardening Philosophy

1. **Take care of your soil.** Organic matter is essential. Add it every year. And don't forget to mulch. This is an excellent method to reduce weeds. Good, sterile compost is the one item that Clay pays low but full price for. He needs more compost than he can make.

2. **Plan your garden in zones.** For example, work around your water source. Plant all of your most water-needy plants nearest your spigot. Put them all together so you can water them at once with the least amount of effort.

3. **Eliminate or minimize turf.** Lawns are the biggest culprit in soaking up pesticides and water. If you want to retain a lawn, switch to a more drought-tolerant variety.

4. **Be informed about your plants.** Know the limiting factors of your site and plants. Which plants are susceptible to disease and insects, which are adaptable to local soils and weather conditions? Find out before you get any plants.

5. **Harvest your water.** There are simple ways to catch rainfall. Clay hooked up a barrel to a downspout from his roof to get about 100 gallons of water a year. For those in dry climates, he recommends using cisterns that capture all of the water on a roof.

6. **Don't waste space.** The tighter you pack your plants, the harder it is for weeds to grow.

7. **Be ruthless.** Pull out plants that don't do well or take too much time, attention, or money.

8. **Be tolerant.** Sometimes a plant that attracts a few pests is worth keeping because its benefits outweigh the effort required to get rid of the pests. "Don't get hung up on having everything just perfect," he says. "A few weeds are okay."

9. **Be frugal, be bold, scrounge, beg, trade, barter, salvage, reuse, and recycle everything.** Anything you can use in your garden can be found somewhere either free or at a greatly reduced cost.

10. **Be creative and innovative.** Break barriers. Gardening is a medium for your personal expression. Do what you feel good with, not necessarily what you think you should do.

Clay has refined his ideas to such an extent that he teaches others how to follow suit. "If you're going to garden, why not do it with the least effort and least cost?" he says. "I want the most beautiful garden I can obtain with the least effort, cost, and amount of resources, like fertilizer, pesticides, water, and electricity. I also want a garden that produces lots of food and provides tremendous beauty."

Sally and Mark Ditzler also love to garden and save money in the process. They bought an older house that had very little landscaping. Both the front and back yards were approximately 40 by 30 feet each. Most of the yard was grass. They decided to hire a designer to get ideas on what to do with their yard. "We told her we had $500 for plants and her design time," Sally says. "She was able to create a plan that fit within that budget." Sally and Mark salvaged some of the plants and equipment and did the labor themselves.

Sally works for a garden store and gets their throw-away plants for free. They also trade plants with neighbors and friends. They pay nothing for manure because they offered to haul it themselves from a nearby horse farm. "We have a little Datsun truck that works very hard," Sally says. "When we first started we hauled 20 truckloads ourselves. It took over a year to gradually fill everything in. People need to remember that they don't need to do everything all at once. Gardening is a process."

The couple built a greenhouse for almost nothing but their labor. The entire structure is built from recycled materials, except the cement foundation. Someone's neighbors had extra gravel to dispose of, so the Ditzlers used it for the floor. They got old single-pane windows from a house that was being remodeled. Those became the roof and windows. The wood was from another old house that had been torn down. They built a potting bench from an old floor out of a demolished building. Instead of paying top dollar at a greenhouse supply for tubs for the plants, Mark bought inexpensive restaurant "bus tubs" (used for busing tables) from a restaurant supply company and drilled holes in the bottom. They salvaged 40 black, five-gallon buckets from a printing company that used the buckets to store ink. Mark drilled holes in the bottoms of the buckets and the Ditzlers use them as solar collectors to start plants, such as tomatoes. They built a grape arbor with salvaged lumber and a pathway from salvaged bricks that came from an old school that was being torn down.

"People often ask us how we find all of this stuff," Sally says. "It's just a matter of keeping your eyes open. Wherever we go, we keep an eye out for discarded things we could use. Even when Mark goes for a swim in the lake, if he sees a two-by-four floating by, he'll scrounge it. We happened to be driving by an old school that was being torn down so we asked the construction supervisor if we could take some bricks. You need to be always looking."

The Ditzlers have used every square inch of their yard for garden space, except for a small lawn ("It's a place for your eyes and feet to rest," says Sally) and a spot for a swing set for their two girls. They use their front yard for ornamentals and the back for vegetables. This year they also got a rabbit. His droppings will be next year's compost amendment.

Sally also plans to earn money from her hobby. She and a friend started a small organic nursery. They've scrounged most of the equipment they need, such as plant pots. "We put the word out and all of a sudden we had thousands of little pots," she says. They'll keep the business small and sell only what they like to grow. "We don't want to be married to our business. We simply want to take a hobby and turn it into a small industry."

Low-Cost Landscape Design

If you don't have a clue what plants go where, or if you have a clue but would like a little help in the design department, you don't need to spend a fortune hiring a landscape design company for this job. You can offer your garden as a high school, voc-tech, or college horticulture project, or pay a design student. These people will be happy to have your work to show in their portfolio. Gil Arter spent $100 (in 1984) having his yard designed by posting a notice at the

Gil Arter in the garden he created with a landscape design student.

Student Union Building at a local university that has a landscape design department. His notice asked for a student who could do a site plan for a low-maintenance yard.

He found a capable student who was a senior in landscape design. They agreed on the price, and one week later Gil had a complete plan for his 3,100-square-foot yard. "My yard was pretty bare: basic grass and a few nondescript shrubs. Ivy on the side and backyard was so thick it was creeping into the house," says Gil. The student did soil tests, sun and shade planning, and created a design with an arbor across the front of the house and medium-low maintenance plants to replace much of the grass. It took Gil three years to begin work on the plan and another three to complete it. He did all of the fence building and terracing himself and bought materials and plants as the money came in. "I would buy a few plants in the spring and a few in the fall," he says. "Some survived and some didn't." He spent a total of about $5,000 to purchase all materials, including those for a large deck in the backyard and two new entry doors for the house.

Gil also found that the student's plan helped jump-start him to come up with other creative possibilities. Today his house sits amid a serene Japanese-style garden. The entrance is framed by a low fence that offers both privacy and openness to the neighborhood. The front yard includes a fountain that Gil built and lots of low-water grasses. The backyard deck holds a hot tub, and the side yard near the kitchen is filled with herbs.

Now Gil spends approximately four hours a month maintaining his yard. "It's always evolving," he says. "I have a friend who is an avid gardener. She says gardening is about moving things around . . . you dig them up and put them someplace else."

Low-Maintenance Gardening

Lazy People's Gardening

Whether they enjoy digging in the garden or not, most people like to have pleasant surroundings. Often what turns many people away from gardening is the perceived notion that gardens take too much time and energy. I know about this problem. The last thing I want to spend my spare time doing is pulling weed after weed. When you're not passionate about installing and moving little plants around, gardening simply becomes a chore of relentless weeding. I have since discovered there is a lot between the kind of yard that is so pathetic that landscape services leave their cards on the doorstep (my true story) and a beautiful, high-maintenance garden paradise. Here are a few ideas.

Gail Smith is one of these people who wants a decent-looking environment but isn't passionate about gardening. After she and her husband, Craig Wyss, bought a house with an acre of land, Gail set to work coming up with a plan that would make the yard look nice but not stress the family. She calls the plan "Lazy People's Gardening." There are five points to this plan:

Native landscapes. Use native plants in your landscape. If you live in the desert, get rocks and succulents that grow by themselves in the wild. If you live in the Pacific Northwest, use what you find in the woods. If you aren't sure what really grows wild, go to the wilderness and find out. (Make sure the wilderness you visit has the same climate as your yard.) If these plants make it out in the middle of nowhere with nobody tending them, they have a good chance in your yard.

Neglected yards. Drive around your area and look for half-neglected yards. Take note of the plants that are thriving. You can assume they will thrive under your neglect too. Look at a number of neglected yards in all variety of sun, shade, and soil conditions. Record your discoveries in a notebook. You will see patterns of common plants. Those are the ones you want.

Invasive plants. Gail went to a nursery and asked which plants were so hardy they were classified as invasive. She figured these too would thrive under her neglect. She also figured they would probably grow normally, not invasively, in her yard because she would pay absolutely no attention to them. She says her theory was correct.

What lives lives, what doesn't, doesn't. Plant your choices in your yard and ignore them. Don't water. The ones that make it are the ones you go out and get more of. The ones that don't obviously need more care than you are willing to give. "We were willing to lose things in order to not have to baby them," Gail says.

Shade. The more shade in your yard, the fewer weeds you'll have. Weeds need sunlight to thrive. One good-size tree or built-in awning arrangement will keep weeds at bay.

It took seven to eight years to get Gail's yard stabilized to the point where she and her husband aren't replacing plants that died. They used pesticides in the beginning stages of their landscaping but soon realized that they didn't want to continue. Five years of never watering took care of the problem. The only time they water is when they first install a plant and when they fertilize the lawn two times a year. As a consequence, the family doesn't have large water or plant bills. They weed twice in the spring for two to three hours each time. Gail says it's important for lazy gardeners to pull out the weeds before they go to seed and multiply. Any weeds that come in during the fall they leave until the following spring.

Rock Gardens

You can create a beautiful, Zen-style garden that will require very little water and very little maintenance. Nicholas Kirstin and his father own a gallery that specializes in Asian art. They borrowed their landscape ideas from Asia and created a Zen garden in the back of the gallery. They turned their parking lot into a beautiful, serene garden.

"The theory of Zen gardens is that the space around plants is as important as the plants," Nicholas says. "That's why there are lots of rocks and sand in Zen gardens."

Zen is a sect of Buddhism. At the core is a belief that everything in the world is connected and interrelated and that we should pay respect to all living things. Zen gardens are purposefully spare, in order that those entering can notice the things in it and develop a deeper relationship with the few things that are there. The gardens create a kind of enhanced condition so you might be able to know a rock or tree in a more intimate way. The point of a Zen garden is to get rid of most of the plants and substitute sand, rock, and gravel.

Richard Daidnsai Kirstin relaxes in his Zen garden.

"Say you have a beautiful tree," Nicholas says. "If you put nothing else around it, you really notice the tree. In painting, you call this negative space. You take away the objects around the tree and the space calls you to notice."

While there are no hard and fast rules to creating a Zen garden, a standard practice is to first get rid of all the grass. Remember that you are erasing rather than adding. Once you have a clear pallet, take a look at the space. Place a tree here, a rock there, and stand back until it feels right to you. There are lots of books available on designing Zen gardens, but Nicholas said he preferred to do it himself, using his intuition. "You look at the space and if it looks right to you, leave it. If not, try something else."

Zen gardens can be less expensive and require less maintenance. Still, Nicholas says you need to maintain what you have. Get to know each object in your garden. Spend time with these things. Go out and pour a little water over your rock, or sit on it. Nurture what plants you do have. "Each item becomes important, as a sacred object," he says. "It simplifies your garden because by having less to deal with, each object can get more of your attention. If you have a house full of furniture, it is difficult to appreciate what you have, versus a room with three pieces of furniture. You'll see those three pieces each day and notice them."

In Asia, Zen gardens are used to create environments that enhance people's potential for realizing their relationship to nature. They become conducive to introspection. Nicholas says: "I think of Zen gardens as the difference between meditating in a very quiet room versus trying to meditate in a downtown office building with ringing phones and noise."

Deck It

Avoid the garden problem by making your yard a deck. Check the yellow pages for wood recycling centers in your area to pick up low-cost lumber.

If you decide to hire a company to build a deck, retaining wall, or help with landscape design, ask if it would be willing to do the work for a reduced fee if you keep a sign in your yard advertising the company for a certain amount of time.

Water

There is no question that we all ought to be conserving water. Whether you conserve for global or financial reasons, it is a good idea to use as little as possible. But most gardens need at least some water. How can you combine the need for conservation and the need for beauty? First, call your city water department for information on water conservation strategies in your area. It may have materials on low-water plants that grow well in your climate. In the meantime, here are a few smart watering tips:

1. Probe the soil with a tool or your finger to see if it's moist or dry. If the soil is moist throughout the root zone, you may not need to water.
2. Water early in the morning or late in the evening to reduce losses through evaporation.
3. Don't water when it rains if the soil in the root zone is moist due to the rain.
4. Avoid runoff and puddling by watering slowly and at spaced intervals. Doing so allows the lawn and garden to absorb water.
5. Water the lawn separately from other plants, which often need less frequent watering.

Three other methods of conserving water include gray water, rain barrels, and low-water landscaping.

Gray water. This is the ultimate in water recycling. You use water from your shower, bathroom and kitchen sinks, bathtub, dishwasher, and laundry room and pour it on your plants. For drought-stricken areas, gray water can be a valuable alternative source of irrigation water for the home landscape. Before you start putting buckets under your shower and plumbing your dishwasher to empty into an outside bin, find out if gray water use is legal in your area. It isn't in some cities. If it is legal, get a book that explains how to modify your plumbing system to adapt to a gray water system.

Rain barrels. Remember the rain barrels our grandparents used for extra water? They're back in style. You can make them very inexpensively. Get one to three 33-gallon cans with lids, PVC pipe to link them and the downspout from the roof, adhesive to seal the cans, a faucet and its fittings, and enough lumber for a stand to hold the cans. The volume of water captured through a downspout from your roof depends on two factors: how much it rains and the size of your roof. The bigger the roof, the more water is collected.

Rain barrels are legal in most states. To be sure, you should call your local water department. You need to cover the barrels with fine-mesh screen or use tight-fitting lids so mosquitoes and their friends can't get in and use the water for a breeding spot. They also need to be secure around young children. Don't put them near stairs where kids could climb up and fall in.

Low-water landscaping. Howard Stenn specializes in helping people create low-water gardens. He devised the following six-step program.

1. Improve your soil. This is one of the major tricks to succeeding and keeping the maintenance down. Good soil allows the water to permeate better and allows the roots to spread out so they can get more water. It also makes your plants healthier so you don't need to spend as much time maintaining them or spraying for disease. The best way to improve the soil is through composting.
2. Select your plants. Get the right plants for the situation. If there is shade, pick plants that thrive in shade. If there is sun, pick sun-loving plants. Above all, choose plants that are native to your area.
3. Reduce your lawn. Lawns are one of the biggest water users in a yard. Replace as much as possible with shrubs, trees, herbs, and groundcovers. Once these are established, maintenance is very minimal.
4. Irrigate effectively. A lot of irrigation is misapplied. People water too much or unnecessarily. To irrigate effectively, you need to get to know your plants. Some need more water, some less. Some need a light sprinkling, others deep immersion. Drip irrigation is a good way to use less water and still provide enough for your plants.
5. Educate yourself. Get books on irrigation or on local plants. Be sure to choose books that specialize in your region. If you learn how to care for your lawn properly, you can reduce the amount of water you use on it. For

instance, using the right kind of fertilizer at the right time and thatching can cut lawn maintenance drastically.

6. Mulch your soil. Mulching means putting organic material on the surface of the soil. This prevents water from evaporating from the soil and keeps the soil loose so the water can penetrate more easily.

Pest Control

Microscopic little beasts cause people to run to their nearest hardware store begging for chemicals to spray on their plants. While pests are a pain in the neck, chemicals are also a pain in the neck when you look at the big picture. They can leach into the soil and wind up in your vegetables' root system and may turn up in your water system as well. There are a few ways to keep the beasts at bay and maintain a healthy environment at the same time. Here are some ideas:

❖ Plant a variety of species. Different insects are specific to certain plants. If you have a wide variety of plants, then you will get a variety of insects. Organic gardeners try to create a whole ecosystem in their yard, so good bugs eat bad ones. This creates balance, which is how organic gardening works. Another reason for diversity is that if you have perennial and annual plants and trees, good insects will have a place to live all year long. If you only have an annual garden, there is nothing for those beneficial bugs to live on through the winter. Your goal is to create a whole ecosystem. You can get information on beneficial bugs in most organic gardening books.

❖ Build good soil and give plants the sun, water, and nutrients they need. Plant bodies are like human bodies; if you eat the right food and take care of yourself, you have a strong immune system, able to resist invasion. The same goes for plants. Insects seem to go for weak ones. Also, stronger plants are more able to withstand a little damage by an insect.

❖ Keep the garden pathway and beds clean and clear of weeds and other objects that may harbor pests.

❖ Rotate crops every year to avoid soil diseases.

❖ Don't expect to kill all pests or have picture-perfect plants every time. Some pests will always be in your garden because they have a place in the ecosystem. Aphids, for example, are good because they attract such predators as ladybugs and lacewings. Your job is to manage them to a level that's not damaging your plants.

❖ When plant damage occurs, be sure to identify the pest properly. The insect you see near a damaged leaf actually may be a beneficial one that eats pests. To find out whether your insect is beneficial, refer to *Rodale's Colored Handbook of Garden Insects* or other guides that include good photos of insects and the plants they are attracted to. If this doesn't help, put the bug in a bag and take to a gardening clinic or hardware store. Some nursery staff are well trained and can identify insects for you.

❖ Try integrating pest management (IPM) before chemicals. IPM is a holistic approach to pest control based on prevention and use of nonchemical defenses. For more information contact your state solid and hazardous waste departments.

Plant and Seed Exchanges

There are secondhand clothing stores, secondhand cars . . . why not secondhand plants? One person's throwaway is—you know the rest. Ruth Pickering is an avid gardener who organized a plant and seed exchange at work. She asked for permission from management and posted notices in the elevator and on key bulletin boards asking people to bring in extra plants and seeds to exchange. Every spring people bring in seeds and starts and every fall they bring in seeds and dividing perennials.

You can take Ruth's idea and incorporate it into your life. Do you belong to a church? A children's play group? Do you go to school? How about your neighbors? There are many, many ways to find groups of people who may be interested in this idea. You could put notices up in grocery stores or local hangouts. Be creative and you'll not only save money by these exchanges, but you'll meet kindred gardening spirits in the process.

Tool Exchanges

Tools can get expensive, especially the kind you need for major landscape work. All of a sudden the cost of a fresh carrot out of your garden begins to soar. An innovative tool exchange was started in Seattle that can be repeated anywhere. In 1977 a university architecture professor and one of his students decided to organize a neighborhood program to assist homeowners and renters with home repair, maintenance, and improvements. They organized with a small group of neighbors who helped form a nonprofit organization. A small educational grant from the state enabled the program to hire a part-time coordinator and purchase a few basic tools. Local contractors and other experts were asked to donate a couple of hours of their time to teach various topics. Some federal block grant money, administered by the city, helped the program to grow steadily through most of the 1980s.

The program offered free classes, free inspection, advice, and service. Annual dues were $25 to those who wanted to join the organization. Members had access to the tool library and labor assistance. A labor exchange was organized to complete minor repairs and major additions. People worked together to help elderly or disabled neighbors.

In 1989 the organization scaled back to become more self-supporting and merged with a community organization. Since then the Well Home Program has limited its labor efforts to helping people and other organizations that are particularly needy. In the past few years they also began to charge class tuition and tool maintenance fees to help support the program. After paying a yearly membership fee of $25, tool rental fees are minor, ranging from $1 for a level to $40 for one week's use of a scaffold set. Most fees are under $10.

Major costs are the coordinator's salary, insurance, tool purchases and repairs, printing, and telephone. Sometimes the program obtains tool-purchase grants from corporations, foundations, local businesses, or direct donations.

If you don't want to attempt organizing this kind of formal exchange, start a tool exchange with your neighbors. Print up flyers explaining your ideas and either call a meeting or have interested neighbors fill out a form stating what tool they are willing to exchange. You'll probably be surprised to discover the wealth of resources right on your block.

My neighbor Barbara and I share my lawnmower and her weed whacker. Why do we each need a full set of tools? Our tool exchange led to a few "gardening happy hours," where we worked together on each other's yards while sipping margaritas. For nongardeners like us, this makes the project a whole lot more enjoyable.

Apartment Gardens

Do not despair if you live in an apartment and like to garden. You can even grow a little food. Start with herb planter boxes. If you don't have roof or patio access, grow a few kitchen herbs in a window planter box. If you have access to the roof, first check with your landlord about watering and drainage. You'd hate to get a nice garden going and find it draining into the apartment underneath you. Because weight is often an issue, some soils have been engineered to be lighter to make planting on roofs easier. Check with your local gardening center. You also can get free five-gallon buckets and grow tomatoes, basil, or other summertime favorites on a patio or roof. Where to get these buckets? Try local grocery stores or warehouse-type discount clubs.

Does your building have a central courtyard, adjacent vacant lot, or other open space? Check with your landlord before digging. Some landlords would be thrilled to have tenants beautifying the yard; others may not. If you don't know who owns the vacant lot, go to the county tax assessor to get the address of the owner. Once you have the okay, join with your apartment neighbors and have fun. You'll not only have a shared garden, but you'll meet your neighbors as well.

Share or Start a Community Garden

Community gardens are thriving all over the United States. They can provide an inexpensive source of fresh vegetables, and having groups of people gardening in the same area provides a feeling of solidarity. Typically a city acquires vacant land and creates garden plots. Throughout history, they have been most popular during times of economic or social unrest. During the Great Depression these plots, known as relief gardens, often were the only source of food for people. After World War II they were called victory gardens, and again they provided a food source during a time of shortage. Today community gardens are popular because of concern for the environment and concerns about our food. The greatest impact, however, on the growth of modern community gardens has been from people who want to halt the rise of urban decay. A vacant lot is a haven for crime, graffiti, garbage, and disease.

They're making people every day, but they ain't makin' any more dirt.

—WILL ROGERS

Rose Murphy writes in *Green-Up Times,* a publication of the New York Botanical Garden, "It takes serious commitment and endless hours of hard work just to get the garbage off the lot. What is astounding is how quickly these lots are transformed into visions of beauty, which become pivotal meeting places in communities. The hard work creates a domino effect, with additional sites being reclaimed by the community and turned into still more attractive open spaces."

Each city responds to its community gardens in its own way. In the East, the

The Story of Ecology Action

In the early 1970s John Jeavons began to wonder about a few things. He took a look at how many people were on the planet and how much land there was. He wondered if there was enough land to feed the people. Some articles indicated there might not be, but not one could tell him just how much land it took to feed one person. So he talked to farmers, agronomists, and academics and researched different farming and gardening methods, thinking that might provide the answer. Finally he discovered a man named Alan Chadwick, who was using a biologically intensive method called bio-dynamic French intensive gardening. Chadwick had transformed a barren hillside in Santa Cruz, California, into a thriving, beautiful garden using this process. John was intrigued.

This intensive method provided a way to produce a lot of food in a small area. John quantified, studied, and simplified this and other methods and explained them in his first book, *How to Grow More Vegetables than You Ever Thought Possible on Less Land than You Can Imagine*, in 1974. A key initial tenet of biointensive gardening and minifarming is double-digging. Most gardens are dug approximately 6 to 12 inches. Biointensive methods dig 24 inches. This aerates and cultivates more of the soil, allowing the roots to grow down rather than out. Thus a gardener can plant crops closer together and enjoy higher yields on less ground.

strategy is to bring people together to make deteriorating neighborhoods more habitable. "Getting people out of their houses to work together and trust one another is a really big deal," says Barbara Donette of the American Community Gardening Association. "When you sweat together over some kind of project, you build bonds that you don't necessarily build any other way."

In San Francisco, there was a need to respond to people living with AIDS, so volunteers installed gardens near the homes of AIDS patients. That city also has a job-training program for low-income youth, where the youth help build and restore community gardens. In the process they learn job skills, such as how to go to work and how to set up a performance record so they can get jobs.

In Albuquerque, New Mexico, a group in the local arts community started a community garden in a housing complex as a way to bring people together. In Seattle, Washington, community gardeners started a program called Lettuce Link, where volunteers collect surplus produce from community gardens and deliver it to food banks. In Cheyenne, Wyoming, a young man was looking for

This became the basis of what was to become John's lifelong work and passion. He gathered with a group of people and eventually settled in Willits, California, where he operates a nonprofit organization called Ecology Action. The group operates a demonstration biointensive sustainable minifarm and garden and offers workshops and classes. They have written more than 30 publications. John's bestselling how-to book is now *How to Grow More Vegetables, Fruits, Nuts, Berries, Grains and Other Crops than You Ever Thought Possible on Less Land than You Can Imagine*. It has been translated into nine languages and is in its fifth printing. The group has conducted workshops in more than 100 countries around the world, teaching people from Mexico to Kenya to grow more crops on less land. It estimates that over 200,000 people are using biointensive practices in Mexico and well over 60,000 minifarmers in Kenya follow it. The idea is growing worldwide. In the Philippines, biointensive gardening has been mandated as part of the school system. Students must be able to use the method before graduating from secondary school.

Jon Jeavons (front middle) and his students at Ecology Action.

For information on workshops and classes and a list of materials (including tools and open-pollinated seeds), write to: Ecology Action, 5798 Ridgewood Road, Willits, CA 95490-9730.

ways for disabled people to fit into the mainstream community. He started the Cheyenne Botanical Garden and hires disabled people to operate the greenhouse and nursery.

The Green Gorillas are a group in New York City whose mission is to collect landscape materials from places that relandscape frequently, such as the Rockefeller Center Gardens. They volunteer to dig up the old plants and distribute them to community gardens.

In San Antonio, Texas, and Miami, Florida, police departments use community gardens as a way to bring people together and reduce crime. They do fund-raising to build additional community gardens. A study in Chicago found that public housing projects that had green spaces and gardens had less crime than those that were surrounded by asphalt.

Socially Conscious Gardening

Anza Muenchow turned her love of gardening into socially conscious volunteer work. First, she started volunteering to manage a garden at her children's school. The school had replaced part of an old playground with a garden for the students and reserved part of it for a community garden. Then she got involved with a homeless youth gardening project. The kids have a plot of urban land for their garden. In the summer, they have a booth at a neighborhood farmer's market to sell their produce, in the fall, they make and sell holiday wreaths. They've even been offered demonstration space at an annual flower and garden show.

The youth are hired by a federal homeless program employment project that takes kids with no skills and pays them to attend two five-week sessions. During that time they learn how to garden and market their produce. Anza's group is working to become self-sustaining. They plan to follow the lead taken by a similar program in Los Angeles in which the group not only grows and sells produce but also sells its own brand of salad dressings. They are called Food from the Hood. The program, aimed at keeping high school students in school, then offers them scholarships to attend college. The kids learn how to grow food as well as all facets of the business, including marketing, labeling, and mixing the recipes. "It's a big community project in the heart of a burned-out area," Anza says. "They get help from a lot of people." A similar program in Colorado is called the Women's Bean Project. There a group of homeless women grow and dry beans to create gourmet soup mixes that are sold through catalogs and in stores.

"We're very happy with the results of our program," Anza says. "I feel really good that we're intervening in some young people's lives. They learn a sense of ownership and belonging that is so important."

Edible Gardening

Don't Garden, but Still Eat Garden Produce

For people who don't like to garden but like to eat (me, for example), this is a favorite. No digging, no planting. Sit on your rear and reap the harvest. Here's how: Join a Community Supported Agriculture Program (CSA). CSAs are based on a concept called *teikei* from Japan, which translated literally means "partnership." The philosophical translation is "food with the farmer's face on it." Teikei clubs in Japan serve thousands of people sharing the harvest of hundreds of farmers.

CSAs are partnerships between consumers and farmers. They are one of the highest forms of symbiotic relationship—one hand literally feeds the other. The farmer has a built-in, guaranteed, prepaid customer base for his or her harvest, and the customer has guaranteed fresh vegetables. When you become a member of a local CSA, it hooks you up with a particular farmer. Members are called shareholders and subscribe to the harvest for the entire season in advance. A share is designed to feed two to four people with a mixed diet or one to two vegetarians by providing all of their vegetable needs for a week. Larger households and restaurants buy multiple shares. The sharers receive a bag of local, same-day-fresh, typically organic vegetables and herbs once a week all summer and once a month all winter if a root cellar or cold storage unit is available. Projects typically provide at least 40 different crops. A five-acre farm in Massachusetts could feed 300 people 43 weeks of the year.

Consumers who like to dig in the dirt can arrange to go to the farm to pick their own vegetables, flowers, and herbs. This arrangement allows city grown-ups and children to experience where their food really comes from, without the responsibility of having to tend a garden themselves.

Make Friends with Overzealous Gardeners

If you like the CSA idea but don't want anything so formal, you can make private arrangements with local gardeners who have surplus vegetables. In some cases you can work a trade and get your vegetables at no cost; in other cases you may work out a payment arrangement. Be creative.

Here are some ideas: Place an ad in your local gardening newsletter saying you'll come and pick excess vegetables and fruit. Or attend gardening meetings. Call your local horticulture schools and nurseries to get an idea where you might find these gardening groups. You also could offer to pick up extra vegetables for local food banks in exchange for enough vegetables for your own family. How about offering to buy seeds or starts for gardening friends and then help them reap their harvest? Or if you have a large yard but would rather do just about anything else than work in it, you could offer your yard to a frustrated, yardless gardener, then split the harvest. Frustrated gardeners and large yard owners can connect by placing notices on bulletin boards of gardening stores, food co-ops, and coffeeshops. If you're the gardener, you could walk around a nearby neighborhood until you see a run-down, suitable yard. Go knock on the door or leave a note about your idea. What a terrific relationship for you both.

Sally Ann Sadler is an overzealous gardener who has formed two informal CSAs for her friends. During the summer, she pays nothing for all of her produce, feeding a family of three, because she sells excess produce to friends, earning enough to offset her costs. "I wanted to garden for my friends and make enough money to support my gardening habit," Sally Ann says. "I also wanted it to be a model for low-income people with little space."

The first arrangement was with a friend who had a large yard. The home-owner had already built a water system, and Sally offered to set up a vegetable garden. She found four other friends who agreed to pay her $10 each for 17 weeks (for a total of $170) for a basket filled with salad greens, a few vegetables, and flowers. Once in a while she would barter with the friends—one gave her a massage in exchange for a basket of vegetables, another built her a greenhouse in exchange for Sally Ann installing a garden at her house.

She uses the biointensive method of vegetable gardening, which can net more produce per square foot than traditional row methods. Sally Ann also uses the successive planting method, in which she has ready a set of transplants to immediately take the place of what she picks. Friends are invited to help at the garden if they choose. "This project is for people who are interested in gardening but don't have the time," she says.

Sally Ann says there is no reason to spend much money gardening. "When I first started gardening I spent tons of money and then I realized it was a total sham. All you need to buy is a good fork, a spade, and a hat. Everything else is nearly free."

She says the first rule is building good soil with the resources that are available. Make your own compost with neighbors' leaf and grass clippings. Collect rabbit manure from a neighbor's pet. Be creative. Sally Ann also collects free manure from the City Police Department Horse Patrol. They are happy to donate it. She gets free wood chips delivered from an arborist. (When arborists cut down trees, they are left with chips they don't need.) Be open to opportunities and flexible. Make your own compost bin with scrap pallet boards. All you need to do is turn and water the compost, and within a year, you'll have good dirt. There are many ways to compost; some people add nonmeat food scraps, others add special mixes. But Sally Ann says the easy, no-cost way works just fine.

"Building soil takes time," she says. "Whether you pay for your compost or make your own, it doesn't happen overnight. After a time you will have good soil."

Sally Ann advises people to start their gardens with only a few packets of seeds. "You don't need to spend money buying vegetable and flower starts at the store," she says. Since the packets often have large numbers of seeds, trade with friends. Start the plants indoors in sterile potting soil, then transfer it outdoors when it is large enough to distinguish from a weed and when the weather is appropriate.

Sally Ann teaches low-income people to garden on little space for little money. "Gardening does not need to be an excessively materialistic lifestyle," she says. "People spend far more than they need to spend."

Buy at Farmer's Markets

If you still like the idea of eating fresh, locally grown produce but don't want to bother with CSAs or personal arrangements, consider shopping at local farmer's markets. Chris Curtis started a farmer's market in her neighborhood four years ago. She began it as a way to get involved in a community project, but now says the most important part of her job is bringing farmers and consumers together without the middlemen. She has become very savvy to the value of fresh produce. "When you go to a traditional grocery store, you're getting vegetables that were harvested six weeks ago and trucked to your store from another state," she says. "When you shop at farmer's markets, you get locally grown produce that has been harvested within 24 hours.

"People read nutrition books and see that broccoli is listed as having all sorts of good vitamins and nutrients, but that is not what you are eating in reality. By the time it reaches your dinner table, a head of broccoli purchased at a supermarket has very few nutrients left."

Chris discovered that the megafarms that supply supermarkets are breeding vegetables not for nutritional value but for shelf life. If they can develop broccoli that will sit for six weeks, they can make more money.

At a farmer's market, consumers have the opportunity to talk to the per-

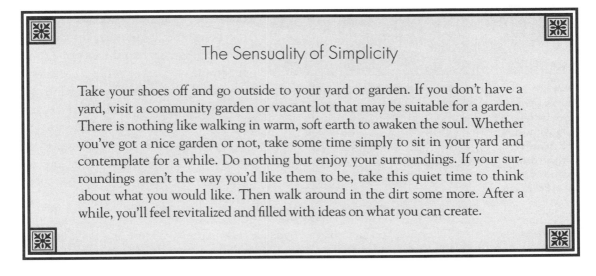

The Sensuality of Simplicity

Take your shoes off and go outside to your yard or garden. If you don't have a yard, visit a community garden or vacant lot that may be suitable for a garden. There is nothing like walking in warm, soft earth to awaken the soul. Whether you've got a nice garden or not, take some time simply to sit in your yard and contemplate for a while. Do nothing but enjoy your surroundings. If your surroundings aren't the way you'd like them to be, take this quiet time to think about what you would like. Then walk around in the dirt some more. After a while, you'll feel revitalized and filled with ideas on what you can create.

son who grew their food. They build relationships. And consumers who buy this way support their local economy. When you buy from a local farmer, he or she will be able to stay in business and be profitable. "People in the city value being able to drive out to the country and see open, green space," Chris says. "They don't want to see the countryside paved over and turned into shopping centers. But that is what happens when we don't support our local economies."

MAKING A LIVING ON AN ORGANIC FARM

Up at dawn, picking strawberries, broccoli, lettuce, and the rest. Still picking, tilling, and farming until the sun goes down. The work is hard and the heat re-

From left:
Thurston Williams,
Artec Durham, 11,
Kyla Durham, 8,
and Annelle
Durham at their
farm in Upper
Lake, California.

lentless. They will sell some of the bounty at local farmer's markets, when Thurston returns home from another long day at 9:00 P.M. Some is sold to CSAs (community supported agriculture programs) and some they will store in the cold room until the next market, when they will try again. After the markets, they count their money. Are they making it? Is their try at organic farming worth the incredible amount of time they spend, and the life they lead, which is so much harder than the city one they left behind?

Annelle Durham and Thurston Williams say yes, definitely, it is worth it. Simpler, yes, in some ways, no in others. But are they more satisfied? "Yes, that's it," they say.

Ten-year-old Artec comes in the door. "You came to write about simple living?" he asks. "We don't live simply. In the city, I didn't have to get up at 6:00 A.M. to pick my strawberries."

"Hmmm," I say.

"But which one do you like better?" I ask.

"Oh, here. You can't run all over the hills in the city. Here, it's much better."

Annelle left her city job and her very organized city play groups that she dutifully brought her children to once or twice a week. Thurston left a very secure, tenured teaching job with the San Francisco school district. They left the city life, where they could walk nearly everywhere . . . to Golden Gate Park, to daughter Kyla's day care, to the library, the health food store, the co-op. They left behind their favorite Greek restaurant where they would walk every Saturday to get Greek pastries and coffee before taking the kids to the park.

"It took us a long time to leave," Annelle said. "We loved it. But then our friends with children started moving out of the neighborhood. The renter in our downstairs duplex moved out. She had a child about the age of one of our kids. We traded child care a lot.

"When she moved out, I really noticed her absence. I realized then that I couldn't even go to the grocery store to buy a carton of milk without making all sorts of arrangements. That's when we started seriously thinking about leaving the city."

When it became clear that Annelle and Thurston both had the same dream, they said yes to a couple who wanted to rent their city place. They had nowhere to go. Two weeks before they were to move out they found a rental in Lake County, California, on 20 acres, 17 with walnut trees.

"Our friends thought we were crazy. I remember joking that I didn't have cold feet about the move . . . I had hypothermia!" Annelle recalls.

The next spring they bought their own 20 acres in Lake County on a little cul-de-sac off a dead-end road in a dead-end valley out in the middle of nowhere. The land was completely undeveloped. The soil and light were perfect. They had their own microclimate. And their kids were safe to roam all over the place because they could see every car that came anywhere near the house.

"Last night at 7:00 a neighbor came over with one kid and our three kids went off to the creek for about two hours. We didn't worry. I like that aspect of this a lot," Annelle says.

"Now the kids have fewer playmates, but when they do play, it is wonderful play. I don't need to know where they are every minute of the day as I did in the city."

The couple agreed to take the risk of learning how to start an organic farm from scratch, but they knew they couldn't also learn to build a house at the same time. Instead they bought a double-wide mobile home and Thurston built a huge garage. They started farming before they moved in, with no power or water. They hauled water in a horse trough and used a milk jug to water the seedlings.

"People said to me, 'You've got an MBA and you're doing stoop labor?'" Annelle remembers. "It was beyond their comprehension that I could enjoy this, but I did and still do."

Annelle and Thurston's only experience with gardening was in their small backyard in the city. They learned by reading and taking classes. They made a garden plan and stuck to it for part of the time, then couldn't keep up. The rest of the time they "flew by the seat of their pants." Annelle says the best way to learn is to start your own farm and make money from what you do. The second best way is to work for someone else for pay.

They moved onto their farm in September and, the following May, they were selling produce at every farmer's market they could find.

"It reminds me of being a parent," Annelle says. "There is just no way to anticipate how hard and how rewarding it's going to be."

The couple earns less money now than they did in the city, but they find they also spend a lot less. "Basically, we just quit spending our money," they say. They had been frugal enough in the city to build a small savings with which to start the farm, but that was quickly used up by paying cash for everything, including all vehicles and equipment. "We were clear that we didn't want to borrow money," Annelle says. "That has been the demise of many farmers, so we decided to wait . . . all things come to those who wait, right?"

Since their first year in business, the couple managed to build their own greenhouse, which enables them to have their own produce year-round. They buy their rice and grains in bulk, and go out to dinner maybe once a month. Their main source of entertainment in the summer is swimming in free places. They have few clothes, since, as Annelle says, "We live on a farm . . . who cares what we wear!"

"It's much better here," she says. "Look out the window. That's one reason. It's beautiful. Absolutely beautiful. We have time to watch the hawks dive. I can watch the rainbows forming and clouds drifting.

"I can do that for just five minutes, and it can totally change my outlook for the day, even if I've been working really hard."

In winter, the couple is religious about getting their kids to bed at 8:00 P.M., so they have time alone. "I read out loud and Thurston brushes my hair. I thrive on it. In summer, the garden controls us."

And the garden is paying off. They're bringing in more than expected. Earlier than expected.

The returns are clear and go beyond money. "I know why I'm working," Thurston says. "I know what is growing, what it's used for, and who buys it. Someone's eating our cucumbers right now, I'm sure."

"I like selling to people with names and faces," Annelle says. "It's all very concrete and tangible, like the dirt under my fingernails."

398

THE SIMPLE LIVING GUIDE

❖ ❖ ❖ ❖ ❖ ❖ ❖ ❖ ❖ ❖ ❖ ❖ ❖ ❖ ❖

Resources

Books

Growing Methods, Harvesting, and Seed Stocking

The Complete Gardener's Almanac by Marjorie Willison (White River Junction, VT: Chelsea
   Green Publishing, 1993)
A thorough reference guide on all aspects of year-round gardening. Author shows how to raise
various vegetables, fruits, flowers, and herbs and explains how to choose the right season for
each one.

*How to Grow More Vegetables, Fruits, Nuts, Berries and Other Crops Than You Ever Thought
   Possible on Less Land Than You Can Imagine* by John Jeavons (Berkeley, CA: Ten Speed
   Press, 1995)
Order directly from Ecology Action, 5798 Ridgewood Road, Willits, CA 95490-9730. Based
on Biointensive gardening techniques developed by horticulturist Alan Chadwick, this book
details the farming method that can produce results on 800 square feet or less and can provide
a family of four with fresh vegetables produced organically while maintaining soil nutrients
for future crops. Jeavons's techniques are being used in 108 countries. A seed catalog is
available.

Lazy-Bed Gardening by John Jeavons, Carol Cox, and Sue Ellen Parkinson. (Berkeley, CA:
   Ten Speed Press, 1993)
Based on *How to Grow More Vegetables*, this is a simpler book with the basic principles clearly
presented for those just beginning to garden or for those who need less information.

Seed to Seed by Suzanne Ashworth (Decorah, IA: Seed Savers Publishing, 1995)
Offers a compilation of seed-saving methods for 160 vegetable crops, including detailed
information on means of pollination, proper methods of harvesting, drying, cleaning, and
storing seeds.

Solar Gardening by Leandre Poisson and Gretchen Vogel Poisson (White River Junction, VT:
   Chelsea Green Publishing, 1994)
Use the sun's rays to help grow vegetables year-round with the "American Intensive" method.
Shows how the grower can extend the season for better yields.

Organic Methods and Farming

Four-Season Harvest by Eliot Coleman (White River Junction, VT: Chelsea Green
   Publishing, 1992)
Explores how to harvest organic vegetables through outdoor gardens, cold frames, tunnel
greenhouses, and root cellars and explains how to grow winter greens indoors. Planning,
preparing, planting, and cultivating are all part of the discussion.

The New Organic Grower by Eliot Coleman (White River Junction, VT: Chelsea Green
   Publishing, 1995)
Popular TV host shows the thinking and methods behind organic farming, including
discussions on which crops work best in the organic garden, dealing with pests, and how
organic farming compares to traditional methods.

The Orchard Almanac by Stephen Page, Joe Smillie, and Steve Page (Morrill, ME: Spraysaver
   Publishing, 1996)
The natural alternative to chemical pest control. Authors advocate use of multifaceted,
indirect, and low-power methods that seek to provide more "balance" on the farm without
the harmful side effects of chemicals.

Landscaping and Planning

Easy Garden Planning by Marjorie Willison (White River Junction, VT: Chelsea Green Publishing, 1995)
Designed for the homeowner with small backyard space, this book bursts with ideas on how to do more with less.

Energy Efficient and Environmental Landscaping. Cut Your Utility Bills by Up to 30 Percent and Create a Natural, Healthy Yard by Anne Simon Moffat, Marc Schiler, and the staff of Green Living (South Newlane, VT: Appropriate Solutions Publishers, 1995)
This book will show you how to cut outdoor water costs by 80 percent, reduce yard maintenance, maintain a lush lawn with less effort and no toxic chemicals, create a yard that's inviting, and grow native plants for the benefit of the local ecosystem.

Composting

Backyard Composting: Your Complete Guide to Recycling Yard Clippings by Harmonious Technologies (Ojai, CA: Harmonious Technologies, 1995).
Latest information on composting and description of current tools available to help you get started on your own composting program. Shows how composting can help reduce household trash and recycle nutrients back into the soil. It also describes all types of composting bins and accessories.

Sustainable Agriculture

Greening the Garden: A Guide to Sustainable Growing by Dan Jason (New Haven, CT: New Society Publishers, 1991)
A practical and entertaining guide to reclaiming control over the foods we eat. Innovative advice for growing high-protein plants, organic growing techniques, ways to extend the growing season, and responsible food choices.

Introduction to Permaculture by Bill Mollison (Permaculture Resources, 1991)
Provides a full explanation of permaculture and how it works.

The Permaculture Activist, P.O. Box 1209, Black Mountain, NC 28711.
This newsletter about permaculture encourages people to live sustainably by using fewer natural resources in a more renewable way.

The Soul of Soil by Grace Gershuny and Joseph Smillie (Davis, CA: Agaccess, 1996)
Discusses learning to manage soils for long-term productivity based on sustainable, ecological methods. Intended for either the home or serious farmer who needs to understand how soil operates in order to have a successful farm.

Nonfarm Farming

The Backyard Berry Book by Stella Otto (Maple City, MI: OttoGraphics, 1995)
Use the backyard to grow strawberries, rhubarb, raspberries, blackberries, blueberries, currants, gooseberries, grapes, and kiwi fruit.

Backyard Market Gardening by Andy Lee (Columbus, NC: Good Earth Publishing, 1995)
You can turn your backyard into a money market by learning how to grow vegetables, fruits, flowers, or livestock. Billed as an "entrepreneur's guide" to selling your own produce.

The Backyard Orchardist by Stella Otto (Maple City, MO: Otto Graphics, 1995)
Intended for the novice and experienced fruit grower, this book explores preparing the soil for planting, pruning fruit trees for maximum growth and production, controlling pests, and harvesting and storing fruit.

A *Patch of Eden* by H. Patricia Hynes (White River Junction, VT: Chelsea Green Publishing, 1996)
A guide for the inner-city farmer that shows how to take unusual spaces (rooftops, sidewalks, decks) and turn them into thriving sources of produce or beauty-inspiring gardens. Stories from community gardens in Harlem, San Francisco, Philadelphia, and Chicago.

Miscellaneous

The Contrary Farmer by Gene Logsdon (White River Junction, VT: Chelsea Green Publishing, 1995)
An explanation of how to be a cottage farmer, or part-time farmer, that mixes with other occupations. You don't have to be "stuck" on the farm full time to achieve its amazing spiritual and physical benefits.

Food from Dryland Gardens by David Cleveland and Daniela Soleri (Santa Barbara, CA: Center for People, 1991)
You too can grow a lot of vegetables in dryland gardens, and this book tells you how.

Gray Water Use in the Landscape by Robert Kourik (Santa Rosa, CA: Metamorphic Press, 1988)
Includes instructions and information on how to set up a gray water system and how to save your landscape during droughts.

Organizations

Seed Companies and Seed-Saving Organizations

Abundant Life Seed Foundation, P.O. Box 772, Port Townsend, WA 98368, 1-360-385-5660
Flower and Herb Exchange, 3076 North Winn Road, Decorah, IA 52101
Native Seeds/SEARCH, 2509 N. Campbell Avenue #325, Tucson, AZ 85719, 1-520-327-9123
Raintree Nursery, 391 Butts Road, Morton, WA 98356, 1-360-496-6400
Territorial Seed Company (for West of the Cascades), P.O. Box 157, Cottage Grove, OR 97424, 1-541-942-9547
Shepherd's Garden Seeds, 6116 Highway 9, Felton, CA 95018

Urban Gardening

American Community Gardening Association helps you turn a vacant lot into a food-raising bonanza. 325 Walnut Street, Philadelphia, PA 19106, 1-215-988-8800
Gardening Angels is an organization dedicated to helping start and maintain community gardens. 3061 Field Street, Detroit, MI 48214, 1-313-921-8071
Green-Up Times Newsletter from the New York Botanical Garden's Bronx Green-Up Program, 1-212-220-8995
The Trust for Public Land supports efforts to create local parks and recreational areas. 116 New Montgomery Street, #400, San Francisco, CA 94105, 1-800-714-LAND, Fax: 1-415-495-4103
The Urban Agriculture Network is a global resource center working to promote agricultural production in urban areas. 17111 Lamont Street, NW, Washington, DC 20010, 1-202-483-8130, E-mail: 72144.3446@compuserve.com

TRAVEL

14
Travel

Happiness is not a destination. It is the attitude with which you choose to travel.

—Yogi Arit Desal

Sometimes my yearning for the open skies has gotten so bad that I get a lump in my throat and a tear in my eye when I see an airplane flying overhead. I'm very sorry I'm not in it, going somewhere. Often when I emerge from the tunnel of one airplane ramp into the airport, all I really want to do is go down another, going somewhere, just for the adventure.

Since adulthood I've arranged my life so I can go when the urge strikes—it's that freedom thing. I've avoided debt like the plague so I don't need to give up my freedom. I have two children and remind them constantly, "Listen, kids, for the umpteenth time, we don't drive an expensive car because I'd rather be able to go to the Yucatan and check out pyramids with you . . . that's a choice."

Traveling is one time I am, indeed, fully and completely "in the moment," as the Buddhists call it. I'm fully present, fully aware, not distracted, not thinking of one thing while doing another. I'm sucking in every sight and sound, I'm ready like a cat waiting to pounce with all systems go. I love checking out new places, new people, new smells, food, sensations, new skies, new roads. I love immersing myself in this newness. I understand what William Least Heat Moon wrote in *Blue Highways:* "On the old highway maps of America, the main routes were red and the back roads blue. Now even the colors are changing. But in those brevities just before dawn and a little after dusk—times neither day or night—the old roads return to the sky some of its color. Then, in truth, they carry a mysterious cast of blue, and it's that time when the pull of the blue highway is strongest, when the open road is beckoning, a strangeness, a place where a man can lose himself."

In *On the Road,* Jack Kerouac called it looking for the pearl: "What did it matter? I was a young writer and I wanted to take off. Somewhere along the line I knew there'd be girls, visions, everything; somewhere along the line the pearl would be handed to me."

Somewhere along the line . . . where the music is different, the light is different. Where your eyes are open and full, rimmed by the wonder of a six-year-old.

I've never had much money, but still I've gone. I've lived on macaroni and cheese dinners in Hawaii. Flew for free to Alaska as a courier. Went to Puerto Rico with the kids for half price because it was hurricane season. Went to Yosemite with six cherished relatives and camped out in a studio room, which made for close quarters, a whole lot of silly fun, and a pocketful of saved money. Drove halfway around the western half of the United States in a free car because it was a drive-away arrangement with a rental car agency. Went to Mexico in a VW bug with the money an insurance company paid me after a lady ran into the corner of my car (decided I'd rather go to Mexico than fix the dent any day). Flew with the kids to the Yucatan for half price because I called endless scores of travel agents until I found that magic pearl price.

It's not like I go away all of the time—I go when opportunity knocks. I can go because I've arranged my life that way—the heart of simple living, staying free. I'd hate not to be able to answer that knock because, gosh, sorry, I have to stay here to make monthly payments on my new TV. Gee, goodness.

Travel and the simple life. Traveling teaches you a lot more about life than any book will tell you. Pages do their best to come alive, but they just don't cut it the way the real thing does. You can try to open your eyes to the state of the world without traveling. You can look at books such as *Material World, A Global Family Portrait,* by Peter Menzel. You can flip through the pages and think to yourself what affluence we have in America as compared to someplace like Bhutan, which is near Tibet. The people who compiled *Material World* sent photographers around the world and asked families in all manner of farflung places if they wouldn't mind hauling all of their worldly possessions out of the house, shack, hut, what-have-you, and put them out in front. There the photographers would take a picture of the family in front of their dwelling, surrounded by their possessions. You can imagine the contrasts in portraits. They did this to show readers the meaning of material wealth around the world and the struggle for survival throughout much of it. They say: "This vivid portrait of humanity at the end of the millennium asks the pivotal question: Can all 5 billion of us have all the things we want?"

> *Don't tell me how educated you are.*
>
> *Tell me how much you've traveled.*
>
> —MOHAMMED

We can scan through this book and say things like "Oh my gosh, will you look at that? These people have hardly anything. Gadzooks, look at the Americans . . . their stuff fills the entire yard and street. What are they doing with so much stuff? How can this family of 10 in Western Samoa live in a place that is only 720 square feet?" Then we can return to cooking our dinner, paying our bills, slumping into bed with a good mystery, going to work.

On the other hand, we actually can go to some of these places and see for ourselves. The place can invade our inner spheres and impact our souls. I know one woman who went to the Amazon for a vacation and wound up adopting a homeless kid. Five years later she and her family love that kid like crazy. I know of another couple who went to Vietnam and returned with a mission to work to disable as many landmines as possible, because the still-live mines were killing and maiming innocent farmers and children. There's nothing like seeing real faces and real eyes up close to get you moving. Traveling teaches us that there are many ways to live and many ways to measure pain, happiness, and affluence.

Travel doesn't always need to change your life in such big ways. You can travel for a lot of reasons . . . you can go to get to know the rest of the folks with whom we share our planet. You can go just because the sky and the road beckon. You can go because there's a beach and a palm tree, or a mountain and solitude. You can go just so you don't have to hear your confounded telephone ring. You can go just because . . .

Veteran traveler Rick Steves says a certain kind of thoughtful traveling can simplify our lives. He says this kind of travel can make you feel alive—and feeling alive is the core of voluntary simplicity. Rick sees the world as a cultural yarn shop—a fascinating global tapestry where you gather threads of different cultures. "If you never travel you don't have much perspective on what's going on around the world," he says. "Travel enables you to paint human faces on what otherwise are splotches on the globe.

"You can go to a cafeteria in Afghanistan and eat with a professor who will point out that just because you eat with a fork and spoon in America doesn't mean you're civilized—after all, one-third of the world eats with their fingers, and the second third with chopsticks . . . and they are no less civilized."

Travel can teach us how to slow down. We can go to a village in Europe and find that a restaurant is closed down during peak season because the owner wanted to take a vacation. We would never think of closing a business during busy season in the United States because here, time is money. In the village, time is life . . . time is the beach.

Traveling thoughtfully means traveling closer to the core . . . like living closer to the core. It means traveling with open eyes, taking in the culture, living like the locals do, as much as a traveler can. Thoughtful travel is not about whizzing through a place or series of places at 90 mph—the old if it's Tuesday, this must be Belgium routine. No, thoughtful travel is slowing down and experiencing the place you are in to its fullest.

"The best kind of travel is a break from the kind of compulsive, habitual movements we make in our daily lives," says travel writer Jim Molner. "Slow down, look around, and notice the details."

Jim says he learned to travel from his son when the boy was four years old. "He taught me to slow down and see details," Jim says. "One time he saw some people out working in a sugarbeet field in Romania. One of the donkeys that pulled a wagon was wearing a straw hat. He thought that was really cool, so we all got out of the car and walked out to the field. The farmers decided to take a break with us, and we wound up having a picnic with them. They didn't speak English, we didn't speak Romanian, but it made for a memorable encounter. That detail is what makes for outstanding travel."

How to Travel Simply

Simple travel is about a lot of things. One is fitting travel into your life without going into debt. What is the point of traveling for the sense of freedom and then harnessing yourself to credit card payments for the next two years to pay for the freedom? Figure out ways to pay for your travel with the money you have. Kirstin Jackson travels frequently and also says she isn't much on budgeting. Since she also isn't much on debt, Kirstin has devised a clever travel payment plan. Whenever she is in a store ready to part with her money for a big-ticket item ($50 or over), Kirstin stops and asks herself, "Would I rather have this thing or would I rather put the money toward my next trip?" Usually the trip wins out. One time she was in an upscale women's

Jim Molner's Simple Travel Tips

❖ Know why you are going to your destination. The simplest and best way to organize a trip is to know what has captured your imagination to visit the place. It could be a poem, a novel you read as a kid, or something you saw on TV. If you know why you want to be there, you will have an easier time organizing your trip. For example, many people want to visit England after reading Jane Austin's novels. Unfortunately, many of these people simply sign up for package tours and never have the opportunity to really experience Jane Austen country.

❖ Make advance reservations for the first and last nights of your trip. Having these nights confirmed is very reassuring; and knowing where you're going when you get off the plane simplifies your life. All you need to do is get a taxi and ask to be taken to your hotel. Who wants to get off a long flight, arrive in a new city, and have to wander around looking for a place to spend the night? On the way home, you're probably tired and will want to repack and organize your things, so it's reassuring to have a place all ready and waiting at this point too. Both places should be fairly close to the airport, depending on the time of day you arrive and depart. In between you can be footloose and fancy free.

❖ Save money by eating, *at most*, two meals a day in restaurants. Look for some kind of central market in your town and buy bread, fruit, and snacks to put in your backpack. Now you have a handy lunch waiting and ready when you are. This is important because in many cities, restaurants aren't open for lunch, or you may be far from a restaurant at midday. You also have more opportunity for local ambience when you have picnic fixings. You can eat in a beautiful park, on a hiking trail, or in front of a monument.

❖ Good maps can simplify, simplify, simplify. Get good city maps and large-scale regional maps. Be sure to get the kind that is appropriate for your kind of traveling. If you are a walker, get a pedestrian-style map; if you spend most of your time driving, get an auto map.

❖ Don't overplan. Allow yourself the flexibility to go when you want to go and do what you want to do. If you plan too much, you'll cut off many opportunities for spontaneity. People tend to overplan because they fear getting lost, but somebody will always be around to help you.

❖ Staying in little villages often is less expensive than staying in major cities. You can find out about these out-of-the-way places from travel agents or guidebooks. Look for the *Rough Guide* series, published in Britain. These include lots of hiking and walking excursions and out-of-the-way budget lodging. The *Lonely Planet* series is good, except that they have become so popular, you will find scores of other *Lonely Planet* aficionados in nearly every place that is recommended. The *Moon Handbooks* are the most detailed of all the guidebooks. They don't have beautiful color photos, but they do have lots of resources.

clothing store, about to write out a check for some very expensive clothes. She had rationalized why she needed these items and took them up to the counter. Just as the clerk was ready to ring them up, a thought struck Kirstin. She realized she could pay for a trip to Europe with the money she was about to spend on clothes. "I'm very sorry," she told the surprised clerk, "but I can't buy these now." Kirstin went to Europe instead.

If you are the budgeting type, you can put aside a few dollars each month for your travel pot. Figure out where you'd like to go at the end of a year or six months, how much it will cost, and then figure how much you need to set aside each month to pay for the trip. For those who lament that they have no extra money for this sort of thing, refer to Chapter 2. Once again, simple living is about living consciously. Simple living is also about making choices and setting priorities. Would you rather have a bigger house or the ability to travel more frequently? Would you rather have lunches out every day, or bring a sack lunch and be able to take off to Tibet in six months? Simple living travelers Bob and Jody Haug say they relish the fact that they don't have much money. Limited money forces them to set priorities. "If you're saving money for the trip and doing without certain things to save, then you really appreciate the trip much more," Jody says. "It just sharpens the decision-making ability. It would be quite boring if you had all the money you wanted; you'd never have to make choices and find out what is important to you."

Once you have prioritized travel, you'll also want to know how to travel for less. You can save money in two big categories: transportation and lodging. The bottom-line rule that applies to both is this: *Pay retail as little as possible*.

Transportation

Air Travel

Get a Good Agent and Dig for Deals

If you want to fly, never take the first quote you get from either an airline or a travel agent. Shop around. First call the airline of your choice and get their lowest retail price offered. Then call a few discount travel agents and see what price they can get for you. You'll find lots of ads for agents in the travel section of your daily newspaper. Call around until you are satisfied that you can't do much better. I have gotten airline tickets for nearly half retail price by this kind of calling marathon. You'll also find that just because a travel agency bills itself as "discount" is not necessarily so. David Huetten teaches a class titled "The Frugal Flyer." Once he shopped around for a good air price and discovered that a man who bills himself as the discount guru of the country actually came up with the highest-price ticket of all the places David called. He ultimately saved $170 because he spent about 30 minutes calling other agents.

If you travel fairly regularly, you will discover after a few trips which travel agents consistently come up with better deals. If you find such an agent, forming a relationship with him or her can simplify your travel life. The agent will get to know your style and budget and will work hard for you.

Often the best deals can be found through agents called consolidators. Consolidators are agencies that have a contract with one or more airline to distribute discount tickets. Usually airlines don't fill their planes completely, so they dump the leftover tickets through consolidators. When you call travel agencies, ask if they sell consolidator or any other kind of heavily discounted tickets. Keep pushing and pushing with whatever agent you have on the line until you feel that she or he has dug about as deep as possible. Consolidator deals usually are best on international flights. Most times you can get a better domestic deal through standard airline price war sales. Whatever your case, get that shovel out and dig until you are satisfied.

Creative Routing

You can also save on airline tickets by creative routing. Once I needed to go to Iowa City, Iowa, from Seattle for a conference. The direct price was out of my range. Through relentless digging, I discovered that there was a sale on round-trip tickets from Seattle to Chicago. I dug some more and discovered a special round-trip deal from Chicago to Cedar Rapids, Iowa. Then I checked for the lowest rental car price. All in all, I saved a bundle by buying two round-trip tickets and renting a car, which I drove from Cedar Rapids to Iowa City. The airline ticket agents never would have told me about this plan—I had to dig it up myself. In general, when you are traveling to a more out-of-the-way destination like Iowa City, Iowa, or Monterey, California, you'll save a lot of money by getting a round-trip special to the closest hub city, such as Chicago or San Francisco. Then, if you luck out and find that the airline is offering a special between the hub city and your destination, you can fly either all the way or close by, as I did. Had my airline not been offering a special between Chicago and Cedar Rapids, I would have rented a car in Chicago. This rule also applies to international destinations. Say you want to fly from Minneapolis, Minnesota, to Nairobi, Kenya. You can call around and get the best possible price from Minneapolis to Kenya. But you can get a much, much better deal by using your thinking cap. If you pay any attention to travel deals or read travel pages in the newspaper, you will recall that very often you have seen fantastic specials from, say, Minneapolis to London. This is because lots of people want to go from the United States to London. Not a lot of people, however, want to go from Minneapolis to Kenya. So book yourself on a bargain round trip to London. Next, check for round-trip deals between London and Kenya. Because many more people travel between London and Kenya, you may be able to get a special fare. You will have saved a bundle by being smart and knowing your geography.

Free Upgrades

There are other ways to save on air fares. David Huetten says he often gets free upgrades to first class simply by asking. He buys himself a discounted coach seat and then, when he arrives at the gate (the one where you actually get on the plane—not the one in the main lobby of the airport), he asks if they have any available first-class seats. David says in every single case except once (during a particularly hectic time at one airport), the agents have always checked for him. He then gives them a reason for requesting the upgrade. He'll say he has lots of work to do on the plane and it would be easier if he had more space. David says, "Every time there are available seats, guess who moves up?"

David says the key to this bold move is to have confidence and a reason. The reason is particularly important. Once a psychological study was done to test the importance of giving a reason along with a request. A study participant went to a copy center where there was a long line to use the copy machine. He asked people if they wouldn't mind if he cut in. People refused. The next time he did the same, only he added a reason. All he said was he wondered if they wouldn't mind if he cut in because he had to make copies. (Hello?) His wish was granted. So if you give the agent a decent, honest reason to be upgraded for free, you may prevail. A retired couple in one of David's classes did the same. During one class, they told David that they had never flown first class. David said they ought to tell this to the agent. Sure enough, a few months later the couple told him they prevailed on their last trip. "Gate agents have a lot of power," David says. "Plus, don't forget, the seat is waiting there for some warm body—it may as well be yours."

The confidence part is also important. David says, "The goal is to sound authoritative and confident, not pushy or bossy, and the world will open up to you."

Get Bumped

Once I heard about a family of five who had gotten rerouted on their vacation because of airline scheduling problems. The entire family was given free round-trip tickets for their trouble. Those tickets were their next year's vacation. You can do the same—it's called getting bumped. Here is how this works. Airlines typically overbook their flights to make up for no-shows and lateniks. When everybody shows up, the airline is stuck with more people than seats, so they ask for volunteers who are willing to give up their seats on that particular flight. They will put them on the next available flight. In exchange for having to hang around the airport for one to a few hours (once in a while longer), the airline rewards these volunteers with a free round-trip, domestic ticket to be used later. If you can be flexible like this, you actually can attempt to get bumped. Reserve your ticket as usual and show up at the airport about an hour early. Go to the boarding agent and say you will volunteer to get bumped if the flight is full. The agent will keep your name on a list of other people who are willing to do the same. Naturally, the easiest times to get bumped are the busiest—on holidays and to popular resorts during high season.

Air Courier

More than once, I flew for free round trip between Seattle, Washington, to Anchorage, Alaska. All I had to do was sit in the airplane seat, which is exactly what I would have done if I paid full fare. Which is exactly what any air traveler does. The only hitch is that you need to take everything with you on a carry-on bag rather than checking it in. This was also no problem for me since I travel light anyway. Here is how air couriers work. The big air courier companies, such as DHL Worldwide, ship this way when they want their packages delivered in a timely manner. When packages are shipped regular air freight (without a passenger), the packages may sit for hours or days on an airline's freight loading dock before being sent to their final destination. Packages checked with a passenger (you) will arrive on the same flight. This is all perfectly legal. Since they ship so much stuff, they need lots of people simply to sit in the seats they have already paid for. Those "lots of people" are folks like you and me. You never see or handle the packages—their employees bring them to the airport and their employees pick them up.

Since this great deal has caught on, some air courier companies now charge couriers for their tickets (at greatly discounted rates), some only use their own employees for the job, and getting the trip you want can be difficult. The most popular routes are, naturally, the most difficult to get. You'll have more choices if you are able to travel on short notice, and in the case of international flights, you'll need to stay overseas for as long as the shipper needs you. Thus, it can be more difficult to try to plan an exotic vacation this way. No matter what, though, this opportunity for budget air travel is worth checking into. See the Resources section for air courier companies.

Airhitch

Airhitch is set up to arrange last-minute "standby" flights on commercial airlines to some cities in Europe. Airhitch was originally set up to help students travel inexpensively, but it now serves everyone.

Airhitch coordinates with regularly scheduled commercial airlines to European cities. Most Airhitch flights land in major cities, such as Amsterdam, Brussels, Frankfurt, London, Munich, Paris, and Zurich. (I can handle this.) After the company receives your payment, you are guaranteed a flight within a certain number of days to either your first-choice destination or one nearby. You need to give Airhitch a window of at least five days during which you can fly. Airhitch, unlike consolidators or other discount agencies that sell reserved seats, sells only standby tickets, which is why you can fly for less. Contact Airhitch at 2641 Broadway, 3rd floor, New York, NY 10025. Call 1-212-864-2000.

Rental Cars

Shop Around

When renting a car, remember, pay retail as little as possible, and shop around. First, call a couple of national rental car agencies at their toll-free number to get the lowest possible retail quote. Pick the lowest one and then call the local number. Often the local office knows about local specials that the national office isn't aware of. Next, always reserve a subcompact car. Here is why. Subcompacts are the cheapest and, thus, the most heavily reserved. Very often when you arrive to pick up your car, you will find that the agency does not have any subcompacts left. Thus, you are entitled to a free upgrade. You can now drive a larger car for the price of a subcompact. If you get to your destination and subcompacts are available, that's a sign that business is very slow. Use this opportunity to bargain some more. Ask the agent if you can get a better price than what was originally quoted. If the agent refuses, say you'll need to check with other rental car agencies at the airport; if the agent wants to save you the time and trouble of checking around, you might get a better deal. If business is slow, it's better to give you a deal rather than have the car sit empty.

I got a great deal on a little tropical island once by taking advantage of their off-season tourist slump. I knew every rental Jeep company on the place had all sorts of cars sitting idle, and I knew I'd be there for a week, so I offered my guy a guaranteed weeklong income if he'd give me a better deal. We both benefited.

Creative Rental Contracts

David Huetten says you also should not be afraid to come up with creative rental contracts, if necessary, in order to save money. Once he arrived at his destination on a Wednesday. The rental car agent gave him a quote for four days. In digging around, David discovered that he could get a much better weekend rate. He asked the clerk about this. The clerk replied that the weekend didn't start till Thursday. "I told him, fine, I'd rent the car for one day at the weekday rate and return it the following day on Thursday, then turn around and write up a new contract to rent again at the weekend rate," David says. "But I also reminded him that if I did that, he'd have to wash and clean my car twice, and that perhaps it would be easier on both of us if he just gave me the weekend rate for the whole time." The clerk agreed and David saved a bundle.

Know Your Destination

Do your homework by knowing a little about your destination. If you are going to a typical business city such as Chicago or Dallas, you will most likely get a better deal on weekends. Why? Most of these cities cater to the business traveler, who travels during the week, when most business is conducted. Business travelers aren't usually there for fun, and they want to be home on weekends. Where does that leave rental car agencies? Empty on weekends. That's the time you show up and offer them a deal they can't refuse. On the other hand, if you are going to a typical tourist spot, such as Orlando, Florida, Southern California, or Hawaii, most rental car agencies there are busy on the weekend and during certain seasons. If you try to negotiate a deal during spring break, for example, more than likely you'll walk away disappointed. Why should an agency give you a deal when people are waiting in line?

Never fear, however, you still may be able to get at least a little discount. Ask if the company offers discounts for frequent fliers, AAA members, or senior citizens. Ask about anything you can think of, and you may prevail. You won't if you don't ask. Also check out local rental car agencies. They don't advertise in the national yellow pages with fancy 800 numbers, but very often they will go out of their way to get your business by offering you a better deal than the big agencies. You can either wait till you get to the airport to locate one of these places, or you can get hold of a local phone book from the library and scout them out. Ask if they'll beat the lowest price offered to you by a national company. Ask what else they'll throw in for you. Before signing up with a small, local agency, however, you should investigate it first. Call the chamber of commerce or Better Business Bureau, and take a look at their cars. If you are driving in an isolated area, you may want to consider paying more for a national chain in case of a breakdown. National chains have ready access to repair and tow equipment that the little place may not have.

Drive-away Cars and Mobile Homes

Once I had a terrific vacation that was shamelessly cheap. A friend and I were students at the time and wanted to go somewhere for the summer. We wanted to spend the equivalent of next to nothing. Since lack of money had never stopped me from traveling before, I didn't see any reason why it should stop me that time either. We contracted with a drive-away company to deliver a car to Los Angeles from Seattle. We were given a certain number of days to deliver the car and agreed ahead of time that we could spend those days seeing other states. We drove from Seattle, through Oregon, Idaho, Utah, New Mexico, over to the Grand Canyon, Nevada, and finally to Los Angeles, where we eventually boarded a flight back home. We paid for nothing except gas for the car and our own personal expenses. A few times we even slept in the back of the car. (It was a hatchback.) We also had plenty of time to see all of the sights we wanted to see, at a leisurely pace. You can do the same. Haul out your trusty yellow pages and look up the Automobile section. Then look up Automobile Transporters and Drive-Away Companies. These companies are in business to connect drivers (you) with people who need their car driven, such as families moving to a new state. Since most people like to fly to their new destination and hire a moving truck for the furniture, that leaves their car still sitting back in their old driveway. They need you to get it to the new place. Rental car companies sometimes need their cars delivered to a certain destination as well.

> *Strong and content I travel*
>
> *the open road.*
>
> —WALT WHITMAN

You also can drive mobile homes the same way. Look in the yellow pages under Recreational Vehicles—Rent & Lease, and call the RV rental companies. Tell them you'd like to be a driver for a motor home. This works the same as the rental car drive-away program: People rent a motor home but don't want to take it round trip. They rent it in City A and drop it off in City B. The rental agency needs the motor home back in City A. The renters are charged a special drop-off rate that includes the cost of three to five extra days rental, mileage, and gas. The company charges this price to cover the cost of hiring someone like you to drive the motor home back to where it belongs. If you can fit into the schedule and itinerary, you can drive a motor home for free plus you sometimes get your gas charges reimbursed. If you want to keep it longer than what the company allows, you can work it out ahead of time with the company though you'll probably need to pick up the extra days' charges. Motor home rentals are anywhere from $130 to $275 a day.

Like any of these bargain travel deals, you need to fit your plans within someone else's parameters. In this case, you can pick your destination and then see if the company has a vehicle that will fit. You will need to deliver it within a certain, agreed-on amount of time. Some firms will allow more flexibility, and others will expect you to take a more direct route. You also will need to be bonded and insured and follow with all of the company rules.

Lodging

Try to never pay retail for lodging. This bears repeating because people in the United States often think bargaining goes on only in places like Mexican open markets. They think they have no options when it comes to paying for hotel rooms. Wrong. The same thing applies to hotels as it does to rental cars and airplanes. If the place isn't busy, you can bargain. If people are waiting in line, you don't have as many bargain options.

There are three basic categories of potential low-cost lodging: college dorm rooms and the like, mom-and-pop motels, and more upscale hotels.

Level 1

The lowest priced lodgings are college dorm rooms ($10–$15 a night), college conference centers, youth hostels, and YMCAs and YWCAs. College dorm rooms are available mostly in the summer only, and the conference centers are available whenever the college isn't hosting a conference. Call colleges to find out what they offer.

Youth hostels may have been strictly for youth in the past, but now anyone, any age, can stay at one. Indeed, I have shared youth hostels with people of every age imaginable. American Youth Hostels recently changed their name to Hosteling International, to link up with the international organization of some 5 million members around the world. There are 6,000 hostels worldwide, including more than 200 in the United States offering dormitory-style, family, and couple rooms, and a range of services from laundry rooms and restaurants, to ski and canoe facilities.

Some of these places are terrific, others are not worth the savings. A lot depends on your bottom-line comfort requirements. One of my requirements is peace and quiet. Once I thought I was saving a bundle by paying $12 for a room at a very cute little youth hostel in a tourist city. Unfortunately, the available room was right on top of a well-traveled thoroughfare, the hostel was in an old (but charming!), poorly insulated house (i.e., noisy) with zero ventilation. The only way to ventilate was to leave the window open. All night long it was zoom, zoom, honk, honk, rumble, rumble. This would have been fine for someone who can sleep through anything, but not for a poor schmuck like me; I saved nothing. On the other hand, I have also paid $12 a night for very wonderful youth hostels. Even the wonderful ones, however, have drawbacks. In most of them, you are locked out of your room all day. You need to be out by 9:00 A.M. and can't return till 5:00 P.M. so the hosts can clean up. Usually you can hang out in the lobby. On the plus side, besides the low price, you will have an opportunity to meet interesting people at youth hostels. You usually cook your meal in a communal dining room along with other travelers, and very rarely have I encountered a shy traveler at a youth hostel. Most have all manner of interesting stories to regale you with while you gobble your pancakes. You don't get this kind of ambience in a stuffy hotel dining room. Nevertheless, sometimes I'm in the mood for stuffy dining rooms. Whatever works for you is the best deal.

Level 2

Mom-and-pop motels where the owner lives on site are usually the cheapest in the next higher level of lodging. This does not include fancy little bed and breakfasts where the owner lives on site. This is basic motel stuff we're talking about. The only way to find these places, however, is through word of mouth, or a sign along the road, or in those little magazines you find in Denny's Restaurant racks. These guys don't have the budget for big-scale advertising.

416

The next level of this category is your standard Super 8, Motel 6, basic Ramada Inn, and Holiday Inn Express. You find these everywhere along the freeway. The nice thing about these places is you can count on a clean, basic room with no surprises. They do not bargain much unless they are really, really empty. But as always, you should ask anyway. You may be able to knock off 10 to 15 percent on a senior citizen or AAA discount.

Level 3

These are your more upscale hotels, and they usually have multilevel prices. Their top-line retail rate is called the rack rate. In California, for example, rack rate is the maximum price allowed by law to charge for a particular room. Nobody pays this rate except people who spend weekends throwing their money out of small airplanes. What's that? You haven't taken up that sport, yet you'd still like to stay at one of these places? Never fear. Here's how:

Off-season discounts. Remember my trip to Puerto Rico during hurricane season? By the way, hurricane season doesn't mean hurricanes are guaranteed to show up. None did while I was there. After we left the out-of-the-way jungle place where we stayed most of the time, we wanted to check out San Juan. I got on the phone and called around relentlessly until I found a first-class hotel willing practically to pay me to stay there. San Juan is empty during hurricane season. Beautiful rooms languish in lonely solitude. Such a sad sight, and I was willing to pay to take one of these rooms out of its misery . . . but I wasn't willing to pay much. We had a splendid time swimming in the nice pool, looking out of our oceanview window, lolling around in a luxurious room, and even having fun in the stuffy dining room because the wait staff was bored stiff and thrilled with any company they could find. We not only paid bottom dollar for our room but went a step further and upgraded on our second night. Why not? They first put us in a room with no view. All I had to say was "Could you please please put us in an oceanview room as soon as one becomes available?" They did. Why not?

If you don't want to even entertain the thought of possibly getting blown off the map by a hurricane (and that is unlikely since you generally have enough notice to take proper cover), you still can get deals on nice places. Remember our car rental scenario? Check your seasons. Not all off season means hurricane season. All hotels in tourist areas raise and lower their prices according to seasons. Not only do you save money during off season, but you have more peace and quiet as well. Scott Stolkanck, an off-season traveler, wrote in the *Seattle Times* about the beauty of the dawn on an island that was deserted because it was off-season. "As dawn broke over the deserted beach, a bald eagle, somewhere in the forest on the bluff, called to its mate. . . . Nothing human broke the silence on this foggy November morning: not a motor, a ringing phone, nor even the sound of a human voice. The off-season had come to Orcas Island."

There are the extreme on and off seasons, and there are also "shoulder" seasons that are in between. Find out what goes on during "off season." Maybe it rains a lot, maybe the temperature goes through the roof, maybe it just means there are no college students on spring break or no wiggling little children on summer break. If you can handle whatever "off" may mean, you can save all sorts of money. On the other hand, if you are going to a business-type metropolitan city, you will get a much cheaper rate on the weekend when the business people go home. Most of these hotels are thrilled to have anyone grace the floors of their lobbies on weekends, and they are happy to entice you to be the one. Whatever money you pay is better than no revenue at all. The general manager of one major hotel said this: "If we have the rooms empty and you look like a person we would like to have come back, you are nice and polite, and no one else wants the room, we are happy to give you a good room at a discount rate."

There you go. If you don't believe me, you ought to be able to believe the general manager of a major hotel chain. Another way to determine whether you can bargain is by simply opening your eyes. Is the parking lot empty? Is the lobby empty? If so, this place may be willing to bargain with you. If you phone ahead to get a bargain rate and arrive to discover your room overlooks the parking lot, don't be shy. Head on down to the desk clerk and ask for a free upgrade. Remember, these people are in the hospitality industry. If you are courteous and reasonable, they will do what they can to make you comfortable. If they can't upgrade you to a better room, maybe they'll throw in a voucher for a breakfast or something. Doesn't hurt to ask. They want to treat you nicely. As David Huetten says, "Your job is to explain to them what 'nicely' means to you."

Other discounts. You also can get discounts in other ways. Ask if the company offers discounts for any of the following: corporate, weekend, off season, advance purchase, frequent flyer, frequent guest, kids-stay-free, senior citizen, student, faculty, clergy and military, AAA and other travel clubs. Remember the study that said people are more likely to acquiesce to your request if you give them a reason? Use it now. You also can use entertainment book coupons. But beware of one thing: Those coupons are discounted from the rack rate. Remember, the rack rate is the *highest possible price* a hotel charges for its room, and it is also a price nobody pays. So your 50 percent discount is not really a full 50 percent in most cases. Before you get excited, see what kind of deal you can get without the coupon first. Most of the time a 50 percent coupon still will be cheaper than many discounts, but as usual, don't believe everything at face value. Check around, check around, and check around some more. Also don't forget to use the same strategy you used for rental cars: Don't stop after contacting the hotel's national toll-free headquarter number. Often the local staff will be aware of local discounts. Many, many times I have been in a city and scanned the local newspaper to discover ads in there enticing local people to come to the hotel for drastic reductions. This is not advertised nationally. Your job is to find these things out by calling the local front desk directly.

You can get discounts through hotel wholesalers. These people are in business because most hotels fill only about 65 percent of their rooms every day. You can imagine that the hotel would rather fill those empty rooms at 50 percent off rather than leave them empty. Since they can't always count on people like you coming in to offer them a deal they can't refuse on these empty rooms, they turn to wholesale companies that are set up just for this purpose. These wholesalers usually operate as clubs, where you need to join to get the deals. For that reason, they make sense only when you travel fairly regularly and you want to stay in standard properties. Also remember the rule: Shop and dig until you are satisfied. You may get a better rate by offering the hotel a great deal yourself rather than joining a club. Check out all of your options before signing up for anything.

Another way you can get good deals on fancy places is in brand-new hotels. Once I wanted to take a stress break and go lie around in the sun. After digging, I found that the cheapest sun fix at the time was in Palm Springs, California. Unfortunately, I needed my "fix" during the Palm Springs high season. Undaunted, I pressed on. An intelligent travel agent knew about a brand-new, first-class hotel that had just opened. You'd think the price would be sky high for something like this, but in fact, often the opposite is true. Think about it. If the place is brand new, that means the word isn't out yet. That means it's probably not packed. That means they want to get the word out fast. How? By offering heavy discounts just to get people like you and me in there who will go home and tell our friends. I stayed for a week in total luxury for the price of a

> *If one must travel,*
>
> *one should do it with eyes of a child,*
>
> *the mind of an ecologist,*
>
> *the heart of a pagan,*
>
> *and the words of a poet.*
>
> —Kirkpatrick Sale

Motel 6. I also have told people about this nice hotel. Ask your travel agent if there are any new hotels in the city you will be visiting. You never know.

Package deals sometimes are another way you can get a better price on a hotel room—you book it along with your air reservation. You'll need to work through a travel agent or an airline vacation desk to find these arrangements. Break down your package into cost for lodging, transportation, and tours. Make sure you actually are getting a better rate on your hotel and air fare by going this way. The only way you can make sure is to do your homework.

Home exchange. You can't get any cheaper than trading houses for a vacation. Lucky for you, some enterprising souls already have done your homework and have found people with houses around the globe, ready for trade. They formed companies and set up databases filled with destinations and houses that are ready to be swapped. I know of a couple in Oregon who wanted to go to London. They joined a home exchange organization and found a man in London willing to trade. Turns out the man lived in a 15th-century stone mansion and even threw a car into the deal. All he wanted to do was come to the United States where the fishing and camping were free (except for permits). The relationship was so successful that the exchangers repeated the deal again and again.

The home exchange "gurus" of America are Bill and Mary Barbour, who have written a couple of books about the subject. In 12 years, they swapped their two-bedroom condo in Florida more than 80 times for different houses around the world. They figured their home exchanging saved them more than $151,200 over staying in hotels.

Your most important job is to find out about the club you decide to join. Since you will be opening your house to strangers, you want those strangers to be decent people. You also want a decent place to stay on your vacation. Call the Better Business Bureau and get references of people who have exchanged with that company. You'll also want to go a few steps further and get to know the exchange family. Exchange references, employment history, and photos of the house. Because you will be developing a relationship with these people, you will need to plan your vacation early to ensure a successful exchange. The Resources section at the end of this chapter provides a list of home exchange organizations.

Innovative lodging. You can get interesting and inexpensive lodging by talking to everybody you know and meet before you leave on your trip. Tell them where you are going and ask if they know anyone who lives there or who might be able to recommend a good, inexpensive place to stay. Most times you will find someone who knows someone who will help you on your trip. People usually are thrilled to play matchmaker this way. If you plan to visit somewhere for an extended stay, you can put ads in local newspapers looking for housing. I know a couple who spent nine months in Norway one year and paid $75 a month for a basement apartment in a farmhouse that they had found by putting an ad in an Oslo newspaper. Be creative and network, network, network.

Gites. *Gites* are an inexpensive way to stay off the beaten path in France. The word *gite* means "home," "lodging," or "resting place." Most *gites* are rustic country houses set in outlying villages away from major tourist centers. They are subsidized in part by the French government. Write to Maison des Gites de France, 35 Rue Godot de Mauroy, 75009 Paris, France. Specify the area of France you plan to visit and ask for a guide in that area. Or contact the French Experience, a specialty tour operator in New York. It charges 25 percent commission on the rental fee to research and book *gites:* French Experience, 370 Lexington Avenue, New York, NY 10017, 1-212-986-1115.

State park cabins and resorts. One well-kept vacation secret is that state parks have some of the lowest-priced resorts and cabins in the United States. Every state in the union has parks that are open to the public, and more than half offer remarkably low-priced cabin accommodations and resort facilities. Call the park department of the state you plan to visit and reserve early.

Family camps. "Call them resorts without the room service, turned-down sheets, or gourmet restaurants—family camps often offer the same range of recreational facilities but without the fancy accommodations or the fancy price," says *The Best Bargain Vacations in the U.S.A.* To find these camps, call your local YMCA, or 4-H organizations, university alumni associations, and city parks departments. There are also private camps listed in the *Best Bargain* book. The degree of luxury and types of accommodations vary considerably. Family camps, found throughout the country, typically are situated in areas of great natural beauty—on lakes, rivers, or seashores. Expect to find swimming, boating, arts and crafts, horseback riding, volleyball, softball, basketball, and evening campfires and sing-alongs.

Hospitality housing. Join a hospitality group, such as U.S. Servas. This organization serves as a clearinghouse for travelers throughout the world who want to stay at each other's houses. You pay a yearly fee to join and, in exchange, you receive names and addresses of overseas members who will accommodate you free of charge at their homes for short stays. By joining, you agree to be a host, too.

The good news about this club is that you need to be screened first. This means your hosts and guests also will have been screened, so you can be more assured of pleasurable exchanges. Refer to the Resources section for contact information.

Sanctuaries. A wonderful book, *Sanctuaries*, by Marcia and Jack Kelly, introduced me to the joy of staying in sanctuaries. The Kellys traveled throughout the United States in search of places to reflect, find solitude, rest, and renew themselves. They visited monasteries, abbeys, and retreats. Listings include places that offer a ministry of hospitality and welcome people of all faiths, with no requirement to attend any services or participate in any activities. Guests are free to join in prayer or just enjoy the surroundings. According to the Kellys, no attempt will be made to urge you to do anything other than what you choose.

Monasteries and abbeys are usually functioning religious communities that have some rooms for visitors, and retreat houses provide a setting for groups to hold meetings or retreats. Often rooms are available for individuals, even when a group retreat is going on. Settings offer everything from seaside estates with exquisite tropical gardens to simple cabins in the woods, reached only by a swaying suspension bridge. Many places have work/study programs; some have work/exchange available for a period of time. Prices range from $15 and up per night.

I used this book once during a car trip. I was traveling alone through a couple of states and wanted to stay somewhere besides Motel 6. I also didn't want to spend a fortune. Through the book, I discovered a retreat set in a delightful hot spring that had been a sacred place used by Native Americans for healing. A communal group maintains the place now. For a very low price I stayed in a little cabin in the woods, enjoyed the hot springs, ambience, and beyond-description hearty vegetarian food. I have since recommended the place to many people. It was just what I was looking for on that trip.

Farm and ranch vacations. Hundreds of farms and ranches across the country welcome city visitors. Here is what the book *Family Travel*, by Evelyn Kaye, says about farm vacations: "City families often choose a farm vacation to show their children where milk really comes from and that vegetables don't grow on supermarket shelves. For children growing up in cities and suburbs, rushing through schedules of school, homework and after-school activities, the pace of farm life is a surprise. Every day is an adventure without a timetable: up early to see the cows being taken out to the fields, go for a hayride on a creaky old wagon, or cool off under the hose. Adults can join in, or just mellow out on the old porch swing." *Family Travel* lists several U.S. farms and ranches that are open to visitors.

Inn-to-inn vacations. If you like hiking, biking, or cross-country ski trips but aren't in the mood for camping, you can hike, bike, or ski inn to inn throughout the world. One U.S. group offering this service is called Country Inns Along the Trail. It offers self-guided hiking vacations with overnight accommodations in charming country inns that are organized so hikers can follow a variety of trails at their own pace and, at the end of the day, find a home-cooked meal, hot shower, and comfortable bed awaiting them. Contact Country Inns Along the Trail at Churchill House Inn, RD 3, Box 3265, Brandon, VT 05733, 1-802-247-3300.

Other Simple Travel Ideas

Volunteer Vacations

Volunteer vacations accomplish two things: They generally, though not always, are a less expensive way to travel, and you can travel and contribute to the state of the world at the same time. You can volunteer for youth programs, health projects, and child care as well as on farm, building, and construction projects. Volunteer vacations are all different, but most require you to pay your round-trip air fare at the very least. Beyond that, most of them provide basic accommodations. Some organizations welcome families with young children, others accept only children over 14 or 16 accompanied by their parents. One volunteer organization is the Sierra Club, which allows you to stay in beautiful parts of the country while you help to restore trails. Another is Volunteers for Peace, which lists over 800 opportunities for volunteering in 37 countries. The range of projects includes renovating a children's home in Romania, assisting on conservation projects in Russia, gathering and repairing second-hand bicycles to be sold to support projects in the Netherlands, restoring a medieval castle in France, and planting trees in Costa Rica. I know one woman who volunteered in Germany right after she graduated from college. She wound up living in a little room in the top of a renovated windmill in a picturesque little village. As a gesture of goodwill, the Quakers had purchased this site from Hitler's Youth Corps and turned it into a peace center.

Learning Vacations

One of the best ways to immerse yourself in a new culture is by organizing a learning vacation for yourself. Depending on where you go, learning vacations can be very inexpensive. Learning vacations can be as simple as a day trip to a

Life at 75 miles per hour
by Janet Luhrs

Chimayo, New Mexico. I wanted to stay and linger. Run my fingers over the wrinkled surface of the red chilies hanging everywhere. Hang around the church and meditate in one of the old wooden pews. Think about life in this serene place. Roam the narrow, curving dirt streets. Watch the brown-haired children play. Smell the tortillas frying.

We couldn't stay. Had to make Gallup, New Mexico, by early evening. Schedule to keep. Life at 75 mph, vacation or not. Always 75 mph . . . always wanting to stop and breathe. Where does the time go? What is life at 75 mph? It's a skimming over the surface life. No time to dig in. No time to feel.

The old church beckoned. Come, stay awhile. Rest here. Follow the long mountain road, find a home in restful Chimayo. A visitor once said: "It's that old country feeling in Chimayo I can't forget. In all the places in the world I have been, this must be heaven." See the beguiling, graceful lines of the adobe and wood church, there since 1813. The centuries-old rafters permeated always with the comforting smell of incense. The candles. Slow down.

Oddly, it takes a lot of energy to slow down our weekday lives. We have to rearrange ourselves, our beliefs. Oddly, it takes time. Often it takes a long time. Our old 75 mph habits are huge boulders rolled into the middle of the path. One thing, though, is easier to change. That is how we take vacations. At least we can simplify our time away from home. We can take the kind of vacation where we get immersed in the life of the place.

As I whizzed through the Arizona and New Mexico desert on this trip with the kids, I picked up a book by Edward Abbey that illustrated the difference between our two views of that same desert. I loved our fast trip through the arid place, but I wanted very much to get to know that endless sweep of barren land. Edward Abbey got to know the desert. He became best friends. Me? I stood on the sidelines. Abbey's book is called *Desert Solitaire*. He spent an entire summer in one part of the desert. He got to know every crawling thing. He and a wild snake became pals. He came to know the sounds of stillness: "the creek of some bird in a juniper tree, an eddy of wind which passes and fades like a sigh . . ." He said: "I wait and watch, guarding the desert, the arches, the sand and barren rock, the isolated junipers and scattered clumps of sage surrounding me in stillness and simplicity under the starlight."

Stillness and simplicity. There are many ways to simplify our vacations. We can pick an area we would like to visit and stay there for the whole time, basking in its personality. For instance, we could have spent our entire vacation hanging around northern New Mexico. We could have gotten to know lovely and charming Chimayo. A Mexican restaurant there is called Rancho de Chimayo. It is a homey adobe hacienda, warm and earthy. Ristras of red chili hanging from the roof around the front door. There is a glow on the terrace in the summer from the brilliant southwestern sunset, the fluffy sopaipillas, the flautas, enchiladas, tamales.

Chimayo tells its history only to those who bother to linger. In the 1930s and '40s it was solidly rooted in its Spanish colonial past. The way of life was similar to what it had been for two centuries, not yet heavily influenced by automobiles, radios, and other 20th-century changes. Do we know the history of the restaurant? It's a folktale, long and colorful. Do we know that the Jaramillo family, long a part of Chimayo, operate not only the restaurant but a bed and breakfast inn called the Hacienda Rancho de Chimayo? Do we know the Jaramillos refurbished the inn using the old methods? They plastered the walls, for example, with the traditional mixture of clay, straw, and wood ash that Epifanio Jaramillo had used a century earlier.

We know all of this only when we bother to stay awhile. Otherwise, at 75 mph, Chimayo looks like a face with no features. Only when we stop and begin poking around corners and into cubbies and out-of-the-way places do we get to know the place.

living history village or cowboy poetry festival, or as involved as participating in a weeklong archaeological dig for Indian relics. The Sierra Club offers more than 300 diverse outings throughout the United States and even more worldwide.

You don't need to sign on with a formal organization in order to create a learning vacation. Susan Nolan discovered her own in San Miguel de Allende, Mexico, where she attended art school. She spent $80 for a month of daily art classes, $60 for her portion of a month's shared apartment rent, and ate her main daily meal in restaurants for about $4. Most schools have lists of people to contact for housing, or you can scout out arrangements for yourself by staying in an inexpensive hotel when you arrive, then getting to know people once you begin to immerse yourself in the new place. Some schools operate on a daily basis, others have monthlong classes in language or art.

Susan discovered San Miguel on a car trip that she had taken a few years earlier. "I fell in love with the city, and I happened onto the courtyard of the school, El Nigro Mante. I never forgot it." When Susan decided she wanted to focus on sculpting, she knew it was time to return.

"You get out what you put into the school," Susan says. "You need to have some idea of what you want to do and learn, and they will help you, but they won't push you. You need to be a mature student.

"I can sit on the beach for about a week," she says, "but after that I want something to occupy my time. . . . I want to feel like I'm engaged in something. I want to be part of the society."

If you would like to study overseas, you have a couple of options. One is to check out a resource such as *Peterson's Study Abroad* books (updated yearly), published by Petersons (Princeton, N.J.). This book lists over 1,500 seminars and year-abroad educational programs. You also can choose your destination, such as Mexico, and pick up a *Lonely Planet* guidebook. These list language and other schools in the region you plan to visit. Then you call or write for information and start saving for your trip. You also can sign up with the Elderhostel program, which offers a wide variety of programs for seniors. Elderhostels offer low-cost, short-term residential academic programs to adults 60 or older and their companions of any age at more than 1,600 colleges, universities, and national parks worldwide. Contact Elderhostel at 75 Federal Street, Boston, MA 02110-1941, or call 1-617-426-8056.

Adventure Travel

Adventure travel can be expensive or very cheap, depending on how you do it. If you sign up with an adventure travel company, in most cases you'll pay a lot of money. On the other hand, you can create your own adventure and give yourself a very inexpensive vacation. Once I packed my bicycle onto a plane and got off in Honolulu, alone. It was great to pull my boxed bike and panniers off the turnstile, put the bike together, and ride off into the sunset while everyone else was waiting for mounds of luggage and taxis. I simply kept riding until I got to a hotel I liked. When I wanted companionship and a trip to an outer island, I called up the local bike club and asked if anyone would be interested in meeting me at the plane and doing a little touring. A great adventure and friendship resulted.

When I wanted to see Alaska by kayak, I signed up for a kayak class in Anchorage, met a couple of local guys who were heading out to Prince William Sound for 10 days, and asked if I could go along. Another adventure, more friendships. Where else can you paddle along with otters, see so many eagles you don't bother to count anymore, and have the best ever blueberry pancakes on your camp stove every morning? On the other hand, where else can you get caught in a storm in the middle of the ocean and end the day thanking all manner of heavenly bodies that you are still alive? This is the spirit of adventure travel—life up close.

Willie Weir has taken budget adventure travel to impressive heights. Willie has traveled over 35,000 miles around the world on his bicycle. He logged 4,000 miles in Mexico, 5,000 in India, 4,000 in New Zealand, 4,000 in South Africa, and more miles in Central America and the Balkans. Each trip took between three and five and a half months. Willie spent very little money on these trips. His total for five months in India was $1,000.

Willie, who spent years earning a living as an actor, says acting trained him to be frugal. "Even when you're successful as an actor, you still don't make much money," he says. "You don't need a lot of money to travel this way. I put 20,000 miles on a bike I bought for $330. People think you need the best bicycle and the best equipment or you can't go, but that's not so. We've gotten so far into the consumer mentality that we think we can't do these things without spending a lot of money.

"I call bicycle travel the great intensifier," he says. "When you travel this way, you have to experience the place whether you want to or not . . . you see it up close, you experience the smells and all of the sensations that you don't notice when you're driving through. When I bicycled through Bosnia after the war, what I saw was incredibly painful but at the same time really valuable.

"As travelers, we often take the easiest path by staying in comfortable places and eating recognizable food, but those don't necessarily add up to an adventure. The reason you go to other cultures is to experience these differences. The bicycle puts you in many more situations that will give you those rich experiences. On a bicycle, the amount of things you'll experience are increased over 100-fold."

Like any adventure travel, bicycle travel has two sides. It lets you experience life at the core, and that essence also makes you more vulnerable. To ensure your safety while bicycling, check out the area you will be visiting by talking to locals or other travelers who have been there recently or investigate through the Internet. Many books have been written about issues relating especially to female travelers. Once you begin your cycle trip, however, you'll likely find that your bicycle will serve as an invitation to join people who may otherwise not open themselves to you. Willie says bicycles are the last innocent form of transportation, and this innocence opens many doors. "People trust you when you are on a bicycle," he says, "and thus, your ability to interact with new people intensifies. Once I spent the night in my tent in an older couple's yard in Canada. The next morning they invited me in for breakfast. The lady told me they didn't usually invite people into their home this way. I asked her why she did this for me. She said, 'Well, you came on a bike and we trusted you.' "

If you think you need to be a bicycling fanatic to travel this way, Willie says not so. He says anyone can do it. The best example is Willie's wife, who had never even been on an overnight bicycle trip before she and Willie cycled the Balkans for an extended trip. "We get caught up in this mind-set that we need to be experts before we can go out and enjoy these things. We miss out on a lot of adventure that way."

Willie says he has learned a lot about life from his cycling adventures. For many years he supplemented his income by leading bicycle trips. This money helped finance his own vacations. "In all the years I worked as a bicycle tour guide, I had dinner with hundreds of people on my trips," Willie says. "Most of them were professionals, like doctors and lawyers. So many of them were very 'successful' but very unhappy. I never once heard one of them say they wished they'd started working 80 hours a week earlier in their lives. Many of them felt trapped, doing things they didn't like, living lives they didn't like. Never once did I feel I made the wrong decision not to pursue a highly paid career. Never once."

Pack Light

Mistakes are our best teachers. I have learned to travel light the hard way by packing too much and having to haul it all over the place. Now I travel with very little. I went all the way to China with nothing but one carry-on bag. I asked myself, "Janet, would you rather put on a fashion show for the Chinese people, or would you rather be able to get from one place to another without hiring a bulldozer for all of your junk?"

It is miserable having to schlep heavy bags through airports, hotel lobbies, down streets, into buses, and here and there. It is so miserable I have refused to do it again. Simple living and traveling are both about having freedom. You cannot have freedom when you are literally loaded down. Here is how to pack light.

Even for the longest trip, pack only two changes of clothes, plus three changes of underwear in addition to the outfit you are wearing. Make your clothes as adaptable as possible. This means stick with basic colors, such as black, brown, or gray. Then you can add a color or two to make the basics more dressy. Take one paperback book with you because you'll always find someplace to trade it for another somewhere along the way. Some people like to take a travel journal along as well, as a way to center themselves at the end of the day.

Pack a bottle of concentrated soap, such as Dr. Bonner's. Use this to clean your clothes, your face, and your body, all in one. The typical biodegradable soap sold in most travel stores is not strong enough to clean clothes.

Soak your clothes overnight in soapy water. This is a good way to keep your socks from getting stiff. What? No plug in the sink? Make those socks wear two hats by using one as a plug. Even if you travel on a budget, 9 out of 10 places will have a sink.

Your next question likely is this: "This cleaning and soaking plan is all very fine and good, but for one problem. I am traveling, and that means moving around. I don't want to haul around a bunch of wet clothes."

Answer: If you are moving around from one place to the next at such a rapid pace that you don't have two days in one hotel, you are not simplifying your life. Travel writer Jim Molner says the most calming, uncomplicated way to travel is to stay in one place. He says: "Give yourself time in a place. Stay there for a while. At least establish a base in the region and then go off on day trips. Don't try to take in as much as you can."

Jim asks, "Would you rather *be* in Paris, or simply say you saw the Eiffel Tower?" Or would you rather be like a birdwatcher or a person who watches birds? The compulsive birdwatcher has one goal: to cross off as many species as possible. The person who watches birds spends time watching and seeing, carefully and thoughtfully.

If you slow down and get to know a place, you will have time to wash your clothes.

Next, pack one long-sleeve shirt and one lightweight wool, cotton, or natural fiber sweater. The right shoes also will simplify your life. Jim takes along one pair of all-purpose leather hiking-type shoes and one pair of sandals. He says the leather makes the shoes a bit more dressy and thus, more adaptable to all occasions.

Bring only travel-size toiletries from home, because no matter where you are, you'll be able to replenish all but contact lens solutions.

Don't forget a Swiss Army knife with a corkscrew and scissors, a small flashlight, a spoon, and about six gallon-size ziplock bags. These can be used for wet or dirty clothes, film, and items you collect, such as rocks or shells.

Add a windproof, waterproof jacket and a fold-up poncho if you know you'll be in a lot of rain.

Travel with Children

When I was 11 years old my parents took me out of school for a month to visit Europe. I learned more about history during that one month than I would have learned in 12 years of sitting in school. I'm all for taking kids on trips. I personally love to explore and learn new things, and I get a double thrill out of exposing my kids to the same. The other good thing about taking kids along is that it forces you to travel at a slower pace. This is a good thing because you can immerse yourself in the culture of the place where you are, and you can calm down. On vacations, it's nice to take life at "hammock pace."

Kathy Merwin, Steve Burtchaell, and their four kids, ages 6 through 12, travel regularly. Each summer they take one extended trip. Usually this is a minivan expedition throughout the United States. They have made huge loop trips around the perimeter of the country, sometimes they go from one coast to the next in a more direct line, sometimes they pick one region. They say their trips are family projects, and the kids are involved in the planning from the beginning. Steve and Kathy pick a general area, choose a few activities they feel are important, and ask the kids what they would like to see. They schedule their trips around the kid's activities, such as baseball or basketball teams. Both Kathy and Steve have flexible schedules, she as a self-employed caterer and Steve as a merchant marine. Steve's last trip of the spring usually finances their summer vacation.

The trips are inexpensive because the family stays with their large extended families or friends along the way, and because they plan and pack carefully. They bring along an ice chest and food box, filled with breakfast items such as milk and cereal, and lots of cut-up vegetables and fruit for snacks. Everyone has a water bottle, and maybe once a day they'll stop for soda pop as a treat. They also pack cooking staples, such as olive oil and basic spices. This way, when they need to stay in a motel, they find those with kitchenettes so they can cook their own meals.

Steve and Kathy also have refined their traveling schedule to harmonize with their children. They like to get in five or six hours of driving time per day, so they get up around 5:00 or 6:00 A.M. and load sleeping kids into the van. This gives the couple quiet, alone time, and it also gives them time to get in almost half a day's driving before the kids wake up and begin the usual barrage of questions, like "When are we going to get there?" When the kids wake up, Steve and Kathy pull off the road and the family eats cereal and milk from their cooler. Starting early also allows the family to stop early and have a good choice of motels when they need one, plus it gives them time to do a little swimming or sightseeing in the new town.

Each child is given one sports-type bag to take on every trip. This forces them to make choices and learn to travel light. Extras such as winter clothing, parkas, gloves, and boots are packed separately. The night before departure, the kids lay their clothes out on their beds and Kathy checks to make sure all the necessities are packed. Each child is also given one small backpack or fanny-type pack for car activities, including books, markers, and games. These are essential during the daily 15- to 20-minute quiet time in the van.

Experience has taught Kathy and Steve how to calm the waters when the kids argue or fight. Two standard methods work well for them. The first is a surprise bag. Before each trip, the couple picks up small gift items, such as inexpensive books, compasses, and car bingo. They keep the bag in the front of the van, and when tempers in the back begin to flare, they toss back one of the surprises. "It's the element of surprise that works," Kathy says. "It's like Mardi Gras for them!" Some trips require lots of the surprises and some very few. What they don't use they stash until the next year. The second method is the last resort. Steve simply pulls over and stops the car. He says nothing and gets out of the car. The kids know this means business because he won't start again until they settle their own dispute. Usually they are eager to resolve the issue because they want to get back on the road too.

The Sensuality of Simplicity

Plan your next vacation so you can immerse yourself deeply in one place. Pick an area rich with the kind of sensations that are invigorating to you, then resist the urge to run all over when you get there, trying to take in as much as possible. Instead, slow down and deeply inhale the sights, smells, sounds, and tastes of your new place. See if you don't return home refreshed and renewed, the way you've always wanted to feel.

A LIFE OF FREEDOM AND TRAVEL IS WORTH THE TRADE-OFFS FOR LOREN AND BECKY SCHMIDT

From the start, Becky and Loren Schmidt knew exactly what they wanted: freedom. Without question. They had not the slightest qualm about the trade-offs they would need to make along the way in order to get the freedom. They would drive their cars for 20 years, they wouldn't buy new furniture for the

Loren and Becky Schmidt outside their home.

house, they wouldn't spend much money on clothing. And neither would pursue a fast-lane career. In exchange, they could come and go as they pleased, travel regularly, spend time getting to know themselves and other people, retire from their jobs in their early 40s, and travel some more.

The Schmidts, now 44 and 45, met their goal without a hitch. The couple married soon after they graduated from college in the early 1970s. They decided not to have children. "We were taken with the idea of having a goal of freedom," Becky says. "We wanted more time and more freedom, and we knew the starting place was our finances."

In April 1975 they set off across the country from their home in Kentucky with two cats, a few belongings, an old van, $500 cash, and no job prospects. Their parents waved good-bye and told them they were crazy. They landed on the West Coast and got jobs, he for $3.50 an hour and she for $3.00. When they saved up $2,500, they decided to buy a house. They found one for $25,000, but no bank would lend them money. "The response was 'You want to do *what* on a salary of $3.50 an hour?' " Loren remembers.

Loren's dad came to the rescue with a bank-rate loan for the remainder of the cost of the house. In nine years, still making little more than $3.50 and $3.00 an hour, the Schmidts paid the loan in full, with interest. "It was easy," he says. "We just didn't spend our money. We turned our backs on a lot of the things that are considered successful in America, like new cars, new clothes, new furniture. We realized that with every purchase we made, we'd be that much further away from our goal of freedom. Before we spent any money, we'd ask ourselves, 'Do we really need it? Is there some less expensive way to get it? Is there a friend who could teach us how to make or fix it?' "

"I think a lot of people are innately good savers," Becky says, "but we live in a culture that encourages us to spend, spend, spend. It is very American to spend. If you travel, you find people in other parts of the world who still live within their means. A woman I met in Asia told me that in her country, it is shameful to be in debt. In America, it is a way of life."

The Schmidts make it their business to know where all of their money goes and how much they are paying in interest. They realized early on that they didn't want to spend vast amounts of their money on interest payments in order to buy a house. "All of our money comes from our time and paychecks," Loren says. "We deal with money we have earned and how much time it takes us to earn that money. We didn't have an inheritance and we didn't win the lottery."

The couple figured out that they weren't buying a house, they were buying a mortgage. The average $100,000 house actually costs over $600,000 by the time a traditional 30-year loan is paid. "All people are doing is supporting some banker's nice lifestyle," Loren says. "I don't know any banker well enough that I want to support that way!"

The Schmidts say anyone can get a payment schedule from a realtor that will show exactly how much of the payment goes to principal and how much to interest.

After the couple's first house was paid in full, they bought a rental house for $100,000 in 1986. Their down payment was from savings. Again they couldn't get a bank loan because their wages weren't high enough. This time they financed on a private contract with the owner and worked out a 10-year repayment schedule. Income from the rental paid the minimum payments for the first year. Then the Schmidts doubled their mortgage payments. Four years and nine months later, they paid that loan in full. "Doubling your mortgage payments doesn't mean what people often think it means," Loren says. "You double only your principal, not principal and interest. For example, if your principal payment is $640 per month, your doubled payment is $904."

While finances are the key to the Schmidt's freedom, they are also clear that money is only one vector in the equation. "To us, freedom is also about looking deeper into how we can keep growing both within ourselves, and in our relationships. We work on ourselves to become the kind of people who enjoy a generous exchange with others," Becky says. "To do that takes time. It takes time to reflect and time to value other people. You can't do that when you come home every day exhausted from work."

Loren says: "It's an old appreciation for neighborliness. If there's something wrong with your house, for example, most people are not skilled enough to do even basic repair. We've all become so specialized that we don't even think of doing repairs ourselves. We ought to be able to call on each other when we need help. Just today I helped a neighbor repair his gutters. When you have time in your life, you can develop these kinds of relationships.

The Schmidts' frugality enabled them to retire from paid work at ages 40 and 41. They live on $25,000 a year, all the result of passive income earned from their investments and rental from the second house. The $25,000 includes regular, lengthy trips around the world, a passion they pursued throughout all the years they were building their nest egg.

"Even though we had this goal of paying off our house," Becky says, "we also wanted to broaden ourselves. One way to do that was by traveling."

Sometimes the couple traveled together, sometimes individually. One evening, about 10 years into their marriage, Becky and Loren sat together and shared tea. Becky asked Loren what he would want to do with his life if he could do anything. He said he'd like to explore the world. "I told him he ought to do it," she says. "We had a very secure marriage, no children, and I wondered how I could hold a person back if this was something they wanted to do. Loren always had a very adventurous spirit. We talked it through and he realized he could do it. He picked a date on the calendar, I dropped him off at a freeway exit, and he hitched around the world for nine months."

Loren left with $100 cash in his pocket and $1,000 in traveler's checks. For the first two months he traveled across America and lived on the cash alone. He offered his services along the way in exchange for hospitality and food. "I'd refuse money," he says, "but I could always help at whatever needed doing, from something as simple as cleaning windows to fixing faucets."

He elevated his hitchhiking to private planes after he got dropped off at a small airport one day. Many of the pilots were flying alone and appreciated the company. He was even offered a ride to Ireland from Maine, but the pilot wasn't leaving for two weeks, and Loren had already found a good deal on a commercial airline to go to London. For the seven months he spent overseas, Loren figures his total costs, including transportation, lodging, and food, averaged $3.85 a day. He camped, bartered, and bought food at grocery stores instead of restaurants.

Since then Becky and Loren have continued to travel extensively all over the world. "We decided traveling is an essential part of life," Loren says. "It's more important than driving a decent car. I think if you added up our total travel expenses from all of these years, we've spent less money than if we'd bought a new car."

Becky worked as an administrative assistant, sometimes on a temporary basis, sometimes as a regular employee. Over the 20 years she worked, her pay increased from $3 to $16 per hour. She would regularly repeat the pattern of working for two to three years, then quit the job and travel. She knew that when she returned, she would have to accept a lower-paying and lower-status job. That was fine with her because the trade-off of freedom was more important than building a career. Loren did the same. He returned to school and learned cabinetmaking. Along the way he learned to build boats too. He would work project to project and take off in between projects. The couple admits that they have never had an argument about money. "About the only time we've even disagreed is once in a while I'll ask Becky to carry more cash with her," Loren says. "I'll say take this $50. She'll say, no I don't want it!"

This year they returned from a three-and-a-half-month trip to Singapore, Nepal, Japan, and India. Their total expenses, including airfare, were approximately $5,000. They spent another $5,000 on carpets and trinkets. They stayed with friends and in medium-range hotels and ate in restaurants three times a day. In Japan they found youth hostels with private rooms for $25 a night. Last year Loren traveled to Europe and the Middle East and spent $2,100, including airfare. They shop carefully for airfare by calling around until they find the best deal. They consult the *Lonely Planet* guidebooks and locals for inexpensive, out-of-the-way places to see, stay, and eat.

The Schmidts' house is open to fellow travelers as well. "For us, our goal is not simply to see if we can save money by staying with people," Becky says. "It's about taking time to nurture friendships. People are welcome at our house too. We often have guests from around the world staying with us.

"If people are interested in simplifying their lives, they ought to travel. They'll find that the rest of the world lives far more simply than we do and yet they can have very fulfilling, more peaceful, and less busy lives. The natural way to live is more simply, but our culture encourages us to be busy, busy. It's not natural to run at the speed we are asked to run and digest all of the information we are bombarded with. No wonder doctors say stress is the number-one reason people come in for office visits."

When Loren and Becky returned from their last trip, they vowed to be more discriminating with their time. They realized how prevalent busyness was in our society when a friend, who was not working, asked them to come to dinner. She had to consult her DayTimer to pick a date off in the future.

"Our goal is to develop a wisdom-based experience rather than a stimulation-based experience," Loren says. "If you completely fill your cup with agitation and activity, there is no room for anything or anyone else. You lose appreciation and contact with the subtleties of life."

The Schmidts find that meditation helps them to feel more grounded. This makes them more aware of when they are overstimulated. Meditation can be a formal sitting or simply being aware of thoughts and feelings while doing the dishes. They also attend meditation retreats every now and then.

This year they plan to finish an extensive remodeling of their house, doing most of the work themselves. To finance the project, they used money earned from a stock investment. When the work is finished, they'll rent that house out too and go off to live in a foreign country for a year, just for the experience. Income from both houses plus interest income will provide living expenses. In the meantime, they're off to the Florida Keys for 10 days to sail on a boat Loren built for a doctor.

"The bottom line for us is, if you can become self-reliant in the basics of life, which are shelter, nutritious food, and clothing—if you have those things covered, then all you have to do with the rest of your time is make yourself a peaceful person, rather than spending that same time buying things you don't need."

❖ ❖ ❖ ❖ ❖ ❖ ❖ ❖ ❖ ❖ ❖ ❖ ❖ ❖

Resources

General Discount Travel

Cheapskate's Guide to Vacations: How to Save Thousands of Dollars No Matter Where You're Going by Stephen Tanenbaum (Secaucus, NJ: Citadel Press, 1996)
Introduces money-saving strategies.

Discount Travel for Dummies by David Huetten and available from him at 2307 114th Drive N.E., Lake Stevens, WA 98258.

Lodging

Budget Hotel Rooms

Budget Lodging Guide (16th ed.) (Los Angeles: B & J Publications, 1996)
Here is a wide-ranging guide, based on pocketbook, taste, and level of adventure.

National Directory of Budget Motels by Raymond Carlson (Greenport, NY: Pilot Books, 1997)
Lists over 2,200 low-cost chain motel accommodations in the United States.

1997 State by State Guide to Budget Motels by Loris Bree (Saint Paul, MN: Marlor Press, 1997)
A guide to cheap motels by a well-traveled writer. Includes motels like Best Western, Days Inn, Roadway, and the like.

Hotel Wholesalers

Quest International, Schinook Tower, Box 402, East Yakima Avenue, Suite 1200, Yakima, WA 98901, 1-800-325-2400

Home Exchange

Books

Home Exchange Vacationing, Your Guide to Free Accommodations by Bill and Mary Barbour (Nashville, TN: Rutledge Hill Press, 1996)
Includes updates and useful resources.

Organizations

Agency Alpha International, 11789 Montana Avenue, Los Angeles, CA 90049, 1-310-472-7216

Intervac, 1-800-756-HOME

Invented City, 1-800-788-2489, E-mail: invented@aol.com

Vacation Exchange Club, P.O. Box 820, Haleiwa, HI 96712, 1-800-638-3841

Camping and Wilderness Vacations

America's Secret Recreation Areas by Michael Hodgson (San Francisco: Foghorn Press, 1995)
Best places to camp, hike, canoe, raft, kayak, fish, spelunk, bike, horseback ride, climb, and observe wildlife.

Woodall's 1997 Plan It Pack It Go (New York: Simon & Schuster, 1997)
Great places to camp and fun things to do.

Ranch Vacations

Ranch Vacations by Gene Kilgore (Santa Fe, NM: John Muir Publications, 1994)
Ranches throughout the United States: guest and resort ranches, fly fishing, cross-country skiing—not always cheap.

Hostelling and Dorms

Books

At Home in Hostel Territory: A Guide to Friendly Lodging from Seward to Santa Cruz by Janet Thomas (Seattle: Alaska Northwest Books, 1994)
Seventy-five of the friendliest and most affordable lodgings—$7 to 12 a night—in Alaska, the Yukon Territory, British Columbia, Washington, Oregon, and northern California.

Organizations

American Youth Hostels, 733 15th Street NW #840, Washington, DC 20005, 1-202-783-6161.

Campus Travel Service, P.O. Box 8355, Newport Beach, CA 92660. Ask for their U.S. and worldwide guides to college dorms.

YMCAs and YWCAs. More than 2,000 Ys across the United States and in 110 countries worldwide provide clean, cheap rooms. Call 1-800-USA-YMCA.

Transportation

Train Travel

Books

Amtraking: A Guide to Enjoyable Train Travel by Mauris Emeka (Port Orchard, WA: Apollo Publishing, 1994)
Highlights many Amtrak rail routes and the splendor of train travel.

Rail Ventures by Jack Swanson (Seattle: Travis Isle Publishing, 1996)
Clickety rides can be fun and cheap, and they get a modern update in this volume that deals with North America in its entirety.

U.S.A. by Rail by John Pitt (Old Saybrook, CT: Globe Pequot Press, 1994)
Complete guide to traveling by locomotive and what the U.S. railway systems have to offer.

Cheap Air Travel

Books

The Air Courier Travel Handbook by Mark Field (Glendale, AZ: Thunderbird Press, 1994)
Couriering may be inconvenient, but you can't beat the prices.

The Insiders Guide to Air Courier Bargains by Kelly Monaghan (New York: The Intrepid Traveler, 1996)
Discusses how to jet for next to nothing and get the best bargains.

Smarter Charters by Christopher Caswell (New York: St. Martin's Press, 1996)
Complete listings for 37 charter companies and brokers and sample charter rates.

The Worldwide Guide to Cheap Airfares by Michael McColl (Berkeley, CA: Insider Publications, 1996)
More bargain air travel and cheap thrills.

Organizations

Now Voyager is an agency that represents courier services. 74 Varrick Street, Suite 307, New York, NY 10013, 1-212-431-1616

Cheap Ocean Travel

Adventure Cruising by Don and Betty Martin (Columbia, CA: Pine Cone Press, 1996)
Thick guide that features all kinds of water-travel cruising, including paddle wheelers, cargo ships, and coastal ferries.

Fords Freighter Travel Guide and Waterways of the World (Northridge, CA: Fords Travel Guides, 1996)
Half the price for passenger cabins and just as nice.

Miscellaneous

Hospitality Groups

Globetrotters Club, BCM/Roving, London, WC1N 3XX, England

U.S. Servas Committee, 11 John Street, #407, New York, NY 10038, 1-212-267-0252.

Sanctuary Vacations

A Guide to Monastic Houses by Robert Regalboto (Ridgefield, CT: Morehouse Publishing, 1992)
Places that are affordable and varying in degrees of comfort.

Sanctuaries by Marcia and Jack Kelly (New York: Bell Tower Books, 1996)
Listings include places that offer a ministry of hospitality and welcome people of all faiths
with no requirement to attend any services or participate in any activities.

Transformative Adventures Vacations and Retreats by John Benson (Portland, OR: New
Millenium Publishing, 1994)
Useful when traveling overseas.

Volunteer Vacations

Books
Short Term Adventures by Bill McMillon (Chicago: Chicago Review Press, 1997)
Profiles more than 250 charitable organizations and 2,000 projects worldwide that need
volunteers.

Organizations
Alternative Break Connection, Vanderbilt University, Nashville, TN, 1-615-343-0385. Call to
volunteer to do something useful during spring break.

Council for International Educational Exchange lists volunteer opportunities throughout the
world. 205 East 42nd Street, New York, NY 10017-5706 or call toll-free 1-888-
COUNCIL or E-mail: info@ciee.org or visit Council's Website, http://www.ciee.org

Sierra Club Service Trips, 730 Polk Street, San Francisco, CA 94109, 1-415-923-5522

Volunteers for Peace, International Workcamps, 43 Tiffany Road, Belmont, VT 05730, 1-802-
259-2759

Index